FRONTISPIECE

THE INFANTRYMAN.

REPRODUCED BY KIND PERMISSION OF THE ARTIST, MR. E. H. KENNINGTON.

HISTORY *of the* SIXTH BATTALION WEST YORKSHIRE REGIMENT

Volume I.—1/6th Battalion
By Capt. E. V. TEMPEST
D.S.O., M.C.

1921
P E R C Y   L U N D,   H U M P H R I E S   &   C O.,   L T D.,
The Country Press, Bradford; And at 3, Amen Corner, London, E.C.4.

Printed and bound by Antony Rowe Ltd, Eastbourne

TO OUR

COMRADES OF THE

6th BATTALION WEST YORKSHIRE REGIMENT,

Who died in the War, 1914-1918.

" And some there be, which have no memorial ;
  Who are perished, as though they had never been ;
  And are become as though they had never been born.
  · · · · Their seed shall remain for ever,
  And their glory shall not be blotted out.
  Their bodies are buried in peace ;
  But their name liveth for evermore.'

Ecclesiasticus XLIV. 9.

CONTENTS.

APPENDICES.

MAPS.

ILLUSTRATIONS.

ILLUSTRATIONS—*continued*.

ILLUSTRATIONS—*continued.*

PREFACE.

The publication of this history of the 1/6th Battalion West Yorkshire Regiment is entirely due to the Committee of the "Old Comrades' Association" of the Battalion. The Committee felt that some account of the Battalion's experiences during the war would be a fitting memorial to those who had fallen. The Old Comrades' Association was formed in July, 1917, when the 1/6th Battalion was at Oost Dunkerque. The project of forming the Association was first discussed between Major R. Clough, Major W. H. Hill and Capts. W. G. Tetley and W. N. Mossop, and it was decided that in spite of the fact that the Battalion was still on active service, and the future very uncertain, an effort should be made within the Battalion to safeguard the interests after the war of comrades who had served overseas. The first meeting was held at Ghyvelde, in July, 1917. Lt.-Col. H. O. Wade, D.S.O., was elected President, Major R. Clough, M.C., Treasurer, and Quarter-Master Sergt. C. H. Woodhead, M.S.M., Secretary, and members were immediately enrolled. Many of these early members were killed in the fighting three months later at Passchendaele and during the battles of 1918, but the Association survived to carry on the work for which it had been originally formed. As President of the Association in 1920, Lt.-Col. R. Clough has given constant support and encouragement in the preparation of this book, which owes much to his advice and guidance. The work of preparing the maps and arranging the illustrations and photographs has been undertaken by Lieut. F. E. Fairbank, a member of the Committee of the Old Comrades' Association, who has also kindly corrected the proofs. Quarter-Master Sergt. C. H. Woodhead, Secretary of the Association, has rendered invaluable assistance by correcting and revising the whole of the Appendices. Without the assistance of these three members of the Committee the book could not have been published.

The list of officers, N. C. O.'s and men who have placed at the author's disposal diaries, letters, notes and advice is too long to enumerate. Special thanks are due to the following :—

Mrs. C. E. Scott, Lieut.-Col. H. O. Wade, D.S.O., Lieut-Col. J. Muller, D.S.O., M.C., Lieut.-Col. F. G. Hornshaw, M.C., Major H. Barker, Major E. D. Stansfield, M.C., Capts. A. Hamilton, Rev. R. Whincup, M.C., F. W. Musgrave, M.C., Lieuts. C. G.

Maufe, G. N. Bisatt, Coy.-Sergt.-Major H. Banks, D.C.M., Sergts. J. E. Yates, J. Ward, M.S.M.

Though necessarily incomplete in many respects, every effort has been made to ensure that the facts and details presented in this History should be accurate, and the proofs have been submitted to several officers and N.C.O.'s for their supervision and correction. Names of individuals have been mentioned only rarely, as it was felt to be invidious, where so many did well, to emphasize the actions of a few. If, on the whole, the names of officers have predominated, it has been because their names happened to be familiar to all ranks, and can be taken as representative of their own particular units in the Battalion. Those who served with the Battalion will know that many hundreds of N.C.O.'s and men, whose names are not found in this or any other history, deserve equally well the esteem and remembrance of the reader. It is owing to the constant and unostentatious self-sacrifice of these men that the 1/6th Battalion has a name worthy of being remembered in the future.

The second volume of the history of the 6th Battalion West Yorkshire Regiment, dealing with the 2/6 Battalion, is now in process of being written by Capt. E. C. Gregory, and will shortly be published as a companion to this volume.

E. V. T.

Bradford, Feb. 10th, 1921.

I am very glad that a history is being compiled of the work of the 1/6th Battalion The West Yorkshire Regiment.

During the recent campaign they formed part of the 49th Division and were under my command in the 2nd Army for a considerable time.

They took part in much of the severe fighting round Ypres, notably in the capture of Passchendaele in October 1917.

They rendered splendid service throughout the campaign and their record is one of which every member of the battalion and everyone connected with it can be justly proud.

Late Commanding 2nd Army, B. E. F.

Malta,
　　11th May, 1920.

In the early summer of 1914, the 6th Battalion West Yorkshire Regiment were about half their proper strength in Non-Commissioned Officers and Men, although greatly to the credit of a band of devoted officers, they were not below the establishment of Officers.

As is well-known, little was thought of War in the industrial districts of England at that time, and I was much impressed by the keenness of the officers struggling against the prevailing conditions of public opinion, who gave up their time and leisure to fit themselves for their position in the Battalion. Too much praise also, cannot be given to those Warrant Officers, Non-Commissioned Officers and Men who also gave up their leisure to learn their military duties, for they had little encouragement and there was nothing to be made out of it, an argument which has always appealed strongly to those engaged in a hard struggle for existence and in places where competition was very keen. Yet, with all these disadvantages, there was the nucleus of a Battalion which, with more training, was developed into the fine Battalion which the 6th afterwards became.

When War was declared there was no lack of Volunteers, and in the first week of mobilization the Battalion was raised to War Strength. By the energy and devotion of the officers and the fine spirit of all ranks, the Battalion was able to take its place fully, if not efficiently equipped, in the 1st West Riding Brigade, when it concentrated at SELBY less than ten days after mobilization. Upon the early difficulties which had to be overcome, I will not dwell further than to say that they were overcome by the fine spirit of the Battalion.

The hardest time came when the Battalion was asked to volunteer for Foreign Service. What this meant to individuals, no one can appreciate until he has been in such a position himself. All their plans of life were altered and they had to face uncertainty and anxiety, not only for themselves, but for those dependent upon them. The fact that they did volunteer is to their everlasting honour. Of all the sacrifices made for England during the War, none I am sure, were greater than those made by the Territorial Force early in the War.

By the time the Battalion was called upon to take its place in the line in FRANCE in April, 1915, it had been trained and had acquired that confidence in itself which made it the fine fighting unit it afterwards proved to be. Although I cannot speak of its doings after 1915, I am convinced that the Battalion owed much to the *esprit de corps* and devotion to duty which characterised all ranks during its early training and the first months of the fighting in FRANCE. Yorkshiremen and the inhabitants of Bradford, from whom the officers and men were recruited, may feel a just pride in the History of this Battalion and should be for ever grateful to those who served in its ranks.

No Commander could wish to be more loyally and faithfully served than I was by all ranks of the Battalion.

This record will keep fresh the memory of the gallant men who gave their lives for the sake of their country, and will be some consolation to those who have lost their health in doing their duty, and who merit our sympathy almost more than those who have left us.

F. A. MacFarlan,
Brig: Gen!

Ceylon,
    25th June, 1920.

GROUP OF OFFICERS, 1914.

TOP ROW.—LIEUTS. HESELTON, DOBSON, MYERS, WATSON, T. E. ARMISTEAD, BIRCH, TETLEY, HAMILTON, MCLAREN, MUSGRAVE, HORNSHAW AND ODDY.

CENTRE ROW.—CAPTS. FELL, BARKER, WALKER, FAWCETT, MAJ. SCOTT, LT.-COL. WADE, MAJ. CLOUGH, CAPT. AND ADJT. G. R. SANDEMAN, CAPTS. ANDERTON, MULLER, AND CAPT. AND QUARTERMASTER W. H. HILL.

BOTTOM ROW.—LIEUTS. SAVILLE, KNOWLES, GRICE, FAWCETT, AND MOSSOP.

I.

EARLY DAYS.

THE 6th Battalion West Yorkshire Regiment was born in the enthusiastic patriotism of 1859, when war was threatened between England and France. England had grown fat and prosperous. Both army and navy had declined in strength and efficiency. France, on the other hand, under Napoleon III., was vastly increasing her military power and adopting an ambitious provocative policy. The early application of steam to ships of war had brought the possibility of the invasion of England within measurable distance. England became violently suspicious of her old enemy. The result was the Volunteer Movement. In 1859, as in 1914, men offered themselves readily for the public service, and a hundred and fifty thousand volunteers were quickly enrolled. Both in 1859 and 1914 England was passing through a time of grave internal trouble and industrial disputes. But in both cases men gave up their social and personal quarrels and joined together to meet the enemy at the gate. Tennyson gave expression to the general feeling in his " Riflemen, Form ! "

> " Let your reforms for a moment go !
> Look to your butts, and take good aims !
> Better a rotten borough or so
> Than a rotten fleet, and a city in flames ! "

Bradford was a small town of a few thousand inhabitants, but she quickly formed two Volunteer Companies as her contribution to the national effort. These Companies were called the 5th and 6th Yorkshire (West Riding) Volunteer Rifle Corps. In spite of many changes of name, this Corps remained a definitely local force, with a strong local tradition, recruited from Bradford mills and warehouses and commanded by officers of the Bradford district. Even after the casualties of the Ypres Salient in 1915, this local tradition survived unimpaired. It was only during the later stages of the battle of the Somme in 1916 that the Battalion ceased to be exclusively recruited from the West Riding of Yorkshire, and even towards the end of the War, in spite of reinforcements from every county of England, the bond between the City and its war-scarred Battalion remained strong and unbroken. This local tradition is a factor of great importance in the history of

HISTORY OF THE 1/6TH BN. WEST YORKSHIRE REGT.

the Battalion. To men in squalid and nerve-shattering trenches Bradford stood for England, and there was a quick understanding and comradeship between men who had worked together in the same mills and taken their pleasures under similar conditions. The Volunteers of 1859, who drilled on the site of Belle Vue Barracks, had true successors in those later volunteers who from trenches in Flanders found the focus of their patriotism in their native City.

In March, 1860, the Bradford Companies were amalgamated with the 3rd West Riding Volunteer Corps under the command of Major Cunliffe Lister (afterwards Lord Masham). Another change took place in 1887, when they became the 2nd Volunteer Battalion of the Prince of Wales' Own West Yorkshire Regiment. It was under this title that in 1900 they contributed their quota of two officers and seventy men for service in South Africa with the 2nd Line Battalion, West Yorkshire Regiment. At this time the Battalion had reached a comparatively high state of efficiency. Annual Camps were held at large Military Centres (Aldershot, 1898, 1900, 1902, 1903), and several of the senior officers and men who served with the Battalion in 1915 owed their experience and self-confidence to this apprenticeship to Army routine and discipline. The 1900 Camp at Aldershot was memorable for the " Black Monday " episode, when owing to the intense heat on a big field day there were over 1,700 casualties amongst the troops, and twenty-eight men died from sunstroke. The Battalion at this time consisted of over 1,000 men, but only fifteen fell out on the march. Several similar tests of endurance and discipline created a good battalion tradition, and bore a magnificent result in the early days of the war. Other Camps were held at Bridlington (1893, 1894, 1895), Scarborough (1896, 1897, 1901), Castleton (1904), Isle of Man (1905), Salisbury Plain (1906) and Redcar (1907).

In 1908 the Territorial Force was organized. At this time the 2nd Volunteer Battalion consisted of nine Companies (one of them a cyclist company), with a total numerical strength of 817 out of an establishment of 1,028. The Battalion was now reduced to eight Companies and became known as the 6th Battalion West Yorkshire Regiment. A year later at Windsor, King Edward VII. presented the Colours to the Battalion. These Colours were the gift of S. Milne, Esq., of Calverley, one of the original officers of the Battalion. Among those who went to Windsor with the Colour party were Capt. H. O. Wade, Lt. H. W. Barker and Lt. W. P. M. Scott. Then followed the usual routine of training. The first Camp under T.F. regulations was at Redcar in 1908, followed by those at Guisborough (1909), Marske (1910), Isle of Man (1911), Hunmanby (1912), Aberystwith (1913).

2

EARLY DAYS

The Camp at Aberystwith was noteworthy, as the Field Operations were on an ambitious scale. There was a record march of twenty-five miles, in which the whole Division took part. For the first time in the land manœuvres of the Division live shell was fired by the Otley and Ilkley howitzer batteries, and this gave a tremendous touch of realism to the army experiences of our so-called "Saturday night soldiers." Unfortunately there was an error on the part of one of the "layers" of an 18-pounder gun, and the shell burst in a farm yard, killing a pig. This was the first casualty caused by our 49th Division Artillery, and gave rise to several witticisms, "God save us from our own Artillery," and so on. In later days the Battalion became very proud of the 49th Division Artillery, as it had every reason to be. On those occasions when we were being shelled by our own gunners, and sanguinary language was flying about amongst the P. B. I. (poor bl—— infantry), we always cursed the artillery of some other Division, never our own.

The Aberystwith Camp of 1913 was in the opinion of many of those who took part in it, the most enjoyable of them all. There was no war-cloud on the horizon, and training was not taken too seriously. It is doubtful whether men of the British race will ever again be able to take military manœuvres in the same light-hearted spirit as in 1913. There were, of course, a great many men who had joined the Territorial Force before the war with deep conviction that military training was necessary and that England was in imminent danger of war. Such men in many cases became Officers and N. C. O.'s, instructors with a keen sense of responsibility, who sacrificed much and often received only the wages of indifference and ridicule. The Battalion will never be able to express its indebtedness to these men, or the country adequately repay them for their fine public spirit. It is almost invidious to mention names, but Cols. G. H. Muller and J. H. Hastings will always be regarded by old serving members as splendidly representative of many others who set duty before comfort, and infused their officers and men with a spirit of soldierly discipline and something of their own seriousness. On the whole, however, men joined the Battalion as a relief from the monotony of civil life, as an outlet for high spirits, and as a means of spending a healthy holiday with good comrades. They were fortunately not impressed with the imminent danger of war. Yet only one year after the Aberystwith Camp, the Call-to-Arms came to every young man in England. Who answered the Call ? The volunteer "Saturday night soldiers," who had been drilling whilst others played, and who had thus prepared themselves for a day of which in most cases they never dreamed ! Few of them are left.

Few have escaped without some scars or some disability. Yet when they paraded on Aug. 5th, at Belle Vue Barracks, and still more when a few days later they volunteered almost without exception for foreign service overseas, the Battalion was formed of some of the finest stuff in England. In spite of individual failures, the spirit of self-sacrifice lifted every man out of the common rut. During the slow progress of the war a steady deterioration in physical strength and morale was noticeable in almost every unit in the British Army. The 6th Bn. West Yorkshire Regt. was no exception. This deterioration was counter-acted to some extent by increased efficiency in armament and methods, and dogged determination and fatalism made up for the lack of the enthusiasm of the early days. But few would disagree with the statement that the Battalion of the late stages of the war, when casualties had thinned the ranks of the original Territorials and early recruits, never quite reached the high standard of 1914 and 1915. The Territorial organization may have been excellent, but the chief asset of the Force lay in the character of the men who had voluntarily joined it in days of peace.

The order for the mobilization of the 6th Bn. West Yorkshire Regt. arrived at Belle Vue Barracks on August 4th, 1914. The following morning, men received the long green envelope franked " MOBILIZA-TION—URGENT," containing the fateful buff Army Form E635 which embodied the Territorial Force. By 6 p.m. on August 5th, a telegram was sent to York reporting that there were present at Belle Vue Barracks 575 all ranks, this being only thirteen short of the strength of the Battalion. It is impossible to exaggerate the significance of this magnificent response to the mobilization order. It certainly sur-passed the most optimistic expectations of the authorities. The adjutant of the Battalion, Capt. G. R. Sandeman (Border Regiment) had taken up his duties in January, 1914, and had been impressed even then with the strong " *esprit de corps,*" and the comparatively high standard of discipline which prevailed in the unit. But some idea of the difficulty of obtaining discipline even in a good class Territorial Bn. can be obtained from the following. The first parade in January, 1914, held by the new adjutant, was called for 2-15 p.m. on a Saturday ; at 2-15 p.m. the Band reported " present," but there was only a handful of men. At 2-30 p.m. a few more arrived, but it was 3 o'clock before the Battalion, consisting of eighty men, marched off the parade ground ! Even this was considered a good attendance ! Yet only eight months later, when the warning orders were issued, practically every man in the Battalion paraded punctually, ready to go anywhere, provided their wives permitted ! Even men quite unfit reported immediately. One man left a sick bed, against his doctor's orders, and walked to Belle Vue Barracks for the 9 a.m. parade on August 5th, simply—as he said—" to show willing." Old members of the 2nd Volunteer Battalion of pre-Territorial days joined up again ; men like Thomas Britton, considerably over-age, yet keener than any youngster : who throughout the war served with the Battalion in France, and who became the Battalion carpenter : who, when asked, in later days, how he was getting on, invariably replied, " Fed up, but *still carrying on.*" The number of officers was soon up to establishment. Col. H. O. Wade had been given command of the Battalion in October, 1913, and Major C. E. Scott appointed second in command. Both were well known in the Bradford district, and before the war had gathered round them a keen and efficient nucleus of officers. One of them (Capt. E.W. Knowles), who had retired from the T. F. in March, 1914, joined up again on Aug. 6th, appointing himself Junior Subaltern, and with the aid of a pen knife made the alterations to his uniform there and then. Probably the cheeriest crowd that has ever been seen on Belle Vue Barracks parade ground assembled there on August 5th, 1914. It was a time of feverish but ordered activity. The Drill Hall was crowded for days with a noisy, dusty, animated mob, in which at first civilian clothes predominated till quickly the men received their khaki, still creased from the Quarter-Master's Stores.

During the first few days of mobilization, the men slept in Belle Vue Schools and in the Drill Hall of the Barracks, or rather, they lay down and waited for morning. There was little sleep for any one, as very few were accustomed to lying in lumps all night on a hard floor— nearly a thousand men !

Some idea of the enthusiasm of those early days can be gathered from the fact that recruits came in at the rate of 100 men an hour. Company Commanders sat at trestle tables, surrounded by piles of blue forms, interviewing men : rushed off for a hurried meal at the Belle Vue Hotel : and slept on the carpeted floor of the Mess ante-room at the Barracks. In the admission of recruits to the Battalion, a high standard was demanded. In pre-war days a number of men had been allowed to join the Battalion who would have been rejected if a strict examination had been enforced. But in August, 1914, the Medical Officer had such a wealth of choice that he could afford to be exacting. Fully twenty per cent. of the volunteers were rejected on medical grounds. The great difficulty was not men, but equipment. Thanks very largely to the foresight and energy of our Quarter-Master (Capt. W. H. Hill, 1st Bn. West Yorkshire Regt.) the mobilization equipment of the Battalion of 1,000 men was completed in four days'

time. Every man on joining, with the exception of the new enlist-
ments, received a bounty of £5, a small-kit allowance of 10/-, and
a pair of boots and two shirts, which had to be bought specially. The
forming of the *personnel* of the Battalion transport was typical of the
quick summary methods of those early days. Captain R. Clough had
been appointed Purchasing Officer and bought all the horses locally.
They arrived on the second day of mobilization, fifty-seven of them
altogether, ten for officers, sixteen pack and thirty-one draught, " the
latter being a good heavy stamp from carters' wagons." The same
afternoon the Battalion was formed up in two ranks, and the order was
given for " any man who knew anything about a horse " to step forward
two paces. In half an hour the *personnel* of the transport was formed,
and the men took over their horses—not always without difficulty.
Occasionally a maddened pony, with pack saddle reversed under belly,
endangered the limbs of everyone within kicking distance, till Captain
Clough came to the assistance of his zealous, but uninitiated, transport.

On August 8th, four days after mobilization, a telegram was sent
to H. Q., York, stating that the Battalion was up to War Establishment,
with a *personnel* of twenty-nine officers and 979 men; fifty-seven
horses, and the necessary transport, *viz.* :—six wagons, five S.A.A. (Small
Arms Ammunition) carts, two tool carts, two water carts and one maltese
cart. It was a proud achievement. The Battalion was the first Territorial
unit in the country to report itself as having completed its mobilization,
and being " ready to move." A special wire of congratulation was
sent to the Battalion from H. Q. Northern Command at York.

The next few days were rather exciting. The air was full of
rumours, and everyone was in a state of credulous uncertainty. The
authorities arranged " test calls " at inconvenient moments. Notices
were posted in the streets and read out in all places of amusement in the
town ordering all men to report immediately for duty at the barracks.
Men had not yet become sceptical with regard to military orders, and
visions of some portentous move filled everyone's mind during these
tests of the Battalion's power of rapid concentration. At last definite
orders came. A billeting party under Captain H. L. Anderton was
sent to Selby. Working hard on an entirely new job they succeeded
in allotting all billets twenty-four hours after their arrival in the town,
and were congratulating themselves on having two or three days longer
in which to put the finishing touches on to their work, when the Battalion detrained, having received orders to move from Bradford earlier
than was expected.

It was 7-30 a.m. on Tuesday, August 11th, when the Battalion
paraded at Belle Vue Barracks, and marched down to the Midland

Station. Rumours of Tilbury Docks and a destination in Egypt or India were very prevalent among the older hands, and there was some surprise when they found the commonplace town of Selby was their destination. There is a kind of poetic justice in the quiet unassuming manner in which the Battalion left Bradford, never to return again till their task was finished, and the War ended. The bands did not play, there were no cheering crowds, no interested spectators, such as used to line the streets on the annual departure for Camp—few friends to wave farewell. The secrecy of it impressed everyone. England was at war ! The Battalion never had the opportunities for spectacular display which fell to the lot of some other units. In the sodden trenches of Ypres and the mud bath of the Somme and Passchendaele, the Battalion did its work thoroughly, with enormous and daily sacrifices of energy and human life, yet without in any ambitious way attracting the notice of the newspaper critics and war correspondents. The quiet departure from Bradford was in keeping with its later history. Not that the citizens of Bradford were to blame ! Few knew the time of the Battalion's departure. Few realized the tremendous part the Territorial Force was destined to play. Fewer still realized the seriousness of the military situation. The war would be over in six months ! The Battalion would not be needed for actual fighting in France. The German advance had been stopped at its very commencement at the gates of Belgium. It was with sentiments such as these that the majority of our citizens bade adieu to the first unit the City provided for the armed forces of the Allies.

The Battalion proceeded in three trains to Selby, arriving at 12-30 p.m. For the first week the men were billeted in private houses, and the inhabitants gave them a splendid welcome, doing everything possible for their comfort. More than one host gave up his best bedroom, and got up before his family in order that the soldier billeted on him should not turn out on early parade without a cup of tea ! More than one old lady, who had been alarmed when soldiers were first billeted on her, probably expecting some kind of wild animal, softened and became very kind, and even wept at their departure !

On August 19th quarters were transferred to a Camp near Selby, a good move from the point of view of discipline. The other units of the 1/1st West Riding Infantry Brigade also arrived, *viz. :* 5th Bn. (York), 7th and 8th Bns. (Leeds Rifles) West Yorkshire Regiment. A careful sifting of the Battalion took place during this period at Selby. Enlisting had been carried out at such a speed in Bradford that it had been impossible to enquire into the characters of many of the men. A few bad characters created a good deal of trouble, and ten men were discharged as " undesirable." A further thirty-eight men were discharged as " physically unfit." It was found that about 100 National Reserve Class II. men had been re-enlisted in the Battalion, and the experience of these old soldiers proved useful to the rest of the men. There were also about 140 recruits, and a special staff was organized to begin recruit training. Training in Camp was carried out under command of Companies, varied occasionally by " Battalion " route marches to harden the men's feet, and accustom them to carrying full kit. Everyone was kept closely to Camp, as German raids were expected on the East Coast. Rapid entrainment practices were also carried out, the record time at Selby being thirty-five minutes. This record was easily beaten only ten days later at York, when the Battalion practised entrainment by night. On this occasion the Battalion and Transport paraded at 9 p.m. The first train took ten minutes, and the second, including horses and wagons, sixteen minutes : complete entrainment thus taking twenty-six minutes. The Battalion was rapidly improving in efficiency and discipline. There was an important S.A.A. depot at Selby, and the Battalion was called upon to provide guards. These guard-duties gave a welcome touch of reality to the soldiering. The magazine was protected by barbed wire entanglements and a kind of " block house " system, and the men had to improve the defences : and on the " alarm," to find their posts quickly by day or night. There was a sentry on duty with field glasses to look out for enemy aircraft. Altogether it was as near an approach to war as one could have in a quiet country town like Selby ! One night an overkeen sentry (supposed to have belonged to the 8th Battalion) fired on a barge which did not respond to his challenge. At least that is the story the sentry told. Perhaps it would be unkind to suggest that he was showing a pal how his rifle worked and had forgotten there was a cartridge in the breach. It was also at Selby that a sentry, on being asked how his rifle was loaded replied, " Four in the tin and one in the funnel ! " This sentry, also, is supposed to have belonged to another unit !

On August 24th, the Battalion moved to the Knavesmire, York, and a week later to Camp at Strensall, where very strenuous training was carried out up to October 24th. It was whilst the Battalion was stationed at York that it volunteered for foreign service, being the first Battalion to do so in the Brigade. Not only that, but it contained a larger proportion of men who volunteered than any other unit. Of these two facts there is every reason to be proud. In Brigade Orders on August 24th, the Battalion had been selected as the Foreign Service Battalion of the Brigade, and had been warned that it might have to go abroad in advance of the Division at any moment. According to

Brigade Orders, this Service Battalion was to have been composed of volunteers, not only from the 6th Battalion, but also from the other units of the Brigade. When, however, practically the whole Battalion volunteered for foreign service, the idea of forming a Composite Foreign Service Battalion was abandoned. It is not easy for us now to realize the full significance of the sacrifice made by these early Volunteers in the Territorial Force. First of all, to offer for foreign service meant offering for all the risks and hardships work in the field involved, and this at a time when the general public had not fully realised the urgency of the need for men, and when there was little public conscience aroused against the " slacker." But that was not all. In the early days of September, 1914, when the 6th Battalion was at Strensall, instructions were issued for the formation of a Reserve Battalion, subsequently known as the 2/6th Battalion West Yorkshire Regiment. The command was given to Lieut.-Col. J. H. Hastings, T.D., who in 1913 had retired from the command of the 6th Battalion West Yorkshire Regt., and who was a very respected and popular officer. Thus any men belonging to the 1/6th Battalion who had had previous experience with the Territorials, and who decided to stay at home, had the best chance of promotion with the second line battalion. This remark applies, of course, not only to officers, but to men who were keen to win promotion as N.C.O's. There were thus many reasons for a large proportion of the men refusing to volunteer for foreign service. It is to the undying honour of the Battalion that when the choice was put before it the very great majority were uninfluenced by personal affairs, and were keen only to serve their country in the quickest, most direct, most dangerous way. It is necessary to state also that all officers and men of the 1/6th Battalion who were passed as medically unfit for foreign service in 1914 and early 1915 were drafted to the second line battalion, and the majority of them went out in 1917 after being passed by the doctor. As is well known, when the 2/6th Battalion went out to France under Col. Hastings in 1917 with the 62nd Division, it quickly became one of the very best fighting units in the Army, and had an exceptionally brilliant career.

The seven weeks' training at Strensall was hard and remorseless. The weather was cheerless ; the Camp had got into a bad state, ground sodden with rain, tents torn, and nights bitterly cold. First inoculation against typhoid, and vaccination, were minor vexations of this period. After parades were over there was absolutely no amusement for the men apart from a tiny Cinema, which held about a thousandth part of the troops on the Common. The fire at Flaxton was an event which varied the monotony a little. Whilst practising an Advance Guard movement, one of the Companies saw a big farmstead on fire, and was in time to check the spread of the fire and put it out. Then they formed up, and each man received a glass of beer from the grateful farmer and his wife. Several weeks later, two shillings reward for each man was sent by an Insurance Company.

No one was sorry when the order came on October 24th to strike Camp and move into billets at York. But it was probably during this strenuous Strensall period that all ranks began to realize the meaning of the word " soldier." It is no exaggeration to say that the endurance and discipline shown during the first winter at Ypres was the result to some extent of the Strensall training. In later days, rules of training were considerably relaxed. Early morning parades before breakfast, and night marches were given up; entertainments and Y. M. C. A. Huts were provided liberally : and in a thousand ways privileges denied to the Volunteers of 1914 were freely given. Men who were with the Battalion at this time remark how interminably long the days of training seemed. The relentless monotony of army discipline tried some of them severely. Parts of the rifle, movements of drill, were learnt till everyone reached utter boredom. Yet obedience was becoming instinctive. The Battalion was being made an efficient machine. Absentee-ism, and other forms of slack discipline, decreased continually. The individual was becoming less, the unit more important. Strensall marks a very important stage in the war history of the Battalion.

Before leaving the question of discipline, it may be useful to warn the reader not to expect from a Territorial Battalion the same type of discipline which prevails in regiments of the Regular Army, such as the Guards. The personal element had been all important in building up the Territorial units. At first commands were obeyed and work carried out simply because of a mutual confidence and respect between officers and men, similar to that in a workshop or any small society. The first bond was personal. Discipline came later, and was used to strengthen and regularize relationships already existing. As one of our Brigadiers (Brig. Gen. M. D. Goring Jones, C.M.G., D.S.O.) said after he had begun to understand his battalions, " Your discipline is one of *good will*." A regular Army officer himself, of long experience, and the severest disciplinarian who ever commanded the Brigade, his words carry unusual weight. The reader will only be able to explain some incidents in this history by referring to that " discipline of goodwill," which remained a tradition with the Battalion.

As mentioned previously, the billets in York proved very comfortable after the Strensall experiences. " Very comfortable " is, of course, only a comparative term. The men were billeted by platoons in empty houses or schools, and palliasses and straw were issued. There was improvement in cooking arrangements. Field Kitchens had not yet been served to Territorial units, and meals had been cooked in Camp kettles. In York, however, good cooking ranges in the billets enabled some variety of dishes to be introduced. There was further improvement in behaviour and discipline, and from several quarters comes the testimony as to the excellent conduct of the men. Training was carried on energetically. The Adjutant was very keen on practising formations for " savage warfare," and if the Battalion had been attacked on the Bootham Park training ground by a tribe of Zulus, it would certainly have carried out some remarkable exercises in " savage warfare " formations. There were also frequent Brigade Field days on the heavy arable ground of the York Plain. The only event of note during · this period was the alarm on November 3rd, caused by a German raid in the North Sea. The Battalion was ordered to " stand to." Two hours after the alarm was given the Battalion was ready to move with transport loaded, but the move was cancelled at dawn. There was another alarm on December 16th, when a German Naval Squadron bombarded Scarborough, and a general " stand to " was ordered in York, and detachments from the Brigade entrained for the East Coast.

On November 22nd, an order came which seemed to bring active operations sensibly nearer. Half the Battalion (E, F, G, H Companies) was ordered to Redcar to dig trenches along the Coast, under the command of Major C. E. Scott. Their place in the Battalion was taken temporarily by four Companies of Home Service men from the 5th, 6th, 7th and 8th Battalions. These Companies arrived at York without equipment or greatcoats, but their wants were quickly supplied. In later days in France it became a standing and bitter joke on the part of quarter-master sergeants and others that all outside detachments joined the Battalion solely in order to be fitted out and re-equipped at their trouble and expense. This was probably, however, the privileged " grouse " of every Quarter-master Sergeant in the Army. On December 2nd the Machine Guns with their detachments, under Captain R. G. Fell, followed the four Companies to Redcar. Everybody enjoyed this period at Redcar. The work was interesting, though fairly strenuous. The men made trenches and dug-outs, " which wouldn't have stopped a Verey Light," and did some excellent wiring, which was regularly washed away by the tide. Several farmers missed fences which mysteriously disappeared during this " occupation." The Companies provided guards for the Cliffs from dusk to dawn, and many mysterious signals and flashes were reported by alert sentries. The trenches were occupied each morning one hour before dawn, and the men were thus initiated into the mysteries of " stand to " at daybreak. It was during this period that the enemy fleet bombarded the east coast near West Hartlepool and most of the men gained their first experience of shell-fire. Gen. Plumer, then G. O. C. Northern Command, visited the trenches and expressed a hope that he would soon see the Battalion with him in France. On December 10th an exchange was made between the Home Service Companies and the half battalion at Redcar, which returned to York, where the whole Battalion celebrated Christmas, 1914.

During the Coast Defence duties at Redcar, an important rearrangement had taken place in Territorial battalions. Up to this time a battalion had consisted of eight Companies, lettered usually A to H. With the introduction of the Platoon System the number of Companies was reduced to four, each being composed of four platoons. In the 1/6th Battalion, A and E Companies amalgamated, and became A Company, B and D became D Company, F and G became B Company, C and H became C Company. The old Company names soon dropped out of use except in the case of H Company, where the old title carried too many associations to be allowed to drop out of memory. H Company was formed very largely from Old Boys of the Bradford Grammar School, and the comradeships of the school and of civilian life were carried into the Army, and were deepened and hallowed by the tragic experiences of War. By the end of 1915 few of old H Company were left. In addition to casualties many of them had taken Commissions in other units. But throughout the War H Company dinners and re-unions in billets behind the line reminded the few who were left of their old allegiance. There can be no doubt that the school tradition and the healthy sporting element which was brought by the men of H Company did good to the whole Battalion. There was keen competition between Companies, and if H Company did not always win, it always set up a high standard.

Early in the new year visible preparations were made for foreign service in the near future. On February 1st twenty per cent. of officers and men were allowed to go on leave. Three days later the Battalion was re-armed with the High Velocity Mark VII. rifle (long rifle converted), and the old rifles were returned to Ordnance. A Letter was also received from H. Q. Northern Command stating that if further re-inforcements were required in France the 6th Bn. West York Regt. would be chosen along with five other Battalions to represent the Northern Command, and the place of the 6th Battalion in the Brigade would be filled by its first Reserve formation (the 2/6th Battalion). This order was not carried out, but it became clear to all ranks that the stay in England was drawing to a close. The most popular marching song of the Battalion up to this time had been, " When the war is nearly over, we'll be there ! " The Battalion arrived in time, however !

On February 26th the Battalion moved to Gainsborough, Lincolnshire, and relieved the 4th Battalion K. O. Y. L. I. (King's Own Yorkshire Light Infantry). The men were billeted on the inhabitants, four men in each dwelling house. This was luxury after the crowded billets in York. The stay at Gainsborough was far and away the pleasantest time the men had passed in England since mobilization. The inhabitants knew the Battalion was about to leave for France, and all classes showed the most generous hospitality. For months later the Battalion post brought letters from Gainsborough, especially of the amorous kind. It may be construed as some kind of acknowledgment of the kindness of the inhabitants that the officers of the Battalion evolved a complicated scheme of trenches, wire entanglements, strong points, etc., etc., for the defence of Gainsborough ! Fortunately, however, it was not necessary to carry the scheme into execution. On the whole, training was not strenuous. These periods of rest and refreshment never augured well for the future : it was the calm before the storm. In later days the men irreverently called it " the fattening-up process," but every one was learning to " live in the present," and the prospect of the slaughter dismayed very few. With the beginning of April preparations entered upon the final stage, and the Bn. H. Q. Staff became busier than they had been since the first days of mobilization. Orders and counter-orders arrived daily. A medical inspection of all ranks for foreign service took place on April 1st. Everyone was inoculated. Forty-five men medically unfit, and who declared themselves under nineteen years of age, were sent back. It by no means follows that all who went out to France on April 15th were medically fit or over nineteen years of age. Quite a number of men who were unfit for digging trenches at Redcar or strenuous training at Strensall declared themselves fit enough for fighting Germans in trenches in Flanders. Boys who were not eighteen lied about their age, and even persuaded their parents that they were fit to fight " Boches " though not old enough by Army standards to do so. The great fear of nearly everyone was of being " left behind " after the weary months of preparation. This enthusiasm was particularly fine, as the prospects of an early victory had become remote. The Neuve Chapelle attack of March 11th had failed. The Russian steam roller was slow to move. And the Territorial Army was needed to fill up the gaps of the line in France.

The men of the 49th Division were about to join their comrades of London and the Midlands (the 46th Territorial Division crossed to France in February, 1915). On April 9th the concentration of the 1/1st West Riding Brigade at Gainsborough was completed by the arrival of the 1/5th and 1/7th Battalions from the coast. Five days later, on April 14th, Battalion Orders were issued for all ranks to parade on the following morning for service overseas with the B. E. F. in France.

The Battalion—less Transport and Machine Gun Section—left Gainsborough at noon on April 15th, 1915 in two trains for Folkestone. The following is a copy of Battalion Orders for the move :—

BATTALION ORDERS
by
Lieutenant Colonel H. O. Wade, Commanding 1/6th Battalion West Yorkshire Regiment.

Gainsborough,
14th April, 1915.

1.
Duties.

Orderly Officer—
On Embarkation to-morrow, Lieut. E. W. Knowles.
Friday, 16th—Lieut. N. Grice.
Saturday, 17th—Lieut. S. C. Savill.
Orderly Officers during moves will report to the Adjutant half an hour after Reveille for orders.

2.
Parade Move.

The Battalion will proceed to-morrow in two Trains :—
No. 1 Train, Battalion Headquarters. "A" Company. "B" Company (less half Platoon).
No. 2 Train, "C" and "D" Companies, and half Platoon "B" Company.
Major C. E. Scott will command second Train.
First Train party will parade, Battalion Alarm Post at 12-15 p.m.
Second Train party, 12-45 p.m.
Dinners 11-15 a.m. and 11-45 a.m. respectively.
Officers Commanding Companies to arrange with landlords for the early dinners, and also for every man to carry a haversack ration.
Orderly Officer, 1st Train—2/Lt. E. Myers.
Orderly Officer and Adjutant, 2nd Train—2/Lt. S. C. Savill.

14

COL. H. O. WADE, D.S.O.

COL. J. H. HASTINGS, D.S.O.

LT.-COL. C. E. SCOTT.

LT.-COL. R. CLOUGH, M.C.

R.S.M. C. L. FREEMAN.

R.S.M. H. BARKER, M.C., D.C.M.

C.S.M. J. POTTAGE.

C.S.M. T. MACKAY.

C.S.M. W. WALMSLEY,
CROIX DE GUERRE.

C.S.M. A. HANSON.

Fatigue parties :—

    1st Train, 2/Lt. N. Grice, three N. C. O.'s, and twenty men " A " Company.

    2nd Train, 2/Lt. W. L. Fawcett, three N. C. O.'s and twenty men, " C " Company.

These fatigue parties will be available if fatigues are required on arrival at Port of Embarkation.

Each of these Officers will tell off two parties from within their fatigues of 1 N.C.O. and 5 men for duty in the holds on arrival, if required.

3. Battalion Headquarters. Unless otherwise ordered, Battalion Headquarters will consist of Headquarters Staff, Signallers, Pioneers, Sanitary men, Machine Gun, Orderly Room and Quarter-Master's Staffs, R.A.M.C. attached.

4. Interior Economy. Kit Inspection Cards, showing complete list of necessaries, are issued to-day to Companies. Every N.C.O. and man will carry this in the pocket of his A. B. 64—Pay Book—The latter to be carried in right breast pocket of service dress jacket. These Cards will be shown by the men at every Kit inspection.

5. Battalion Standing Orders. (War). Battalion Standing Orders embodying field work, marches, duties in the trenches, etc., are issued to all Officers and N.C.O.'s to-day. All ranks will be lectured in these Orders, and N.C.O.'s must work them up *thoroughly*. They will be carried in the Haversack.

6. Voluntary Church Service. A voluntary service—Celebration of Holy Communion—will be held at Holy Trinity Church at 8 a.m. to-morrow morning. Men can take their relatives or friends.

Officers Commanding Companies will arrange interior economy work to allow men to attend this service.

7. Railway Station. Arrangements cannot be made, on account of limited accommodation, at the Railway Station for civilians to enter the Station to-morrow. No civilians will be allowed in the Station.

8. Farewell message from Honorary Colonel. " Good luck and best wishes to all ranks in my Battalion."

    From Col. Sir Geo. Helme.

(Signed) G. R. Sandeman, Captain and Adjutant,
1/6th Battalion West Yorkshire Regiment.

HISTORY OF THE 1/6TH BN. WEST YORKSHIRE REGT.

In Part II. Orders there are a few significant " changes of name," where men declare their " true names " officially through the medium of Battalion Orders :—a detail significant of many other preparations made by every man for his unknown dangerous future. The trains proceeded *via* Lincoln and London (Liverpool Street). The journey to London was marked by never-ending demonstrations of enthusiasum, and every house along the route seemed to be flying the allied flags. As the train passed through towns and villages amidst incessant cheering, many of the men remembered with regret how some eight months earlier the Battalion had marched out of Bradford almost without notice. During the short stay at Liverpool Street Station the evening papers were being sold giving the heavy casualty lists of the battle of Neuve Chapelle—an untimely subject, hardly the sort of mental stimulus for new troops leaving for France! The Battalion reached Folkestone at 9-30 p.m., and the embarkation on the s.s. *Victoria* was rapidly and smoothly carried out. The troopship was escorted by torpedo boats, but their number could not be ascertained in the darkness. The rules were those for night operations, all lights extinguished, and no noise. The sea was very calm, and the passage was over in an hour and a quarter. About midnight the men marched up to the ST. MARTIN'S rest camp, situated about two and a half miles from Boulogne, on the hill top. Though a short march, it was rather a trying one. Everyone had left England loaded with equipment of all kinds. At the last moment friends had sent numberless packages of " necessities for soldiers on active service," including anything from patent periscopes and " knuckle dusters " (a fiendish instrument for killing Germans at close quarters), to condensed meats and vermin killers, with the poems of Ella Wheeler Wilcox thrown in. In spite of orders to the contrary, everyone had accumulated stores of these things, partly from sentiment and chiefly from ignorance of active service conditions. Naturally the four-kilometre march up an exceedingly steep hill after hours of parades and over-crowding brought home forcibly to everyone the folly of being laden like a pack animal. Many things were left at Boulogne which had been guarded with tender solicitude in England !

The following message from the City of Bradford was sent to Lieut. Col. H. O. Wade, on April 14/15 :—

Officer Commanding Officers and Men of the 6th West Yorkshire
Regiment.

Gentlemen,

On the eve of your departure for active service abroad I have the honour to address to you the heartfelt good wishes of the citizens of Bradford. During the period of your training I am informed that your general conduct has been exemplary, and that you have now attained a high state of efficiency.

Bradford is justly proud of her sons who have so nobly answered the call to duty, and in now taking leave of you we have full confidence that you will serve your country with distinction on the battlefield.

We should very much have preferred to give you a public send off; but the circumstances of your training have prevented this. You may rest fully assured, however, that our good wishes for your welfare are none the less sincere, and we pray that when the purposes of your mission are fulfilled you will have a safe and speedy return to your homes.

In the meantime we shall follow with close interest your progress at the front, in the full assurance that you will maintain the proud traditions of the city you represent.

Yours faithfully,
GEO. H. ROBINSON.

April 14/1915.   Lord Mayor, Bradford.

"A safe and speedy return to your homes" was not to be! But we shall see in the story that follows how the Battalion "*fulfilled the purposes of its mission.*"*

---

* A List of all Officers and Men who crossed over to France on April 15th, 1915, is given on page 280.

CHAPTER II.

FIRST EXPERIENCES IN FRANCE.

THE story of the Battalion's first few days in France is worth describing in some detail, as although there is nothing very unusual to relate, our men passed through experiences typical of those of most untried units in a foreign country under active service conditions. The movement of 1000 men with transport and other details is a complicated affair, demanding patience and forbearance in a marked degree on the part of each individual. Especially is this the case when officers are new to their work, and when men are not trained in making the best of bad circumstances. During the first few days one thing was extremely noticeable. Everybody was in great spirits. Whether the men were packed—forty-four of them—in a railway truck for over thirty hours, or whether they were searching for their billets at 2 a.m. on a cold wet morning, they never lost their first keenness and enthusiasm now that at last, after eight months' weary waiting, they were " on active service." Naturally, it was only after several months of " the real thing " that they could rise to the high philosophy of—

> " Old soldiers never die
> They simply *fade away*."

For the first few weeks no one could be bored : everything was too strange, absurd or exciting. There were no crimes of any kind : no insubordination ; any amount of " grousing," of course, but no bad temper or ugly spirits. These humours came later, when the enthusiasm wore off. In the meantime, the men were amazingly cheery, ready on the slightest excuse to turn their misfortunes into a joke.

First of all, let us deal with the early experiences of the Battalion Transport. The misfortunes of the Transport were always a legitimate theme for jest and sarcasm on the part of everyone except the Transport men themselves. We were proud of our Transport and they served us magnificently, but it was our special privilege often to turn their exploits to a jest. Immediately before the Battalion left England, the Transport Officer (Lieut. F. W. Musgrave) had an extremely anxious time. All the arrangements had been left to the last few days. A few hours before the Battalion left England six chargers and twenty-nine mules, to replace animals cast as " unfit for active service," arrived at Gainsborough. At the same time wagon after wagon load of equipment rolled in, harness, picketing gear, buckets, nose bags, head ropes, tail ropes, officers' saddles, bridles, bits, horse shoes, mule shoes, harness tools, saddlers' tools, etc., etc. Most of the men had never seen the Army pattern of harness in their lives, and as it was all new and had to be fitted, the work was made doubly difficult. However, after superhuman exertions, everything was sorted out in time. The Transport and M. G. section left Gainsborough the day before the Battalion, at 3-50 on the morning of April 14th, 1915. They embarked at Southampton on the s.s. " Archimedes " at 7-30 p.m., and arrived at Havre the following day 2-45 a.m. There was only one casualty on the passage, a mule being badly bitten on the upper lip.

At 5 p.m. on April 15th, the Transport entrained at Le Havre on their way to meet the Battalion at Pont de Brique, near Boulogne. There were eight horses as usual in each cattle truck : four horses facing the engine, and the other four with their tails to it ; men, forage, and harness being placed in the middle. Wagons and limbers were on trucks at the rear of the train : then came about ten horse wagons : about twenty-five trucks for the Battalion, empty of course : and four empty compartments for officers and senior N. C. O's. At 7 a.m. next day the train reached Amiens, and seven hours later arrived at Pont de Brique Station, where the rest of the Battalion was waiting to entrain. The train then continued its slow progress, and arrived at Merville at 10 p.m., where everybody detrained and set out to find their billets. Before dealing with the adventures of the Battalion, we will give a brief *résumé* of the experiences of the Transport.

The Transport had been thirty-six hours in the train and everybody was fed up. It was a very dark night, and the detraining of transport, never an easy job, was rendered unusually difficult to inexperienced troops. The story of the next few hours is tragi-comedy of no mean order. The first difficulty was to find the harness in the darkness of the trucks : the next to fit it on. Nobody had flashlamps—that most essential part of an officer's or N.C.O's equipment—and condensed foods and Ella Wheeler Wilcox's poems did not help. The train steamed out of the station before some of the things lost could be found, and before anyone could explain to the driver in lucid French that his train would be needed for some time longer. The R. T. O. (Railway Transport Officer) could not be found. One of the limbers was minus a breastpole, and some men of C Company were detailed to man-handle the limber, and march ahead of the rest of the Transport with the guide. At last, however, everything was ready. The transport had just started, when a Staff Officer's Car, with huge head-lights, came round a corner suddenly. Whereat the mules in a couple of limbers shied, reared up, slipped their harness and faced their respective limbers. This little stoppage having been rectified, the procession carried on for about half a mile, when the first limber with mules absolutely refused to cross a wooden bridge. Tremendous efforts were made to drive, cajole or carry them across, but they wouldn't have any of it. All this time the man-handled limber and the guide—in blissful ignorance of the situation behind them—carried on in the darkness. The woes of the harassed Transport Officer were only just beginning. He had galloped on the cobbles for some time in an effort to find his man-handled limber and guide, when he was stopped by the inevitable Staff Officer, turning up as usual at the awkward moment. He informed the Transport Officer that his Transport had stopped. " Why?" he demanded curtly. Then followed an energetic and brief explanation. " You had better stop your front limber, and find your guide," says the Staff Officer, and rides on, conscious of rectitude. The guide was found. The limber was man-handled over the bridge, and the refractory mules harnessed on the other side of the canal. The rest of the mules caused difficulty, as this seemed to have been the first bridge they had ever crossed in their unnatural lives. By this time the Transport was rather scattered. Up comes another Staff Officer, and demands of the T. O. " Did he know his transport was all over the streets?" This information was not new, but he added, " You had better take on what you have, and leave the rest to come on later." Captain N. Muller thereupon stayed behind with two or three limbers and mules which were still trying to precipitate themselves into the canal, and the rest of the Transport marched on. It was black darkness, and pouring with rain. Everyone was wet through, but trials had only commenced. Another half mile, and the pole of one limber ran through the tail board of the next. A few yards further, and one of the wagons turned turtle into a ditch. Eventually the guide stopped, and informed them they had arrived, and he pointed into the darkness. The Transport Officer dismounted, felt his way to a gate and discovered in time two deep ditches on either side of it. The first wagon which entered the field went straight into a quagmire up to the axles. The driver had not learnt that first golden rule, which experience in France quickly taught everyone,—to shout out to those behind immediately anything unforeseen lies in your own way. Result—two other wagons followed him, and also sank up to their axles in the mud. Then Captain N. Muller (who had arrived with the remainder of the Transport) volunteered to flash his lamp in a safe part of the field. Unfortunately some one made a mistake, and followed the flash before it was intended, with the result that a fourth limber came to grief, this time in the ditch. In his effort to save the next limber the T. O. himself followed the other limber in the ditch, and confusion was complete. When dawn broke on the scene it was still raining heavily, everyone was still working, and the field presented something of the appearance of a battlefield. It was hours later before the limbers and wagons were rescued from the ditch and the bog, and the men could have a few hours of rest. The field was near LE SART, a small village one and a half miles from Merville. The Battalion had also arrived during the same night. Their billets were only a few hundred yards away from the field where the transport was parked.

The immediate result of their experiences of the first night in France was that for two or three hours each day during the stay near Merville, the mules were practised in pulling limbers across bridges, and the use of dubbing to soften harness was popular for a short time. Probably one cause of the animals' bad temper was the awful galls they had received with the new harness served out the day before they left Gainsborough. Quickly, however, the Transport adapted itself to new conditions, and became thoroughly efficient, one of the best in the Brigade. But none of the Transport men will forget the experiences of that night. On countless later occasions they had similar difficulties, with the added complication of danger; but it is usually the first experience which is remembered most vividly.

To return to the remainder of the Battalion, whom we left at the Rest Camp near Boulogne. The men lay down in their greatcoats on the grass under canvas. The night was clear, but there was a cold wind and no one was tempted to sleep too long. The Battalion paraded early next morning, and marched to Pont de Brique Station, three or four miles from Boulogne, where they were to entrain. The day was very hot. The Frenchwomen, who ran alongside the column selling oranges, did a roaring trade. When the Battalion arrived at the Station, and the command was given " forty-four men to each truck," the first impression was one of frank incredulity that so many men with full equipment could be crammed into so small a space. However, it was done. Nobody could either sit or stand with any degree of comfort, and of course to lie down was out of the question. Occasionally on these journeys men who were near the door, or who tried to get some fresh air, fell out of the train, or were pushed out. This was not usually serious, as the troop trains were notoriously leisurely, and took hours to cover a few miles. The crowding into trucks also had the advantage of keeping men alive, who might otherwise have been frozen to death during the cold nights of winter. Two men, belonging to one of the other battalions in the Brigade, fell out in their sleep on this same journey, but were uninjured, and joined their battalion a few hours later in Merville! The 6th Battalion had no accidents, and reached Hazebrouck about 4 p.m. There was a hospital train full of wounded in the Station, and this may have damped the ardour of a few of the men—it was rather a harsh reminder of the direction in which they were moving. But the men were in great spirits, and had been singing for hours. At one point our train was passed by a train going to Boulogne, packed with men on leave. These fellows shouted out, " Are you downhearted ? " and received a tremendous " No," from the men of our Battalion. " Well, you damned soon will be," was the fervent reply from scores of throats, as their train passed on. After a short while our train stopped about six miles from Merville, waiting for darkness before nearing the town, which was only about seven miles from the line. Another grim reminder of the fact that the Battalion was nearing the battle zone was given here. Night was approaching, and our men saw for the first time the Verey lights of the line, about twelve miles away. As many thought they were going straight into the firing line, the flares awakened great interest and some seriousness. During this hour's wait, one or two resourceful people borrowed hot water from the engine boiler, and made themselves tea. The train arrived at Merville at 10 p.m., and the Battalion detrained immediately.

They marched through the town of Merville in good order, but their troubles began when they left the town behind them, and approached the long straggling village of Le Sart, in expectation of quickly finding billets. Billeting is a fine art, and needs a long apprenticeship before it is thoroughly understood. A special type of officer and N.C.O. is needed to billet a battalion properly, especially in a French village. He must be a man of initiative and resource, with a good " bump of locality," first-class memory and an aptitude for unselfishness in giving the best billets to other people (especially his Colonel, Company Commander, Quartermaster and Sergeant Major) and never thinking of himself. He must also have a knowledge of French, and be able to bully the Mayor, and use infinite tact with " Madame," convincing her that his battalion is very polite and very rich, ready to pay for everything and be satisfied with anything. We discovered in later days three ideal billeting officers, who possessed all the above qualifications, Lieuts. Scales, Mitchell and Higgins; but unfortunately, the arrangements for the Le Sart billets were in other hands. It is difficult to say exactly what happened. The billeting party had been sent on in advance, but had lost both the Battalion and

FIRST EXPERIENCES IN FRANCE

FIRST EXPERIENCES IN FRANCE

the Battalion's billets. It was probably all the fault of Brigade H. Q. Staff, as is usually alleged by battalions on these occasions. Anyhow, when the Battalion arrived at the long straggling village of Le Sart no one could find their billets. For that matter no one could see Le Sart, as the darkness was of that blackest kind, in which a man six feet away is lost. The rain came down in torrents and it was bitterly cold. Everyone realized that to arrive in the village in which one is billeted is very different from reaching billets. French villages consist usually of one main street, sometimes with many turnings, and often two miles long. Le Sart was such a village. Men went by sections and platoons to any barn which was handy. Billeting became the individual affair of every platoon officer and sergeant. It was not till hours later, when the cocks began to crow, and a miserable dawn appeared on the horizon, that the Battalion could be said to have settled down for rest. Men were sleeping near pig styes and in cattle sheds, anywhere, everywhere. Half-a-dozen men climbed up to the loft of a rickety barn, and lay close together for warmth. In the early hours of the morning, the matchwood floor boarding gave way, and they fell in a heap on to some frightened horses fifteen feet below. No one was injured. O. C. 'A' Company passed through experiences on this night which, though not in any way remarkable, provided food for mirth in later days. Though temporarily lame in one knee he had refused to stay behind in England, and had marched with his Company to Le Sart. In the centre of the village, on the side of the road, there was a very deep and particularly filthy sewer. He fell into this, in the darkness, up to his shoulders, and was only extricated with difficulty. He was then taken to a barn and one of the men of his Company gave him some hot coffee. He said he never tasted a better cup of coffee in his life! Later on he learnt that his drink had been made of water taken from the aforesaid sewer. It was on this night that Sergeant W—, a steady married man with a family, was found by the Colonel in " compromising circumstances." The Sergeant was trying to find a billet for his platoon and had lost himself in the darkness. At last he saw a woman coming out of a farm house, and in his best French he explained that he wanted a shelter for the night for himself and any men he could find. He confessed later that he had little hope of finding any men, as he was lost too completely himself. The woman was just beginning to understand, when the Colonel arrived on the scene. He had been at work for some hours, trying to produce order out of chaos, and was not disposed to cheerfulness on finding one of his senior sergeants alone with a woman and hopelessly lost. Matters were soon explained, however, and the sergeant got his billet.

23

For several days the Battalion stayed in Le Sart. The men began to accustom themselves to billet life in France. They lived in barns all over the village, forty or fifty in each farmyard. The degree of discomfort of such billets depended almost entirely upon how much clean straw there was available, and if the barns were well built. During the first few months the Battalion was in France every barn had a good supply of hay or straw, and the billets were therefore tolerably comfortable. Unfortunately, owing to frequent outbreaks of fire, the privilege of hay and straw in billets was withdrawn in later days. As the inhabitants had not at this time left the Merville district, the farm buildings were on the whole comfortable; but nearer the line, where the barns were in many cases falling to pieces, the men had little shelter from the rain, and on cold nights were frozen stiff. Even in good barns it was impossible to sleep the night through in winter, and men were frequently compelled to walk about half the night to exercise their frozen limbs. When the Battalion was in reserve, one blanket per man was issued, and of course everyone slept in his great coat. It is impossible to exaggerate the cheerless discomfort of this " barn-life." This discomfort was greatly increased when fires were prohibited, owing to the carelessness of a few individuals who would easily have burnt down the whole village if the regulation as to fires in billets had not been strict. The barns were very inflammable, as they were not built of brick, but of wood laths covered with " torchis," a kind of baked clay. As we shall notice later three or four incendiary shells falling on this inflammable material would burn out a village in two or three hours.

On the other side of the line the Germans lived in comfort, " stabling " themselves in the best rooms of the houses, and graciously allowing the inhabitants to live in the cellars!

All French farms in the North were constructed on the same model. A hollow square of buildings—dwelling house, barns, pigstye and stables—surrounded a large open space, in the middle of which was the manure heap. As Bairnsfather describes it :—" a three or four-sided red-tiled building, with a rectangular smell in the middle." The wealth of the farm could very largely be estimated by the extent, depth and pungency of odour of the manure heap. All day long hens and pigs rummaged in the heap, and fed on the slops which were thrown on it daily from the kitchen. The Company Officers' Mess was usually in one of the two living rooms of the farm, and the officers slept on the floor. Occasionally two or three of the more fortunate officers were able to sleep in one of the bedrooms. The men, numbering from fifty to two hundred, slept in the barns round the manure heap.

FIRST EXPERIENCES IN FRANCE

It was 10 p.m. on 16th April, 1915, when the Battalion arrived in Merville. During the next few days the concentration of the 49th Division in the Merville district was carried on and completed. For the sake of convenience we will in future refer to the Brigades of the Division by their final titles. On May 7th, 1915, the 1/1st, 1/2nd and 1/3rd Infantry Brigades were re-named the 146, 147, 148 Infantry Brigades respectively. Major–General T. S. Baldock was in Command of the Division, which was re-entitled, in the same War Office Letter, the 49th West Riding Division. The General in command of the 146 Brigade was Brigadier-General F. A. Macfarlan, C.B. The Division arrived in France at a critical moment. Six weeks earlier the battle of Neuve Chapelle had been a failure and everyone was beginning to realize the probability of a prolonged struggle. The first gas attack, heralding the second battle of Ypres, began a few days after the Battalion reached Boulogne. For a week the struggle continued, and our line was withdrawn for a depth of two miles on a semi-circular front of about eight miles. This battle was raging whilst the Battalion was going through its first experience of the line at Fauquissart, and a constant stream of traffic and reinforcements was moving north, always north, towards " The Salient." Thus the Battalion went into the trenches when the horrors of gas had just been added to modern methods of war, and when the shortage of shells had been admitted by our G. H. Q. in France. The infantry in the line had realized it some time previously !

Two days after arriving at Merville the order came to Battalion H. Q. that Company and Platoon Officers were to go for twenty-four hours' instruction into the line near Fauquissart, and to be attached to the 2nd Yorkshire Regt. (Green Howards), 21st Brigade of 7th Division. On April 22nd, the Battalion marched from Merville to Estaires (five kilometres), and from the latter place platoons and companies were sent into the same Fauquissart sector for instruction. The first platoons to go in for twenty-hours were one each from A and B Coys. on the 25th April, under the orders of the 2nd Border Regt, 20th Infantry Brigade. The next day one platoon from each of the four companies went into the line, and the two platoons of A and B Company returned to the Battalion. On the 27th April the whole Battalion marched into the line, and relieved the 2nd Border Regiment for twenty-four hours.

Before dealing with the experiences of these first twenty-four hours in the line, let us consider the general characteristics of the sector. Fauquissart was probably the quietest part of the British line in France. When the Battalion returned two years later to this sector, those who remembered the line in 1915 were surprised to find the same dugouts still intact and in use. Throughout the war the sector was regarded as a good training ground for new troops. For instance the Portuguese in 1917 tried to learn their first lessons in war here ! The chief towns behind the line were Merville, La Gorgue, Estaires and Laventie, small industrial towns in the heart of a rich agricultural district. Before the war Laventie must have been by far the pleasantest town of the four—with wide tree-shaded streets, and a few handsome villas and public buildings. The country was flat and well-watered, with dykes along the edge of every field, and long lines of willows and poplars : a closed-in landscape, where trees confined the view to the limit of a few fields, and where red-roofed farms were dotted every few hundred yards over the country side. When our men first went to Laventie in 1915 there were few inhabitants in the district, owing to the battles of Neuve Chapelle and the preparations for the battles of Aubers Ridge and Fromelles. But when the sector took on again its wonted calm the inhabitants returned, and tried to live again a normal life two or three miles behind the line. Old men and women worked in the fields and gardens within a few hundred yards of our advanced guns.

Between the opposing trenches at Fauquissart there was a dyke about fifteen feet wide—dignified by the name Rivière des Laies—which occasionally in times of heavy rain flooded both lines of trenches. The trenches were about 150 to 200 yards apart. Our men looked over the enemy line to a ridge of low hills, about three miles away, which constituted the enemy's last natural defence west of Lille. Lille was about thirteen miles distant from Laventie. Owing to the low-lying ground and the fact that the trenches quickly filled with water, the defences in the Fauquissart sector were chiefly built up above ground, in the form of breastworks, made of millions of sandbags, supported by almost as many wood and iron stakes, and defended by miles of barbed wire. In April 1915 there were practically no reserve lines or communication trenches. Reliefs were carried out by night across country. By day small parties of men could walk fairly freely a few hundred yards behind the line, and canvas screens erected along the road sides gave some protection from view by the enemy. Ruined farms on the Fleurbaix—Neuve Chapelle Road (called Rue Tilleloy) were used by our men as observation and machine gun posts. The great danger of the sector was not artillery, but machine gun and rifle fire. At intervals by day, and persistently throughout the night, enemy machine guns swept with fire the approach areas to the front trenches, and gave reliefs and ration parties a bad time. There were few dugouts, and those were poorly constructed : the men lived in lean-to shelters over the fire-step. A few days of heavy artillery fire would have blown all the dug-outs and defences to pieces, but the days passed quietly on the whole.

By day sniping was constant. Every few moments the sharp crack of a rifle spoke harshly of an alert watch : an ever-threatening danger.

One of the most striking things about this part of the line was the extraordinary irrelevance of a charming countryside in time of war. Flowers could be plucked in the trenches. A nightingale was heard in the front line on the morning of the battle of May 9th. The orchards were full of fruit (for a few hours only) within a hundred yards of the guns. Yet death struck men down with remorseless frequency even in this pleasant corner of La Belle France.

When the Battalion took over the line for twenty-four hours at Fauquissart, the absence of all the expected signs of a battle front rather disconcerted our men. They saw no Germans, and had nothing to shoot at except rats. As one of our Sergeants wrote in his diary, " The veterans of the Border Regiment took their relief as stolidly as woolcombers on the nightshift at Isaac Holden's ! " No Man's Land was a charming continuation of quiet country scenery, and the dead were hidden in the long grass. This impression of pleasantness of course quickly vanished. During the second night in the line the enemy began shelling—heavily, as it seemed then. Impossible to describe the first experience of being shelled ! The old " sweats " of the Border Regiment seemed to ignore shelling. During one bout of shelling a few of them even played football between the traverses, and if the ball went over the parapet jumped over and brought it in. Our men thought this indifference to shelling was a magnificent affectation, and they tried to be indifferent also, and to refrain from asking too anxiously, "Where did that one go to?" But it was impossible for them to maintain this indifference. Every shell seemed to have " one's name written on it." No one had learnt to discriminate between dangerous shells, and those which were likely to burst harmlessly a few hundred yards away. It was even difficult to tell whose shells they were, and the invariable question during those first hours was " Whose was that ? " as a missile shrieked overhead. The shelling on this occasion lasted about three-quarters of an hour : yet it seemed to last for hours. Later on, when nerves had become dulled, everyone was tempted to ignore the effect of the everlasting strain which men went through during a tour in the trenches, even in so-called quiet sectors. Yet the trace was on every man's face. The lack of sufficient sleep accentuated the strain. Men grew older visibly. The youngster became unnaturally flushed, and carelessness passed from him. Upon the older men the result was much more marked. They often aged years in as many weeks. But a week's rest worked marvels : the face lost its hard lines, and the eyes relaxed. Unconsciously, however, reserves of mental force were consumed in the trenches, which normally would have been used in later life against the demands of middle and old age.

During the first twenty-four hours in the line everyone was impressed with the morning and evening " Stand-to." At the approach of dusk the word was rapidly passed down to all ranks by the officer and N.C.O. on duty and the trench became the scene of sudden activity. Men came out of dugouts, and got up from the fire steps where they had been resting : examined rifles and bayonets : looked at their ammunition : prepared for the unknown adventures of the night. Sentries loosed off a few rounds at the enemy : M. G.'s fired one or two rounds from their night emplacements (the M. G.'s were strictly rationed in ammunition in those days !). The enemy replied, and a desultory fire began along the whole front from Nieuport to Switzerland. Then the first star shells were sent up : after which the minutes passed uneventfully : darkness came on rapidly, and the sentries could not see beyond their own wire : there was " nothing doing." Men said to each other, " Fritz seems quiet enough to-night" The hour of danger passed, and the order was given to " stand down." The trenches again became silent, except for the whispered talk of sentries : the occasional rat-tat-tat of a M. G. : or a sentry's rifle-fire, caused by a suspected enemy patrol, or a desire to keep himself awake during his two or three hours' watch. The first night in the line seemed long to our men : the dawn inexpressibly grateful. Again the " stand to " order was passed down the line : all patrols were in : the enemy's trenches could be dimly seen through the mist. Rifles and ammunition were again examined : everyone was again on the alert during the dangerous hour when there is enough light to guide men for a big attack, yet enough darkness to give shelter from accurate fire. Then followed the usual " morning hate." Those hours from dawn to breakfast were nearly always the worst part of the day for the wretched infantryman. The gunners and trench mortar experts always seemed to have passed a refreshing night and to be full of energy before breakfast. Light was good and ammunition had been brought up in the darkness. So they shelled us merrily and registered fairly good hits. Voice in enemy Observation Post :—" No. 2 Gun. Four six hundred. Ready. Fire. Drop one hundred. Ready. Fire. O.K. four rounds— " or some such jargon, followed by a grunt of gutteral Bosche satisfaction. Voice in our trenches, " Oh Hell ! where is the next one coming to ? " Then a direct hit. Trench fills with smoke, and the pungent smell of picric acid. Confusion for a moment, and the inevitable " Stretcher bearers this way ! " Then follows the usual slow-moving procession : corporal and two men carrying a stretcher, covered with a ground sheet, under which a pair of regulation boots show stiffly and rigidly. The Battalion had seven casualties—all wounded —during the first twenty-four hours in the line : no N. C. O.'s or Officers : but the men began to realize how grim was the trade to which they were serving their apprenticeship. Men learnt their lessons quickly. The first twenty-four hours in the line at Fauquissart taught more than as many days in Camp in England as to what were essential qualities in a soldier :—a rifle always ready to shoot accurately : an intelligent discipline : a capacity for making oneself comfortable anywhere : and a self-control which never allowed a man to show how much afraid he really was.

Three things were always welcome after the " stand to " in the morning :—First, the Rum Ration. Second, the sight of our own aeroplanes, as usually the enemy guns then became silent so as not to give away their position by gun flashes. Third, breakfast. Even the enemy breakfasted, and the world for a short time was at peace. The first Rum Ration in the history of the Battalion was issued at 11 a.m. on a very hot morning. The night had been very cold and the ration would then have been very welcome, but some humorist in the Battalion remarked that the Authorities desired to see in broad daylight the effect on the men of the first rum ration.

The regular troops in the line were very good to our Territorial Battalion. They were liberal with their cigarettes and, as our men had received none in the rations, their generosity was welcome. They also gave us much information : and their word was law.

After the first tour in the trenches, the Battalion went into reserve billets in Estaires. On May 1st, the Brigadier inspected the equipment of his Brigade very thoroughly, and introduced one or two innovations. An order was given for the men to hand in their winter clothing (greatcoats, etc.), and to cut short their trousers below the knee, for greater coolness when marching. Scissors were used freely, but not always accurately, with the result that the length of trouser varied with every man throughout the Battalion. A further order came to remove the wires out of the service cap. Caps of all shapes and contours began to appear in the Battalion. In those days, everyone wished to appear old in experience of active service. A worn-out uniform, or a shapeless mass of a cap, distinguished the wearer from the crowd at the Base, or from new reinforcements from England. Moreover, these details marked a definite advance in the eyes of the men from the wearisome " eye-wash " of home service training, where smart buckles and puttees were final proofs of efficiency. Needless to say this slackness was only temporary. The stage in discipline quickly came when it was a matter of pride to get rid of the mess of the trenches as quickly as possible : when the most efficient battalion was the one which could appear most quickly with clean equipment and shaved faces on the morning after a relief. The order to remove the wires from the service cap was a very necessary one, as the flat regular round showed very clearly in the trenches, and was easily picked out by enemy snipers.

During this stay at Estaires our men came in contact with the 3rd Lahore Division, and were very favourably impressed with the Indian troops : their courtesy and splendid physique. Few of our men will forget the march through Estaires of the 1st Lahore Division on its way to the battle in the Ypres Salient. There were one or two English battalions attached to the Lahore Division—such as the 2nd Battalion Manchester Regiment and the 4th Battalion Suffolk Regiment (the latter one of the earliest T. F. units to go into action) ; but the physique of the tall turbaned Indians seemed to surpass that of our own men, and they marched with a wonderful spirit and élan. Our men also became acquainted with the French people, and were fleeced and overcharged for everything, till Estaires got a very bad name. As often happened in villages near the line, the French shopkeepers were amongst the worst of their class : people whose cupidity had made them willing to risk danger, and who were trying to make a fortune quickly. Very often they were not natives of the town, but speculators from other districts, who installed themselves in houses evacuated by their original owners during the German advance. The inhabitants of Estaires had suffered considerably during the eight days of German occupation in October, 1914. Our men read notices on the walls of Estaires Town Hall asking for the names of all women and girls who were enceinte as a result of the German occupation, to be given to the Mayor. The courage and cheerfulness of most of the natives very much impressed our men and was beyond praise. In spite of a constant succession of often very careless soldiery Madame kept her temper and carried on her work unceasingly. But some people have short memories, and there were doubtless many shopkeepers in Estaires who regarded the invasion of their town by English soldiers in much the same light as they would have regarded an invasion by Germans—with this supremely important difference, the English had money and would pay handsomely for everything ! And the English paid handsomely for everything—for their " luxuries " in reserve, and even for the hire of their trenches in the front line system ! In the meantime the profiteers of Estaires and of England carried on gaily and unashamed, and the sacred thing called business was even " better than usual."

CHAPTER III.

PERIOD OF APPRENTICESHIP—NEUVE CHAPELLE AND FLEURBAIX.

AFTER another move and a few days' stay at Bac St. Maur, a village about four miles from Estaires, the Battalion marched to Laventie, where orders were received to take over the Neuve Chapelle sector of the line. This was done on May 5th, 1915, and for ten days the Battalion remained in this sector.

The 146th Infantry Brigade held the line from Neuve Chapelle to La Cordonnerie Farm inclusive, a front of about 7 kilometres. Apart from one or two isolated platoons in reserve positions, all the Battalions of the Brigade were in the front line. It is interesting to compare this method of holding the line with that adopted in 1917. The Brigade front two years later (1917) was only three kilometres long, or less than half the 1915 front. Moreover, in 1917 only four Companies were in the front line—two Companies from each of the two front line Battalions. The third battalion of the Brigade held a series of posts in support, and the remaining battalion was in reserve at Laventie. It can easily be seen that, whereas in 1915 the front line was held in strength with all available men, there was an entire change of tactics later on in the war, and positions were held in depth, the front line being regarded as an outpost line only. In 1915 every bay had a sentry post, and the line gave one the appearance of being crowded with men. In 1917 one could walk along several bays of the front line trenches without being challenged, and without meeting a soul. This latter method saved many casualties.

Another reason for the concentration of men in the front line was that in 1915 there were practically no men extra-regimentally employed. The personnel of the Transport and Q. M. Stores was also cut down to the minimum. No one had heard of the Lewis Gun, and there were only two Maxim Machine Guns per battalion. Bombs were rarely used, and were of a very primitive pattern. Thus attention was concentrated upon the use of the rifle, and every extra rifleman in the front line was regarded as the surest economy. During the Neuve Chapelle and Fleurbaix periods there must have been at least 700 men in about 1,500 or 1,700 yards of trench. At "stand to" the firesteps were crowded, and must have resembled the line of spectators at a football match.

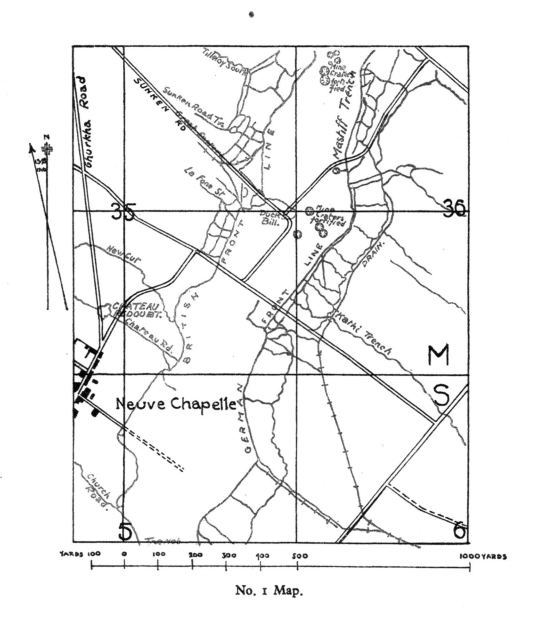

No. 1 Map.

LIEUT.-COL. R. A. HUDSON, D.S.O.

LIEUT.-COL. W. A. WISTANCE, D.S.O., M.C.

LIEUT.-COL. F. G. HORNSHAW, M.C.

LIEUT.-COL. AND QUARTERMASTER
W. H. HILL, M.C.

V.

CAPT. R. WHINCUP, M.C., C.F.

MAJOR G. R. SANDEMAN, D.S.O., M.C.

MAJOR R. A. FAWCETT, M.C.

CAPT. A. HAMILTON, R.A.M.C.

vi.

DEPARTURE FROM BRADFORD.

SCENE OUTSIDE BELLE VUE BARRACKS.

MOBILIZATION SCENES.

LOADING TRUCKS.

ARRIVAL IN SELBY.

MOBILIZATION SCENES.

PERIOD OF APPRENTICESHIP

Shortly after the May 9th battle it is interesting to note there were five battalions of the West Yorkshire Regiment next to one another in the line. They were in the following order from right to left:—

2nd Bn. West Yorkshire Regt.
1/6th Bn. West Yorkshire Regt.
1/8th Bn. West Yorkshire Regt.
1/7th Bn. West Yorkshire Regt.
1/5th Bn. West Yorkshire Regt.

Neuve Chapelle was similar in most respects to the Fauquissart Sector: the same breastworks: the same flat, enclosed country: the same method of holding the line. There was one great difference however: the tide of battle had flowed over the countryside and left its horrid debris everywhere. The front line occupied by our Battalion formed originally, before the advance in the battle of Neuve Chapelle, the enemy third and fourth support lines. Behind this front line lay the ruins of the village and the battered remains of the original German front line system, where our men wandered for souvenirs and occasionally unearthed tins of provisions, especially rice—a great asset to trench diet. In front of the line lay the dead, rows and rows of them, mostly British, though German dead lay thickly enough in some parts. What is the most enduring memory of the Neuve Chapelle sector? There could be only one reply:—"The Dead." Our men existed for ten days in a vast cemetery where no one had been buried. In front and behind the line, along communication trenches, everywhere, putrescent bodies! The parapets were built up with them: they served as directing points to dugouts and sentry posts, and even helped to give direction to patrols across No Man's Land. The heavy sickly stench, which could be felt miles away, lay like a cloud over the trenches where men ate and slept. The heat during May was terrific: men gasped and sweltered under it, and the ration of tobacco and cigarettes soon gave out. Amazing that there were no cases of disease, but everyone was very fit and hardened. A peculiar callousness to the dead came over everybody. Their bodies were rifled for useful parts of equipment, matches and cigarettes. Considerably more than half the men in the Battalion fitted themselves out with the new Short Rifle issued to the troops who attacked on May 9th, and the long rifles were returned to Ordnance. There was rivalry among the Companies as to how many short rifles could be salvaged, and unfortunately, there were more than enough of them to equip many battalions. The only difficulty was that the dead lay out in No Man's Land, and the rifles were frequently salvaged at the risk of our own men's lives.

There was much heart burning at Head Quarters on the question of these salvaged rifles. The Authorities ordered the Battalion to give up all their short rifles, and at the same time tried to persuade us that the " converted long Rifle " (already in our possession) was a better weapon than the short rifle, which was being then issued to all units in the New Army. This was adding insult to injury. The Battalion carried out several tests, which proved conclusively that the short rifle did not jam in " firing rapid " to anything like the same extent as the long rifle. This freedom from " jamming " outweighed any inferiority there may have been in accuracy of fire, and made men willing to risk their lives to obtain the new rifle. Also the long rifle could not be used for firing rifle grenades, as these were constructed to clip on to the short rifle. After considerable difficulty, permission was obtained by the Battalion to keep the salvaged rifles, and in this way the Battalion was put on an equality with units of the New Army. In a few other respects, let it be said in passing, T. F. units did not receive in the early days either the equipment or consideration given to New Army units. As the Earl of Harewood stated after the Armistice at a Meeting of the West Riding Territorial Association, the 49th Division held a vital sector for six months in the Ypres Salient in 1915 with only thirty-six 15-pounder guns (these restricted for considerable periods to three rounds a gun per day), when Divisions formed of Regulars and the New Army had fifty-four 18-pounder guns. The chance of promotion too for junior officers was naturally more difficult in a T. F. unit, with its pre-war cadre, than in a New Army one, and this gave rise in some cases to bitterness which was based on a misunderstanding of the nature of the T. F. by younger officers and N. C. O.'s. On the other hand, there was a feeling in some quarters that senior appointments were not given with sufficient impartiality to T. F. officers, and their years of service not taken into account. Although these things did not alter either their loyalty or keenness, it is necessary to mention them, as they were matters of common knowledge in every unit.

To return to the Neuve Chapelle sector, and the conditions of trench life in that vast cemetery of " unhouseled dead."

Men became initiated to the strange effects of shell fire and other methods of killing men. Some men had been torn by bullets, bombs and shells till their bodies were unrecognizable ; others had been untouched, dead from concussion. Some had been killed in the midst of fight, every muscle stretched ; some seemed literally to have fallen asleep, with a smile. Wherever possible they were buried, and though it was done in haste there was no lack of sympathy. " Things that involve a risk are like the Christian Faith : they must be seen from the inside." Our men knew it was quite possible they, too, would quickly share the same fate, and the callousness towards the dead, which we have mentioned above, was only superficial.

The most dangerous section of the Neuve Chapelle line was an advanced post, called " The Duck's Bill." A sap about 150 yards long ran out from our front line towards the enemy, and formed three sides of a square approximately seventy yards each way and about ninety yards from the German front line.   It was commonly supposed that the whole area had been undermined by the enemy and would probably " go up " any time.   The feelings of the garrison can be imagined, but not described.   One night (May 13th) No. 11 Platoon was ordered to evacuate it, as the R.E. expert said " the time had come."   Owing to some delay in receiving definite instructions, the garrison remained a further two hours before evacuation : and even then a small sentry post was left. The mine did not go up during the Battalion's stay in the sector, but such experiences test every faculty of the soldier.   The fact that on this occasion every man stayed at his post without hesitation needs no comment.

In the centre of the Duck's Bill was an old broken-down farm house. A member of the M. G. section which occupied the post writes :—

" I can recall the excitement caused after one of our men had visited this old farm.   The troops in Duck's Bill could distinctly hear a whirring buzzing sound, which they naturally put down to the evil work underground of the enemy.   Much excitement. It appeared, however, that there was no ground for anxiety, as on investigation it was found that in the old house was a milk separator, which had been left in good running order, and which one of our men had set going ! On another occasion a member of our section was acting as cook's orderly and he found quite a decent supply of good dry timber for his fire in this farm house. A piece of the upstairs floor boarding was hanging down within reach of the ground floor.   Taking a tug at this, the man pulled down the entire bedroom flooring, and one outside wall of the farm, burying under the debris the equipment of a platoon of C Company.   This caused No. 12 platoon to be on fatigue the whole morning, and also caused our friends the Bosches across the way a little excitement.   They began rapid fire upon the farm with M. G.'s and rifles, and as the parapet was very low at this point the situation was not comfortable, but no one was hit."

The Neuve Chapelle sector introduced our men to the horrors of trench mortars.   One of them describes the occasion as follows :—
" I was on sentry duty, and was looking over the parapet one

evening, when to all appearances a Verey light was fired from the German lines. This caused a certain amount of interest, as it did not burst into flame and light up No Man's Land as other Verey lights had done. Instead, it described a wobbly course right over our lines and dropped behind the parados near the farm. The sentry turned round to see what happened, when there was a deafening explosion, and earth and bricks were thrown in all directions. The light was of course from the burning fuse of a ' football,' as the medium weight Trench mortar of 1915 was popularly called."

Trench mortars had a peculiarly demoralizing effect upon even the best troops. It was useless trying to avoid shells, but trench mortars gave you warning, and several seconds of infinite anxiety. You heard distinctly the first dull " pop " from the enemy lines as the huge missile left its gun, and then everybody looked anxiously into the sky, as there was just enough time for an expert to run for protection to the shelter of the next traverse. Men grew old after an hour or two of this grim game. Philosophy and fatalism were little use : no one could avoid watching tensely for the arrival of the ugly twirling brutes. One humourist described a trench mortar as " setting off on its stocking feet and landing on its clogs." This kind of understatement appealed to everybody ! So what with trench mortars, machine guns and snipers, Neuve Chapelle left us no pleasant memories.

One or two typical incidents of these ten days are worth recording. A man was sighting his rifle to fire over the front trench when something struck him—hard, and he rolled from the fire-step into the bottom of the trench. Naturally he thought he had been hit and wondered where. After a few seconds' astonishment, he pulled himself together, examined himself and found he was uninjured. Then he looked at his rifle and found a German bullet embedded exactly in the muzzle ! In almost all the casualties during the first weeks in France, the very high percentage of head wounds was very noticeable—wounds from which the steel helmet of later days would have saved men frequently.

An officer writes :—

" It was in the Duck's Bill that I first saw a man wounded. Pte. S— was observing, whilst I sniped from a place which we had been warned by the outgoing tenants was a dangerous corner—when, crash ! I saw S— struggling in the bottom of the trench, his periscope smashed to atoms, and his face a mass of blood. Happily his only injuries were bad cuts about the face, caused by the shattered glass from the periscope. We decided to snipe from a fresh place in future."

The most amusing episode connected with the " Duck's Bill " is probably the following :—No. 2 Platoon of A Company had been holding this part of the line for twenty-four hours, and in the ordinary way of trench routine would have been relieved by No. 4 platoon, as the " Duck's Bill," being a very unhealthy spot, was only held for short intervals without relief. The O. C. A Coy. (Major R. Clough) asked the officer commanding No. 2 Platoon (Lieut. N. Grice) how things were going on, and was surprised to receive not only a particularly cheerful reply, but a request to stay in the sector for a further twenty-four hours without relief. Feeling that this self-sacrifice was the result of a keenness shared by no one else in No. 2 platoon, Major Clough asked the platoon sergeant how he liked the line. He received an even more enthusiastic reply, and the same request to hold the line a further twenty-four hours. A sentry also volunteered the same information. The O. C. A Coy. was mystified, as there had been fairly heavy shelling and some casualties. However, he departed pleased with his platoon's fighting spirit, and cancelled the order for relief. Three years later, a signaller of No. 2 Platoon, who had then risen to be Adjutant of the Battalion (Capt. E. D. Stansfield, M.C.) informed Col. Clough that the reason why the platoon had been so magnificently bellicose in 1915 was because a cellar full of wine—good pre-war quality—had been discovered underneath a ruined house in the " Duck's Bill " area, and had gladdened the heart of everybody. Such a find was obviously worth a second twenty-four hours ordeal. As Battalion Head Quarters at that time were drinking a nasty mixture of strong tea, bad water and chloride of lime, those bottles of good Sauterne and Bordeaux must have been extraordinarily welcome in the front line.

Ration fatigues always were unpleasant, and seemed particularly so at Neuve Chapelle, on account of the unusually long communication trench to the front line, and the uncomfortable bulk of the ration loads. Rations in those days were not sent up in the small portable sandbags used later and which could easily be carried by one man. For instance the bread ration of one company was carried in a huge sack about 6 ft. × 4 ft. × 4 ft.—an unwieldy load which needed four men to carry it. On one occasion the unlucky ration party struggled with the load up the long muddy trench, getting " stuck " immovably several times on the way, till everyone became utterly exhausted and lay down in the trench and fell asleep. They were wakened some hours later by a very irate quarter-master sergeant. Another incident in connection with rations at Neuve Chapelle ought to be told, though the joke is against the Battalion. There was a narrow gauge tramway behind the line, and on this occasion the rations were pushed up on small bogies by a party of our men. All went merrily till they came to a junction in the line, one arm of which led to the sector on our right, then occupied by a battalion of the Manchester Regiment. At this point some Manchesters met our men, and told them the enemy had come over, and taken the front line. They advised us to " quit " as rapidly as possible. Our guileless innocents did so, but as nothing seemed to be happening, they returned half-an-hour later, only to find of course that the rations had disappeared. The wily Manchesters had an extra issue that night. That ration party was anything but popular for some time.

One of the perils of these early days was sleep. Days of strange excitements and incessant tension : nights of sentry-duty, when it was impossible to obtain more than two hours at a stretch off duty, resulted in an overwhelming need for sleep at all costs. Later on, the men became inured to long bouts of wakefulness : could sleep at odd moments during the day, and had learnt the tricks by which, when necessary, sleep could be kept at bay. But during the first tours in the line the danger of falling asleep on sentry was a constant agony to men who were fresh and enthusiastic. There were a few cases of men who found their comrades asleep and voluntarily undertook extra turns of duty with a pal in order to keep him awake. Company signallers were particularly liable to the danger : and they had more temptations than most. They were confined in the heavy warm atmosphere of the signal dug-out, with their comrades asleep all round them ; and the impression of safety which a dug-out always gave powerfully assisted the craving. Signallers throughout the war were notorious for three things : skill in the science of " chatting," which consisted in picking obnoxious insects from your shirt and putting them carefully on the ground : novel reading, and letter writing. They passed their long spells of duty in these three occupations, the most effective antidote to sleep certainly being the first. Rightly regarded, the everlasting wakefulness of our Army, day and night always alert, is seen to be the result of truly heroic qualities. Many thousands of men would have given all they possessed to close their eyes at some critical moment and sleep. But they *determined not to do it*, from no fear of punishment, but from a sense of duty and responsibility.

During the tour in the Neuve Chapelle trenches the Battalion took a minor part in the battle of Aubers Ridge on May 9th. If the French and British plans had not completely miscarried, the 49th Division would have taken an important part in the development of the attack. The battles of Aubers Ridge and Festubert formed part of a great offensive concerted between General Foch (as commander of the French Northern Group of Armies) and Sir John French. The French attacked near Notre Dame de Lorette and Souchez, with their objective Lens. On May 9th they captured Carency and the spur of the Moulin-Topard, and thus permitted their African troops to pass through Souchez and capture Vimy Ridge. There are no bloodier names in French history. They were taken at a cost which staggered the whole of France. The British attacked on a smaller front, and with smaller forces. Their objectives were the capture of the ridges S.E. of Lille, and thus, with the help of the French, relieving the difficult situation in the Ypres Salient, and cutting into the Lille-Douai communications. The attack was in the hands of the 7th and 8th Divisions of the IV. Corps of the 1st Army. The 49th Division took over the greater part of the trench line held by the IV. Corps, with the 7th Division on the left and the 8th Division on the right. The 146th Inf. Brigade was the right Brigade of our Division, and the 6th Bn. was the right battalion of the Brigade. The task of the 49th Division was to assist with their fire the Divisions on each flank and to make a demonstration, so as to mislead the enemy as to the exact sectors of attack. In case of success the 147 and 148 Brigades were to occupy the German trenches and exploit the success. Sir John French declared " It was not a local effort for the capture merely of Fromelles and Aubers, but was part of a much larger operation designed to break the enemy line on a wide front." The arrangements for the attack were not kept secret, and they were a matter of common conversation in every estaminet in France. We learnt wisdom later. On May 8th, the enemy put up one or two notices along our front—" Attack postponed till to-morrow." And so it was. This was in spite of the fact that our Intelligence Police were very energetic. They even arrested " Jim " Walker, our Battalion postman, as a German Spy ! On May 9th the Bombardment began at 5 a.m. According to one eye witness, " It was the most wonderful bombardment yet seen in Western Europe. It ate up the countryside for miles." Unfortunately this concentrated bombardment was very short, and lasted for only a few minutes, though a slow rate of fire was continued till 10 a.m. As the attack failed, the 49th Division remained in their trenches. The Germans bombarded the Battalion front throughout the attack. Fortunately A Company had been moved up during the night from the support positions to the front line, and owing to this wise precaution the Battalion escaped with few casualties, as the enemy fire was concentrated chiefly on the support lines, in order to prevent reserves from entering the battle. Our trenches and dug-outs had also been strengthened and repaired in preparation for the attack. May 9th was a day of excitement for everyone, as the Battalion was in the midst of a great battle, though not taking an active part in it. The Adjutant wrote the following laconic report in the Battalion War Diary. " Bombardment commenced 5 a.m. Battalion remained in its trenches. The men are splendid : very cheery, and behave like seasoned troops. They feel the strain more than regulars in my opinion, but they are willing to work and obey orders." The Battalion was relieved on May 15th, after an unusually prolonged spell in the line, and marched into billets at Laventie. There had been remarkably few casualties, *viz.* :—eight killed and twenty-one wounded. The first serious casualty in the Battalion had been on April 28th, when Pte. C. Burgess of B Coy. was mortally wounded. A few minutes before A Coy. was relieved on May 15th, Sergt. J. Hammond was killed by a German sniper.

On May 18th the Battalion was again in the line, near La Cordonnerie Farm, and Battalion Head Quarters were at Le Trou. With the exception of three or four brief intervals of rest in Reserve billets on the Rue du Quesne and Rue du Bois, about two miles behind the line, the Battalion remained in this sector over five weeks, till they were relieved on June 25th, by the 2nd Northampton Regt. This period was as uneventful as trench warfare could be. Reliefs were easy, and carried through without much interference from the enemy. Tours in the line lasted about five days, after which four days were spent in reserve billets. There was a good pond near the reserve billets where men had the unspeakable luxury of a bathe. Occasionally, whilst in reserve, a few fortunate people were given leave to visit Armentières, the largest town our men had seen so far in France, and which was only about six miles from Fleurbaix. Though very near the Front, Armentières at this time was one of the " liveliest " towns in France, and life was carried on under almost normal conditions. Anything could be bought there. Burberrys, with their usual initiative, had established a branch in the town. Tennis by day, dancing by night : restaurants and cafés always crowded : and this within little more than two miles of the line ! One of our officers described the town as being " as gay as Paris."

In the Fleurbaix sector the Transport brought rations up to within 500 yards of the front line, and although the Transport suffered their first battle casualty in this sector—one mule wounded—the risk was well worth the trouble saved to the infantry. The Ration Party was a popular institution, as the men sat in an estaminet till the Transport arrived.

Was there ever in any part of the front a more welcome method of beginning a ration fatigue than this—beer and female society in a cosy estaminet a few hundred yards behind the line ! It was about this time that someone "far back" had the brainy idea of giving battalion transports some worn-out motor tyres to bind round the wheels of their ration limbers, to enable them to approach near the front line with the minimum of noise. One evening a pair of mules was pulling one of these motor-tyred limbers when a rubber tyre worked loose at one end. Every time the wheel went round the loose end hit one of the mules. The mules became frightened, began to trot, finally to canter, and being lashed all the harder by the rubber tyre—bolted ! The driver pluckily stuck to his saddle and finally gained control without accident. But the tyres were not popular.

There was, of course, a certain amount of shelling and trench mortar fire, and snipers and machine guns were always busy. But the comparative quietness of the sector gave an excellent opportunity for learning the necessary routine of trench warfare. An enormous amount of work was done, and the Battalion left the trenches much more comfortable for the incoming unit. When our men arrived in the line there were few dugouts : the trenches were broken down : there were gaps in the wire : and the ground was covered with dead after the May 9th attack. Miles of trench grids were laid along C. T.'s (communication trenches) and front line bays : wiring parties were out every night : old dugouts were rebuilt, trenches revetted, sniping posts made : the dead buried. The Battalion at this time was very fortunately situated for trench building and improvements, as there were several skilled men—bricklayers, joiners, and engineers—in all ranks. Capt. H. W. Barker, a well-known Bradford civil engineer, was able to render valuable service by superintending the trench works, and it was owing to such assistance that the Battalion made use of a form of A frame for revetting long before they were supplied by the Royal Engineers. Above all, our men practised patrolling : learnt how to move about in No Man's Land : observed the enemy trenches and learnt to snipe effectively. Battalion scouts had not yet been organized. It was seven months later before General Head Quarters were convinced of the necessity of having specially trained men in each battalion for patrolling and observing, and at this time patrols were carried out by volunteers and on the initiative of Company Commanders. Small patrols of four or five men went out from each Company front every night and, creeping to within twenty or thirty yards of the enemy line, reported presence of enemy working parties and sentry posts. Our sentries also were trained to observe the enemy trenches, and details of enemy work and movement were sent down in the Company Situation Reports to Bn. Head Quarters. A great deal of this work may have been unsystematized and unscientific, but everybody took part in it, and lessons were learnt which increased self-confidence, heightened morale and prepared every one for the stern ordeal which was quickly to come in the Salient.

One or two incidents stand out during this period. On June 3rd a Feu de Joie was carried out along the whole Divisional front in honour of the King's Birthday. Every available man " stood to " on the fire-step, and a ripple of rifle fire ran three times from one end of the Divisional front to the other. The effect was rather fine, and relieved the monotony of things. On June 18th an order was issued that the troops were on no account to fraternize with the Germans owing to the day being the anniversary of the battle of Waterloo. If the order had not reminded everybody of the fact, nobody except a few leisured people at the base would have remembered it. However the order did not reach the Battalion till 5 p.m., so could not have been of much use. Moreover, the Germans showed no inclination to fraternize.

It was in this sector that the Battalion had its first officer casualty, Lieut. Savill. He came into Battalion Head Quarters with the idea he had been hit through the ear by a spent bullet. Col. Wade asked him if he would have a drink, and he accepted and sat down, resting his head on his hands. Suddenly he jumped up and said, " I believe the bullet is really in my neck." The Medical Officer (Capt. A. Hamilton) came in, and examined him, and there it was in his neck all right. The wound was not serious, but he was sent to England. Most people expected that the first officer who was wounded and sent to England would become Adjutant of the 3rd line Reserve Battalion, then at Skipton. This appointment was in due course given to Lieut. Savill, and held by him for nearly two years.

The following almost incredible story of human endurance refers to this sector. On the 25th May, an hour or two before B Company was relieved by a Company of the 1/5th Bn. West Yorkshire Regt., one of our sentry posts saw something moving in the grass a few yards from our parapet. After some suspense they saw it was a wounded man, evidently belonging to the 7th Division, who had gone over the top sixteen days before in the attack on Aubers Ridge. He was almost unrecognizable as a man, and nearly dead. He had just enough energy to crawl to the trench top, and was carried down to the First Aid Station, where he died. As he did not know which was the English and which the German line, and was unable to move in No Man's Land by day, as movement attracted the fire of both sides, he had remained out in the open for over two weeks. He had lived on the rations of dead men, but had found practically no water. The sufferings of this man can hardly be imagined. The weather was so hot that on May 23rd there was a case of sunstroke in the trenches.

Another incident is typical of the tragedies incidental to war, though in this case everything ended fortunately. An old man—a French civilian—arrived at Battalion Head Quarters with a " safe conduct " pass, giving him permission to visit his house near the front line. He was given a guard of three men, but when he arrived at what had been his house he found nothing but a pile of stones which had been built into a shelter and barricade by our men. However, he set to work frantically with a shovel, removing sandbags from the barricade, and eventually unearthed a large amount of money, and three bottles of cognac. He departed with his money, but minus his cognac. His case was similar to that of thousands of others who had hidden their treasures during the German advance, but this man was more fortunate than most.

On the same day, a shell killed one of the men of the machine gun section in a communication trench. His remains were picked up and buried in a small soldiers' cemetery on the spot. The grave had been dug for some time, and the body was laid on a stretcher by the side, whilst a number of comrades grouped themselves round with bared heads. Everything had been arranged quickly, with no preparation, and there was no officer present. A volunteer was called for to read " something " from the Prayer Book, *if* a Prayer Book could be found. At last one was discovered, and a long time was spent turning over leaves, till at last one man said, " here it is !, " meaning the Burial Service. He then read the last prayer, after which the small group repeated the Lord's Prayer and lowered the body reverently into the ground. This impulse to bury a comrade with fitting dignity was never altogether lost, even in the worst sectors, although it could only rarely be satisfied by infantry in front line conditions. The scene may remind the reader of that other unconventional religious ceremony where Tess baptises her child in Thomas Hardy's " Tess of the D'Urbevilles." This burial incident had an important sequel. One of the men described the scene in a letter home, and the letter was censored by one of the officers, with the result that never again—where burial was possible—did it take place without the presence of an officer and a simple ceremony. Thus the much-abused censorship of men's letters by officers was occasionally the means of bringing about an immediate improvement and recognition of some complaint or requirement.

On June 25th, the Battalion left the Fleurbaix sector, and marched to Sailly-sur-la-Lys, where the whole Battalion was billeted in one huge farm. No one was cold that night. The next day they marched to

Doulieu, about four miles away, where they stayed the night. The Church at Doulieu had been entirely gutted, having been set on fire wantonly by the Germans before they left in 1914. The most remarkable event in Doulieu was connected with the Mayor. He was a friendly gentleman, keen to show interest and hospitality. As the Battalion was marching out of the town the next day, he asked if the Band would play the National Anthem for him. Whereat the Band struck up, and everybody marched at attention. The Mayor was very disappointed. " But I wanted ' Tipperary'," he said, " your proper National Anthem." So the Band played " It's a long way to Tipperary," and the Mayor was satisfied. When the Battalion left Doulieu, the period of apprenticeship may be said to have been concluded. The men were hardened and experienced—for one learns much in two months in the trenches. The 49th Division was transferred from the Indian Corps of the 1st Army to the VI. Corps (Sir John Keir) of the 2nd Army (Sir Herbert Plumer). It was on June 28th, on the march from Doulieu to Proven, that the Battalion first entered the Second Army Area. Before leaving the First Army the Division received one or two complimentary messages. The Adjutant-General at General Head Quarters wrote :—

> " The Commander-in-Chief notices with gratification the record of the 49th (West Riding) Division for the month of May, which shows that no single conviction by Court Martial has occurred, a condition which does not obtain in any other Division of the Armies. He desires that his appreciation of this fact be duly conveyed to the 49th Division.

Our Divisional General was informed by the G. O. C. First Army—

> " Sir Douglas Haig wishes to add an expression of his great satisfaction at the state of discipline in the 49th (West Riding) Division, and also desires to congratulate the Division on its soldier-like bearing, and efficiency."

In the merit of these compliments the 1/6th Battalion West Yorkshire Regt. may justly claim a share.

It is probable that, on reading these two congratulatory messages, some one will be tempted to say, " If there was no conviction by Court Martial in the 49th Division for a whole month, discipline must have been very slack ! " Such a criticism entirely ignores what we have pointed out previously, viz., that in the typical Territorial unit during its early days of active service there was an unusual " *esprit de corps*," and sense of personal responsibility. Men refused to disgrace their platoons or companies, or " let down " their Officers and N.C.O.'s whom they had known personally in civilian life. That very highest form of discipline, " *the discipline of goodwill* " to which we have previously alluded, worked like leaven in the lump of our immature Battalion, making it from the very first worthy of a high place amongst battalions of the British Army.

CHAPTER IV.

THE YPRES SALIENT.

FOR the British Army there was only *one* Salient. So much misery, mud, murder was nowhere else compressed in so small a space. The ground reeked with gas : was polluted with dead and the debris of a hundred battles : was tortured by an everlasting storm of shells. There was no possibility of peace or safety in the Salient. No Regular Division had stayed in the line for more than six weeks, even in summer, and the Battalion looked forward to an early move when it first arrived there. For nearly six months, however, during perhaps the worst winter of the war, the Battalion remained, in deepening mud and rising water, till the grand finale came in the Gas Attack of December, and the line was held and the Salient saved. It is not easy to appraise justly the importance of different phases of the war. The spectacular events of 1918 will always receive the praise and special attention which great victories merit. But the victories round Cambrai and Valenciennes were made possible by the endurance and self-sacrifice of battalions, who, in the dark days of the war, held a thin line against a much stronger foe and under incredibly vile conditions. Throughout these six months, the men of the Battalion were faced with two tasks ;—First, to keep back the enemy : second, to live and still preserve their sanity in a sea of mud.

One of our Battalion (Sergt. J. E. Yates) wrote :—

" If I were to pick from a variegated career the period when physical wretchedness reached its stark bottom, I should choose the last five months at Ypres in 1915. We started in exuberant health and spirits. At Christmas those who were left crawled out, broken in body and almost in heart, staggering and falling like drunken men after a march of five miles. Rain fell incessantly."

An eminent statesman once said he was never impressed by a case unless it was understated. It would be impossible to overstate or exaggerate in any way the misery of conditions in the Salient in the winter of 1915.

When the Battalion marched out of the Fleurbaix sector on June 25th, most of the men thought they were going to Festubert, but when orders came four days later at Doulieu to march to Proven, they began to realize there could be only one destination—the Ypres Salient.

And very few at the time were sorry. Changes of sector (even when it was from Fleurbaix to Ypres) always meant a short relief from the monotony of trench life; and everyone thought more of the days in reserve, and the interests of a " long trek " North, than of the dreary prospect of a winter in the Salient. But the move began badly; was " all wrong " from the beginning. With the exception of the short first stage of the journey from Doulieu to Meteren, the march to the footsore men was one of the worst in the history of the Battalion. The Battalion paraded at 7-30 p.m. in Meteren, and everything went well till nightfall. The country was pleasant and the roads not too bad. Then it began to rain heavily, and continued for over two hours, till everyone was wet through. As the Battalion approached the Belgian frontier—Berthen, Boeschepe, etc.—the peculiar horrors of the Flanders pavé on a dark wet night became almost unbearable. Men slipped and floundered on the slimy cobbles, and the luckless right files, trudging in the mud off the pavé, were in continual danger of falling in the ditch. A sixteen-mile march in England on a bright cool day in a walking suit is nothing, but sixteen miles with heavy pack and rifle, in pouring rain at night on the worst marching roads in Europe, needs every ounce of endurance a man has. Our Medical Officer (Capt. A. Hamilton) brought up as usual the rear of the Battalion, and was a great asset to the other officers and N. C. O.'s. Few stragglers were able to " wangle " round our M. O., and when they dropped back towards the rear and his presence, they became less tired than they had imagined they were. During the later stages of the march the cry throughout the Battalion was " How far to Wateau ? " a town East of Poperinghe and just within the Belgian border. The answer invariably was " two kilometres." This question and answer had run many times up and down the weary column, when a wag, hearing the answer for the umpteenth time, at last shouted out, " Thank God, we're keeping up with the damned place ! " Equipments became sodden : the greatcoats heavy as lead. The men threw away everything that could be thrown, even to the concertina that was the joy of one Company. One man, who had less sense of property than some of the others, threw one article after another into the ditch till he came to a shirt which an aunt had just sent him, and as this also went into the ditch, he muttered grimly :—" My false teeth go next ! " But everything has an end. A few hours' sleep, and the Battalion woke up, refreshed, to find they were in Proven, one of the pleasantest villages in Flanders : rich, well-wooded, agricultural country. It was a great change to see hops, flax and tobacco growing freely. In France, except in the Pas de Calais where there are many restrictions, it is

" défendu " for the villagers to grow tobacco : but in Belgium every farm has its small tobacco plantation, which is untaxed by the state. Hence the cheapness of Belgian tobacco—the only thing in Belgium which was cheap to our men! During the five days' rest at Proven the 146th Infantry Brigade was inspected by Brig. Gen. Macfarlan, C.B., Sir John Keir (VI. Corps) and Sir Herbert Plumer. Rightly or wrongly, Sir Herbert Plumer was always supposed to have a special interest in the 49th Division. A good deal of its training in England had been carried out when he was G. O. C. of the Northern Command. And the 49th was the first Territorial Division to be detailed for a long spell in the Ypres Salient.

On July 4th at 6 p.m. the Battalion left Proven in motor busses, 800 all ranks, debussed at Vlamertinghe, and marched to the Canal Bank, one mile North of Ypres, where they arrived 11 p.m. The Battalion was attached to the 12th Brigade, 4th Division, till the 146th Brigade had completed the relief—two days later—of the 12th Infantry Brigade. The 1/7th Bn. West Yorks. Regt. were in the front line on the left, the 1/5 Bn. on the right : the 1/8 Bn. in reserve, and our own Battalion in support on the Canal Bank. The 49th Divisional front extended from the East bank of the Yser Canal near Boesinghe to Morteldje Estaminet on the Ypres-Langemarck Road, a front of about four kilometres. The 148th Infantry Brigade was on the left, 147th Infantry Brigade in the centre, and 146th Infantry Brigade on the right. The Brigade Boundaries are given on Map No. 2. On the left of the 49th Division the French were holding the line with the 45th Division : the 49th was thus the left Division of the British Army. On our right was the 6th Division, which included the 1st Battalion West Yorkshire Regt. The above were the dispositions when the 49th Division entered the Ypres Salient. Major General Baldock (O. C. 49th Division) was wounded by a shell at Divisional Head Quarters at the Chateau des Trois Tours about half a mile west of Brielen, only seven days after taking over the line. Major-Gen. E. M. Perceval, C.B., then took command, and remained with the Division till after the Passchendaele battle in October, 1917.

It is unnecessary to state that the Ypres Salient was a vital point in the British Defences, and that for eight months before the Battalion entered it the Salient had been a battle sector, where British and German Divisions were massed together, holding only narrow frontages, and where there were permanently concentrated probably the heaviest armaments on the Western front. The morning after the Battalion took over its billets on the Canal Bank the " Wiper's Express "—from a 15-in. German naval gun—was heard whistling over

THE YPRES SALIENT

their heads into the ruins of Ypres. There were no 15-in. shells in the Fleurbaix sector ! In the Railway Station Yard at Bac St. Maur our men had become acquainted with " Granny," a British 15-in. gun which fired into Lille. But " Granny " was severely rationed, and her voice could only be rarely heard ! The following day the 11th Infantry Brigade attacked the German line, and the first memory of the Salient our men had was this battle on their left, filling the whole Salient with its din and unpleasantness. One day later the Battalion had their first experience of gas shells, and several men were gassed, some seriously. And not quite a week after the Battalion entered the Salient the first D.C.M. (Distinguished Conduct Medal) which the Battalion received was given to Pte. E. Preston. Incidentally this was the first D.C.M. in the Division. We mention these details to prove how quickly the Battalion entered into the true Salient " atmosphere " of constant fighting. In that very expressive phrase, the Salient was " all wrong." In addition to special actions, we are told that Sir Herbert Plumer was pleased if the Second Army casualties in the Salient alone did not exceed 200 men a day, in ordinary trench work. As the Salient in 1915 was a small half circle of not more than four kilometres (two and a half miles) radius some idea of the daily sacrifice can be obtained. Nor was the defence of Ypres merely a sentimental affair—persisted in for the sake of preserving British prestige, as so many people at one time alleged. The town, with its network of roads and canals, formed at once a natural centre and barrier in the British system of defence on the Western Front.

Before the war the country round Ypres, though rather monotonous and flat, had the charm of rich, cultivated, well-wooded landscape. Even in July, 1915, some corners of the Canal Bank, lined with poplars eighty feet high, gave one the delusion of peace and safety. Men, for a few days of the summer at least, bathed in the Canal, where there were fishes and water-lilies. In the shelter of the East Bank men in reserve moved freely on quiet days. When the Battalion first took over the line, the trenches had not fallen in, and were deeper and narrower (for protection against heavier shell fire) than those further south in Fleurbaix. In fact, in the middle of summer the trench system at Ypres seemed tolerable. There were support and reserve lines, organized in depth in a way not adopted by this time in the Fleurbaix sectors : communication trenches : and shelters, which, though far too few, were not needed urgently in the height of summer except as protection against shell fire,—and very few of them were much use for that. The precautions which began to be adopted on a big scale in 1916 to preserve trenches from collapsing in the winter months

E   49

(such as A frames and other systems of revetting) had not been taken in the Salient. The Division arrived too late to organize draining and revetting on a sufficiently elaborate basis. The result was disastrous. When the Autumn rains began in August, the trenches disappeared, or became canals. The whole Salient, as General Perceval reported officially, was " permanently flooded." The line could only be held by a system of detached posts, where men were prisoned till nightfall, up to the knees in water day and night, and without room for any exercise. Tremendous efforts were made throughout the Division to combat the most serious danger of water-logged trenches—" trench feet,"—and the Division had a very good record. In spite of the sector being probably the worst on the British front, the Division reported fewer cases of trench feet than any Division in the Army. This was entirely due to good morale, and the fact that in the Salient the danger was so obvious that everyone took the utmost trouble to avoid it. Thousands of tins of anti-frostbite grease were sent out to the Division from the Territorial Association at York : gum boots—though never in sufficient quantities—were issued in thousands : efforts were made to compel all ranks to take every precaution against the disease, even to the point of threatening to make it a criminal offence. Each man took with him three or four pairs of socks into the trenches, and Divisional arrangements were made for drying and cleaning them. Soup kitchens : thousands of boxes of " tinned heat " : a portable bath house, where sixteen men at a time were stripped, given three minutes under a hot shower bath, underclothing changed, uniform cleaned and fumigated— these were all efforts to palliate the danger. Pathetic attempts were made to drill and do physical exercises in a line where men could hardly lift one foot after another without pain or extreme effort.

With regard to " Soup Kitchens " and " gum boots," it is regretfully necessary to add a word of explanation, as these remedial measures existed to some extent only on paper. Elaborate plans and arrangements for Soup Kitchens and hot food were made with the best intentions at Divisional Head Quarters, but, as was unfortunately often the case, failed to materialize in the front line system. In mud where it took an hour for a man to move one hundred yards, it can easily be imagined that no one would face the almost incredible exertion —let alone danger—of going back to reserve positions for hot soup or a cup of tea. In later trench warfare Hot Food Containers solved the difficulty, and the front line garrison by this means received hot tea at midnight in addition to other times of the day.

The gum boots arrived in November, in the nick of time. In the two days before they were received the Battalion had forty cases of trench feet ! The distribution of the gum boots was a matter of some difficulty, though it worked fairly successfully. There was only a supply of gum boots sufficient for the battalion in the front line. The result was that on relief the outgoing battalion took off their gum boots at Essex Farm, and laid them out in heaps for the incoming battalion. The incoming battalion then marched up in the darkness and each man changed into the first muddy gum boots he could find, being fortunate if he got a decent pair, and no odd numbers. The confusion round Essex Farm on a pitch dark night, with heavy rain, fields everywhere over the ankles in mud, and with frequent bursts of enemy shelling, may be left to the reader's imagination. Every effort was made to organize the distribution, but it was too complicated to work smoothly under bad conditions. More than one fellow marched to the line every relief night with a left boot on a right foot : or became stuck in the mud on the way up, and had to leave his gum boots behind him, and finish the journey in his stockings. However, as a result of these and similar methods to counteract the effects of the " mud-life " of the Salient, there were only 760 cases of " trench feet " in the Division, although this means the average loss of six men per day—a sinister total !

As mentioned previously, two days after the Battalion arrived on the Canal Bank, on July 6th, the 11th Brigade attacked the German system near the point where our front line touches the Yser Canal, East of Boesinghe. They made an advance on a three Company front to a depth of about 500 yards, capturing three lines of German Trenches. They established a new front line, which was later called the " International Trench," an unpleasant spot, about fifty yards from the enemy. During this attack the Germans shelled the Canal Bank heavily, especially Bridge Four—the most important bridge from Ypres to Boesinghe, immediately north of which were the Battalion dug-outs. In this shelling we suffered about fifteen casualties : a fitting welcome to the Salient. During the next week there was no peace. At 10 p.m. on the 10th July, the Germans massed and recaptured their old front line from the 5th Bn. York and Lancaster Regt. (148th Infantry Brigade), after a heavy bombardment. The 5th Bn. promptly counter-attacked, and in a brilliant show succeeded an hour later in again taking the International trench and all their former positions. A night attack at Ypres was always an awe-inspiring sight—from a distance. The whole Salient was lit up like a devil's smithy. Thousands of Verey lights of all colours, and the flames of bursting shells, drew a ring of fire round the City of Ypres, the ruins of the Cloth Hall—gaunt and naked in the glare of bursting shells—being clearly seen by our men from their shelters on the Canal Bank. Three nights later the Battalion took over from the 1/5th Bn. West Yorks Regt. the front line on the right of the Brigade in front of Turco Farm and Morteldje Estaminet. The front line was divided into numbered sections, and D 19, D 20, Willow Walk and Canadian Dug-outs became quickly notorious for varying forms of acute unpleasantness. The whole of this section of the line was overlooked by what was known as " The High Command," though the name appears on no official maps. The High Command was a slight rise in the ground (twenty-nine metre contour) which had been very strongly fortified by the enemy, and was only about 250 yards from our front line near Willow Walk. There dwelt enemy snipers, who, from a dry point of vantage, picked off our men as they ran from post to post across broken-down water-logged trenches. The greatest delight—a joy too deep for expression—which could be given to our Battalion, was to see the German parapets at this point plastered with " rafale " fire from the French 75's after some unusually trying and prolonged enemy trench-mortaring.

This French aid was particularly useful when the Battalion was on the extreme left of the Divisional Front near the Canal. After some particularly heavy bombardment of our line, the French did not need to be asked for retaliation. They cleared their infantry from the front line, and threw over every missile they could lay hands on, and as they were well supplied with trench mortars and artillery ammunition, their retaliation was very effective. No one seemed to enjoy loosing off ammunition more than French gunners, who were never satisfied till they had blazed off their last round.

Our own artillery made good use of their shells, but shells then were few, and our retaliation was usually insignificant, and generally limited to four rounds per gun. As mentioned previously our Divisional Artillery only had thirty-six 15-pounder guns, and a ration of three shells per gun per day. As one of our Colonels expressed it—" our shelling was like *barking* against thunder," though he actually used a more vigorous word.

The Battalion was relieved after ten days in the line, and went into reserve in the grounds of the Chateau des Trois Tours, near Brielen. Divisional Head Quarters had been moved the day before to Hospital Farm, about two miles further west—as the Chateau grounds had been shelled and General Baldock wounded. The Battalion found their billets comfortable and peaceful after their tour in the line, although the " billets " consisted merely of holes in the ground which were gradually converted into shelters by successive battalions. The grounds were quite charming : the chateau was surrounded by a wide moat full of fish. C. Coy. played a cricket match with the Officers, and won. The six days of relief passed pleasantly enough, and on July 25th, the Battalion went again into their former sector of the line near Turco Farm, where they remained six days, and were relieved by the 1/5th Bn. W. Y. Regt.; whereupon they again returned to support on the Canal Bank. Relief followed relief: bombardment succeeded bombardment; the toll of casualties from shellfire, sniping and trench feet grew daily. Two small batches of reinforcements totalling one officer and fifty-nine men, arrived in August. On August 24th the 1st Bn. K.S.L.I. of the 16th Brigade 6th Division took over the Turco Farm and Morteldje Estaminet front, and the Battalion relieved the 1/5th Bn. West Yorkshire Regt. on the Canal Bank. When they again went into the line six days later it was to relieve the 1/7th Bn. immediately on the left of their old sector. The usual routine of Trench warfare followed for ten days, till the 146th Infantry Brigade was relieved by the 147th Infantry Brigade, and the Battalion marched to the Rest Bivouacs in Coppernolle Wood, about three miles east of Poperinghe, where they remained for eleven days. This was the first period " out on rest " since the Battalion had landed in France, five months earlier. This rest was made possible by a Divisional re-arrangement. The 6th Division took over part of the front of our right battalion, and the 49th Division front was held by two instead of three Brigades, the third Brigade then being allowed a twelve days' rest. Under this arrangement, each Battalion would receive about twelve days in support, twelve days in reserve and twelve days in the front line, but it was found impossible to keep strictly to these reliefs.

These eleven days in Coppernolle Wood were a great success. The men were crowded fifteen in a tent in some cases, but as the weather was very fine, everyone was content. Apart from occasional route marches and the necessary " interior economy " parades, there were few restrictions. Parties of men were told off to work on building wattle " torchis " huts under the guidance of half-a-dozen Belgians, but as most of the necessary tools and materials were lacking, work proceeded slowly. A number of men went " on leave " to England, and " leave " was a magic word which improved wonderfully the morale of the Battalion. Lieut.-Col. H. O. Wade took command of the Brigade in the absence on leave of Brig. Gen. Macfarlan. There were two ceremonial parades by General Keir (VI. Corps) and General Plumer (2nd Army), when a D.C.M. and Gallantry Cards were presented to men of the Battalion. There were, of course, football, cricket, and sports of all kinds. Men renewed their acquaintance with civilization by visiting Poperinghe, about four kilometres away. There was a cinematograph in Poperinghe, and above all, the 6th Divisional Troupe, " The Fancies," whom every man in the Battalion went to see on every available occasion. At this time " The Fancies " were giving an extremely good show, and some of their songs became immortal, for example " Ho Roger Rum." Two Belgian girls—christened " Lanoline " and " Vaseline "—were in the troupe, and during the few months they remained with " The Fancies," were a great attraction. The peculiar pronunciation they gave to English songs, especially some doggerel like Vaseline's " Which is the switch for Ipswich," convulsed nightly a crowded house.

The 49th Divisional Concert Party, " The Tykes," gave their opening performance on August 22nd, at Peselhoek, near Poperinghe, and some members of the Battalion probably regard that as one of the most important events in the history of the Division. From that date to February 2nd, 1919, " The Tykes " performed in almost every sector of the Northern Front. They easily rivalled in general excellence any other troupe of their kind in France. They carried a rather elaborate apparatus with them : electric motor : dresses and simple theatrical scenery : and quickly made a tolerable theatre of any barn, hut or schoolroom they could find. During their three years of existence, the profits were 80,000 francs, which went to the Divisional " Institutes " for the provision of extra comforts, sports, etc. They were the first Concert Party in the British Army to perform at Arras in the Salle des Concerts (an enormous amount of rubbish, plaster and broken furniture had to be removed before a performance was possible), and also in Cambrai during the advance of 1918. Probably the names best known throughout the Division were those of men belonging to " The Tykes," such as Lt. J. P. Barker, and Marsden, Coates and Smith. It was an incredible luxury, after the mud and horror of the trenches, to come to the small theatre behind the line : to hear good music and singing, and humour often highly seasoned : and to see Barker arrayed in the latest robes from Paquin, showing a finely turned leg, shapely enough to have been the envy of a chorus girl at the Empire. Occasionally French civilians watched the performance from the back of the crowd, and were mystified with the appearance of a charming girl, altogether English, who sang with a captivating innocence, whose smile seemed charming in the half-light of the stage, and who bore her dresses like a mannequin in a West End show room. If it is not true that Barker was more than once offered a card by some old beau on the lines of Communication after one of his turns—it deserved to be ! In 1918 the 1/6th Battalion provided one of the best artistes " The

Tykes " ever possessed in Pte. Moyes, who superseded even Lieut. Barker as a girl-impersonator. His song " Take a look at me now," was of a dangerously exciting character. Some of the items in " The Tykes' " programme played quite a definite part in improving the morale of the Division—though such methods may not be referred to in Army text books. Such songs as " James William Maconochie," " Charlie Chaplin's Walk," Moyes' " Roses of Picardy," Marsden's " I murdered him," and " I wish I were a dog like you," Smith's " Chrysanthemum," the duets with Barker, " We're so glad to see you back, dear lady," and " Number 1 Gerrard,"—will never be forgotten by men in the Division, and livened the atmosphere in many a dull barn or mess, dug-out, or on a route march.

" James William Maconochie ran a monarchy, on his own :
Folks crowded to live on that island, with James on the throne.
He loved them like anything, and a kindly king was to them :
But the one he loved blindly, and treated most kindly, was
—— J. W. M."

Such songs became a disease, though the results were generally good : they were certainly a better narcotic than the vile wine, weak beer or copious whisky which usually characterized other " magnificent evenings " in reserve billets, and which were inevitably followed by a headache, or an " orderly room." The most noticeable feature about every Tykes' Concert was the audience. One way of appreciating the effect of trench warfare was to watch carefully the rows of faces of the infantrymen at a Tykes' concert near the line : the pathetic eagerness to be amused, and to forget everything : the intense way the men took their pleasures : in many cases the slight hysteria : in all cases the occasional look of strain or gloom : which, though only momentary, expressed more than the average onlooker knew.

When the Battalion marched to the line on September 20th, they took over what were known as the Pilkem trenches, on the extreme left of the British line, where they relieved a Battalion of the 148th Infantry Brigade. This sector was probably the most dangerous on the front : some of the trenches had been captured from the Germans in July, and were in a very broken-up condition. For three weeks the Battalion remained in this sector, with the exception of two short periods of five days each in support. Owing to the discomforts of the line reliefs were carried out every four instead of six days, and were often extremely unpleasant and dangerous. With ominous accuracy the enemy seemed to time his bombardments with the hour of relief, notably on October 9th, when the relief of the 1/7th Battalion was delayed two hours, and on October 13th, when the 1/7th Battalion relieved us on our final departure from this sector. The dispositions of the Battalion when in support were :—Head Quarters and one Coy. at Malakoff Farm, one Coy. on Canal Bank, one Coy. at Modder and Saragossa Farms, and one Coy. in trenches at Hull's Farm. Whilst in support the Battalion provided carrying parties for rations and R. E. stores to the battalion in the line, which was generally the 1/7th Battalion West Yorkshire Regt.

On the extreme left of the Pilkem sector was the " International Trench," where our men were within twenty to thirty yards of the enemy, and where our posts passed some anxious hours. In many ways trenches so close to the enemy had compensations. There was an entire freedom from artillery fire, as no gunners—English or German —cared to risk killing their own men. Heavy trench mortar fire was also absent, as there was not sufficient margin of safety. But bombs were so easily lobbed over at that convenient range of twenty yards, that during bombing " stunts " the trenches became intolerable, and casualties certain. The German bombs at this time were better than ours, and they had a more plentiful supply. Our Mill's Hand Grenade was not yet in use, and we had to rely on the " Gas Pipe " Bomb, French " Pear " Bomb, and Hale's Hand Grenades—less serviceable and more dangerous to use. At night, the tension was extreme, as a distance of thirty yards was rushed in as many seconds. Wiring was, of course, impossible at such proximity to the enemy, and ready-made *chevaux de frise* were pushed out from the trench over the parapet. The Battalion war diary during this period is full of daily " affairs " of bombing and sniping, in which we gave and suffered casualties in a line where the " wearing down " process of trench warfare could be seen at its worst. The enemy took nothing lying down, and invariably retaliated if one of our platoons became demonstrative,—very often on an innocent platoon which had arrived just in time to receive the reward of their comrades' pugnacity. If we sniped a German, we were certain to receive a shower of rifle grenades or bombs to remind us someone " over yonder " had noticed our little effort. No quiet-ness : little time for sleep—even if one could sleep in trenches without dug-outs, up to the knees in water, where hot food was impossible, and where drinking water was often taken from the shell holes, and was powerfully dosed with chloride of lime. Moreover the long cold nights of winter were setting in and the weather had broken. The Salient also had a bad reputation for the use of gas, and when the wind was from the east, occupants of these front line trenches must have felt completely helpless, full of foreboding, rather like the soldiers of Henry V., the night before Agincourt, who could only

THE YPRES SALIENT

" round their watchful fires sit patiently,
and inly ruminate the morning's danger."

Under such circumstances a painfully anxious attention was naturally given to the gas mask. The original "gas mask"—if it could be so called—simply consisted of a handkerchief dipped in urine and tied round the mouth. This was the protection during the first days in the Fauquissart and Neuve Chapelle trenches. Later on cotton waste which had been soaked in photographic fixing solution, was wrapped in black gauze and bandaged over the mouth. Opinions varied as to how this should be worn :—the fashion seemed to be to fill as much of the mouth as possible, and stuff what was left up the nostrils. This no doubt kept much of the gas out, but unfortunately kept out the air too—and was almost as asphyxiating as the gas itself. Then came gas helmets without mouth pieces, which suffered from very similar defects. The P. helmet was the next development, but as it had no outlet valve, it was very difficult to breathe through, and if the single mica window was broken the whole helmet was rendered useless. Finally, three or four weeks before the December 19th Gas Attack, the "Tube Helmet" with valvular mouthpiece and flannel soaked in elaborately prepared anti-gas solutions, was issued in time to save the lives of hundreds of our men.

This Tube or new P.H. helmet had two strong glass eyepieces and an outlet valve. As there was only an issue of one P.H. helmet per man, it was decided that all ranks should continue to carry the old P. helmet as a reserve.

On September 25th the French attacked on a wide front in Champagne, and made a tremendous but unsuccessful attempt to drive the Germans back to the Aisne. On the same day the British attacked in the neighbourhood of Loos and Halluch (between Lens and La Bassee) with the 1st, 7th, 9th, 15th and 47th Divisions, but the attack was broken up amongst the pits and mines around Hill 70. In order to divert attention from this battle, minor engagements were carried out on other sectors, notably against the German positions between the Ypres-Menin Road and the Ypres-Roulers Railway. In these engagements the 3rd and 14th Divisions of the V. Corps took part, and successfully reached and held their objectives. At the same time all other units in the line in the Salient made a demonstration. The bombardment began at 5-30 a.m., and at the same time thousands of smoke bombs were thrown from our front line trenches, covering No Man's Land with a thick almost impenetrable mist. The ruse was successful : the Battalion sentries report seeing the enemy stand up on his fire step and fire " rapid " into the mist, and as the smoke cleared away our snipers did considerable execution amongst the enemy, who was moving about fairly freely, anticipating an attack. This was our first use of phosphorus smoke bombs on a big scale. Parties of men had been at work all night detonating the bombs. One of the men who, on the following morning, was engaged in lighting the fuses before throwing the bombs over the parapet, was very short-sighted, and caused alarm amongst his section by holding every bomb close to his face in order to see when it was " sizzing ! " Smoke bombs were used later with wearisome frequency for every " false " attack, till the enemy became sceptical, and often never even fired a rifle in acknowledgement of our elaborate efforts to mislead him.

The entries in the War Diary at this time describe baldly the life of the Battalion. The following are typical :—

October 1st. Enemy shelled Battalion Head Quarters and C. Coy. One man killed, nine wounded.

October 3rd. Our left Company attacked enemy working party with bombs. One German sniper killed. Our right Coy. landed several bombs in enemy trenches with " West " bomb thrower. Wind S.E.

October 4th. Enemy bombed our left Coy. with hand bombs and large trench mortars, " Rum Jars." Bombs fell in our trenches, " Rum Jars " behind. We replied energetically with hand bombs, and got retaliation from our Artillery, 12-30 a.m. Bombing attack on left Coy. begun by enemy. We replied with two bombs to Germans one, till he gave up. Probably enemy bombing attacks were to cover working parties. Enemy doing a lot of wiring in front of his line : noise of driving of stakes fairly continuous. 12 noon. Enemy put heavy and light trench mortars into F. 31. We replied with rifle grenades and trench howitzer bombs, silencing him effectively. Enemy shelled our Coys. in F 31 and F 32 with H. E. Enemy seen lading water out of his trenches. Heavy rain. Trenches collapsing in many places.

Partly from a natural pride, the War Diary invariably dwells on the bombing duels where we silenced the enemy—but this was naturally not always the case.

On October 13th, the Battalion was relieved and again went back with the rest of Brigade to Divisional Reserve, N. E. of Coppernolle Wood. The Battalion remained in reserve for seventeen days, but the weather was bad, and working parties were sent up to the front to work on reserve lines and communication trenches. Elverdinghe village was being destroyed, but in an entirely peaceful and orderly manner. The bricks of the houses were being used to form horse-lines and shelters for the Brigade Transports! The building of wattle huts went on slowly. On the 27th October, His Majesty the King reviewed representatives of all the Divisions in the VI. Corps at Abeile, and our party of one Officer, Regt. Sergt.-Major and twenty-five other ranks was inspected by the King and the Commander-in-Chief. On November 2nd the Battalion was again in the front line trenches, this time in their original sector near Turco Farm. A great deal of work had been done in the front line system by the 148th Infantry Brigade. Second line trenches such as Vicar Lane, had been improved, and new dug-outs and living-in trenches constructed, such as " Dawson's City," named after Brig.-Gen. Dawson of the 148th Infantry Brigade. But the rain and bombardments destroyed everything before the work could be made permanent, and when the Battalion took over the line, the discomforts of the sector had reached their almost unbearable limit. The history of the next six weeks (with the exception of seven days' rest in reserve at Poperinghe from November 20th to 26th) is one of prolonged " suffering," though no one would have tolerated the word then, as it would have sounded too sentimental. Even the Battalion Transport was living in an absolute quagmire of mud. The horse lines were some distance from the road, and to get from one to the other it was necessary to wade up to the knees in liquid mud. It was beyond the strength of any horse to pull a wagon into the horse lines, so all the food both for men and horses was conveyed from the Quarter Master's Stores on pack horses. Early in November Brig.-Gen. Macfarlan ordered that the front line should be held as lightly as possible, though this was inevitable, as for hundreds of yards the front line had disappeared, and it was only possible to hold the sector by a series of isolated posts at about fifty yards' interval. Even these were always two or three feet deep in water. There were a few cases in the Division of men being drowned in Communication Trenches. Several times men lost their footing in two or three feet of water, and would have drowned but for a comrade's help, as they were too exhausted and loaded with equipment to save themselves. Naturally it was impossible to move along " the front line " in daytime, or to get from one post to another across the open. Our Chaplain (Rev. R. Whincup) again and again in later days stated that when he visited the front line trenches (which he often did, as no one in the Battalion is likely to forget), and when he realized the state of misery in which men were existing and their dogged optimism, he was amazed and could hardly believe such endurance possible.

The following extract from a letter will give some idea of conditions. " You may think I am in trenches. Disabuse yourself of that idea at once. We are inhabiting canals which are of four varieties.

1. Full of water.
2. Full of mud.
3. Full of earth.
4. Drains.

"The ones full of water are easiest to move in, but rather disappointing as places of habitation. We sit on the Firing Step all night, and wheeze and spit and smoke. Cigarettes save the situation. Fires are impossible : sleep impossible. To keep warm is only possible occasionally—to keep dry a farce. It rained for four days, and filled up the trenches—canals I mean—and then it stopped and froze. Trench feet and frost bite claimed five out of our section of nine. When I tell you that we took to walking across the top in daylight, you will see that we cared nothing for our lives at the time. No one uses the trenches at night—they are too dangerous. One might be suffocated or drowned. One of our engineers' fatigue parties came in the other night from the German trenches. They had wandered up to the enemy wire carrying sheets of corrugated iron. Our sentries challenged them—luckily, as sentries are used to seeing mobs strolling all over. . . . . If any man can get through this really bad dose, he can hang on for good. If any one can do it, I can, being built like a lamp post. Don't be worried about me." (E. M. Kermode). Another inhabitant of this region writes :—" Of late we live in a marsh handed over as a trench area. On our occupation the rain began its winter session, and we ran up against a simple little bit of arithmetic. ' If two inches of rain per diem brings down one quarter of a company's parapet, and one company, working about twenty-six hours per diem, can revet one-eighth of a company's parapet, how long will your trenches last, given the additional premises that no revetments to speak of are to be had, and that two inches of rain is only a minimum ration.' We have indented for a fleet : and even a few auxiliary cruisers and some packets of torpedoes would be better than nothing, which is what we have got so far." One incident illustrates the spirit of the average infantryman in the Battalion at this time, and incidentally shows the regard the men had for our Adjutant, Capt. G. R. Sandeman. He was going round the " trenches " one night—a task demanding immense physical strength apart from anything else—and in his cheerful way asked a sentry how he was getting on. The sentry was standing in a foot of water, surrounded by a sea of mud, and a heavy bout of trench mortaring had just passed. Without looking at his questioner, the sentry snapped out " Damned fed-up." Then the man turned round and saw it was Capt. Sandeman and he became confused and apologetic.

No. 2 Map.

YARDS 100 0 100 200 300 400 500

2000 YARDS

1000

BOESINGHE

FROM DIXMUDE

C

GERMAN FRONT LINE

HINDENBURG FM.

BULOW FM.

NORMAN COTTAGE

NEW COMMAND

YPRES

CANADIAN DUG OUTS

MONTELIQUE
MORATELLE
ESTAMINET
CANADIAN FARM.

ALGERIAN COTTAGE

GAWTHORPE ROAD

THE PUMP ROOM

CLIFTON GATE

CLIFTONS TOWER

HAREM

KNARESBORO CASTLE

THE WILLOWS

CARLIN

CARL FM.

BOAR LANE

CASTLE LANE

DELLE

ALLIANCE

ST.

FOCH FM.

26

BURN'T OUT FARM.

CONEY

CONEY ST.

JOFFRE FM.

SPANKY FM.

LANCASHIRE FM.

DAWSON CITY

FUSILIER FM.

ELSON FM.

LILY FM.

LILY FM.

LONDON FM.

14

13

WELLCATE

INTERNATIONAL TRENCH

BARNSLEY

SOUTH ZWAANHOF FM.

NORTH ZWAANHOF FM.

THE FORKED TREE

SKIPTON ROAD

HUDDERSFIELD

MIDDLESEX ROAD

HALIFAX ROAD

MOROCCO FM.

STREN LL.

19

F

BRIDGE

4

CANAL

YSER CANAL

WYAT'S LANE

OLD BRITISH FRONT LINE

TIGER FM.

TALANA FM.

MUDDER FM.

TO MALAKOFF FARM.

Facing page 60.

They talked for some time, and when the Adjutant went away, the sentry was heard to say, "I would have given anything for the Adjutant not to have heard me say that." The incident needs no comment. The men refused to give in. The officers heard no complaints and took their turn of duty with absolute confidence that their platoons were with them to a man. If we were to narrate the more conspicuous deeds of self-sacrifice and bravery during these weeks, we should need the rest of our space. Men who never failed to bring up rations in spite of shell fire and appalling conditions : who volunteered for dangerous work when sullenness would have been almost excusable : who took messages without delay by the direct route, shelling or no shelling : who maintained signal lines in spite of bombardments—these all carried on a daily tradition of which any battalion could be proud. On November 19th the first V. C. in the Division was gained by Cpl. Meekosha, of B Coy., and the three other N. C. O.'s with him each received the D.C.M. In this supreme decoration a compliment was also given to the general rank and file of the Battalion. The official mention is as follows :—

"He was with a Platoon of about twenty Non-Commissioned Officers and men who were holding an isolated trench. (The Pump Room—see Sketch Map, No. 2). During a very heavy bombardment by the enemy six of the platoon were killed and seven wounded, while all the remainder were more or less buried. When the senior N. C. O. had been either killed or wounded, Cpl. Meekosha at once took command, sent a runner for assistance, and in spite of no less than ten more big shells falling within twenty yards of him, continued to dig out the wounded and buried men in full view of the enemy and at close range from the German trenches. By his promptitude and magnificent courage and determination he saved at least four lives."

About this time an incident happened on the right of the Battalion front which has several points of interest and is somewhat amusing. Our post near Morteldje Estaminet was only about twenty yards from the enemy, and the garrison there was always expecting a "cutting out" operation by the enemy in order to capture this small salient. One afternoon A Coy. received a message from Battalion Head Quarters stating that, from a prisoner's information, an enemy attack was being prepared that night with the object of capturing the Company front and the Morteldje Estaminet Salient. Double sentries were therefore posted, and an extra one hundred rounds ammunition served out per man. But as prisoners' tales were always received with scepticism, and there had been other alarms of this kind, the " attack " was not taken too seriously.

As it happened, however, a newly joined junior officer of the 6th Division (immediately on the right of A Coy.) who, like all officers fresh from England, took these alarms very seriously indeed, heard in due course of the expected attack. Towards midnight this officer must have misunderstood the ordinary night fire of our sentries against any enemy wandering in front of our wire, and he immediately became convinced we were trying to repulse a heavy counter-attack. About midnight, Major R. Clough (O. C. A Coy.) received an anxious telephone message from the Adjutant at Battalion Head Quarters. In the first place the Adjutant appeared astonished that Major Clough was still living. He then asked, " Have you got your line back "?, to which the Major replied that he did not know he had ever lost it ! " Yes, you have," replied the Adjutant. " Brigade has rung up to say the Bosches have taken Morteldje Estaminet." This news was so astonishing, that O. C. A Coy. instantly led the way with one or two runners towards his front line, and was unspeakably thankful to find his men in position, and that there was only the usual night fire—exactly as he had left everything an hour earlier. He asked the officer on duty if the enemy had attacked. " No," he replied, " but something queer is happening to the 6th Division on the right." They went to the right, and found a strong block had been made in the trench against them : they were nearly shot by very alert 6th Division sentries : and they found everybody on the *qui vive*, and the whole 6th Division " standing to." They were greeted with the anxious enquiry, " Have you been wiped out ? " Things were rapidly explained and the alarm was traced to its source. The news of the " attack " had travelled from 6th Division to 49th Division Head Quarters with commendable rapidity ! As a result of the night's excitement one or two literary people in A Coy. wrote essays as to how they escaped capture in the Morteldje Estaminet line.

During this period the dispositions of the 146th Infantry Brigade were as follows : Two Battalions were in the front line, the left Battalion holding D21 and D22, the right battalion D19 and D20. The right Battalion had three platoons of one Coy. in the front line : another Coy. at Knaresborough Castle and The Willows : third Coy. and Head Quarters on Canal Bank : fourth Coy. and one Platoon near La Belle Alliance. The left Battalion had two Coys. actually in front line, two in support, and Battalion Head Quarters on Canal Bank. The support Battalion had two Coys. and Battalion Head Quarters at Elverdinghe Chateau, one Coy. at Hale Farm and one Coy. on West Bank of Canal, South of Bridge 4 ; all the men at the Chateau were in tents, and a few of the officers lived in the Chateau.

On the night of the 15th December, the Battalion moved into D19 and D20 for the last time, with the 1/5th Battalion West Yorkshire Regt. on their left, and the 1/7th Battalion in support. The following four days saw a fitting culmination to the five months' ordeal in the German gas attack of December 19th, 1915. The German object was probably to rely upon the cylinder gas overpowering our infantry, and gas shells our artillery, and then to follow up with small parties their demoralized enemy, and drive in the N.E. line of the Salient by an advance in force.

Fortunately, great improvements had been made, as we have seen, in the anti-gas mask since the Spring of 1915 when the enemy first used poison gas. On that occasion a comparatively weak concentration of pure chlorine was employed, but the new P.H. helmet issued to the Battalion had been devised as a protection not only against chlorine, but against phosgene also. The bombardment which preceded the gas attack extended from the Canal Bank near Boesinghe as far south as Wieltje. Some authorities say that it was the strongest concentration of phosgene cylinder gas sent over by the enemy during the war : the ground over which the cloud passed was covered with powdered crystals like hoar frost, and Canadians on parade at Bailleul, twelve miles back, felt the effects. But the attack failed entirely and not a yard of ground was lost. Small parties of Germans were seen to leave their front line, but were met by such a withering rifle and artillery fire that an advance in force was impossible. The 19th December will always remain one of the great days in the history of the Battalion, as something very definite and tangible was done on that day towards achieving ascendancy over the enemy.

December 17th, two days before the attack, the enemy shelling was unusually heavy. Shelters all along the line were blown in : the "tramcar," the officers' dug-out for the left front Company was smashed up, and Lieuts. Turner and Speight wounded. C. Coy's. No. 12 Platoon was reduced to seven men. In many places what was left of the front line trench became merely a row of shell holes. A year or two later the Artillery Intelligence methods of registering the presence of new German batteries, and thus estimating the probability of a big attack, would have confirmed the general expectation of trouble. Fortunately, however, information from prisoners captured a few days before the attack, gave warning and led to precautionary measures being taken. The fact that the Battalion had fewer casualties than any other unit speaks well for the steadiness and efficiency of officers and men. Special mention should be made of Major C. E. Scott, who was "O. C. Gas Masks," and who insisted upon the most minute examination and constant replacement of every defective helmet in the Battalion. This "excessive" punctiliousness and devotion to detail did not at the time make him popular with either officers or men, though after the attack there was no one in the Battalion regarded with more gratitude or confidence. The first message which was got through by telephone at 10 a.m. to advanced Company Headquarters after the attack was from Major Scott :—" How many gas masks are in your possession ? " Instances of an almost uncanny foresight could be given. O. C. A. Coy. records that he attributes the comparatively few casualties in his Company to Sergt. B. M. Riley, who had heard that the Germans had gas cylinders on their front, and had read in the papers that the Kaiser was coming to Belgium on the 19th December. On the evening of the 18th the wind changed in favour of a German gas attack. He told his platoon there would be an attack between 4 a.m. and daylight the next day, and though he admitted he was surprised when it came, his prophecy was certainly useful.

The bombardment of the 17th December was followed by an unusually quiet day and night. Hardly a shell was fired by the enemy and the silence seemed ominous. No Verey lights were put up and both sides were working hard, our men repairing wire entanglements, and the enemy arranging for the attack in the morning—our sentries reported seeing him move about on his parapet. Inter-Company reliefs took place, A and B Coys. taking the place of C and D in the front line. At 5 a.m. one of the sentries of the left Company (A Coy.), heard a peculiar hissing noise, and saw a white vapour rising between the German line and ours. Otherwise there was nothing to show anything unusual was likely to happen. The alarm was given, and the whole line stood with gas masks ready. A few moments later the " show " began, and everything was pandemonium. Gas was hurled over in bombs and shells of all calibres, in addition to the cylinders. In Brigade Head Quarters two miles from the front line, on the Canal Bank, the message was put through to Division only one minute before all signal lines to the guns were down under the heavy shelling. The Canal Bank was bombarded heavily, and the 1/7th Battalion, ordered to move from Elverdinghe up to close support near Bridge 4, was fortunate to escape without many casualties. Thanks to the promptitude of the Staffs concerned, our guns got to work almost immediately, and as a good supply of ammunition was available, they made a magnificent field day of it. The French 75's joined in, and swept the German parapets with a hail of shells which gladdened the heart of every Tommy in the front line, who was firing his rifle till the barrel was almost red-hot. The enemy gas-shelling began in earnest about half an hour after the cylinder gas was let off, and the shower of these " deadly quiet shells, coming through the darkness like

LT.-COL. H. L. ANDERTON. T.D.

CAPT. L. ODDY.

MAJOR N. MULLER.

CAPT. T. E. ARMISTEAD.

LIEUT. C. G. HIGGINS.

CAPT. W. A. SCALES, M.C.

LIEUT. E. M. KERMODE, D.S.O.,
M.C. AND BAR, D.C.M.

CAPT. L. SPEIGHT.

X.

GROUP OF SERGEANTS, 1914.

BACK ROW.—SERGTS. SANDBACH, KELLET, KELLY, PARSEY, FLEW, FINNEY, WATSON, MURPHY, SMITH, WALMSLEY, DERWENT, RILEY, CLARKE, BUCKLEY, MOORHOUSE, WILMAN, MIDDLETON.

3RD ROW.—COL.-SERGT. KERR, MERRALL, SHIPTON, HUGHES, HETHEN, SIMPSON, CONSTABLE, HAMILTON, RENDELL, GRIFFITHS, BEANLAND, JOWETT, SERVANT, OVERTON, COL.-SERGT. CHECKLEY, COL.-SERGT. DAWSON.

2ND ROW.—SERGT.-DR. BUTTERFIELD, BD.-SERGT. ABBOTT, COL.-SERGT. WOODHEAD, RHODES, COL.-SERGT. BARKER, COL.-SERGT. HANSON, WRAY, CAPT. G. R. SANDEMAN, LT.-COL. H. O. WADE, R.S.M. FREEMAN, COL.-SERGT. MACKAY, PACKETT, COL.-SERGT. POTTAGE, JENNINGS, HARDAKER, ATTWELL.

IST ROW.—SERGTS. BANKS, R. VIRR, DALGLEISH, MARTIN, VAUGHAN, W. VIRR, KIMM, KING, STEVENSON.

(All Sergeants unless otherwise stated.)

xi.

CAPT. W. N. MOSSOP, M.C.

MAJOR E. D. STANSFIELD, M.C. AND BAR.

CAPT. G. SANDERS, V.C., M.C.

CAPT. F. W. MUSGRAVE, M.C.

xii.

rockets and exploding merely with a dull splash," added a new horror to the scene. Men in some cases were gassed by them before they had realized what kind of shells they were, or had adjusted their helmets. Everyone stuck to his post, however. There were no stragglers that day from the 49th Division. Instead of the enemy finding a trench line full of the gassed and dead, and a clear way to the canal, he was checkmated before he left his own trenches, and the few enemy parties who got on to their parapets melted away before the storm of our bullets and shells. The cylinder gas came over for about forty or fifty minutes, and the concentrated enemy bombardment lasted about an hour. At 7 a.m. all was comparatively quiet, and remained so till 2-30 p.m. when a heavy bombardment with H. E.'s began, and continued intermittently till 3 a.m. next morning. By that time, however, the Battalion had been relieved by the 1/7th Bn. West Yorkshire Regt. and had moved to support on the Canal Bank. Throughout that night the sky was " one great glow like a vast electric light, and the atmosphere was laden with a choking, sickly heaviness."

The Army Commander said later that the steadiness of the Division had averted a great disaster, and that undoubtedly the Germans had relied upon creating a panic. The result is particularly noteworthy, as it came after several months of trench life calculated to destroy the morale of almost any regiment. The 1/6th Battalion escaped with comparatively few casualties—nearly one hundred men altogether, of whom eighteen were killed : the proportion of casualties in this one action being about one in four men holding the line. The total casualties in the Division were fourteen officers and 343 men. As a result of the action ten Military Crosses and twenty-nine D.C.M.'s were awarded.

The following extracts from letters give the battle from different points of view :—

" I am able to see quite well once again, after being practically blinded by gas. I was just out of hospital, and when I joined the platoon they told me....to expect a gas attack. *They* shelled like fury. Things looked like business. Result : one day quiet and a quiet night. Orders to have all belts on, guns filled, and reserves ready. More bombs up, and smoke helmets ready for 4 o'clock. 5 a.m. Alarm signals all along the line. Then the gas came hissing along in clouds, and huge trench mortars full of it. Our battalion was ready. I tell you frankly I was physically shivering, although I could keep good control of myself. They sent thousands of rifle grenades, I, like the rest, cowering down in the trenches..... The next Company had a gas mortar right in their trench : the stretcher bearers were all killed, and no one left knew anything of bandaging. It was day-light, and no help could come to their wounded. I took the job on: got to work: but had to take my helmet off. My eyes streamed all the time, and I was coughing and spitting and drinking rum to keep me going. Poor fellows! I could do nothing for three of them, so we gave them cigarettes and rum, and they died. The rest (three) I trussed up with tourniquets, pad splints and bandages, and got them under cover. The whiz bangs were awful, and an enfilade machine gun fire swept the top of the trench, so they had to be dragged along in the mud, using their hands,—all leg and body wounds. There they lay all day, but it finished me. The stuff was hanging round that trench all day. The agonies some men went through with the gas was utterly hellish, fiendish. I was sick and blinded and had to be taken away. I lost all my kit. I was rushed straight here, where I was six days with my eyes bandaged, spitting and coughing all the time. Then I began to mend. This hospital is a fine affair—used to be a casino. The nurses are fine and the doctors good: the equipment is magnificent, and the food A.1. I am clean—clean!, and in bed, hot water to wash in, no work! We had a concert at Christmas, and although I could see nothing, I enjoyed the music immensely."

(Edgar M. Kermode, Sergt., awarded D.C.M. for above action. Later Commissioned and received D.S.O., M.C. & Bar).

"I will give you some recollections of the gas attack, before I forget it. On night 18/19th I took duty (against my usual custom) between 11 p.m. and 2 a.m., and went round the line. The only way to get about was to walk on the remainder of the parapet, and even then your feet were caught in bits of broken wire blown away from the wire entanglements by the bombardment of the previous day. Fortunately it was moonlight. About 5 a.m. 'The Babe' (Lieut. W. H. Scales) who was on duty came to the dug-out, and said there was a report of gas about and we heard heavy rifle fire on the left. All officers went to their platoons, and I made my way to No. 3 platoon in front of our telephone dug-out. It was still dark. Artillery fire was commencing, and heavy rifle fire all down the line.... Scales came from No. 4 platoon and reported he had so far escaped without a single casualty, which shows splendid discipline, and promptitude in getting all the men out, and gas helmets on in a few minutes in the dark. About 7-30 a.m. (Lieut.) Harold Mitchell turned up, having come in full daylight through bog and in full view of the enemy in many places from my right, and reported Nos. 1 and 2 platoons all right. He also brought messages from B Coy., who asked for stretcher bearers, but I could not allow any to go. Mitchell was the only man who came

down from the right all day, and if he had not come I should not have known what happened to B Coy. and my two right platoons. Before this (Lieut. H.) Jowett, the bombing officer, had turned up slightly gassed from ' Dawson City.' He reported that he had set out with (Lieut. T. E.) Armistead, but had found that the eyepiece of his tube helmet had dropped, and let the gas in. He had lost Armistead, and was done up. Mitchell reported A. had turned up at No. 1 platoon absolutely knocked up : he had lost his way and been unconscious for half-an-hour, but was not seriously gassed. At 3-30 p.m. a stretcher bearer said there were some men buried. We all rushed out and found two dug-outs blown in. We pulled off sandbags and from one dug-out removed six men all wounded or crushed. We were in full view of the enemy, but fortunately our artillery was giving them socks, and they did not fire on us. The other dug-out contained three dead men and one mortally wounded, three of them tip-top men and the other a rein-forcement. Our men were all cheerful and hoping the Bosches would summon up courage and come over to us ; we would have wiped them out.....I am quite fit, and got through the Christmas dinners safely (more deadly than gas) and have made many speeches, fortunately to very indulgent audiences. If any of you want to send woollen things, send socks. If we can keep our feet warm we can hang on anywhere. Our chief enemy out here is mud, and the Bosches make a bad second."
(Major R. Clough, M.C.).

Christmas in No. 4 Camp, Coppernolle Wood, near Poperinghe ! What memories of much pig at heavy Company Dinners (dangerous certainly, as Major Clough suggests) : of limitless beer : of impromptu concerts in the Church Army Hut at Peselhoek : of frequent pay-days, regular mails, and the prospect of at last one month's rest : and far away the black Ypres battlefield—suddenly removed to the uttermost part of the earth ! Only modern war and Flanders mud can plunge 500 men into such an abyss of wretched-ness, and then fling them—in the twinkling of an eye—into a pleasant peaceful corner of the earth where a menu such as the following could be discussed and ecstatically enjoyed :—

Potage.
Homard, Lobster Mayonnaise.
Roast Beef and Yorkshire Pudding.
Sauce madère aux champignons.
Purée de pommes de terre.
Petits Pois.
Omelette au rhum.   Fromage.
Café Cognac.   Vins and Liqueurs.

Usually active service menus do not give the literal truth. Often they were a poetic exercise on the part of a literary member of the Officers' or Sergeants' Mess : a Coy. Scout or Signaller : and these gentlemen were not always in liaison with the cook, who had to vary his dish according to rations, or the capacity of Madame and the village épicerie. But generally speaking these festive dinners were master-pieces : and the menu was regarded as an extra hors d'œuvre, which whetted the appetite and helped to strengthen the beer. The men cheered the Colonel : though rather an august individual he was a fearless leader, and a friend who thought more of the Battalion than of himself. They cheered their officers and N. C. O.'s because they too had not been found wanting in the crisis : and, in cheering every-body else, they cheered themselves, because, especially after a Christmas dinner, they knew they were thoroughly good fellows, and that without their help the best-laid schemes and leadership would not have saved the Battalion from inglorious retreat.

On December 31st, 1915, the Battalion crossed the Belgian Frontier and spent the night in Houtkerque, and on January 1st reached Worm houdt, where fourteen days were spent in one of the pleasantest towns of French Flanders. The Battalion was very comfortably billeted in farms, and the ' Tykes' performed every night in the town. On January 15th began the long march to Calais, in three stages of about seventeen kilometres each on successive days. The first halt was at Bollezeele : the second at Zutquerke : and on the last day the Battalion reached the Rest Camp at Calais. These three marches were extremely trying to all ranks. The men's feet were in a terrible state after months in the mud and water of the Salient. In several cases they marched the last few miles to Calais in their stockings, as boots were impossible on such swollen feet. Practically no one fell out on these marches, one of the finest records in the history of the Battalion. It was a case of good morale triumphing over physical weakness. For the last mile or two before reaching Calais, the men marched in close fours, bands playing, as though they had just left billets. When they reached their tents near the Dunes some of the men collapsed—but not before. During the next fortnight at Calais the weather was fine, though cold, and exer-cises on the Dunes and sea air wrought the inevitable cure. The Camp was on a very dry sandy common, rather like Strensall, and covered with gorse bushes. A Belgian Aerodrome was next to it, and our men saw a good deal of practice-flying.

The Commanding Officer started an officer's riding school, and nearly all the officers attended it. Every available hack in the Bat-talion was turned out, and almost every subaltern in the Battalion was thrown, to the great delight of the grooms and a small keenly interested crowd of O.R.'s, who watched " afar off " from among the gorse bushes.

When we left Calais on February 1st and moved down to the Somme the Battalion had regained a good deal of its fitness and endurance. In some respects the stay at Calais was disappointing. The Camp was four miles from the town, and there were several vexatious restrictions imposed on British troops in visiting Calais, all the more burdensome because it was the first large town the Battalion had had the opportunity to visit in France. Only small numbers of men were given leave from the Camp, and they were marched there and back in parties, having only a few hours of liberty in the town. They were not allowed to use the civilian tramcars except with special permission. French and Belgian troops who were in the town received much more liberty. Our men laid the responsibility for these restrictions at the door of the French Authorities in Calais. But " Authorities " always seemed to move in a mysterious way, and their decrees were accepted, like Providence, philosophically. For the favoured few who had " thé à l'anglaise " at the Sauvage : dinner at the Continental : who could practise their French on the pretty demoiselles in the lace and lingerie shops of the Boulevard Jacquard : or who had numerous shampoos and " frictions " in the coiffeurs' shops,—Calais seemed a place of ineffable charm. On January 30th, after presenting decorations, and on the eve of the Division leaving the Second Army, General Sir H. Plumer gave the Division the following farewell message :—

" This is a very pleasant ceremony to me, and I hope to you, with which to finish for the time being my connection, and that of the Second Army, with this Division. I have had the pleasure on two occasions lately : one some weeks ago when you came out of the line, and one the other day, when I gave ribbons representing decorations to Officers, N. C. O.'s and men of the Division after the recent gas-attack : of expressing briefly, but I hope quite distinctly, my appreciation of the way in which the 49th Division has carried out the duties entrusted to it during the last few months. But now that it is settled for the time being that the 49th Division is to leave the Second Army, and go into another area, while I have nothing to add as regards appreciation of the work you have done, I should like to say how sorry I am that you are leaving the Second Army. I cannot expect you to share my regret. No one so far as I know has felt any deep regret at quitting the Ypres Salient. But while you will not regret your change of scene, when you look back at the time you have spent up here, notwithstanding the arduous times you have gone through, notwithstanding the losses of your comrades, which we all deplore, you will, I know, have some pleasant memories to carry with you of your comrades of the Second Army. We, I can assure you, will follow your doings with the deepest interest, and shall always feel a kind of reflected glory when we hear of the gallant deeds which I feel sure you are going to accomplish, both individually and as a Unit. I say Good bye to you, and I wish you all the best of Luck. Good bye ! "

CHAPTER V.

PREPARATIONS FOR THE SOMME.

WHEN the Battalion was training in England, moves from one part of the country to another did not cause much interest or anxiety, except to lovers and married men. After eight months in France this indifference entirely disappeared. Men developed a very keen interest in the way G. H. Q. moved units up and down the chessboard of France. They discovered that " one place was *not* as good as another," and that some sectors had fathomless capacity for every variety of unpleasantness. They had begun to like sectors which were not well-known at G. H. Q., and which were never mentioned in official Communiqués. When the Battalion moved south from Calais on February 1st, 1916, the Somme Front had quite a pleasant sound in the ears of the British soldier. It gave him the grateful impression of a place not too much talked about, and he was inclined to think that the trenches there might probably be of the inglorious but comfortable kind where the Kaiser sent his tired Divisions. He possibly hoped that the 49th was regarded as a " tired " Division, though he could not feel certain on this point, as he had already enjoyed a month's rest, and red-tabbed staff officers had been very complimentary—always a dangerous sign ! However, anything was better than another dose of Flanders mud, so the Battalion received their sealed movement orders very cheerfully, and entrained at Fontinettes Triage, a small station near Calais, at 5 p.m. on the afternoon of February 1st. Three days' rations were carried on the train, in addition to the usual iron ration on each man. The journey was accomplished very quickly, and the train arrived about 1 a.m. next morning at Longeau Station, about three miles east of Amiens. The whole Battalion was fast asleep, as every one had expected a longer journey. The night was fine, but bitterly cold, and there was no moon. Detraining was carried out quickly. The detraining party will remember vividly a vociferous R. T. O., who was in a very bad temper. Within half-an-hour of the arrival at Longeau, the Battalion was on the march to Ailly-sur-Somme, a small manufacturing town on the south bank of the river, about seven miles N.W. of Amiens.

This march rouses no pleasant memories. Very few officers or men knew the destination, or how far away Ailly was from Amiens. As hour succeeded hour without sign of billets, the patience and endurance of everybody was sorely tried. The ten minutes halt each hour was a time of mingled relief and dread so far as the officers and N.C.O.'s were concerned, as the men lay down on the roadside and fell asleep, and it was extremely difficult to find out if platoons were complete when the " fall in " had sounded, owing to the darkness of the night. It was also impossible to give stragglers a definite idea as to destination apart from " keep straight on this road till you reach the Battalion's billets in the morning." However, about 6 a.m. Ailly was reached. The billets were scattered over a wide area, one or two Companies being in isolated farmsteads two or three miles from the town. By daybreak the whole of the 146th Infantry Brigade was concentrated in the district. The 1/5th and 1/6th Battalions were at Ailly-sur-Somme, the 1/7th Battalion at Picquigny, the 1/8th Battalion at Breilly.

The pleasant " rolling plains of Picardy," not unlike the Yorkshire Wolds, but richer and well wooded, were a grateful contrast from the monotony of the Flanders plains. Ailly was a rather dirty town, but there were compensations. The Amiens tramway came as far as Dreuil, which was little above a mile from Ailly, and it was thus possible to spend a few hours in the afternoon in Amiens. There were good baths for all ranks in a factory on the Ailly-Dreuil Road. There were at least a score private houses and half as many estaminets where one could obtain excellent " Eggs and chips " and coffee for a franc, and this meal always made the average infantryman feel " at home," or at least, near civilization. The men also found that " le franc Picard " was a good type of Frenchman, who did his best to make them comfortable without charging outrageously for it. In short the Battalion was favourably impressed with the experiences of the first few days in the Somme district.

When the Battalion arrived on the Somme, one or two important changes had taken place in the personnel of the officers of the Brigade. Brig. Gen. F. A. Macfarlan, C.B., relinquished command of the Brigade on December 20th, 1915. It is not often that one can say sincerely that the loss of an officer of General's rank was regretted by all ranks under his command. Yet such a statement would be strictly true in the case of Brig. Gen. Macfarlan. He was a man of powerful physique, and day and night during the months at Ypres, in every kind of weather, he visited his battalions in the line, and was as thoroughly acquainted with front line conditions as any Company officer. He was bluntly outspoken in praise or blame, and meant every word he said. " If you're going to soldier, *soldier*. If not, go and clean latrine buckets out," was his sharp rebuke to some men for slack discipline on the march. He had a remarkable facility in remembering the names of all ranks under him, and N.C.O.'s and men very much appreciated the uncommon personal interest shown in them as individuals by their burly Brigadier. One of his outstanding merits was that he regarded every order from the point of view of the infantryman in the line : this was done as a definite policy, with justice and without sentimentality. He regarded the Staffs of his own and higher formations as servants to the infantryman, and combated at every point the evil—which grew to such terrible proportions as the war continued—of unnecessarily inflated Staffs, often conscious only of their own importance. He believed that honours should be for the fighting soldier, and that faithful work in the organizing branches of the Army carried sufficient reward in increased comfort and safety. Though not a new doctrine, and one shared by every great soldier since the world began, considerable tact was needed to make it palatable to the higher authorities. He was loved and respected by the Territorial officers under him : and no one else in a time of crisis could have got more out of his Brigade than General Macfarlan. His successor was Brig. Gen. M. D. Goring Jones, C.M.G., D.S.O., who had been in command of the 2nd Bn. Durham Light Infantry for one year, and who remained in command of the 146th Infantry Brigade up to October, 1917. A few days later he took Capt. G. R. Sandeman (who, as we have seen, had been Adjutant of the 1/6th Battalion from 1914) to be his Brigade Major.

Everyone was pleased that Capt. Sandeman would still remain in close touch with the Battalion, but his loss as Adjutant was a very serious one. For the first sixteen months of the war he had been one of the outstanding characters of the Battalion. As Adjutant in peace time he completed the ground work of the Mobilization Scheme, which had been conceived and begun by Capt. T. M. Ellis, and infused into others his own interest in musketry. There was always something about which he was enthusiastic, and he had the rare gift of making others enthusiastic about the same thing. On several occasions his influence saved the Battalion from utter boredom. Most men will remember his familiar figure, when, with swinging walk and hunting crop in hand, he made his daily and nightly round of the trenches in the Ypres Salient. One of his Officers (Captain J. Muller) writes of him as follows : " I venture to think the general impression is of a little man, with a prematurely bald head, who was loved by the whole Battalion in 1914 and 1915, and who was chiefly known by his energy, good temper, sense of duty, and ability for getting things done. Of Sandeman's youth we know very little except that he had a violent temper and that he was ' soldier-brained.' That so few people, who thought they knew him well, discovered he had a violent temper is a proof of his self-control. Careless of his own comfort (the most petrolly tea the writer has known was drunk in Sandeman's dugout facing the High Command Redoubt in the Ypres Salient) he was always considerate of that of his men." One of the deep reasons for the good influence Capt. Sandeman exerted in the Battalion was the simplicity and directness of his dealings. He never became a " paper merchant," sending out long " chits " where a personal interview would have served much better. He knew how to deal with men, and did not seek refuge in multiplying piles of correspondence.

Early in 1916 an important change had taken place in the arrangement of the Machine Guns in the Brigade. Each Battalion previously had its own Machine Gun section. The Lewis Gun was to some extent taking the place of the Machine Gun within battalions, and under the new orders all the Machine Gun sections were amalgamated into one Brigade Machine Gun Company, forming an entirely separate unit in the Brigade, with separate transport and administration. The command of this very important unit was given to Captain John Muller (subsequently Lieut.-Col. J. Muller, D.S.O., M.C.), who took with him from the Battalion, Lieuts. Dobson, Hill and Thresh. Lieut. (after Major) Dobson, or " Dobbers " as he was familiarly called, was one of the most unselfish and loyal officers the Battalion had. He refused recommendation for promotion on more than one occasion because it would have entailed separation from the M.G. Company he had done so much to make. Mesopotamia and pneumonia caused his death two years later.

About the same time as the formation of the Brigade Machine Gun Company, the Scouts were organized as a separate unit in each battalion. The 1/6th Battalion Scouts were placed under the leadership of Lieut. Harold Mitchell with Sergt. F. E. Fairbank (afterwards Battalion and Brigade Intelligence Officer) as Scout Sergeant. Lieut. Mitchell was very popular, and the Scouts quickly justified their existence.

The Brigade, thus re-organized, marched from Ailly-sur-Somme on February 10th to Rubempré (20 km.), thence by buses to Bouzincourt (20 km.), and on February 12th relieved the 16th Lancashire Fusiliers in the sector opposite Thiepval. Till the end of the month the Battalion remained in the line in this sector. Though the actual time spent in the Thiepval trenches in February was thus only a little over a fortnight, more than usual interest is attached to this introduction to

74

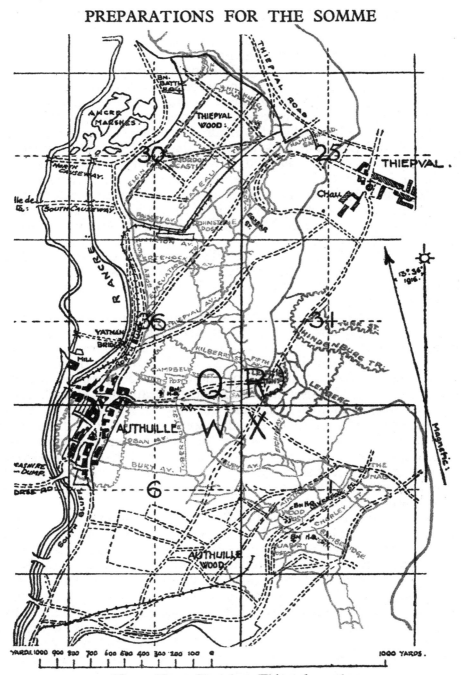

No. 3 Map. Trenches, Thiepval, 1916.

Thiepval, where, later in 1916, the Battalion lost more men in casualties than in any other sector during the war.

The arrival of the 49th Division opposite Thiepval in Feb./Mar., 1916, was a preliminary stage in preparation for the battles which opened in July 1st. During these weeks the Division obtained an idea of the ground and the enemy fortifications it was to attack three months later. The battle of Verdun began on February 21st, nine days after the Battalion took over the line at Thiepval. During the anxious months which followed, the Allied plans for an offensive on the Somme as a relief to the situation at Verdun, were being matured. In March and April the 49th Division was engaged in the construction of strategic roads and railways behind the Thiepval sector, and the prolonged training which followed at Vignacourt was of course part of the same preparation.

The 36th (Ulster) Division, which relieved the 49th in March opposite Thiepval, was the Division which attacked from Thiepval Wood on July 1st. Thus, early in 1916, the pieces were being arranged for the great game.

It is not necessary to describe at present the country round Thiepval, except to say that it had all the usual characteristics of Picardy, being hilly, well-wooded, with a series of long irregular spurs and deep depressions which ran in a S. and S. W. direction to the main valley of the Somme River. In one of these deep depressions the River Ancre ran past Miraumont, Grandcourt, Beaumont Hamel, Albert, and other names famous in military history, till it reached the Somme near Corbie. The German trenches were sited very skilfully on the crest of the high ground east of the Ancre, and from a defensive point of view had every advantage of position. It will easily be understood that the effect upon the morale of British troops of being compelled to cling painfully to the western slope of positions dominated by the enemy, was not good.

The Battalion had arrived at Bouzincourt late on the afternoon of February 11th. There had been heavy rain during the journey, and everyone was soaked to the skin. Billets were not comfortable, as the village was only three miles behind the line. A false sense of security was given to many of these villages by the undulations of the country, and the fact that the enemy had no direct observation. Englebelmer, Martinsart, Bouzincourt were fairly well occupied by civilians. Even in Albert during the battle of the Somme hundreds of civilians remained in spite of frequent shelling. Bouzincourt and Martinsart were further sheltered from the enemy by Aveluy Wood, which reached down to the Ancre, and contained more than a 1000 acres of fine timber and thick undergrowth, where an infantry Division and a score of batteries were easily concealed during the final preparations for July 1st.

On the 12th February before dusk, the Battalion marched out of Bouzincourt, through Albert, and along the Albert-Aveluy road about the same time that battalions in the line were " standing to," and the nightly " strafe " was commencing. There was little shelling, but considerable rifle and Machine Gun fire, and the hope that Thiepval would be a quiet sector for " tired " troops did not seem to have much foundation ! In Authuille a few of the houses could still boast roofs, though most of the town was a shambles—as could only be expected 700 yards behind the line ! The inevitable sentries on the out-skirts of the village warned reliefs to split up into small parties at 40 yard intervals, and progress became slow. Occasional shells come low over the hill side and plunged harmlessly into the marsh below with a shrill cry and weird echo which became a familiar and nerve racking sound to anyone who inhabited the Ancre Marshes. Enemy Machine Gun fire had an extraordinary way of being effective at unexpected points, owing to the fact that most of the valleys were re-entrants, which the enemy commanded from one part or another of his trenches. Everyone was agreeably surprised to find how deep, dry, well-revetted and comfortable—comparatively speaking—most of the trenches were, especially after the experience of the Ypres " canals," and the flimsy Fleurbaix and Neuve Chapelle breastworks. In the Thiepval sector the trenches were eight to ten feet deep, with good firesteps, and the hard chalky nature of the soil made them fairly resistant to heavy rains. They were also easily drained, being on a rather steep slope. The 1/6th Battalion took over the right of the Brigade Front, from Hamilton Avenue to Hammerhead Sap inclusive. There were three companies in the line, and one in support. The 1/8th Battalion was on the left, and held the line to Peterhead Sap, with a post near " The Mill " in the Ancre Swamp. The 1/7th Battalion was in support, with Battalion Head Quarters and two com-panies in Authuille : one company in support to the 1/6th Battalion at Johnstone's Post, and the other company in support to the 1/8th Battalion at Gordon Castle. The 1/5th Battalion was in reserve in Martinsart. On February 20th the Battalion was relieved for four days by the 1/5th Battalion. Again on February 24th the Battalion took over the same sector, and remained till the end of February, when the 1/5th Battalion relieved them for the last time. After four days in support at Authuille, Johnstone's Post and Gordon Castle, the Bat-talion was relieved by the 9th Battalion Inniskilling Fusiliers (109th Brigade, 36th Division) and marched back to Bouzincourt.

One or two features of this period require special mention. During the whole time the Battalion was in the line the cold was intense, and there were fairly heavy snowfalls. The men's feet were still in bad condition after the Ypres trenches, and the cold weather resulted in a great number of cases of trench feet of a very severe kind. During the second long eight days spell in the line, there were two or three cases where men would have frozen to death on the firestep but for the prompt attention of a corporal or sergeant, prolonged rubbing, and a stiff dose of rum. As there was only an average of one tolerable mined dug-out on a Company front, the only protection against the extreme cold consisted of shelters on the fire-step. These shelters were of the flimsiest kind, and consisted merely of a few pieces of corrugated iron laid over the trench, with some waterproof sheets fastened at each end " to keep out the cold ! " The line was held extremely thinly, as the average strength of platoons during the last tour in the line was only fourteen or sixteen men. This resulted in longer hours of " sentry-go," and after three hours watch in driving sleet and freezing cold a sentry came off duty more dead than alive, and usually stamped up and down the trench for an hour to restore circulation before creeping alongside a comrade on the fire-step. The thinness of the line, and the insecurity of our position on a slope dominated by the enemy, and which would have been almost impossible for such small numbers to hold against attack, combined to make all ranks unusually anxious. Later on, when we passed over No Man's Land, and saw the German defences on the other side, we found that whilst we had been shivering on the fire-step, he had been able in the coldest weather to sleep soundly in his elaborately-mined dugouts, and had had no necessity to keep on the ceaseless " alert," owing to the strength of his defences.

There was another respect in which his mined dug-outs gave the enemy a great advantage. Trench Mortars of a particularly noxious type were an unpleasant feature of the sector. An enormous 140 lb. minen-werfer—the biggest missile of its kind the enemy used—was active on this front, chiefly near Hamilton Avenue. The thing was like a huge cigar in the air, and lurched slowly over No Man's Land in such an indefinite wobbling way that the wretched garrison was uncertain as to where exactly it would fall. In any case a few yards one way or another did not matter, as the destruction caused was enormous. Men who were caught disappeared entirely ; in some cases it was necessary to parade a platoon in order to find out who was missing, as there was no other method. Candles in dugouts 300 yards from the explosion were blown out and men lifted off their feet and thrown against the trench side by the concussion. A rather good description of Trench-mortar fire is the following—given by a victim.

"You sit in a somnolent condition watching the humid disintegration of your dugout, when there is a rushing through the air from above, and a noise like someone lifting the plug of an enormous bath, followed by another like Vesuvius exploding bodily. You rush outside when the lava has stopped coming down, and find that a Trench Mortar has dropped a young mine about the size of an hotel a few yards off your dugout."

A 17-in. shell penetrated deeper, and probably caused more damage, but a large Trench Mortar made more noise, and produced a bigger " sensation." The worst Trench Mortar casualties during this period were inflicted on the 1/5th Battalion on February 29th, when a whole platoon of sixteen men was wiped out by one " rum jar " which fell on the head of a C. T. as the platoon arrived to take over the line. The 1/6th Battalion had suffered frequent Trench Mortar bombardments, and had only been able to obtain feeble artillery retaliation, when a Trench Mortar enthusiast " fra' Scotland " went round the Battalion front trying to choose an emplacement for his engine. Each Company was very pleased to see him, and anxious that he should fire off all rounds possible, but they were even more anxious that he should not fix his " beastly engine " in their own Company front, as the enemy was sure to retaliate. The Trench Mortar enthusiast informed D. Coy. Head Quarters that he had received instructions to " settle down " on their front, saying affectionately " Wait till I fire my little football." Everyone got on the fire-step to watch " his little football " throw the enemy parapet about. He fired. The football flew beautifully, and fell nicely on top of what we thought was a German dug-out. Prolonged silence: a dud! The next—a dud! The third and last made amends, exploding magnificently, but the stick of the " football " flew back to our line, nearly wounding the Coy. Sergeant-Major. Our Trench Mortar's ration for that day was three shells. The ration improved later, and although the infantrymen had the job of carrying the " footballs " from a dump in Authuille to the front line— a great labour—it was not altogether an unpopular one, as the carriers were cheered by the prospect of being able to see the footballs burst on the enemy parapets in the morning.

When the " pop " of our Trench Mortar had given the enemy warning of a shell coming over, he blew a horn, evidently to warn everyone in his trenches either to keep in the dugouts, or watch for the Trench Mortar. This horn was the same used by French porters in French Railway Stations, and gave the " Tykes " material for one or two jokes. But it was probably a good invention from the enemy point of view. Sentries had very anxious moments in a line which was being trench-mortared. Some of them became experts in calculating exactly where a T.M. was going to drop, and were often able to save not only their own lives, but those of other men. Our padre (Rev. R. Whincup) owed his life on one occasion in the Thiepval trenches near Hamilton Avenue, to the nice calculation of Pte. R. Howard, a D. Coy. sentry. The padre was walking cheerily along the front line, when he heard a sudden shout from a sentry telling him to " double round that traverse." He did so—just as an enemy T.M. landed clean in the bay he had left, and made a shambles of everything in it.

The newly formed scout section, under Lieut. H. Mitchell, did extremely good work in this sector. They had bad luck during the first tour in the line, as their dugout was hit by a Trench Mortar and three of them killed outright, the rest being badly shaken. Patrols were out every night, especially to Oblong and Diamond Woods. No Man's Land was efficiently " mapped," and the reporting of purely " Intelligence " matters in Daily Intelligence Reports was for the first time begun throughout the Division. A great deal of quite useless " Intelligence " was probably sent back to Head Quarters, but the principle that war is a science in which knowledge of the enemy trenches is quite as important as knowledge of your own line, was being generally understood by Officers and N.C.O.'s. For the first time in the Battalion War Diary notes such as " much movement seen at R 25 d 55 " begin to appear, and artillery shoots were arranged as a result of Infantry observation. Up to this period throughout the British Army Infantry " Intelligence " had not been systematized : patrols had been sent out on the initiative of Company Commanders who only rarely wrote any report on the result of the patrol. Artillery and Machine Guns had to rely almost entirely upon their own observation for suitable targets. By the end of 1916 a great advance had been made in co-ordinating information from all sectors of the front, and when a sector changed hands the continuity of the " Intelligence " regarding it was not broken. During the first year or so of the war the enemy " Intelligence " was superior to ours. The morning after the 1/6th Battalion took over the trenches at Thiepval, some Germans shouted across No Man's Land near Hammerhead Sap " Hullo, West Yorks. ! " And this kind of information as to our reliefs and movements does not seem to have been very rare during 1914 and 1915. But towards the end of 1916 we achieved definite superiority in purely " Intelligence " work.

BRIG.-GEN. M. D. GORING JONES,
C.M.G., D.S.O.

BRIG.-GEN. G. A. P. RENNIE, C.M.G.,
D.S.O.

BRIG.-GEN. F. A. MACFARLANE, C.B.

PTE. E. J. WILKINSON, D.C.M., L./CPL. E. JOHNSTON, D.C.M., CPL. J. SAYERS, D.C.M.,
SERGT. S. MEEKOSHA, V.C.

xiv.

ROUTE MARCH, STRENSALL.

SCENES ON COAST DEFENCE DUTIES NEAR MARSKE.

XV.

PANORAMA—AUBERS RIDGE, 1916.
(VIEW FROM O.P. TILLELOY RD.).

xvi.

PREPARATIONS FOR THE SOMME

After relief in the Thiepval sector, the Battalion stayed a night in Bouzincourt, and then marched to Varennes, a village about five miles away, where they stayed for a week. Varennes had the distinction of being one of the dirtiest villages in which the Battalion was billeted. The civilians seemed to have no sanitary arrangements in their farms—so far as the uninitiated eyes of our men could discover ; and there were very few such facilities for troops. The week passed quickly with easy Company parades and sports. Whilst at Varennes the authorities prosecuted their campaign against cameras with more than usual vigilance. O.C. Companies signed certificates that no cameras were in their possession. We have heard of a battalion in which O.C. A Coy., remembering his friendship for O.C. B Coy., sent him three cameras as a present, and then signed the certificate : whereupon O.C. B Coy. sent seven cameras to O.C. C Coy., and signed likewise : D eventually receiving eleven cameras, which were sent to A Coy. in due course. Naturally, this could not have been a battalion of the 49th Division ! But some cameras must have escaped, as photos of the Somme battles in 1916 are still fairly numerous. It is charitable, however, to hope that these cameras belonged to reinforcements who came out immediately before July 1st, and knew no better ! On February 14th half the Battalion (A and C Coys.) marched to Buozincourt. The remainder (B and D Coys. with Battalion H. Q.) marched to Senlis. There the Battalion remained till April 2nd, constructing a new road from Bouzincourt to Martinsart. This road, under the name of " Northumberland Avenue," proved most useful as a means of lateral communication during the battle of the Somme. The work was not interfered with by the enemy: the men worked well, as it was too cold to be anything but energetic. The stone was quarried near Bouzincourt, and the road, about two miles in length, was eventually finished by other units of the Brigade. The other Battalions of the Brigade were also on working parties. The Brigade Head Quarters and 1/8th Battalion were at Beaucourt sur l'Hallue, 1/5th Battalion at Behencourt, and the 1/7th Battalion at Fréchencourt, engaged in the construction of a new railway from Daours (on the Somme) to Contay.

Senlis was a pleasant town with good billets and a friendly population, and even the two companies at Bouzincourt had a good time, playing several games of football, watched by large crowds, within four kilometres of the front line. For relaxation men visited Albert, and looked at La Vierge Dorée, " the Virgin of Albert Cathedral," which had fallen at a perilous right angle with the Cathedral tower, and which—according to the prophecy which was never fulfilled—would remain gazing sadly down upon the market square till the Day

G

of Victory, when it would collapse on the pavement below. In those days Albert was full of troops. It was easy to buy fresh vegetables, rosaries, and silk-embroidered cards beloved as souvenirs by the British Army. There was also a quite comfortable estaminet, where one could get tea and coffee, and a game of billiards on a vile billiard table, and even—if fortunate—have a talk with " Marianne," famous for miles round for her smile and " prettiness ," though she used more than a " soupçon " of powder and paint. As always when the Battalion was in rest billets behind the line, there were " adventures " of an amorous kind, one of the strangest being that of a certain officer with " Marguerite " of Varennes. " Marguerite " was a charming and entirely respectable young lady who was very popular with a certain Company Officers' Mess. One of the officers—married and conduct beyond reproach—was startled to receive one day a long letter from " Marguerite " proposing marriage in such a diffident, delicate way as quite to disarm criticism. She had evidently no idea that Lieut. X— was married, and must have been misled by the ordinary courtesies of billet life usually paid by any average British officer to a charming French girl. The result was a very awkward situation. The said officer gravely examined his past conduct, and after anxious deliberation, decided to ride over to Varennes (the Battalion was then stationed at Senlis) and explain the situation to the misguided girl. Just in time, however, a friend told him it was a hoax, and the letter had been written by another officer, who had an excellent knowledge of French. After the first shock of relief, Lieut. X— was probably a little piqued that after all his attractions had not proved so irresistible !

While the Battalion was at Senlis, the 16th Bn. West Yorkshire Regt. (the " Bradford Pals ") reached Mailly-Maillet, about four and a half miles away, and several of our men walked over to see them, and welcome them to France. The 31st Division was also fated to take part in the attack on July 1st near Gommecourt.

On April 3rd and 4th the Battalion moved to Molliens-au-Bois (12 miles) and thence to Vignacourt (9 miles), where they stayed till June 9th. The other units of the Brigade were also on the march. The 1/5th and 1/7th Battalions were inspected on the Behencourt-Fréchencourt Road by Lord Kitchener, who had been attending the Allies' Conference in Paris. The other Battalions of the Brigade were also concentrated with Brigade Head Quarters at Vignacourt, with the exception of the 1/7th Battalion, which for the first month was attached to the IVth Army Infantry School at Flixecourt for demonstration purposes and fatigues.

This period of eight weeks at Vignacourt was the longest

continuous rest the Battalion had in France, and was probably the most enjoyable for all ranks. If we looked at this Vignacourt period from the point of view of the official War Diary we should dismiss it in a few words, something as follows :—" Training carried on vigorously : Battalion and Brigade Field Days weekly : Reinforcements of three officers and 170 other ranks received in May : two officers and 100 other ranks provided for work on New Railway Sidings at Vignacourt : Battalion provides Brigade Head Quarters' Guard every fourth day, etc., etc." The War Diary would thus compress the life of eight weeks into as many lines, whereas a few lurid hours in the Leipzig Salient on July 15th would fill a page. Most members of the Battalion would reverse the emphasis, however, and become eloquent on a joy ride to Amiens : a favourite estaminet at Vignacourt : an anniversary dinner : a jolly billet ; and they would dismiss the affair in the Leipzig Salient with a shrug, as hardly being worth mentioning in comparison.

Vignacourt was a typical village of Picardy, with a main street over two miles long and of extraordinary width. The houses were of irregular height, colour, and form. There was the one-storey white-washed cottage of the peasant : the long windowless wall of the farm out-building : the two-storied stone house of the " rentier " : the villa of the proprietor of the local mill : and the chateau or country house of the gentry of the district. In the middle of the street there were half a dozen pools surrounded with willow trees, giving an additional touch of the picturesque to the village. A few great lime trees, over a hundred years old, towered over the houses, and gave a welcome shade during the hot afternoons of summer. Battalion Head Quarters were in the doctor's house opposite the church. The " Tykes " gave their show every night in the " Salle des Concerts," which was crowded by men from all other units of the Division, billeted in Naours, Flesselles, Havernas and Flixecourt. The Battalion training grounds were near the Forêt de Vignacourt—a fine wood about three miles in extent and only half an hour's march from the village. As Vignacourt was on the summit of a plateau 500 feet above sea level, the air was healthy and bracing. Amiens Cathedral nine miles away could be seen on a clear day, and Vignacourt Church was the most prominent landmark for ten miles round. The natives of Vignacourt were particularly friendly, and did everything in their power to make the Battalion's stay comfortable. The 146th Infantry Brigade was practically the first British unit which had been billeted on them, and this accounts to some extent for the warmth of their welcome. Leave to England was regular during this period, and comparatively few officers and men were unable to get leave before July 1st. The Adjutant (Capt. W. N.

Mossop) was away on a Special Course, and his place was taken temporarily by Lieut. N. Dodd, of D Company.

There was an astounding amount of common sense shown in the training during these weeks, and as a result of it the Battalion reached a level of efficiency and physical fitness which surpassed even that on the departure from England. War experience had hardened the men, and the reinforcements from England were of a very good type, and soon settled down with the rest. For the first two or three weeks the Battalion was trained by Companies. As many of the Officers and N.C.O.'s had been on courses at the IV. Army and 49th Divisional Schools (the latter under Commandant Major Bousfield, 1/7th Bn. West Yorkshire Regt.) the Battalion reaped the benefit of the latest improvements in methods of training. The watchword of the new training methods seemed to be " variety," and after a few minutes strenuous drill or physical exercises, a number of games were introduced, which entirely saved the men from any feeling of boredom. Scouting and Bombing Competitions were arranged in the Division, and the 1/6th Battalion Bombers carried off the Divisional Prize. To tell exactly how they won the Divisional Bombing Competition would require the use of a considerable vocabulary. In bombing up a trench the leading section became so enthusiastic and bloodthirsty that they came out with a very purple flow of language, the full force of which fell on the Divisional General and our Brigadier, who were watching the show. The Divisional General reported that he was much impressed with the " earnestness and good morale " of the Bombers, and awarded them the prize accordingly. Whilst throwing a bomb for practice a few days later, our Bombing Officer, Lieut. H. A. Jowett, was wounded in the arm. His loss was very regrettable. Under his influence the Bombers had become a keen efficient unit, and as we shall see later, did great work in the fighting in July.

The country near Havernas and the St. Ouen—Pernois Valley was excellent ground for manœuvres. Brigade field days in Vignacourt Forest were followed by elaborate Divisional attack practices on " taped trenches," near Naours. There were also one or two night operations, but as they were over before midnight they could not be called strenuous. Usually these manœuvres produced a very vocal enemy in the shape of a French farmer—or his wife—threatening enormous claims for damaged crops.

Various efforts were made to instil the true " attack " spirit into the men. Lectures on " morale " were given by everyone, from the Brigadier in the Salle des Concerts, to the newest subaltern in the platoon barn on a wet day. The famous Major Campbell gave us a most bloodthirsty lecture on the use of the bayonet. He detailed the whole science of butchery, and seemed to enjoy describing the most horrible details of bayonet fighting. He explained in a quiet bloodthirsty voice exactly how to pierce the liver or kidneys or "lights" of the enemy, and described with a ghoulish gurgle the soft thud of the bayonet as it was pulled out of the quivering body of a German. He told many funny stories, which made his large audience in the Salle des Concerts at Vignacourt roar with laughter. His story of " Where's 'Arry? " is perhaps the most typical. There was an attack on some German trenches, and many Germans were killed coming out of a dug-out. The Sergeant had orders to "blood" all his men, and had been able to do so very successfully on this occasion. But 'Arry was a shy new recruit, who had evidently been overlooked. So the Sergeant shouted out during the killing, "Where's 'Arry? 'Arry hasn't had a go yet." So 'Arry got to work......and became a man-eating tiger in future, and never needed inviting again! Great laughter usually followed this story of "the blooding of 'Arry." We also had lectures on the use of German words of command, and we learnt many useful adjectives to apply to Germans in the forthcoming attack. When the Battalion left Vignacourt, it was as well-prepared for "business" as any unit in the British Army.

During the stay in Vignacourt, steel helmets were issued to the Battalion. They were of course quite a novelty, though two steel helmets after the French pattern were issued per Company in the Ypres Salient, but these had been kept in the Quarter-Master's Stores, as no one wished to appear "odd" in wearing them. As it happened, the steel helmets were first issued on one of the hottest days of the Summer and before one of the longest and hardest field days the Battalion ever had. The result was much perspiration and bad language, and steel helmets were not popular for some time. The Battalion postman (Cpl. J. Walker) reports that he was trying on his helmet in the barn before the field day mentioned above, when " one of the boys " hit him on the head with a spade, " to see if it hurt." The blow took no effect. Whereupon another man took the helmet, and told the same fellow to hit him also. This was promptly done, and, to every one's surprise, the blow took immediate effect, and laid the man out, senseless. He was brought round after some natural anxiety. Walker explains it by saying the other fellow's head was much smaller than his own, and the helmet therefore fitted him too closely, with the result that he received the full force of the blow. For some weeks later a few hard-headed men in the Battalion took on bets from one franc upwards that whilst wearing their helmet they could stand any blow on the head with an entrenching tool handle ! They usually won, but there were occasional casualties.

Another innovation adopted in May throughout the British Army was the use of coloured markings on the right sleeve near the shoulder, and in the middle of the collar at the back of the tunic. The letter adopted for units of the 146th Infantry Brigade was T, and the Battalions were distinguished by different colours, 1/5th Battalion being green, 1/6th Battalion yellow, 1/7th Battalion red, 1/8th Battalion blue, and red and blue for the 146th Brigade Machine Gun Coy. (Later on in December, 1917, at Etaples, the 146th Infantry Brigade Trench Mortar Battery (Stokes' Gun) received a yellow and green T as their colours). So far as civilians were concerned, the units in the Brigade became known as " green " or " yellow " T's, etc. These signs were adopted in order to assist Officers and N.C.O.'s who were not familiar with their men to reorganize them rapidly after the attack.

The Anniversary of the Battalion's arrival in France on April 15th, 1915, was duly celebrated at Vignacourt by a series of Company dinners. A smoking concert was held on April 14th, for all members of the Battalion, and the Sergeants had a dinner on April 16th. B. Company produced a menu which would have done honour to the Godbert Restaurant at Amiens, and D. Coy. attracted nearly all the Officers of the Battalion to their Company Mess by a wonderful Champagne Cup which loosened the tongues of many present, and impelled them to give eloquent speeches to an audience which could not be called critical. Anniversary Dinners do not occur often, and perhaps it was fortunate that April 16th was a quiet day, without any complicated field operations.

On May 9th, 430 Officers and other ranks left Vignacourt for Martinsart, Englebelmer, Bouzincourt and Forceville, to work in the forward areas on cable trenches and assembly positions for July 1st. From this date, the thoughts of everyone were concentrated on the battle which was believed imminent. The news of Kitchener's death came early in June, and a Battalion Memorial Service was held on June 11th, our buglers playing the Last Post. Officers wore crepe arm bands for some days in honour of his memory. Five days later the Battalion marched from Vignacourt *via* Rubempre to Puchevillers (13 miles) where they camped in an orchard on the outskirts of the village. Here they were re-joined by the working parties which had left the Battalion five weeks earlier.

This period at Puchevillers was the final calm before the storm. No one could overlook the signs of the approaching conflict. The most potent reminder was the enormous Casualty Clearing Station which had been built within three minutes' walk of the Camp. For weeks this Casualty Clearing Station had been accumulating stretchers and other paraphernalia, and during the ten days the Battalion remained at Puchevillers men walked up every evening to watch the Casualty Clearing Station orderlies working overtime digging graves. The Battalion wags used to speculate as to which of the new recruits would fill them ! Another portent was the enormous new Railway Sidings, with scores of thousands of shells of all calibres. An even more ominous sign was the entire absence of parades at Puchevillers. " Enjoy your-selves," said our Colonel, and the implication was that we should not have much opportunity for enjoyment in the future. The Vignacourt days had been altogether " too good." " They're fattening us up for the slaughter," the men said. And so " they " were, and everyone, in spite of the prospect, seemed to enjoy the process. The Camp in the Puchevillers Orchard was a very lively place—games and horseplay of every variety. Champagne corks popped merrily in the village and in Beauquesne (2 miles away), for, as one of the Battalion put it, " There's no sense in being killed with money in your pocket." Some of the men brought out " knuckle dusters," and knives, and any other mur-derous implements which they thought would help them to give a good account of themselves in the coming battle. A few people wore " safety waistcoats " of steel, and other protections, but these expedients were not generally approved. " If your turn's come, you can't do nothink to get out of it," said the philosophers in the Battalion. And the men preferred to take their chances all together, and with a rather fine unselfishness, would have refused protection which everyone else could not equally have enjoyed. The men were as eager to attack on July 1st as they had been to come out to France fifteen months before.

On Sunday, June 25th, Church Parade was held in the Orchard. It was probably the most impressive Church Parade ever held in the history of the Battalion, and practically no one was absent. The Padre never had a more attentive audience, and gave a simple and moving sermon. War offers many strange contradictions, but surely none more strange than bloodthirsty lectures from Major R. Campbell on the use of the bayonet and inspiring sermons on Christian principles from our Chaplain ! The next day the Brigadier addressed the troops in the customary " go in and win " style, and after his speech the men gave three lusty cheers for the King, which would have brought victory if shouting could have done it. Preparations were by this time com-plete. Instructions had been received that not more than twenty-five Officers per Battalion were to go into action, and that the remainder, with extra Signallers, Lewis Gunners, Bombers and Scouts, were to remain behind as a reserve to replace the inevitable casualties. The

Final Maps had been issued. These were small leaflet maps giving the First, Second and Third objectives of the attack (Map No. 4). In addition there was an issue to Battalions of the Douai—St. Quentin 1/100,000 Scale Maps for use after the advance of the first day, when the war would have reached the " open country " stage, and the 1/10,000 scale Trench Map would have been discarded for ever. As a matter of fact these 1/100,000 Douai-St. Quentin Maps were left behind in the Quarter-Master's Stores on July 3rd, and never looked at again till the last few months of the War ! The day before the Brigade left the Puchevillers area, Lieut. Rigby (Brigade Intelligence Officer) gave a lecture—a résumé of General Head Quarters' publications—in which we were told that the enemy had practically no guns left—they had been blown to pieces at Verdun : that the German Infantryman was tired of the war—extensive quotations in proof of which were given from German prisoners' correspondence : and that on the second day after Z day, our cavalry would be careering through Bapaume after the German Army in full retreat to the Rhine. And we all believed it ! The Somme was to finish what Verdun had so magnificently begun—the break-up of the German Army !

On June 27th, at 8-30 p.m., the Battalion marched out of Puchevillers. The noise of the bombardment twelve miles away had been heard very distinctly all day, and as the Battalion marched towards Varennes the red glow in the eastern sky showed unmistakably that things were being prepared for us. Civilians came to the doors and windows in Toutencourt and Harponville to watch the march past of the Battalion. Lighted direction signs in the villages gave one the impression of being in the London Underground Railway. The men were in great spirits, singing and shouting, till the hill between Harponville and Varennes was reached, when the column quietened down, and everyone became almost mesmerized by the thousand lights and flashes of the battle front, stretching north and south as far as the eye could see. The Battalion reached Varennes in heavy rain and darkness, and the men quickly filed into their crowded and dirty billets to get as much sleep as possible before morning. This was the night of X Day. The battle was timed to begin on June 29th. Owing to the heavy rain, however, Z day had been postponed forty-eight hours to the morning of July 1st, and the Battalion therefore remained in Varennes for two days longer. At 9 p.m. on June 30th the Battalion marched from Varennes, reaching the Assembly Trenches in Aveluy Wood about midnight. No one will ever forget the experiences of this march from Varennes to Aveluy Wood. Special tracks across country from Hedauville to Martinsart had been carefully allotted to each unit marching into the battle. In order to avoid any possibility of delay or loss of direction the tracks were marked every five hundred yards by lamps, and each track was distinguishable by a different coloured light. The way for the 1/6th Battalion was marked by a line of green lights. Thus throughout the night long lines of men in parallel columns moved east towards Thiepval. There was little noise, but the darkness seemed full of movement and excitement. On all sides the streams of men seemed never-ending, inexhaustible. The roads were reserved for artillery and other traffic, and were crammed with double lines of limbers and general service heavy wagons all moving in the same direction—eastwards. The Battalion waited a short time before entering Martinsart, as the village was being shelled. When the march was continued, the green lights led the Battalion into Aveluy Wood, and white tapes tied to the trees guided companies to their assembly trenches. Everything seemed to have been arranged excellently, and the preparations were on a gigantic scale. There was no foreboding or pessimism. The Morrow was to be the day of victory ! Did not the signboards to the Ancre Bridges say " Thiepval-Bapaume-Berlin ? " Henry V. was not more confident of victory, when he rebuked Westmoreland for wanting more reinforcements, and gave utterance to the conviction of all high-spirited soldiers on the eve of a battle.

" O do not wish one more !
Rather proclaim it, Westmoreland, through my host,
That he which hath no stomach to this fight,
Let him depart ; his passport shall be made,
And crowns for convoy put into his purse.
We would not die in that man's company
That fears his fellowship to die with us.
This day is called the feast of Crispian :
He that outlives this day, and comes safe home,
Will stand a tip-toe when this day is named,
And rouse him at the name of Crispian....
This story shall the good man teach his son ;
And Crispin Crispian shall ne'er go by,
From this day to the ending of the world,
But we in it shall be rememberèd,
We few, we happy few, we band of brothers ;
For he to-day that sheds his blood with me
Shall be my brother ; be he ne'er so vile,
This day shall gentle his condition :
And gentlemen in England now abed
Shall think themselves accursed they were not here,
And hold their manhoods cheap while any speaks
That fought with us upon St. Crispin's day."

CHAPTER VI.

THIEPVAL.

DURING the first six months of 1916 the enemy launched two great offensives. The first at Verdun began on Feb. 21st and culminated in a last effort to capture the town on June 23rd, a week before the opening of the battle of the Somme. The second was the Austrian attack in the Trentino during May and June, which drove the Italians to the edge of the Venetian plain. The Allies replied quickly. On June 4th the Russians under Brussiloff attacked the thinly-held Austrian lines between the Pripet Marshes and the borders of Roumania. The whole of Bukovina and several towns in Eastern Galicia were captured by the Russians, and the situation on the Italian Front was greatly relieved. Nearly a month later began the Franco-British attack on the Somme which eased the situation at Verdun. And in August the Italians attacked on the Isonza, and captured Gorizia. Thus during June, July, August, the Allies launched three great offensives on three fronts against the Central Powers.

The object of the British Army in the opening phase of the Somme battle was the capture of the Ridge stretching from the village of Thiepval, near the Ancre, in an E. S. E. direction through Pozières, Bazentin, Longueval and Ginchy. The strongest part of the German defences was near Thiepval. From Beaumont Hamel and the Schwaben Redoubt the enemy could overlook the whole of the Ancre Marshes, and command the bridges across the river. The attack was in the hands of the IV. Army (Sir Henry S. Rawlinson), and the task of the X. Corps (Lieut.-Gen. Sir T. L. K. Morland) was the capture of the Thiepval defences. The left of the X. Corps front was the River Ancre, and the right was bounded by a line from Mouquet Farm to the German front line immediately South of the Leipzig Salient. The three successive objectives of the attack on the Corps front are given in Map No. 4. The 36th was the left and the 32nd the right Division in the attack. The 49th Division was in immediate reserve, and the remaining divisions of the X. Corps (the 12th and 25th) were in readiness to exploit the success of the first three attacking Divisions. Naturally the orders of the 49th Division were not definite, as everything depended on the measure of success gained by the 36th and 32nd Divisions. It was expected however that the 49th would come into action on approximately the Green Line (3rd objective), and the attention of the 146th Infantry Brigade was focussed on the high ground south of Grandcourt to Mouquet Farm. In addition to the assembly trenches in Aveluy Wood an elaborate system of trenches had been dug 300/400 yards behind the front line in Thiepval Wood. After having served for the assembly of the 36th Division, these trenches were regarded as convenient halting places for the 49th Division on their march from Aveluy Wood to Bapaume.

Throughout the night of June 30th, the artillery bombardment continued with unabated intensity, but in their narrow trenches in Aveluy Wood the Battalion was undisturbed, except by occasional machine gun bullets. At 6-30 a.m. July 1st, our artillery began the final hour's bombardment. Guns, hitherto silent, opened up from all sides of the Wood, and east of Albert. There was intense excitement. At 7-30 a.m. the whole front line went " over the top." An hour and a half later the Battalion moved out of Aveluy Wood, across the Passerelle de Magenta (a bridge over the Ancre Marshes) to their trenches in Thiepval Wood. There was heavy shelling, and the full inferno of battle. Major R. Clough had been wounded just before the Battalion left Aveluy Wood, but there were few other casualties. The spirits of everyone were high. The full significance of the tremendous rat-tat-tat of enemy machine guns, which broke out almost immediately after our infantry attacked at 7-30 a.m. could not then be realized by anyone in the Battalion. But that ominous sound dominated even the artillery bombardment, and told only too clearly of enemy machine gun emplacements either unobserved or missed by our artillery : and of an enemy garrison still capable of using the most deadly weapon of modern warfare.

What actually happened is now well known. The 36th and 32nd Divisions reached the Schwaben and the Leipzig Redoubts, and even penetrated to Grandcourt. But enemy machine-gunners came out of their dugouts behind our infantry, and took the attack in the rear : the enemy barrage was appalling : our casualties enormous, and our men were too few to consolidate positions they had reached. If the 49th Division had been sent into action earlier, when the forward Divisions (36th and 32nd) were in Grandcourt and the Schwaben Redoubt, the result might have been entirely different. But the enemy's strength was under-estimated and our reserves were used too late. Criticism however is easy and futile, and the fact remains that when the 49th Division entered into action on the afternoon of July 1st the attack on the X. Corps front had practically failed. A few hundred yards of the Leipzig Salient was all that remained permanently in our hands in the Thiepval Sector as a result of July 1st.

The story of the next two days is one of confused superhuman effort in the nerve-racking tumult and discord of battle. An entirely false impression of sanity and ordered movement is apt to be given in

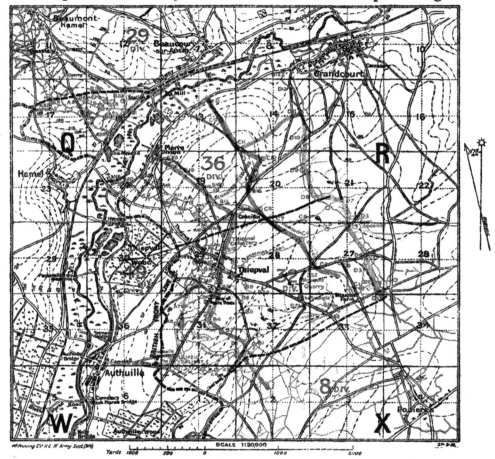

No. 4 Map. Operation Map, July 1st, 1916.

all accounts written after the excitement of the battle is over. The reader too often is given an impression of sequence, as though plans were being properly carried out, whereas what really happened from the infantryman's point of view was almost hopeless uncertainty as to positions of Companies on the flanks or in front : quick movements

THIEPVAL

followed by hours of suspense : confused masses of men of all units : everlasting rain of shells and bullets, and contradictory orders and rumours. In this particular battle everything was still further complicated by the failure of the attack : the congestion of men in the front line positions : the multitude of wounded : the stunning disappointment of the blow to the hopes and preparations of months.

The Battalion lay in the assembly trenches in Thiepval Wood from early morning to late afternoon on July 1st, and the extent of the disaster gradually became realised.* No orders had been received to advance and consolidate a line south of Grandcourt! The enemy shelling never ceased, and the predictions as to the enemy shortage of artillery were obviously falsified. At 3-30 p.m. a brief order through 146th Infantry Brigade Head Quarters came to our Colonel that the Battalion was to make a frontal attack upon Thiepval with the 1/5th Bn. West Yorks. Regt, and one of the units of the 36th Division—zero hour 4 p.m. !

The following is a copy of the order :—

146th Infantry Brigade Operation Order. 3-30 p.m.

1. The Brigade will attack Thiepval village from the West at 4 p.m. exactly. Preliminary bombardment will be carried out from 3-30 to 4 p.m. One battalion from another formation will be ordered to co-operate from North.

2. Attack will be carried out as follows :—Front line—1/5th Battalion West Yorks. Regt. on right and 1/6th Battalion on left. 1/8th Battalion in support. 1/7th Battalion in Brigade Reserve. Frontage of attack 600 yards. 1/5th Battalion and 1/6th Battalion each on a frontage of 300 yards. Dividing line between battalions is due East and West through Cross Roads in centre of Thiepval.

3. Brigade Head Quarters will remain at Belfast City (Thiepval Wood) during operations. O.C. Signals will arrange a system of runners to follow attacking troops, and run back by relays or otherwise direct to Brigade Head Quarters.

G. R. SANDEMAN, *Capt.*,

B.M., 146th Inf. Bde.

---

*The following Officers went into action with the Battalion on July 1st and 2nd, 1916 :—
Bn. H.Q.—Lt.-Col. H. O. Wade, Maj. C. E. Scott, Capts. W. N. Mossop, A. Hamilton (M.O.), Lt. N. Dodd, 2nd/Lt. G. E. Milner.
A. Coy.—Maj. R. Clough, Lt. N. Grice, 2nd/Lts. W. A. Scales, H. Mitchell, R. Moore, Todd.
B. Coy.—Capt. E. W. Knowles, Lts. J. L. Oddy, E. Myers, 2nd/Lts. C. R. Harper, H. Speight.
C. Coy.—Capt. R. A. Fawcett, Lt. F. G. Hornshaw, 2nd/Lts. C. G. Higgins, S. Hickson, J. Taylor.
D. Coy.—Capt. J. L. Heselton, Lts. T. E. Armistead, W. G. Tetley, E. A. Turner, 2nd/Lt. E. V. Tempest.

So Thiepval had not fallen. Many argued swiftly that a fortress which had withstood the attack of two Divisions would hardly be likely to fall to the efforts of three battalions. Moreover, half-an-hour's warning gave no time for any consultation between the Colonel and Company Commanders : quite apart from preparations within Companies. On paper the assembly of a battalion from trenches near Belfast City and Ross Castle for an attack in half-an-hour upon trench lines a kilometre away may seem to be practicable under favourable conditions. But an order which gives no single officer in the battalion a few moments to consult with his subordinates is only too likely to lead to failure. But not an instant was wasted. Within five minutes of receiving the order the whole Battalion was on the move. C and D Companies were in front, B in support and A in reserve. The vast majority of the men, and many of the officers, had only the vaguest idea of the direction in which Thiepval lay. Flanks of attack and positions for consolidation could only be considered by officers and N. C. O's. as the Battalion was moving forward. Between the high ground of Thiepval Wood and our front line near Gourock Street and Hamilton Avenue there is a deep valley or re-entrant from the Ancre, half way up which is Johnstone's Post. In extended order and as steadily as though on parade, the Battalion doubled across this valley. The enemy could see the whole Battalion from his trenches in the front line and near the Schwaben Redoubt, and a murderous Machine Gun and Artillery fire was opened upon our men. But no one wavered. The intense enemy shelling and Machine Gun fire led many of the men to think they were crossing No Man's Land, and as they rushed up the slope near Johnstone's post, they were surprised to find the trenches there were filled with our men, and that our front line was some hundreds of yards away. Whilst crossing the valley Col. H. O. Wade and Capt. A. Hamilton (Medical Officer) were wounded, and our Signalling Officer (Lieut. N. Dodd) was killed. The last glimpse some of the Battalion had of the Colonel was seeing him running to overtake the Battalion before it went " over the top," minus one puttee, with his leg tied up, and the end of the bandage flapping behind him. But there was no time to lose. At 4 p.m., C and D Companies " attacked Thiepval." The result was a foregone conclusion. Hardly a man came back unwounded from No Man's Land and no one advanced more than a hundred yards. 2/Lieut. S. Hickson of C. Coy. reports that every man of his platoon advanced with him, but after a few dozen yards he looked round and could not see a soul. Every one of his men had been killed or wounded. He himself was dangerously hit a moment later, and remained all night in a shell hole, only succeeding in crawling to our lines before dawn on July 2nd. Both Company Commanders of C and D Coy. (Capts. Fawcett and Heselton) were wounded. The men dropped down in rows, and platoons of the other companies following behind remained in our lines, as to do anything else was suicide. It is impossible to describe the angry despair which filled every man at this unspeakable moment. The rat-tat-tat of enemy Machine Guns searched every corner of No Man's Land. A Division would have done no better than a Company against that deadly fusillade. Very shortly after the remainder of the Battalion reached the front line, the responsibility of giving the order to cease the attack was taken with most commendable promptness by Capt. E. W. Knowles, who was the next senior officer left in the Battalion.

There is little variety in the testimony of those who took part in the attack. One of them (J. E. Yates) describes it briefly as follows " The order to attack was given. Men sprang to the parapet, and were at once in the zone where machine gun bullets swept like rain. Here and there a man dropped back into the trench. Others fell in swathes on the parapet. A few struggled further. I think the furthest would hardly make more than a few dozen paces. Again and again men climbed the parapet and added their bodies to the pile. It was useless. Thiepval was not to be taken until the army had laid its finest manhood in the shellholes of the Somme. On the left other Bradford battalions had fallen in heaps as we had. The splendid Ulster Division of the morning had become a broken remnant under our eyes, its dead being scattered over these lines of trenches."

The Battalion was warmly congratulated by the Corps and Divisional Generals on the speed with which an almost impossible order had been carried out. The 1/6th Battalion was the only one which succeeded in obeying the order. We were told that it was a " feint " attack to relieve the pressure on the 32nd and 36th Divisions, and had been entirely successful in drawing the enemy fire. Thus the Battalion learnt that essential but often bitter lesson, viz., that it is impossible to judge the general position of a battle from what may be happening to one's own particular unit ; the sacrifice of a battalion may be justified from the point of view of larger operations. But within twenty-four hours every third man in the Battalion had become a casualty, and the results seemed nil. Thanks, however, to the prompt decision of our Colonel and the disciplined obedience of all ranks the attack took place according to orders. Col. H. O. Wade received the D.S.O. in recognition of his services on this occasion, and the work of his Battalion. There are few actions of the 1/6th Battalion West Yorkshire Regt. in France of which we have more reason to be proud.

The night which followed was one prolonged nightmare. Thiepval

Wood, which on the morning of July 1st was thick with trees, giving excellent cover, had become a mere congregation of bare stumps, and the ground was covered with a mass of broken branches, pounded and lashed by high explosive and shrapnel. The Battalion before midnight had been concentrated again in the trenches near Gordon Castle and Belfast City, and those who were not detailed for ration or ammunition parties lay in heaps trying to sleep under a continuous bombardment. The 1/5th Battalion was ordered during the night to occupy the Schwaben Redoubt, which had been reached by men of the 36th Division earlier in the day. This was done, but the position was found to be untenable, and the survivors cut their way out on the night of July 2nd. The fate of men of the 1/6 Battalion in Thiepval Wood was only a little more fortunate. The ground was soaked with gas fumes, and in the deep communication trenches of Inniskilling and Elgin Avenues the gas was so thick that men had to wear gas masks, and floundered along in stifling darkness. The Wood was crowded with men of the 36th and 49th Divisions, and every communication trench was full of lost or weary wretches who waited for the dawn in order to find their whereabouts. Further down at " Paisley Dump " the confusion was almost incredible. All the trenches in Thiepval Wood, and the tracks to Authuille and across the Ancre, met at this point. The wounded lay there in hundreds waiting to be evacuated: scores of them died where they lay. Reliefs, reinforcements, fatigue parties, congregated there like sheep: and a thick mist of gas and smoke covered the whole valley of the Ancre. The enemy had never previously shelled this spot, but he began to do so that night, and every shell, falling amongst such a dense mass of men, added casualties to the heaps already lying on the road side. The place was an Inferno. As one approached Paisley Dump, one became " aware of noise—a noise inhuman. A wail as of enormous wet fingers on an enormous glass: a wail that rose and fell, interminable, unbearable. Then suddenly one became aware whence that wail came. All along the muddy roadway they lay—the wounded: hundreds of them: brown blanket shapes: some muttering: some moaning: some singing in delirium: some quite still."

The Battalion reinforcements had been left behind at Bouzincourt, and their march to rejoin the Battalion through Aveluy Wood, past Lancashire Dump to Black Horse Road and the Passerelle de Magenta, was an unforgettable experience. As the long single file marched slowly through the narrow rides of Aveluy Wood, they were met by incessant streams of walking wounded. These wounded men were in many cases hysterical, and such cries as " It's bloody murder over

there ! " or " Thank God, I'm out," were amongst the mildest ejaculations. When the reinforcements reached the bewildering chaos of
men near " Paisley Dump," it was found impossible to keep together,
Only after wandering about all night were most of the men able
to find their companies, and lay down at dawn to sleep. Hardly had
they lain down, however, when the Battalion again moved across the
valley shortly after dawn to Johnstone's Post, where Major Scott (now
in command) awaited further orders. Several men were killed and
wounded whilst waiting at this point. An officer of another unit,
mortally wounded, was being carried to the small First Aid Station
there, and one of the men with him yelled out to a crowd of wounded
men who were in the way, " make room for Capt. ——," whereupon
the wounded officer called out, " Shut up, and don't make such a noise.
I'll be dead soon ! " And he was, in a few minutes. At last orders
arrived, and before noon the Battalion had taken over the front line
from Hammerhead Sap to Gourock Street, and the men had settled
down for the first rough meal since they left Aveluy Wood on June
30th. The trenches were crowded with men—twelve to fifteen in each
bay. The afternoon passed slowly under a constant bombardment.
The shelling increased about 6 p.m. : companies were reduced
to platoons, and platoons to sections. Word came round that an enemy
counter attack was expected. Probably the enemy was expecting an
attack as well, so the artillery duel went on furiously, and reached the
climax about 9 o'clock in the evening. The enemy had just obtained four
simultaneous direct hits on one of our bays, killing and wounding about
twelve men of D Company, when the first men of a relieving Company
of a Cyclist Battalion arrived at the head of the communication trench,
and took over the shambles we were only too glad to leave. The
remainder of the Battalion was relieved by the 7th Battalion Duke of
Wellington's Regiment. Thus ended so far as our Battalion was
concerned the first phase of the Somme battle. The approximate
casualties for two days were 14 Officers and 250 other ranks. The
Battalion reached Aveluy Wood in the early hours of July 3rd, and
found that our Quarter-Master had brought up plenty of rations, and
a good post for almost everybody. Only too many of the letters, alas !
could never be delivered ! Aveluy Wood had not yet been shelled.
It was not until July 6th that the enemy artillery paid attention
to the Wood—probably they had learnt from prisoners or captured
maps that it was being used as an assembly place for our troops.
    The following gives a vivid impression of July 2nd. " Almost
imperceptibly the first day merged into the second, when we held
grimly to a battered trench and watched each other grow old under the

H   97

day-long storm of shelling. Big shells landed in the crowded trench. For hours, sweating, praying, swearing, we worked on the heaps of chalk and mangled bodies. Men did astonishing things at which one did not wonder till after. Here is an instance of fortitude. A man had his right arm and leg torn off clean. His mind was quite clear as I laid him on the fire-step. His left hand wandered over his chest to the pulp where his right shoulder had been. ' My God,' he said, ' I've lost my arm.' The hand crept down to the stump of the right thigh. ' Is that off too ? ' he asked. I nodded. It was impossible to move him at the time. For five hours he lay there fully conscious and smoking cigarettes. When at last we tried to carry him out the stretcher stuck in the first traverse. We put him on a groundsheet and struggled on. But our strength was gone ; we could not hold his weight. ' Drag me,' he suggested then, and we dragged him along the floor of the trench to the medical dug-out.

" At dawn next morning we were back in a green wood. I found myself leaning on a rifle, and staring stupidly at the filthy exhausted men who slept round me. It did not occur to me to lie down until some one pushed me into a bed of ferns. There were flowers among the ferns, and my last thought was a dull wonder that there could still be flowers in the world." (J. E. Yates).

On the afternoon of July 3rd the Battalion marched back from Aveluy Wood to Martinsart, and were billeted in deserted houses. The next day was spent in cleaning arms, ammunition and equipment, and was quite peaceful till late in the afternoon, when the enemy dropped a few 5·9's in the village, and hit A Company Head Quarters, wounding Lieut. J. S. Gordon. Another shell burst on Martinsart Chateau and slightly wounded the Brigade Major, Capt. G. R. Sandeman, who however remained on duty in spite of a rather painful wound in the head. At this time Captain J. L. Oddy was in command of A Company, pluckily endeavouring to carry on notwithstanding some shrapnel in his thigh. He was ordered to hospital before the Battalion left Martinsart. The next move was on July 5th to Hedauville, and the Battalion took over some not very clean huts near the Chateau. On the morning of July 7th the Divisional Band came to play in the Chateau grounds, and was still playing a very lively waltz when the order to " stand to " was received, and in half-an-hour the Battalion was on the move in fighting order towards the front line. It began to rain heavily. After rather over an hour's march the Battalion reached Martinsart Wood, where they waited all day for further orders in pouring rain. Towards evening a party of about two hundred German prisoners passed through the Wood escorted by men of the Worcester Regiment.   At 10 p.m. another move was made a stage nearer the front to the Aveluy-Hamel Road, south of Aveluy Wood, and here again the Battalion remained for several hours.   The night was very cold, there was incessant rain and everyone was chilled to the bone.   There was little grousing, however, as everyone believed the Battalion was going to attack in the morning, and the men were keen to wipe out the memory of July 1st by some dashing victory.   Nearly everyone passed the night in walking up and down the Aveluy road smoking and talking : a few lucky ones were able to fall asleep in the mud and the rain on the roadside.   Some men of A Company found an abandoned dugout, and by breaking up empty Stokes bomb boxes, were able to light a fire and issue tea to the rest of their Company. R. S.-M. Barker and some others convinced A Company that they were still on its ration strength, and therefore entitled to share in the Company's good fortune.   At daybreak the third stage in the journey to the line took the Battalion across the Ancre, past a signpost with the familiar legend " Authuille, Thiepval, Berlin," to " Quarry Dugouts," a series of shelters in the chalk cliff side near Crucifix Corner on the Aveluy-Authuille Road.   Remnants of the 3rd Worcester Battalion (32nd Division) were occupying these dug-outs when the Battalion arrived early in the morning of July 8th.   These men had been in the line continuously since July 1st, and were in a state of extreme exhaustion. They were asleep and crowded together in the small stuffy dugouts. It was almost impossible to waken them.   Only one officer was left and he roundly declared that he would not disturb his men " for any damned battalion in the British Army."   There were about eighty of them, all that was left of his battalion.   They marched off at noon, covered with mud and blood, and decorated with German helmets and bayonets, and other souvenirs of the Leipzig Salient.

When the Battalion returned to the Thiepval area on July 8th it formed a unit in what was called the " Containing Army," under the command of Sir Hubert Gough.   After the opening phase of the Somme battle on July 1st the two northern Corps of the IV. Army (Sir H. Rawlinson) had been allotted to the V. Army (Sir H. Gough) with the instruction that the V. Army was to " contain " the enemy by maintaining a steady pressure on the front from La Boisselle to Serre.   Few will be likely to dispute that during the next few weeks this " pressure " was very well maintained.

During the afternoon of July 8th the situation was explained to all ranks in the Battalion.   The 1/7th Battalion had relieved three Companies of the 8th Bn. Loyal North Lancashire Regiment and one Company 3rd Bn. Worcester Regiment in the Leipzig Salient, and the enemy were expected to counter attack the following morning. The counter attack did not come off, but the Battalion relieved the 1/7th Battalion about 10 a.m. July 9th. The instructions were brief. " The Leipzig Salient must be held at all costs." Thus began the second phase of the Somme battle—so far as the 1/6th Battalion West Yorkshire Regt. was concerned—The Leipzig Salient.

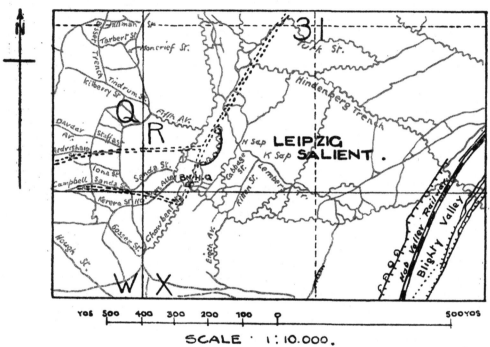

SCALE · 1 : 10,000.

No. 5 Map. Leipzig Salient, July, 1916.

This Salient was emphatically one of " the high places of the field." Apart from the fact that it was the only part of the Thiepval defences which had been gained as a result of July 1st it was of very great military importance. Looking from H or K Saps we could observe the whole German support and reserve positions from Mouquet Farm to Pozières, two very important centres of German communications. The valley between the Leipzig Salient and Pozières had been previously free from our observation, and during the first few days the Battalion was in the line the Germans still walked fairly freely on the road in R 32 d : cyclists and even men on horseback could be seen there, and were easily killed by our machine gun fire from the Salient.

THIEPVAL

By July 15th as many as thirty machine guns were massed in the four hundred yards area of the Leipzig Salient, which became one of the strongest and most interesting parts of the battle front. A French war artist fixed his easel on the firestep in K Sap, within forty yards of the enemy, and in the intervals of trench mortar and rifle grenade fire, painted quite elaborate canvases of the view of Mouquet Farm and the Wonder Work. He carried on his work as calmly as though in a studio, and the platoon holding this section of the line came to regard him as either a lunatic or an extraordinary case of artistic perversity. Our hold in the Salient was always threatened by the commanding positions the enemy held on the rising ground immediately to the north of our trenches. He occupied three strongly fortified lines of trenches, rising one behind the other, *viz.* Hindenburg and Lemberg Redoubts and the "Wonder Work"—so called from its elaborate dugouts and defences. It seemed as though a determined rush from the enemy would sweep the whole Battalion down the slope and across the old No Man's Land. For some days it was found extremely difficult to place exactly on the Map the forward positions held by our troops, and there were many cases of our artillery firing into our own lines. Close Artillery support during constant enemy attacks was vital, and eventually signboards were placed at such points as 68 and 45 (Map No. 5) in order to guide the artillery observers. The Salient contained several deep mined dug-outs with thirty or forty steps, and at least two, sometimes three and four, entrances. Some of these dugouts were fitted up with electric light, and with mirrors and other furniture from French houses. Battalion Head Quarters was in one of these near point Y (Map No. 5). The enemy knew the exact position of these dugouts, and shelled them constantly with high explosives and trench mortars. On more than one occasion a shell burst half way down the entrance steps, killing and wounding the usual crowd of waiting orderlies, and completely blocking up one entrance. As quickly as possible strong sand bag breastworks were built to protect the entrances. It was always a "close call" entering the more important of these mined dugouts when a "strafe" was on, as Battalion runners knew to their cost. In order to connect the Salient with the original front line, trenches across No Man's Land were dug in feverish haste. This work was nerve-racking and dangerous, as it was done under direct enemy observation, and by night working parties were swept with machine gun fire and shelled heavily. The original communication with the Salient was by a low narrow underground "Russian Sap," dug before the July Offensive. This was blown in several times, and was of course quite inadequate for the traffic to and from the Salient.

The general aspect of the Salient when the Battalion entered it was gruesome and chaotic. Trenches had been ploughed out of recognition by our own and the enemy bombardments. The ploughed earth had become deep mud during the heavy rains : the dead were rotting in every corner, unburied for over a week. A large crater three hundred yards wide in the middle of the Salient gave everyone who walked across it a feeling of utter defencelessness and insecurity, as the enemy constantly shelled it with shrapnel. Every man on " sentry go " felt he was " up against it," and the tension was extreme. Whilst the 146th Infantry Brigade was holding the Salient (from July 7th to July 20th) the S.O.S. was sent up every night, sometimes even two and three times. Pozières was captured by the 1st Australian and 48th Divisions on July 25th, and this advance naturally somewhat relieved the situation near Thiepval. But it was not till towards the end of August that the enemy ceased constant efforts to throw us out of the Leipzig Salient. By that time the enemy had been compelled to evacuate his trenches in the valley in X 2, and the Salient had become the left flank of the whole British attack from Thiepval to Lesboeuf. The holding of the Leipzig Salient during the critical days of July is one of the most noteworthy actions of the Battalion—perhaps even its most important achievement.

The first spell in the Leipzig Salient was from July 9th to 12th, and the second for three days from July 13th. Thus the Battalion was only six days actually in the Salient. Immediately afterwards however, on July 16th, the Battalion took up positions in front of Authuille Wood for twelve days, and another period of nearly three weeks was spent immediately opposite the Liepzig Salient near Oban Avenue. These were virtually reserve positions to the Salient, and shared many of its discomforts. Some idea of the casualties caused during the first six days may be obtained by the fact that 289 men came on July 15th as reinforcements from the Durham Light Infantry, in order to keep the Battalion to fighting strength. On the same day, in one small action, the Battalion lost four officers and fifty other ranks killed and wounded. Not an hour passed, day or night, from July 9th to July 15th, without several casualties.

To return to the morning of July 9th, when the Battalion moved *via* Campbell Avenue and a shallow newly-dug trench across No Man's Land, into the Leipzig Salient. The men were in fighting order and without packs, which were brought up a few days later by a carrying party of the 1/7th Battalion West Yorks. Regt. One of these packs (belonging to Capt. J. L. Oddy) contained 2,500 fcs. for C Coy. As Capt. Oddy had gone to hospital wounded, there was great excitement at his Company Head Quarters regarding the said 2,500 fcs. However, the pack was eventually found on a front line parapet, having lain there untouched for two days! The 1/7th Battalion had very little to hand over except thousands of Mills Bombs, S. A. Ammunition, and the curiosities of the place, such as corpses, German rifles, bayonets, gas masks. Some platoons were fortunate in taking over unconsumed quantities of German Soda Water in the platoon dug-outs. There were many evidences of Homeric combats all over the place. In one Company Head Quarters' dug-out were found the bodies of a British subaltern and a German officer still locked together, and in one trench lay the body of one of our men who had killed two of the enemy and had then himself been bayoneted by a German who must have been killed immediately after, as all four bodies lay together. There was considerable shelling during the relief, so the formalities of "handing over" the sector were quickly rushed through.

Apart from continuous shelling nothing happened till July 12th, when the enemy made a heavy bombing attack near H Sap. The 1/7th Battalion had brought up thousands of bombs during the day, and almost every man in the Battalion had plenty of practice. There was some delay in getting our artillery to open fire, owing to all wires being cut by the enemy shelling. S.O.S. rockets were sent up, but in the smoke of the battle, and amongst the hundreds of other Verey lights of all kinds which went up in streams it was found impossible for our artillery to distinguish the all important S.O.S. signals. On this occasion it was forty minutes before our artillery opened S.O.S. fire, although the time usually supposed sufficient was only thirty seconds. In later actions our artillery had instructions to open out on the S.O.S. lines the moment heavy enemy shelling and bombing was heard in the Salient, and as this happened several times a night, the gunners had no rest. In the morning of July 13th the Battalion was relieved, and went into support in the South Bluff dugouts near Authuille. The respite was only for a few hours. The 1/7th Battalion was ordered to make an attack on the area A B C D (Map No. 5) on the 14th inst. The 1/6th Battalion was to support them, and to consolidate the ground taken. About 10-30 p.m. the Battalion moved up again to the Salient, every officer and man carrying as much trench material as he could stagger under. Our men then lay down in the trenches near the crater, and waited developments. Our barrage began at 2-15 a.m. on the positions the 1/7th Battalion were to attack, and lifted ten minutes later on to the enemy support lines. On the right flank the 1/7th Battalion reached the objective, but on the left they met strong opposition from several enemy bombing posts which inflicted severe casualties. About 2-45 a.m. a message came from the successful right flank of the 1/7th Battalion that we were to go forward and consolidate. " A " Company of the 1/6th Battalion was ready almost immediately with their material, when a second message came that the enemy had counter-attacked on the left, and that the 1/7th Battalion was hard pressed. So down went barbed wire, pickets, sandbags and shovels, and our men began to use their rifles. The enemy counter-attack had evidently been carefully prepared, and was well executed. Their men showed considerable bravery and resourcefulness. The 1/7th Battalion had already suffered over 100 men killed and wounded, and the situation was serious. At this moment the 1/6th Battalion Bombers advanced at the double across the open, and with very fine dash and combination drove back the counter-attack. The 1/7th Battalion reported that " the Battalion Bombers of the 1/6th Battalion came quickly up to reinforce and speedily drove back the enemy from our flank at point C, thus enabling us to hold our own trench again." The bombers during this action were under the command of Lieut G. H. Speight, and in recognition of their good work Lieut. Speight received a well-deserved Military Cross. For some months the bombers had been a very dependable unit in the Battalion, and on this occasion their training and good morale saved the situation. During their time of training in Vignacourt they had as their officer Lieut. H. A. Jowett, who was very largely responsible for their good work. The bombing Sergeant, Jock McIvor, was one of the best known Battalion " characters." He used to attend the parades in pre-war days in his kilts and spats, and never forgot that he belonged to the Highland Light Infantry. He was killed whilst serving with the 9th Battalion West Yorkshire Regt.

This action was part of the great night attack of July 14th, which began at 3-25 a.m., and in which the 18th Division captured Trones Wood, the 9th Division reached Longueval, and the 3rd, 7th, 21st and 34th Divisions advanced on the whole front from Bazentin-le-Petit to Pozières. It is easy to understand that the attack of the 146th Brigade on the left flank of our line, exactly an hour before the main attack further east was launched, would have considerable effect on the enemy, and would greatly increase his uncertainty and divert his attention from the main attack. He put down a tremendous barrage on our reserve positions between Aveluy and Authuille, and evidently expected a bigger attack than was actually made. The following message came from the 49th Division—

" The Divisional Commander wishes me to tell you that he considers that the attack by your Brigade last night, and the stubborn fighting that followed, materially assisted in the success of the larger operation on the British front."

During the rest of the 14th July the Battalion remained in the Salient, B Company of the 1/6th Battalion relieving one Company of the 1/7th Battalion in the section of the line from which the Leeds Rifles had attacked earlier in the morning. The remaining three Companies of the 1/7th Battalion remained in close support near the crater and were placed under the command of Lieut.-Col. C. E. Scott (commanding the 1/6th Battalion after Col. H. O. Wade had been wounded on July 1st). The battle between Longueval and Pozières was still continuing. From the German point of view the whole line depended upon Thiepval being retained. On July 15th the enemy made the last determined effort to drive us out of the Leipzig Salient, and make his hold of the Thiepval defences more secure.

The first signs of dawn were in the sky on the morning of July 15th, and the order to " stand to " had just been given, when sentries in B Company heard a sound " like a sharp gust of wind," and there was a startling burst of flame and clouds of dense smoke along the whole German line opposite B Company. A Liquid Fire Attack was being added to the devilry of the few previous days in the Salient ! Apart from the hiss of the liquid fire projectors there was no sound on the front for several moments. Then the enemy artillery opened out on the whole sector, and especially on the Communication Trenches across the old No Man's Land. On the flanks of the liquid fire attack our Lewis Guns and rifles began firing almost immediately. The whole Salient was aflame with every kind of shell, bomb, grenade, and thousands of Verey lights. There was no need for our S.O.S. rockets this time ! The Salient was one of the most conspicuous parts of the battlefield, and our artillery opened out immediately. A few minutes after the beginning of the attack half a platoon of B Company came doubling towards the crater from the front line, and headed straight towards Capt. N. Muller (O. C. A Coy.), saying that " someone had given them the order to retire." When Capt. Muller ordered them back again with a sharp denial of any such order, the men turned round immediately, and doubled to the line again. The incident is eloquent as to the effect upon morale of a liquid fire attack after a fortnight's almost continuous experience of a battle sector, and at the same time shows finely the effect of discipline and a sense of duty. " A " Company moved forward to the front line : the Battalion bombers came up and were soon hotly engaged : the supports near the crater " stood to " for any emergency. Invaluable assistance during the attack was given by the 146th Infantry Brigade Stokes Mortar Battery under Captain Pike. On one or two previous occasions the Stokes gun had proved very useful against targets at close range, and its rapid rate of fire had a bad effect upon the enemy morale. On this occasion Capt. Pike brought up one gun himself to within close range of the enemy, and as there was not time to fix a base plate he held the gun in his hands whilst it was being fired. The barrage of Stokes' shells was very well ranged, and caught the enemy as he was retreating and caused him a great number of casualties. In the middle of the attack 289 reinforcements of the Durham Light Infantry arrived. There was no time for organization or explanation. They were met at the top of communication trenches in the Salient, and divided off into platoons and sections, and sent off into the most hard-pressed parts of the line. Several of them were killed before there was any possibility of taking their names. The introduction of these reinforcements to the Battalion was thus not made under favourable auspices. They were from a miscellaneous number of units in their regiment, and some of them had only received two or three month's training in the Army. But they seemed stout fellows, and did well that night. The following summary of messages and reports received at Battalion Head Quarters from 4-10 a.m. to 6-10 a.m. during the above action gives a good idea of the type of messages and information which usually reached Battalion Head Quarters. The attack began at 4 a.m.

4-10 a.m.   From 2/Lieut. Speight. Attack on our left preceded by liquid fire. Have driven Bosches off once, but am slightly wounded. Please reinforce.

4-15 a.m.   C Coy. report they are all right.

4-25 a.m.   C Coy. ready to move to support.

4-27 a.m.   Sent visual message " Short of Bombs " to Q. L. (146th Infantry Brigade).

4-40 a.m.   C and A Companies report O.K. Situation unchanged.

4-55 a.m.   To A Coy. Fifty Boxes of Bombs are on their way to the Crater.
Lieut. Hornshaw reports that B Coy. have no officer, and he has sent 2/Lieut. Maufe.

5-4 a.m.   B Coy. keep sending on to C Coy. for Bombs, and C Coy. say they cannot spare them.

5-5 a.m.   To Lieut. Hornshaw. Major Scott sent an order that C Coy. should send on fifty Boxes of Bombs to A Coy. Why has this not been done ? Answer. Lieut. Hornshaw reports that his Bombs are not in Boxes, and that he is sending on as many as he can, but he has only 400 Bombs left.

5-10 a.m.   Got on with Brigade. To Brigade Major. Any amount of Bombs wanted. Brigade Major says 1/5th and 1/7th Battalions are bringing them. Told Brigade Major to keep barrage on.

5·25 a.m. Bombs arrived by 1/5th and 1/7th Battalions.

5·35 a.m. Telephoned Capt. Muller to tell Lieut. Fawcett to return to Battalion Head Quarters quickly as possible as Major Scott wants to write report of operations.

5·36 a.m. Asked for barrage to be made slow. 150 rounds are being sent up for the Stokes Mortars.

6 a.m. Brigade Major wants to know if we are on the alert during the fog : sending out patrols, etc. Major Scott replies in the affirmative.

6·10 a.m. Brigadier wants short barrages at intervals during fog. Brigade Major says Germans are sending Gas Shells into Ancre Valley—men must be warned to have helmets handy.

Thanks to mined dugouts and good telephone communication Battalion Head Quarters were thus kept continuously in touch with the situation. The following is a description of the action by one actually in the front line.

"No two men have the same memory of an engagement. For me it opened with a kick in the ribs and the shout of a sentry : ' Stand to ! They're comin' ower.' It was exactly 4·10 a.m., and the grey tint of dawn was creeping down the long shaft of stairs to the dugout which by good chance had been allotted my platoon for the short night. I kicked every one within reach and ran up the stairs. A moment later we were crouched in single file in a trench some twenty yards behind the front line, awaiting orders.

Shell fire has its own language for the soldier. This morning there was a vicious intensity in the screaming of the shells as they skimmed our parapet which told us we were in for something serious. A warm sleep in a dry dugout followed by a plunge into a mixture of cold grey dawn and bursting shells is about as bad a thing for morale as anything can be. Personally, in those few minutes of waiting I was more unhappy than I wanted anyone to know.

A sharp crackle of rifle fire broke out, and a dark figure dashed round a corner. ' Give me your bombers quick,' it shouted. My bombers disappeared towards the front line. Another figure arrived. ' Is that so-and-so ? ' it inquired languidly. ' Yes, sir.' ' Good. Go to the dump, draw two boxes of bombs each and take them to C Company.' The drawling unconcerned voice amused me. I laughed as we hurried to the dump, and felt myself again.

On the way back we passed a man whose leg seemed to be attached to his body only by a red puttee. I recognised a friend. ' Can't help you, old man,' I shouted, as he hugged the side of the trench to let us pass. His tortured face twisted into a grin. ' All aboard for Blighty,' he half sang, half sobbed.

We staggered into the front line, and each man of us as he rounded the corner roared his approval of the sight he saw—a long fire-step and above it the hinder parts or boot-soles of C Company as they craned over the parapet towards the enemy or lay bodily on the top, using their rifles as in the range at Strensall. There were uglier sights in the trench bottom where stretcher bearers were busy.

We dumped the bombs and jumped on to the fire-step. To the left was a wide depression—a blown-in trench probably—up which the Germans were crowding in mass, to be met and broken by a shower of bombs. Time after time they rallied and returned to the attack. In front the enemy lay in heaps where they had advanced in the open. Suddenly the dead came to life. A number of the still grey figures jumped up and rushed forward, hurling bombs as they came. A storm of bullets broke on them, and they fell again. Finger on trigger we watched them for I know not how long, but this time they did not move.

Further on the left the attack was still strong. The defence was weakening. Our bombers had suffered badly, and we could not reach the enemy with rifle fire. But now came reinforcements. ' Where are the blighters ? ' barked an officer with the trench mortar badge, jumping on to the fire-step. ' There, sir.' ' We'll plaster 'em,' he said, and stepped down. A moment later Stokes mortars were raining into the attacking mass. To escape this new terror the Huns scurried even into the open—and into the murderous hail of our waiting rifle-fire.

That was the end. At eight o'clock ' Stand down ' was passed along the weary line. We lit our pipes, found out which of our pals were still alive, and set about making breakfast." (J. E. Yates).

With this action the direct connection of the Battalion with the Leipzig Salient ended. Other battalions in the Division carried on the good work. Trench after trench was captured. It was not until September 17th however that a firm hold on the Salient was assured by the capture of the Wonder Work by the 7th Battalion West Riding Regt. (147th Brigade). From this trench the great attack which resulted in the capture of Thiepval was launched on Sept. 26th.

The next section of the line held by the Battalion was N. E. of Authuille Wood. Battalion Head Quarters for the first day or two was near Wood Post, but as it was a most unhealthy locality and heavily shelled, a much safer Head Quarters was quickly found near Quarry

Post, a few hundred yards further south. The front line from approximately Boggart Hole Clock, Mersey Street and the Nab to Bamberbridge Street, was held by two companies, and the other two companies were in support in Authuille Wood. The most interesting part of the line was " The Nab," a sharp salient consisting of a maze of battered trenches with Company Head Quarters in Liverpool Street within a few yards of the front line. It was near this point that the Battalion lost one of its most valued and experienced officers in Lieut.-Col. C. E. Scott, who was fatally wounded during one of his tours of duty round the line. He had reached the front line near The Nab in company with his second in command (Capt. E. W. Knowles) when the enemy began shelling with heavy high explosives and shrapnel, and Lt-Col. Scott was mortally and Capt. Knowles dangerously wounded. By this time the men in the Battalion were too inured to casualties to regard them in any but a fatalistic way, yet as the Colonel was being carried down on a stretcher, men took off their helmets, and muttered sincere words of sympathy, and felt a keen sense of personal loss as Colonel Scott passed on. Almost the only words he uttered as he was carried past Battalion Head Quarters were words of anxiety as to the fate of the Battalion deprived of both Colonel and second-in-command. The three weeks during which Col. Scott commanded the Battalion was a period of extreme difficulty. Crisis followed crisis, and the heaviest responsibilities were laid on the Battalion Commander. But Col. Scott was equal to the emergency. He added greatly to his reputation for thoroughness and unselfishness. It can be said with absolute sincerity that he thought first of the comfort of his men, and last of himself. The command of the Battalion was taken over for a few hours by Capt. N. Muller till Lieut.-Colonel R. A. Hudson, D.S.O., second in command of the 1/8th Bn. West Yorkshire Regt. arrived, and remained in command till the Battalion left the Thiepval sector.

The chief work of the Battalion during this period in the line was the digging of a communication trench across No Man's Land south of the Nab. The Division on our right was advancing trench by trench in a due north direction from Ovillers la Boisselle, and from the right of our Battalion front we looked across the No Man's Land of July 1st to our own men in the original enemy front line. The new trench was dug to connect the two positions, and contained several fire bays, as it was regarded as a reserve line south of the Leipzig Salient. An embankment about six feet high ran half-way across No Man's Land at this point, and received the name " Dead Man's Bank," as our men had been shot down there in hundreds by enfilade machine gun fire during the July 1st attack. The new trench ran alongside this bank, and was dug literally through a mass of putrefying bodies. The work was urgent, and no one spared themselves in digging the first three feet of trench which gave some protection against machine gun and rifle fire. The part of the trench nearest our line was the most popular, as it was seven feet deep, and within easy reach of our front line. Lewis gun covering parties lay out in the shell holes north of the new trench to protect the digging parties. The scene during the digging of this trench defies description. Verey lights were being sent up from all sides, and during their brightest glares everyone in No Man's Land became silent and stationary : men crouched at their digging, and the covering parties cowered in the shell holes. A few seconds later, and the darkness was again filled with movement and noise. The Leipzig Salient a thousand yards away was lit up constantly with bombs and shells, and behind the digging parties the sombre line of Dead Man's Bank stretched across the country like an unclean reptile.

After relief by the 1/5th Bn. West Yorks. Regt. on the 27th July, the Battalion moved into billets at Forceville, and for four days endeavoured to re-organize, and carried out Company Training on the fields immediately south of the town. On August 1st a sudden move was made to Hèdauville, and on August 3rd the Battalion took over the line from Thiepval Avenue to Oban Avenue with Battalion Head Quarters at Campbell Post : A Coy. on left, B on right, C in support, and D in reserve near Authuille. The trenches in this sector were almost non-existent, and constant shelling was the order of the day. Tobermory Street, Bissett Trench, Durham Street look well on the map, but in reality they consisted of collections of shell holes, in full view of the enemy near the Chateau, and too open to offer any protection. About this time the Army Authorities began to show great interest in the construction of mined dugouts of the German type, and 2/Lieut. Melhuish took charge of the construction of one or two in 5th Avenue Communication Trench. This was not an altogether enviable job, as the attention of everybody, from the Brigadier General upwards, seemed to be concentrated upon these mined dugouts, and there was a superfluity of excellent ideas as to methods of quick construction. On August 18th the 49th was relieved by the 25th Division, and the 1/6th Battalion by the 3rd Battalion Worcester Regt. After relief the Battalion marched back to Lealvillers, where seven days were spent in constant training. The men were jaded and exhausted, and though still keen enough, needed a rest. However, instead of a rest, the Battalion was put through the mysteries of attacks on taped trenches representing the German lines near St. Pierre Division on the Ancre. Red-hatted Staff Officers of high rank took

THIEPVAL

a personal interest in the Battalion. The Divisional Band played cheerful ditties. The die was cast. The Division was again to attack on the grand scale. The scene was to be the Thiepval sector! On August 26th the Battalion moved to Hèdauville, and waited for some hours in heavy rain till orders were received to relieve the 2nd Bn. Royal Irish Rifles in dugouts in the South Bluff, Authuille. The relief was completed about 7 p.m. in heavy shelling, during which an A Coy. dugout was blown in, killing five and wounding four others, including Coy. Sergt.-Major Banks. Thiepval thus received the Battalion suitably after its prolonged absence of seven days, and sustained its reputation for being a " sale trou," or " dirty hole " in the expressive French phrase.

Before the war French people spent their summer holidays at Beaucourt and Grandcourt. The Ancre was then a broad and pleasant river, not a derelict marsh. There was a well-known confectioner's shop in Thiepval, where people ate delicious " patisserie " and took " thé à l'anglaise " on summer afternoons, when their children had finished gathering hyacinths in the wood, or bathing in the river. Our men had bathed too in the Ancre near the South Bluff, but it had been an uneasy bliss. There was a South African 6-inch battery on the hillside near the Bluff, and enemy shells intended for our guns fairly frequently fell amongst our bathers, and stirred up mud and bad language. Men, clothed only in their " tin hats," rushed about for their equipment, and ran for shelter to their dugouts, arranged in galleries in the cliff side, where they waited till the strafe was over.

Up to the end of August, 1916, the Battalion had only known the section of line west of Thiepval Wood, and in the vicinity of the Leipzig Salient. In preparation for the attack of September 3rd, however, the Battalion was introduced to another part of the sector, on the north side of the Wood (see Map No. 6). This part of the line had been fondly regarded as comparatively " quiet." In the opinion of most of the officers and men of the Battalion it would probably have remained quiet if the 49th Division had not become interested in it, or if our Brigadier had been of a less combative disposition. By this time Brig. Gen. Goring Jones was always alluded to by the men as " Thiepval." The Brigade's constant preoccupation with Thiepval was laid at his door, for the General was supposed to have set his heart on capturing Thiepval " regardless of cost." The result was that our Brigadier was almost as unpopular as the German Fortress. As a matter of fact no one was more pleased than Gen. Goring Jones when his battalions left Thiepval for ever. In any case, from August 20th onward this sector became a battle sector, with incessant working and carrying parties, interminable shelling, and constant " excursions and alarms."

Before dealing with the details of the preparation for the attack, some description of the ground is necessary. Our original front line ran along the north edge of Thiepval Wood, about 400 yards distant from the enemy. To the west the line ran steeply down the hillside to the Marshes of the Ancre, and on the east reached its highest point in front of Thiepval village. Between the two lines the ground rose slightly, so that from our lines the enemy trenches could not be seen. To get a view of the enemy front line it was necessary either to cross over the Ancre to the hills near Hamel, or to go across No Man's Land to the Sunken Road, which ran between the opposing lines of trenches. This sunken road is worthy of special mention. Few localities earned a more sinister reputation.

On July 1st this road was one of the bloodiest parts of the battle-field. During the attack men jumped into it for shelter from frontal machine gun fire, and were killed in hundreds by enemy artillery firing in enfilade from east of Beaumont Hamel. On the same day a German doctor worked magnificently in attending to our wounded in the front line and the Sunken Road. He had been captured early in the attack, and stayed in the line voluntarily till the morning of July 2nd—a very rare example of practical Christianity on the part of a German Officer. Then followed weeks of quieter warfare during which there was "nothing to report." Working parties gathered up the salvage of the battlefield and buried the dead. Patrols carried on their grim uncertain game. Working parties of hundreds of men began digging the first and second parallels in preparation for the attack of September 3rd. The distance from the original British front line to the German trenches had been nearly 400 yards, but by digging these advanced parallel trenches our front line was brought alongside the Sunken Road, and thus the distance was reduced to about 200 yards. Success in the attack depended upon our first "wave" following the barrage very closely, and only three minutes were allowed in the attack time-table for our men to reach the German lines : thus it was very necessary for our "jumping off" trenches to be as close as possible to the enemy front line. In addition to the parallels the K. O. Y. L. I. West sap was re-dug under the very nose—so to speak—of the enemy. Then followed the attack. A few months later the Sunken Road north of Thiepval Wood—so long a nightmare to infantrymen—became a commonplace feature of a "back area," where men could light their pipes in safety, and admire at leisure the desolation of the Ancre valley.

The attack on Sept. 3rd was entrusted to the 39th and 49th Divisions, north and south of the Ancre respectively. Each Division attacked on a front of about one kilometre, and the objective in each case was the

AEROPLANE PHOTO—NO MAN'S LAND NEAR FAUQUISSART-TRIVELET.

xvii.

COAST DEFENCE. WIRING AT MARSKE,
1914.

A GRAVE NEAR THE TRENCHES, YPRES, 1915.
PTES. H. S. CRYER AND A. NEWBY.

ESSEX FARM CROSS ROADS, NEAR YPRES, 1915.

COPPERNOLLE WOOD, NEAR POPERINGHE.

"CHATTING" ON THE YSER CANAL BANK, YPRES,
1915.

NO. 4A BRIDGE, YSER CANAL, YPRES,
1915.

DUG-OUTS ON THE YSER CANAL BANK, YPRES,
1915.

THE SUNKEN ROAD, THIEPVAL,
1916.

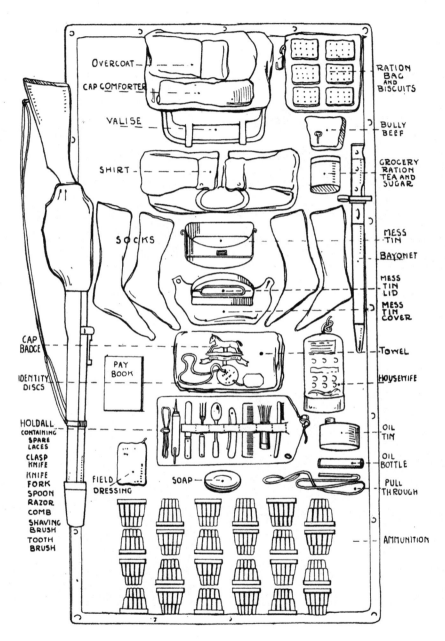

OVERCOAT

CAP COMFORTER

VALISE

SHIRT

SOCKS

CAP BADGE

IDENTITY DISCS

HOLDALL
CONTAINING
SPARE
LACES
CLASP
KNIFE
KNIFE
FORK
SPOON
RAZOR
COMB
SHAVING
BRUSH
TOOTH
BRUSH

PAY BOOK

FIELD DRESSING

SOAP

RATION BAG AND BISCUITS

BULLY BEEF

GROCERY RATION TEA AND SUGAR

MESS TIN

BAYONET

MESS TIN LID

MESS TIN COVER

TOWEL

HOUSEWIFE

OIL TIN

OIL BOTTLE

PULL THROUGH

AMMUNITION

LAY-OUT FOR KIT INSPECTION.

XX.

German second line, approximately 600 yards behind the enemy front line. Success depended upon both Divisions reaching their objectives, as either objective alone would have been untenable owing to enemy enfilade fire. The right battalion of the 39th Division was the 4/5th Bn. Royal Highlanders. The 147th Infantry Brigade attacked on the right, and the 146th Infantry Brigade on the left of the 49th Divisional front. The battalion attacking on the right of the 1/6th Bn. West Yorkshire Regt. was the 1/4th Batt. Duke of Wellington's Regt.

The following is a selection from the final Brigade Orders for the attack :—

1   The Brigade will capture and consolidate the German front lines from R. 19. c.1. 6. to River Ancre and support line from R. 19. c.3.8. to River Ancre—The 147th Brigade being on our right.

2   The 1/6th Bn. West Yorkshire Regt. and 1/8th Bn. West Yorkshire Regt., will carry out the attack. 1/6th Bn. West Yorkshire Regt. on the right, 1/8th Bn. West Yorkshire Regt. on the left.

1/5th Bn. West Yorkshire Regt. will be disposed as follows :— One Company to hold original British Front line from Q. 24. d. 8.1. (top of Sandy Avenue) to River Ancre, both inclusive. This Company will deal with prisoners coming back from captured trenches, in event of their giving trouble.

Battalion Head Quarters and three Companies in Brigade reserve at Gordon Castle.

1/7th Bn. West Yorkshire Regt. in reserve in Assembly Trenches, Aveluy Wood.

3   ATTACK :—

1/6th Bn. West Yorkshire Regt. and 1/8th Bn. West Yorkshire Regt. will attack in two lines on a frontage of 250 yards each. Each Battalion will have one and a half Companies in front line in single rank and one and a half Companies in the second line. 1/6th Bn. West Yorkshire Regt. will have one extra platoon to follow second line and mop up X communication trenches which meet a R. 19. c.0.9.

1/8th Bn. West Yorkshire Regt. will have one extra platoon to move along the Marsh between River Ancre and the left of the 1/8th Bn. West Yorkshire Regt.

The first line will take the German Front line. The second line will go over through the German Front line and take the German support line.

4   MOPPING UP :—

One Section in each platoon in Battalion first and second lines

I   113

will be told off to mop up, place guards over dug-outs, and evacuate prisoners. A proportion of bombers to be attached to these
sections. When the trench is taken and mopped up the whole
party, less the sentries, to consolidate without delay.

5 SPECIAL PARTIES :—

1/6th Bn. West Yorkshire Regt. and 1/8th Bn. West Yorkshire
Regt. will each tell off special bombing parties to move
with the second line and be placed opposite the following points :—
1/6th Bn. West Yorkshire Regt. opposite Q.24.b.9.0.
1/8th Bn. West Yorkshire Regt. opposite Q.24.b.5.3. and
Q.24.b.4.4.
Each of the above bombing parties will have six extra men to
carry bombs.
On arrival at the German support line these parties will at once
bomb and make blocks 100 yards up communication trenches
towards the enemy.
1/6th Bn. West Yorkshire Regt. will in addition detail strong
bombing parties on right flank of both first and second lines to
block trench or form defensive flank in case 147th Brigade on our
right fails to reach objective.
In addition special parties consisting of one Lewis Gun, one
N.C.O. and six men carrying bombs and four bombers will move
with the second line—each Battalion will have four of these parties,
dividing the distance along Battalion front. On arrival at support
line these parties will at once push out about thirty yards and
take up their positions—dig in and consolidate, after which they
will dig back communication trenches to German support line.

6 CARRYING PARTIES :—

Immediately the position is captured dumps of Small Arms Ammunition, Mills Grenades, R. E. Stores and water, will be formed
in the German front line at the junction of communication trenches
running from German front to support line, points Q.24.d.8.7.,
Q.24.d.6.7., points 5.7 and Q.24.b.2.1. Officers Commanding
1/6th and 1/8th Bns. West Yorkshire Regts. will detail the
necessary carrying parties from the reserve platoons.

7 COMMAND POSTS.

Battalion Head Quarters of 1/6th and 1/8th Bns. West
Yorkshire Regts. will be at Q.24.d.05.15.
1/5th Bn. West Yorkshire Regt. at Gordon Castle.
1/7th Bn. West Yorkshire Regt. at A Group Assembly Trenches
in Aveluy Wood.
Brigade Headquarters—at Q.29.d.4.4. on Aveluy—Hamel Road.

8 EQUIPMENT AND RATIONS :—
Every man in the attack will carry the following—
Emergency ration—One day's preserved rations in haversack.
Filled water bottle.
170 rounds S.A.A.
Four sandbags in belt.
Two Mills Grenades.
Every other man in the attack will carry either a shovel or a pick tied on to his back or slung with a rifle sling.
This order also applies to the 1/5th Bn. and 1/7th Bn. West Yorkshire Regt. who will carry everything as above laid down.

9 OFFICERS :—
Not less than sixteen or more than eighteen officers to go into action with Battalions.
1st Echelon—(Second in command and one Officer per Coy.). to remain at Martinsart Wood.
2nd Echelon—(remainder) and fifteen per cent. N.C.O.'s to Forceville.

10 MAPS :—
Special Operation Map No. 20, and 57D.S.E 1/20,000 should be carried by all officers. No other map is to be taken and no copy of orders.

11 After the capture of the Front line the Peterhead Sap and K.O.Y.L.I West Communication Trenches are reserved for " Up " Traffic. " Down " Point 57 along Sunk Road to Thurso Street.

G. W. SANDEMAN, *Captain,*
1-9-16.　　　　Brigade Major, 146th Infantry Brigade.

In order to understand correctly the failure of the Division to carry the objectives, it is essential to bear in mind that all the battalions were very exhausted, not only by the incessant trench fighting from July 1st, but by the seven days working parties immediately before September 3rd. It is almost a truism that battalions cannot be expected to work for a week on nerve-racking digging and fatigue parties and then succeed in capturing lines which had resisted fresh troops with weeks of special training behind them. But such was the task set the 146th and 147th Brigades. Night after night from August 27th all available men were employed in carrying ammunition and reserve rations from Lancashire Dump to Speyside, and thence to forward dumps in Elgin Avenue and the parallels. Between Elgin Avenue and the Ancre a series of assembly trenches were dug in the hill-side, and a mined double Battalion Head Quarters dug-out was constructed near Peterhead

Sap. All this was done under constant shell fire, and of course at night. Hundreds of men paraded each night at Lancashire Dump in Aveluy Wood, or the North Bluff near Authuille : were met by guides at Paisley Dump : and loaded with ammunition and all the paraphernalia of battle, began their two hours march to the parallels, or spent all night digging trenches. They returned an hour or two before dawn so exhausted they could hardly walk, and would have laid down in hundreds on Speyside or Paisley Dump, anywhere, but for Officers and N.C.O.'s, who were compelled to urge on the men to other fatigues and preparations during the daylight. It can be said without fear of contradiction that no officer or man looked forward to the hour of attack with anything but misgiving. There was no enthusiasm. " We've been through it before, we can go through it again," was the usual sentiment. It was said if the men reached the Assembly trenches on the morning of the battle it would be a feat worthy of praise ! And the most that was hoped for was that with an extra rum ration, and the excitement of the moment, the attacking waves would reach the enemy support line and remain there from sheer physical inability to go back. Moreover, the Battalion was no longer the Territorial unit of July 1st, but a mixture of reinforcements from twenty-seven different battalions from all parts of England, who had had no opportunity of shaking down into one efficient unit during the past few weeks of trench warfare.

On the night of August 29th there had been unusually heavy working parties, one of which consisted in the placing of ladders in the second parallel in order to help men to get out quickly from the very deep and narrow front line trenches immediately before zero. The attack was arranged to take place on August 31st. On the 30th August however, zero day was postponed, and the Battalion ordered to move to trenches in Aveluy Wood. This move was also cancelled within a few hours of receiving it, and the 31st was spent in the usual fatigues. On September 2nd the Battalion moved to Aveluy Wood, having received orders to be clear of North Bluff by 3 p.m. Heavy shelling began at 2-30 p.m. along the Bluff and Authuille Bridge (Black Horse Road). There were several casualties, Capt. J. L. Oddy being killed and three N.C.O.'s wounded. The loss of Capt. Oddy was serious. He was one of the very finest types of British officer, courteous, cheerful and fearless. He had returned to the Battalion before he was physically fit to do so after his wound early in July. He may be singled out as typical of a great number of Officers and men who sacrificed themselves continually, without the faintest hope of reward, in clear response to an idealism which too many men affected to despise.

THIEPVAL

On the morning of September 3rd at 1-30 a.m. the Battalion left Aveluy Wood, crossed the Ancre by the South Causeway (the 1/8th Battalion crossed by the North Causeway), and reached the parallels *via* Sandy Avenue, Thurso Street, and K. O. Y. L. I. West Sap ten minutes before zero, which was fixed at 5-10 a.m. A few minutes before zero the whole of the front line (one and a half Companies) lay out in the open in front of the 2nd parallel, and the second line (one

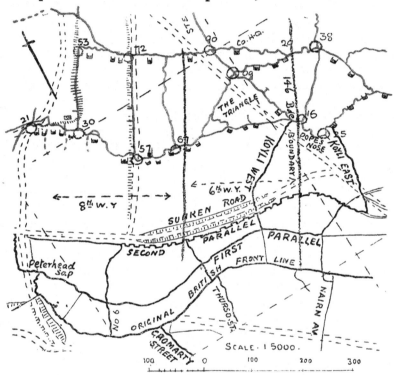

No. 6 Map. Attack, Sept. 3rd, 1916. Thiepval.

and a half Companies) moved from the 1st to the 2nd parallel. Everything was very quiet. There had been no enemy shelling during the massing of the battalions in the front line positions. The night was very dark. There had been a certain amount of confusion in the assembly positions, but the men were quietly ready and waiting a few minutes before zero. The darkness was of the blackest kind which immediately precedes dawn.

All officers and men were thoroughly acquainted with the objectives, and were "word-perfect" so far as their instructions went.

The 5th Bn. Duke of Wellington's Regiment on their right had the difficult task of capturing the " Pope's Nose," an important Salient in the enemy line. Our own Battalion had a trench system called " The Triangle " as an objective, and an alleged Company Head Quarters in the German support line.

The artillery barrage began promptly at 5-10 a.m. and was accurate and magnificent in volume. The men were lined up within forty yards of it, and we had no casualties from " shorts." As the barrage moved forward our lines advanced in regular order and steadily. But the enemy was thoroughly on the alert. His barrage came down three minutes after zero, and his machine guns opened out from the Pope's Nose immediately our barrage lifted from the enemy front line. The preparations for our attack had been obvious, and from several parts of his line the enemy had been able to range with absolute accuracy on our parallels and front line. The result was that our second line was badly caught in the barrage as it was leaving the front parallel and crossing the Sunken Road, and the other second line groups (machine gunners, trench mortars, carrying parties) were not able to advance, or were so badly cut up that the disorganized remnants never crossed No Man's Land. Practically the whole of the first line reached the enemy wire without many casualties, and for a few seconds everything seemed likely to go well. Then enemy machine guns suddenly began firing in direct enfilade down their wire from the Pope's Nose, immediately on the right flank. The line wavered, and what had been only too sadly anticipated happened : sections of men retired towards the Sunken Road. Some of these men reported they had been ordered to retire, and they believed the order must have been given by some German disguised as a British Officer. It is impossible wholly to discredit the report, though the evidence in support of it is not very strong. A great number of the men pushed forward, and entered the enemy lines, but the impetus of the attack was lost. The number of men who retired was not great, but the casualties had been very heavy, with the result that comparatively few were left in the enemy front line to deal with the situation. Almost all the Officers and N.C.O.'s with experience in the Battalion reached the enemy line with groups of men round them who knew and trusted them, and whose morale had survived the shocks of the previous weeks. But these groups were not sufficiently supported. The second wave, as we have seen, had been badly caught in what was a truly terrific enemy barrage, with the result that the few who remained in the enemy line felt themselves " in the air " and deprived of supports. There was a good deal of hand-to-hand fighting, however : several of the enemy were killed : but few of the officers or men who reached the German positions came back. Lieut. Hearne (A Coy.) reported seeing Lieut. Senior with several men busily bombing German dug-outs, but Senior was killed a few minutes later. Lt. Hearne also reported that we had held fairly strongly Point 16, but the enemy counter-attacked and drove us out. No. 10 Platoon (C Coy.) reached the front German trenches, but was compelled to retire after suffering several casualties in a hot engagement. Lieut Chas. H. Mitchell with about twenty of his men reached the enemy line, and seems to have stayed there longer than anyone else. By about 6-30 a.m. most of his platoon had become casualties, and the enemy were surrounding him on all sides. He told his men one by one to try and get back to our line, but most of them in doing so were killed by enemy rifle fire. In fact only two of his party survived, and reported they were the last to leave him. He had evidently refused to go till all his men had left the trench, and he must have been killed in the final rush of the enemy. He was called " The Professor " from an air of studiousness about him, but he died the death of a soldier. Lieuts. Melhuish (B Coy.) and Hearne with a few small groups of men remained in the enemy lines till about 6-30 a.m., but by this time the situation was hopeless, and the strong German counter-attack mentioned previously compelled the remnants of the Battalion which still remained in the enemy front line to retire. Lieut. T. E. Armistead, one of the most fearless and reliable officers the Battalion ever had, scrawled the following message at 5-40 a.m.

" We got part of the front wave into the enemy line. But the rest of the front wave had stuck in front of the enemy wire, and then retired, leaving only a few scattered men in front line, who have had to come back. I am trying to collect men into front parallel, but there are very few." Lt. Armistead had stayed in the enemy line till the position was hopeless. His message was the first to be received at Battalion Head Quarters at 6-10 a.m. By 7 a.m. the attack was over. A similar fate befell the 1/8th Bn. West Yorkshire Regt. on the left, and on the right, in spite of the success of small parties in reaching the enemy front line, it was found impossible to maintain their positions. The 4th Battalion Duke of Wellington's Regt. on the extreme right flank of the Division seem to have advanced furthest, and were in the German support line at 11-10 a.m., but they also were compelled to retire, as they were dominated by the enemy from the Schwaben Redoubt. Thus the attack on the 49th, and also the 39th Divisional front north of the Ancre, failed, and in almost every unit the story was the same :—The German second line not reached, and the front line held too weakly to resist the German counter-attacks, and enfilade fire. The terrific enemy barrage completely cut off the arrival of supports, and made it almost impossible to keep Battalion Head Quarters in touch with the situation, as very few runners were able to get back. At noon the average strength of Companies was only from thirty-five to forty men, and these were widely scattered up and down the first and second parallels.

A platoon sergeant who took part in the battle, but who was seriously wounded crossing No Man's Land immediately after Zero, writes as follows :—

" I believe the experience of my platoon was an average one. When we marched into support on August 27th this platoon was thirty-three strong and in fair condition. After a week of working parties, etc. there remained to go over the top eighteen decrepit old men. The rest were dead, wounded or in hospital. It was my unfortunate duty to wake my men up and parade them for the fatigues (The word should be written in capital letters !). The British infantryman seldom wakes with a cheery smile, but towards the end of that abominable week, my men could be roused only by the sort of brutality one likes to think is a German monopoly. They lay like men drunk or dead. For instance, there was one decent average man who, I knew from experience, always pulled his last ounce. One night I could wake him by no ordinary means, and in the end he had to be pulled on to his feet, held there, and kicked into consciousness. " I can't do it, sergeant," he said, in reply to my language, " I'm done." I knew he was done, but there were stacks of trench mortars to carry across the marsh up to the line, and I had seen men do miracles before. So we dragged him out to the railway where the other men were waiting. He made an effort to pull himself together, and he moved off with the party—to collapse after a few steps. But he was one of the eighteen in my platoon who went over the top two days later !

Everyone was loaded up for the attack with sandbags of bombs, coils of barbed wire, wire cutters, red or white flares, Verey lights, Verey pistols, picks, shovels, etc., etc. When everything was ready, and one could not have pushed a tooth pick into a pocket or haversack, the mail came, and most of us got parcels. We ate what we could, and dumped the rest !

By this time several of us had come to the conclusion that victory would depend mainly on any one of three things—(*a*) the extermination of the enemy by our own guns, (*b*) the instant paralysis of the enemy at sight of us, (*c*) a miracle. After a four hours' march we arrived at the assembly positions. No one then complained of fatigue, though we had felt desperately unfit when we had set out. The men took off their breach covers, fingered their rifle bolts, and chatted quietly. But there was a peculiar note almost of exaltation in their whispers which told of the tremendous excitement of the moment. I felt as though my veins were filled with electricity. It was rather pleasant than otherwise. Then the barrage started, and the world seemed to be breaking up...."—J. E. Yates.

Such an experience as this explains a good deal which happened during the battle.

Two or three facts are indisputable. The enemy held the Pope's Nose throughout the attack, and the failure of the battalion on our right to capture this dominating position seriously prejudiced our chances of success. Our men also had been overstrained and overworked, and their morale was not equal to the task of capturing some of the strongest enemy positions on the Somme battlefield. Several divisions during the next few weeks attacked equally unsuccessfully the same objectives as those of the 49th Division on September 3rd.

The scene in the first and second parallels after the failure of the attack baffles description. The narrow assembly trenches were choked with dead and wounded, and the small groups of unwounded men were silent and exhausted. At 8-45 a.m. a message from 146th Infantry Brigade Head Quarters ordered a second attack to be prepared on the 1/6th Battalion front by two Companies of the 1/7th Bn. West Yorkshire Regt. The attack was to have taken place from the old British front line, as the enemy barrage on the parallels was murderous and would have destroyed any chance of success. Fortunately the attack was cancelled later in the day, when the extent of the casualties suffered by even the two reserve battalions (1/5th and 1/7th) was realized. During the action the double Battalion Head Quarters in the mined dug-out in Speyside was crowded with the usual dense mass of runners, liason officers, R. E. signallers, and all the other details whose work only begins in case an attack is successful, and who otherwise have nothing to do except try to keep cheerful, and out of harm's way. Lt. Col. Hudson (1/6th Bn.) and Lt. Col. Alexander (1/8th Bn.) tried to make out a coherent story from the confusion of reports. The dugout was lit by candles, and occasionally tables and candles were knocked over by the concussion of High Explosives. The seriously wounded lay outside in rows, and the less severe cases poured down in hundreds to the tramway line in the valley and the First Aid Station there. Out of an approximate strength of 350 men in the 1/6th Battalion who actually went " over the top " at 5-10 a.m. there were three officers, thirty other ranks killed, three officers and 172 other ranks wounded and thirty-three missing. Thus two out of every three men who attacked became casualties.

Towards midnight the 146th Infantry Brigade was relieved by the 148th Brigade. The 1/5th and 1/7th Battalions moved to Martinsart Wood, the 1/8th Battalion to Hèdauville, the 1/6th Battalion and Brigade Head Quarters to Forceville. Thus ended the blackest day in the history of the Battalion.

After a fortnight's rest at Forceville and Hèdauville the Battalion moved again into the Thiepval sector on September 20th. The great attack of September 26th on Thiepval was being prepared. Sir Douglas Haig describes the attack as follows :—

" .... a brilliant success.... In Thiepval and the strong works to the north of it the enemy's resistance was desperate. Three waves of our attacking troops (11th and 18th Divisions, II. Corps) carried the outer defences of Mouquet Farm. On the left of the attack fierce fighting, in which Tanks again gave valuable assistance to our troops (18th Division), continued in Thiepval during that day and the following night, but by 8-30 a.m. on the 27th September the whole of the village of Thiepval was in our hands. Schwaben Redoubt was assaulted during the afternoon of the 28th September, and.. we captured the whole of the southern face of the Redoubt, and pushed out patrols to the northern face and towards St. Pierre Divion."

During this attack the 146th Brigade was holding the Thiepval sector from the Ancre on the left to the trenches opposite " Thiepval Chateau " on the right. The 1/6th Battalion put out observation posts from the second parallel, and the other battalions in the Brigade sent up observers to remaining posts on the Brigade front. The whole of Thiepval village, and the line of the Schwaben and Stuff Redoubts, could be seen from our line, and this view of one of the greatest battles of the war was certainly unique. Only eleven days earlier, on September 15th, Tanks had been used for the first time during the war, in the attack on Flers. There was thus great excitement when at zero hour (12-25 p.m.) two Tanks were seen " waddling " into action near the " Apple Trees " immediately south of Thiepval village, having arrived at Gordon Castle 11-30 p.m. the night before. The enemy fought stubbornly, especially near the " Crucifix," north of Thiepval, and our men looked across No Man's Land to points only 300 yards away, where through drifting smoke and amidst a debris of trenches and bricks, groups of men could be clearly seen bombing and fighting. Our machine guns near Chateau Trench were able to fire in enfilade on the enemy, and caused him considerable annoyance and casualties. The 146th Infantry Brigade took a definite part in the victory, as the 1/5th Battalion was detached to support the 7th Battalion Bedfordshire Regt. of the 18th Division in the attack on the Schwaben on

THIEPVAL

September 27th, and received a very warm letter of appreciation from Major-General T. H. Shoubridge (18th Division) for their " splendid support."   A Coy. of the 1/6th Battalion crossed over No Man's Land on the night of September 26th, and helped to consolidate the position in Thiepval, and on the following day B Coy. dug a trench across No Man's Land to the former enemy line near Thiepval Chateau.

Thus some of the Battalion (but how few !) who had attacked Thiepval at 4 p.m. on July 1st, had entered it on September 26th and 27th with victorious troops.   The final scene of the victory was only one of a long and terrible drama in which the Battalion had played a worthy part.   And if there was disappointment that the Battalion had not been able to share directly in the glory of victory, we took comfort in the thought that the war was bigger than any one day's battle, and the opportunity of victory would always remain the privilege of the few.

The following message to the 49th Division was received from Lieut.-General C. W. Jacob (II. Corps) on October 3rd, when the Division moved out of the Somme area.

" .... The conditions were trying, and your casualties heavy. The calls made on units necessitated great exertions which were always cheerfully carried out.   The gallantry of the officers and men is shown by the large number of decorations won by them, and the spirit of all ranks is good.   The clearing of the Liepzig Salient, the prompt way all calls for raids on the enemy trenches were met, and the heavy work done by the Division in the preparations for the final attack on Thiepval are gratifying records....It was unfortunate that the Division as a whole could not take part in the final capture of Thiepval, but you will all be glad to know that your representatives in the battle, the 49th Divisional Artillery and the 146th Infantry Brigade, did excellent work, and added still further to the good reputation of the Division."

CHAPTER VII.

TRENCH WARFARE. GOMMECOURT, MONCHY-AU-BOIS, RANSART.

WITH the fall of Thiepval on September 27th, the Somme battle may be said to have ended. The capture of Beaucourt and the southern slopes of the Beaumont-Hamel Spur on November 13th and 14th was an isolated battle of great importance, but the rest of the Allied line on the Somme had settled down to unusually miserable conditions of " static " warfare. When the 49th Division left the Thiepval front at the end of September, 1916, they were expecting a fairly prolonged period of rest. The 146th Infantry Brigade concentrated in the Warluzel area, two or three miles north of the main Doullens—Arras Road. The 1/6th and 1/7th Battalions were at Sombrin, 1/8th Battalion at Humbercamp, and the 1/5th Battalion and Brigade Head Quarters at Warluzel. Sombrin was uninteresting and rather more than usually dirty. The countryside was littered with dumps and transport lines, and all the mess of a much used billeting area. Lt.-Col. H. O. Wade took over command of the Battalion, having recovered from his wound of July 1st. His arrival was welcomed by all who had served under him, though the Battalion was sorry to lose Lt.-Col. Hudson, who was very popular, and who took over command of the 1/8th Bn. West Yorkshire Regt. After a rest of only ten days at Sombrin, the 1/6th Battalion marched to Pommier, five miles nearer the line. On October 18th the 146th Infantry Brigade took over the Fonquevillers—Hannescamps sector, with Brigade Head Quarters at Bienvillers. The Brigade front extended for about five kilometres from Gommecourt to Monchy-au-Bois, and was held by three battalions in the line (1/6th Battalion, 1/7th Battalion and 1/5th Battalion) and one battalion (1/8th Battalion) in Brigade Reserve in Bienvillers. The 1/6th Battalion was the right battalion of the Brigade, and took over the line opposite Gommecourt, which the 31st Division had vainly attempted to capture on July 1st.

The first duty of the Battalion was an elaborate reconnaissance by all Officers and N.C.O's., of the defences of Fonquevillers and the old assembly trenches south of the town, used for the July 1st attack. This reconnaissance was ordered because it was expected that the 49th

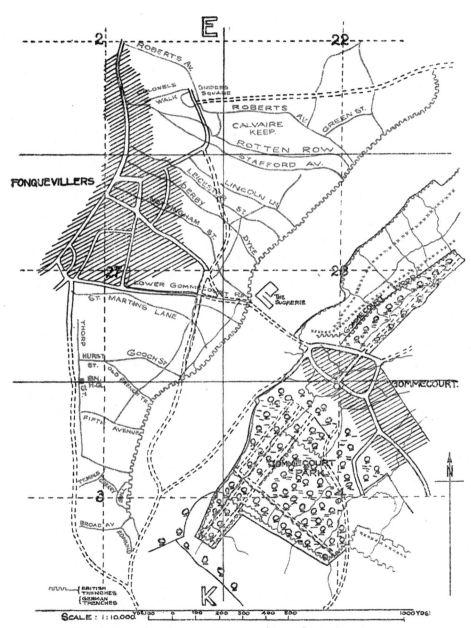

No. 7 Map.   Trenches, Fonquevillers-Gommecourt, 1916.

Division would attack Gommecourt in the near future, and thus assist in the development of the advance which was being made by our armies on the Ancre. The project was not carried into execution, and the right subsector remained an average unpleasant specimen of trench warfare. The Gommecourt sector has often been described. The enemy held strongly constructed and well-sighted trenches in front of Gommecourt Wood, and about 250 yards from our own front line. The wood itself was full of barbed wire entanglements and machine gun positions, and the Gommecourt Salient was defended by three or four successive belts of barbed wire each thirty to forty feet thick. The inter-battalion boundary between the 1/6th and 1/7th Battalions was the Fonquevillers—Gommecourt Road, down which an enemy concrete machine gun emplacement had an admirable field of fire. Immediately north of the road and in No Man's Land was a ruined distillery with one or two deep wells, down which men on patrol had been known occasionally to disappear for ever on dark nights. The Battalion frontage was rather over a thousand yards, and the right boundary was " The Mousetrap," opposite Gommecourt Park. Gommecourt was in ruins : Fonquevillers was in ruins : yet in both places there were a few houses with roofs, commanding good views of the country side. Several houses in Fonquevillers were used as billets, in spite of fairly frequent and terrific blasts of enemy shelling. The only really safe places in the town were the enormous caves beneath the Church, used as an Ammunition Store and an assembly place for troops before July 1st.

One of the great games in the Fonquevillers and Hannescamps sectors was the exhilarating one of trying to find one's way in the endless maze of trenches. Division and Corps Head Quarters were beginning at this time to show a great interest in Trench Maps, and as the sector was a " static " one, there was every chance that a Trench Map would remain useful for some weeks at least. The game was complicated however by the fact that several old French trenches were still existing, down which the uninitiated warrior plodded wearily till he came to a cul de sac. Then he swore deeply and savagely. Also, every Brigadier had different points of view as to the siting of trenches, with the result that several schemes of trench fortifications had been begun, worked on with energy for several weeks, and then left severely alone in disgust by the next incoming Brigadier who began constructing trenches more in accordance with his own theories. To complicate still further the trench system, boards were put up at junctions giving the names of trenches, such as " Crawlboys' Lane," " Rotten Row," " Landleague Avenue," " Leeds Road," etc., and perspiring ration carriers on

TRENCH WARFARE

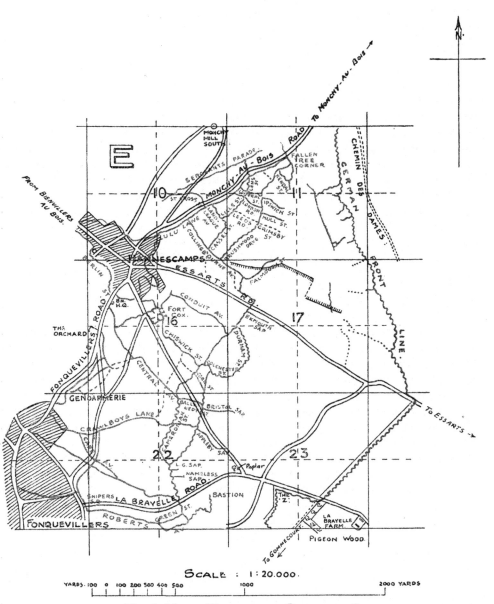

SCALE : 1:20.000.

No. 8 Map. Hannescamp Sector, 1916.

some dark night knocked the boards down. Whereupon some enthusiast next morning put them up again, but only too frequently in entirely wrong positions. Sometimes an R. E. party, with several neatly inscribed boards from Army Head Quarters, fixed them up according to a plan known at some Head Quarters thirty miles behind the line, but which was entirely different from the one at Battalion or Brigade Head Quarters. The result can be imagined ! A visit to a strange part of the line was an adventure. You never knew exactly where you would come out. Instead, for instance, of reaching a front line Sap or Lewis Gun Post, you found on looking with infinite precaution over the parapet that you were still some hundreds of yards behind a support Company Head Quarters. Whereupon you approached the aforesaid Company Head Quarters, and with the camaraderie of the trenches, helped yourself to their whisky, spent an hour trying to understand half-a-dozen damp filthy maps handed over by as many different units, and departed with the conviction that if we could not find our own way about our lines the enemy would find it practically impossible : the war would therefore end in a stale-mate.

Runners, lance-corporals and junior officers passed through some of the most awful moments of their lives in mazy trench systems like Fonquevillers. Such moments occurred when, after leading a choleric Colonel or Brigadier for some hours in a vicious circle in trenches which you believed you knew as well as what would come up in the night's rations, you found yourself lost, irrevocably. In halting accents you then began to murmur that the map must be wrong. If the enemy took the opportunity to begin shelling or trench mortaring your Colonel or Brigadier, your life was not worth living. Experience taught most orderlies one excellent excuse for not taking visitors to intricate parts of the line, or trenches they did not feel sure they could find. "Very unhealthy place, Sir : B Coy. lost three men there an hour ago"; or "They usually begin trench mortaring there about this time, Sir !" In many cases the ruse served : the visitor decided that some other part of the line was more interesting : and the orderly retained his reputation for omniscience.

One of the features of our trench system near Fonquevillers was the sunken road immediately behind the front line, with shelters in the bank side, and two or three newly constructed mined dugouts, which it had been proposed to use as forward Battle Head Quarters in the attack on Gommecourt. The enemy had the exact range of this road, and plastered it heavily and frequently with trench mortars. As it was an important thoroughfare, the trench mortars claimed casualties every day, and the sunken road was not popular. Everyone

THE JAM TIN GRENADE
(1915)

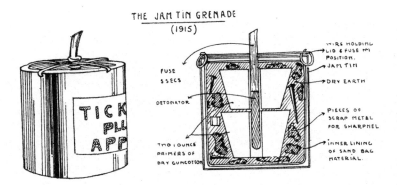

FUSE
5 SECS

DETONATOR

TWO 1 OUNCE
PRIMERS OF
DRY GUNCOTTON

WIRE HOLDING
LID & FUSE IN
POSITION.

JAM TIN

DRY EARTH

PIECES OF
SCRAP METAL
FOR SHRAPNEL

INNER LINING
OF SAND BAG
MATERIAL.

THE GAS PIPE GRENADE
(1915)

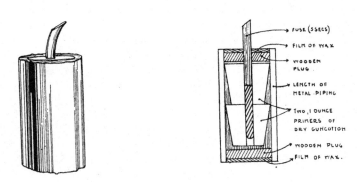

FUSE (5 SECS)

FILM OF WAX

WOODEN
PLUG

LENGTH OF
METAL PIPING

TWO, 1 OUNCE
PRIMERS OF
DRY GUNCOTTON

WOODEN PLUG

FILM OF WAX.

THE HAIR BRUSH GRENADE.
(1915)

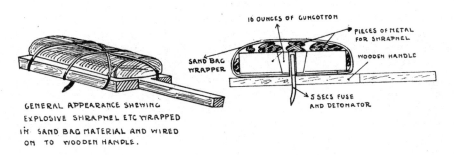

16 OUNCES OF GUNCOTTON

PIECES OF METAL
FOR SHRAPNEL

SAND BAG
WRAPPER

WOODEN HANDLE

5 SECS FUSE
AND DETONATOR

GENERAL APPEARANCE SHEWING
EXPLOSIVE SHRAPNEL ETC WRAPPED
IN SAND BAG MATERIAL AND WIRED
ON TO WOODEN HANDLE.

ILLUSTRATIONS OF GRENADES IN USE IN 1915.
(DRAWN BY CAPT. H. A. JOWETT.)

OBLIQUE AEROPLANE PHOTO—YPRES, 1918.

R.Q.M.S. G. WELCH.

R.Q.M.S. C. H. WOODHEAD, M.S.M.

C.Q.M.S. E. A. PACKETT.

C.Q.M.S. C. ST. JOHN VAUGHAN.

C.S.M. H. BANKS, D.C.M.

C.S.M. E. BRADLEY, D.C.M.

C.Q.M.S. A. MOORHOUSE.

C.S.M. C. G. FINNEY.

xxiv.

continued to use it, however, as movement was slower and more wearisome in the trench which ran parallel to it. The Battalion Head Quarters was in one of a line of dugouts on the Fonquevillers—Hébuterne Road, commonly known as Thorpe Street. One of these dugouts was famous for its Bairnsfather cartoons. Like most of them it was comfortable and fairly well constructed, and contained a certain amount of furniture from ruined houses in Fonquevillers. Bairnsfather had evidently drawn the cartoons in crayon, or with the end of a red-hot iron, on the whitewashed timber walls. The other dugouts in Thorpe Street were also adorned with pictures, though of a different kind :— usually noble arrays of Kirchner prints or coloured drawings from " *La Vie Parisienne.*" Hours of animated conversation were spent in discussing the respective merits of these different types of female loveliness. When the Padre visited the dugout, his chair—or biscuit box— was carefully placed so that his eye should not be " intrigued " by the more scantily dressed figures.

The most exciting event of the tour was an enemy raid on our front line near Lincoln Lane on October 22nd. The enemy had evidently become alarmed by our extensive digging operations—new trenches and the mine shafts of tunnels under No Man's Land which were being sunk at this point. The enemy attack was preceded by a heavy bombardment of trench mortars for one and a half hours which blew our front line to pieces. The enemy failed entirely either to capture prisoners or to examine our line, chiefly owing to a prompt and well-executed counter-attack across the open immediately after the enemy barrage lifted. The counter attack was led by Lieut. T. E. Armistead, with his Coy. H.Q. details and support platoon. In recognition of this action, he received the M.C., a decoration which he had earned many times. The day but one after, the Battalion was relieved by the 1/4th Bn. West Riding Regt., and after four days in St. Amand, the Battalion moved into the left sector, taking over the line from the Bienvillers— Monchy Road on the left to the Hannescamp—Essarts Road on the right. The Battalion remained in this sector up to December 6th, with occasional intervals of rest in billets at St. Amand or Bienvillers.

Trench warfare on this front offered more variety than in any other sector occupied by the Battalion since its arrival in France. On the left, near the Bienvillers—Monchy Road, our line was only 100 yards distant from the enemy. On the right, the lines were over 1,200 yards apart. On the left, trench mortars and shelling was the order of the day : on the right, extreme quietness, with uneventful patrolling at night. The trenches sloped up to high ground near Monchy on the left, and high ground near Exmouth Sap on the right.

In the Valley between, a trench ran out beyond the front line for about 350 yards into No Man's Land, and was called Falmouth Sap.

Long grass, bushes, and undulating country gave excellent opportunity for practising patrols, the only disadvantage being that the enemy was not in the habit of sending out small sporting patrols of four or five men, but usually moved in formed bodies of at least forty men, slowly, taking no risks. Our patrols made several efforts to get in touch with enemy posts in advanced trenches in No Man's Land, but without tangible results. The game of " winkling " was being introduced into warfare by the Canadians during the 1916-1917 winter. The game was a good one, and later on the Battalion played it quite successfully. It consisted in small parties of resolute fellows surprising the sentry of a detached enemy post, and then picking prisoners out of the dugouts behind him, as one picks winkles out of shells. But the Monchy sector was not favourable for this kind of game. The enemy was on the defensive, and was only holding his support lines in strength. The positions of the few advance posts he was holding were constantly being changed, and it was therefore impossible to raid any point with the certainty of finding the enemy in occupation. A little diversion in patrolling was caused by one of our Scouts—a powerful boxer—who developed alarming, though temporary, signs of insanity. On one famous patrol, he carried on a great fight in No Man's Land with several other members of the patrol, and was only brought in with difficulty. Before he was finally sent to the base, he entered the Battalion Head Quarters dugout one day, and threatened the Colonel himself with grievous bodily injury. With his usual presence of mind our Colonel offered him an orange, and told him to " be a good boy " : whereat he remained quiet till an orderly led him away. A few hours later, when he was being escorted to hospital, he told some of his escort that " he was not so mad as they were, sticking it in those damned silly trenches,"—a remark which gave the escort " furiously to think."

Occasionally enemy snipers were known to creep out before dawn to within two or three hundred yards of our line, and lie out in the long grass, picking off our men near the Essarts Road. One instance is worth recording. For two or three hours after dawn a thick mist had covered the whole of No Man's Land, and offered an invaluable opportunity to one of our men to examine the state of our wire near Exmouth Sap. Under cover of the mist he walked straight down the Essarts Road, past the Lewis Gun team at the Sap head, and continued alone for about two hundred yards further down the road :— a mad thing to do, but the mist seemed to give protection. He was busily occupied in making notes of the ground and the wire, when he saw something move in the grass about forty yards away, and was disturbed to find it was the head and shoulder of a German. Whereupon he turned round and walked slowly back to our sap head, afraid every second of hearing the crack of a rifle and feeling the inevitable bullet. Evidently the German was incapable of believing that a man could be so mad as to walk openly in No Man's Land without some hidden escort, and the bullet was never fired. A Lewis Gun from the sap head was turned quickly on to No Man's Land when our barbed-wire-entanglement expert reached safety, but the result is unknown. A minor incident, but typical of the line.

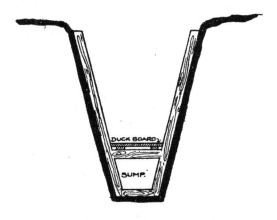

"A" FRAME.

The usual winter campaign against mud and falling trenches had begun in earnest when the Battalion took over the line opposite Monchy. In the Ypres Salient during the previous winter there had neither been men nor material enough to carry out a systematic repair of the trenches. In the Bienvillers sector however, "A" frames and trench grids by the thousand were being sent up, and in addition to the work of battalions actually in the line, work on the main Communication Trenches was carried on by Royal Engineer Companies and labour battalions. Lulu Lane and Chiswick Road, together with countless other smaller Communication Trenches were revetted and trench gridded in a thoroughly workmanlike manner, and in the wettest days of winter, when other trenches were quagmires, ration parties and visiting "Staffs" could walk up to the front line without getting more than the soles of their boots wet. The trench grids were lifted two or three feet above the floor of the trench, and the water thus remained underneath the grids (see diagram). Only direct hits on the trenches by High Explosives could destroy the draining system, or disturb quick access to the front line. Lulu Lane was probably the best piece of trench revetting the Battalion ever saw. There were one or two cases of broken legs when some of the laths in the trench grids were missing, and men slipped through the grid at night; but instead of ration parties taking over three hours to walk the two kilometres from Hannescamp to the front line (as was the case in the Ypres Salient), rations could be taken up in twenty-five minutes. Of course the whole trench system was not revetted, and the front line in places like Brushwood Drive and Durham Street was two and three feet deep in water during November. But Bienvillers was the first sector in which the Battalion saw scientific revetting carried out on a comprehensive scale.

In this sector there was also a well-organized system of cooking, which tremendously revived men's spirits. The use of hot food containers for the first time gave every man a hot meal in the trenches, and hot tea at midnight. The kitchen was built in the side of a sunken road on the eastern outskirts of Hannescamps, and the food containers were carried up quickly by men of the reserve company. Thus food was practically as good as in reserve billets. Battalion Head Quarters was a few hundred yards away from the cook-house. It was a very cosy place, dug into the bank of the Hannescamps—Fonquevillers Road. The walls were lined with mirrors and the dugout furnished with red plush. It was approached by a glass porch. A 4·2 would have made short work of the whole affair, but fortunately the enemy did not know it was there.

The outstanding event in this period was the German attack on November 23rd on the extreme left, near Kendal Street and Lulu Lane, —one of those terrible convulsions always liable to happen in the quietest trench sectors, and which often surpass big engagements in local intensity and destructiveness.

No Man's Land near Lulu Lane and Kendal Street was flat, and narrowed down to a width of about 150 yards. Our wire was good, but had to be constantly repaired as the result of enemy trench mortar fire. An advanced Battalion Observation Post had been built near Kendal Street Sap, as it was realized that this was the most important position on the Battalion front, and gave the best view of the enemy defences south of Monchy. For a week before November 23rd this part of the line had been heavily shelled, and the observers had reported that the enemy appeared to be registering several new trench mortar positions. Reports had also been sent in to the effect that there was

TRENCH WARFARE

unusual enemy activity in the trenches opposite Kendal Street : fresh earth thrown up : blasting heard as though concrete Machine Gun or Trench Mortar emplacements were being prepared : and at night increased traffic on the light railway immediately behind the enemy front line. Both Battalion and Brigade Head Quarters were expecting an attack, and Divisional Artillery was asked to shell the sunken road south of Monchy, which seemed to be the centre of the enemy activity. Unfortunately the Corps Heavy Artillery could not also be prevailed on to bombard the enemy positions, and thus his preparations for attack were carried on without serious difficulty. The Corps " Heavies " were notoriously " difficult to move," and in obedience to the Higher Powers, they continued to shell Ayette and Achiet-le-Petit, several miles behind the line, whilst the enemy continued to concentrate his " travelling circus " of field guns and trench mortars in the sunken road. At 5-5 a.m. on Nov. 23rd the show began, and the row was certainly heard at Corps Head Quarters eleven miles away. An avalanche of Trench Mortars and High Explosives of every calibre ploughed our lines from Lulu Lane to Hull Street and as far back as Landleague Avenue, till the wire was destroyed, our trenches had disappeared, and practically the whole garrison of this small salient was blown up and buried as though in the crater of a volcano. It is doubtful if anyone in the Brigade can remember a bombardment which, on a small scale, was so thoroughly destructive. The bombardment ceased at 5-40 a.m. and by 5-55 a.m. everything was quiet, apart from a few shells on back areas. The convulsion passed as quickly as it came, leaving a wreckage rather like that of the Leipzig Redoubt after a fortnight's bombardment ! An enemy raiding party entered our lines near Kendal Sap, but as the garrison had disappeared, neither side obtained any prisoners. A number of German wire-cutters were found in the remains of our wire, and also several stick bombs—evidently thrown hurriedly into our front line with the fuses still in the safety position. Apart from one or two men, who by some miracle had escaped with wounds only, there was no one left who could tell what actually happened in the front line. The enemy had simply been able to report the effect of their bombardment, and had withdrawn quickly, not one of our men having seen a single German during the forty minutes the affair lasted.

The 49th Division was relieved a week later by the 46th Division, the 1/6th Battalion being relieved in the line by the 4th Battalion Leicester Regt. After a night's halt at Pas, a charming country town six miles east of Doullens, the Battalion reached Le Souich, remaining there till January 6th, 1917. The billets on the whole were poor and very crowded, as the 1/8th Battalion and Brigade Head Quarters were also billeted in the village. The 1/5th and 1/7th Battalions were in Bouquemaison, a larger and more straggling village. The weather was extremely cold : the barns in a dilapidated condition : and the only method of passing time tolerably was in hard work and much exercise. The first was provided by wood-cutting parties in Lucheux Forest : the second by furious games of football in a muddy field south of the village. The chief games were inter-Brigade ones, in which the 1/6th Battalion was successful, and beat the 1/5th Battalion by eight goals to nil, and the 1/8th Battalion by three goals to one. The Battalion training ground was between Bouquemaison and Lucheux near the Bois de Robermont, and there were rifle ranges in the hill side south of the wood. The river Grouches ran down the Grouches-Lucheux-Humbercourt valley, and was a favourite scene for field operations and patrol exercises. The scenery was as charming as any part of Picardy, and in the valley near Humbercourt the war seemed hundreds of miles away. Doullens was within two hours' walk of Le Souich, and for the first time since the Battalion left Vignacourt (where they could visit Amiens), our men were able to pass a few hours in a fairly large town with all the advantages of civilization, *viz.*, the latest papers, magazines, La Vie Parisienne, etc. : new gramophone records : re-fills for electric torches : shampoos : patisserie in a score of little tea-shops : lunch at the Trois Fils D'Aymon : and the privilege of chaffing French girls behind the counter—girls who seemed nearer the conventional French type than the over-worked women who toiled all hours in filthy farms a few kilometres behind the line. These few and rare visits to such towns as Doullens, Amiens, Dunkerque, St. Omer, are amongst the most precious memories of the war. The men were able to stroll, and not " march " or " proceed." The moment the last sign of Le Souich or the billeting village was left behind, everyone breathed an exhilarating atmosphere of liberty and excitement, a mixture of the feelings of a schoolboy escaped from school, a convict leaving his prison and an explorer discovering a new world.

Before the Battalion left Le Souich, an event happened which to the original officers and men who came out with the Battalion seemed nothing short of a calamity. Lieut.-Col. H. O. Wade, D.S.O., relinquished his command of the Battalion. He was the last to leave the Brigade of the original Territorial Colonels who brought their battalions to France in April, 1915. Of the eight officers who at one time or another commanded the Battalion in France Col. Wade was easily the longest in that position, being in command from April, 1915, to January, 1917, with the exception of ten weeks interval during the battle of the

Somme. He had also borne the burden of the months of preparation in England in 1914 and 1915. Tall, athletic, an excellent horseman, he combined the sportsman's fearlessness and love of fair play, with the reserved non-committal attitude of the lawyer. He received the respect of everyone who served under him, and he deserved it. The Battalion was fortunate in having commanders who maintained Col. Wade's very high standard, but in some cases, not being original members of the Battalion, they could hardly be expected to realize how much of their own success was due to his influence and training of the Battalion during the first two years of the war. Major Wistance of the 1/5th Battalion South Staffordshire Regt. succeeded Col. Wade in command of the Battalion. Christmas was celebrated with the usual uproarious festivities. Many pigs were slain: many hundreds of bottles of champagne drunk : the village estaminets reaped a harvest which made every farmer in the district jealous : and every Company Officers' Mess made such huge levies for the feasts of the season that few subalterns in Le Souich had not to mortgage some at least of the three January instalments of 125 francs which parsimonious Mr. Cox allowed them to draw on account of their Army Pay.

On January 2nd, 1917, Brigade Orders were sent round to battalions instructing them to prepare for a move on the 7th inst. into the line immediately south of Arras, then being held by the 21st Brigade of the 30th Division. Thus after a rest of exactly one month, the Battalion moved again into the line.

When the 146th Infantry Brigade first took over the sector opposite Ransart, the dispositions were as follows :—The 1/7th and 1/5th Battalions occupied the front line from the Bellacourt-Ransart Road to " Renfrew Road," about three kilometres further south. The 1/6th Battalion was in Brigade Reserve in billets at Bailleulval, and the 1/8th Battalion in Divisional Reserve in billets at Bailleulmont, pronounced popularly " Ballyoolamon." The reserve billets were notable for their wire-beds—a great boon. During the five weeks the Brigade remained in this sector battalion reliefs were carried out every four days with unfailing regularity. The line was fairly quiet : there were heavy falls of snow and considerable frost, the weather thus being too bad for any operations on a big scale.

The dispositions of battalions mentioned above were rather peculiar owing to the nature of the ground. Between the two front line and the two reserve battalions there was a distance of three kilometres without any occupied defences. The two front battalions occupied a line a few hundred yards east of and parallel to the Berles-Bellacourt Road, called popularly " Ridge Road," as it ran on the top of a crest.

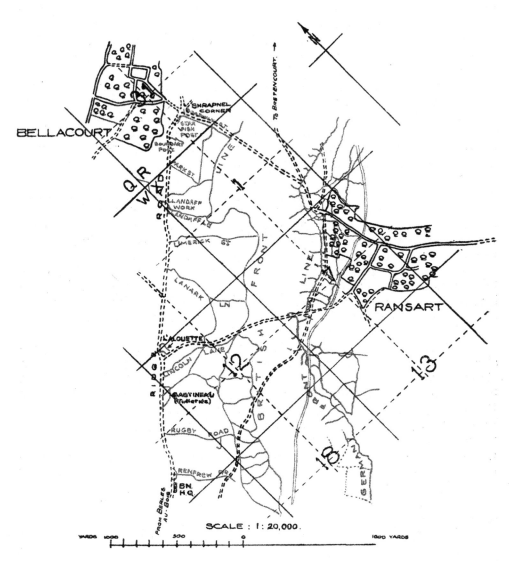

No. 9 Map. Trenches opposite Ransart, 1917.

TRENCH WARFARE

Between our line and the German trenches there was a fairly deep depression, and the enemy support line was half-way up the eastern slope of the valley. A long line of trees on the Ransart-Monchy road stretched across the horizon opposite our line. Behind our line the configuration of the ground was similar, ridges running S.W. and N.E. parallel to the front, and affording us excellent defensive positions in case of attack. The two reserve battalions were thus able to rest in comparative peace and quietness, with one or two series of strongly wired and entrenched positions on successive ridges between themselves and the line. Cross-country tracks from Bailleulmont and Bailleulval led to Gastineau, L'Alouette, and Shrapnel Corner, three well-known points on the Ridge Road, about 400 yards behind our front line. The gaunt red-brick gable-ends of the ruined Tilery called Gastineau were the most prominent landmarks on the whole front. When the Brigade first took over the sector the Ridge Road had not been shelled, and a hot canteen was installed in the Gastineau buildings, and became a rendezvous for every kind of unit and ration party on the brigade front. L'Alouette, a ruined estaminet about 500 yards further north, was used as a store and drying place for gumboots, and was a minor centre of activity. Then suddenly the enemy opened out rapid fire with 5·9's on Gastineau, and peppered L'Alouette with high explosive and shrapnel, causing several casualties and great commotion. Up to this time men had considered themselves entitled to lounge about the Ridge Road very much as they liked, though only 500 yards behind the front line : but the enemy shelling was repeated at all hours of day and night, till Gastineau and L'Alouette became the least popular places in the sector.

In no other sector since Fleurbaix in 1915 was the Transport able to bring rations so near to the front line as opposite Ransart. Every night the Battalion was in the line the Transport brought the rations up to Ridge Road, and although there was fairly often a certain amount of shelling and machine gun fire, there were very few casualties, and the work of the Transport was very much appreciated by every man in the Battalion.

The trench system opposite Ransart was extremely simple and easy to understand. The front line ran practically parallel to the Ridge Road along the whole front, and the communication trenches were never more than 600 yards long. There were no cases of lost rations or orderlies. The worst feature of the sector was the awful state of the trenches. The revetments had been badly constructed and in some places had bulged in during the winter rains, and completely blocked the trench. In other places the trenches had become a great mass of liquid mud, of a peculiarly adhesive and treacherous kind. It was almost impossible to move along a trench which was more than one foot deep in mud, and if a man made a false step he was often in serious difficulties and needed the assistance of two or three others before he could be extricated. The Divisional Commander (Major-General E. M. Perceval) was once bogged in Limerick Lane for over half-an-hour, in spite of the efforts of five or six people to rescue him. The men stood the conditions very well, chiefly owing to a plentiful supply of gumboots, elaborate anti-trench-feet precautions, fairly good dugout accommodation, and hot food brought up in food containers. A ruined house near Bn. H.Q. was turned into an inspection and " drying room " for socks, etc. and incipient cases of " trench feet " were there promptly treated by our Medical Officer, Capt. H. E. Robinson.

In February an exceptionally hard frost set in, and completely changed conditions on the whole sector. The water in the trenches froze into solid sheets of ice, and the liquid mud hardened into a jagged broken mass of earth with the consistency of iron. Snow froze on the trench grids till they became so slippery that it was almost impossible to walk on them without wearing sandbags tied over the boots. Patrols went out over No Man's Land wearing white cloaks, and during the long nights many men on " sentry go " on the firestep thought they might very possibly freeze to death before " stand to " in the morning. One day Lieut.-General Sir F. I. Maxse, our Corps Commander (XVIII. Corps, IIIrd Army), visited the sector with several other officers of his staff. One of them, a Royal Engineer Officer of high rank, could not believe that the infantrymen passed the night on the trench fire-step, almost without shelter. " But they *must* freeze to death ! " he said. It was only after talking to several sentries that he began to realize something of what was, after all, only a minor horror of trench warfare. Most men preferred frost to the misery of mud and rain.

Yet the misery of this frost period was very great. It is easy to under-estimate the terrible effect of keen and prolonged frost on men living in trenches such as those opposite Ransart. If the men had been able every four days on relief to go back to luxurious billets in Bailleulmont with the certainty of good fires and excellent food, the hardships of the intense frost during the 1917 winter would have been comparatively easy to bear. But reserve billets were not luxurious, and men who slept on wire beds in draughty barns had few chances of being really " warm " ! The only regular sensation of heat was given by the rum ration after " stand to " every morning ! Even if for a few hours both day and night men had been able to shelter in warm dugouts in the trenches, the privations would have been more easily endured. But dugout accommodation was limited to a few, and for most of the men the nights were spent on the firestep. The result was that the men's vitality was undermined. Exposure which to a normal healthy man in England would have been endurable, proved nearly fatal to scores of half-starved men in the Ransart trenches. Their limbs were in a chronic state of numbness, and their hands and feet were terribly swollen. Sections were put through regular physical drill and bayonet fighting, but these exercises were frequently real agony to some of the men. A numbness also came over the mind as well as the body. Only officers living in front line conditions could estimate what it was possible for the men to perform. It was easy for energetic people from Head Quarter formations, who visited the line after a good night's sleep in a warm house miles behind the line, to enjoy the bracing atmosphere of the trenches and criticise the small amount of work done by front line units. But if they themselves had lived in the same conditions for days and weeks they would have probably been equally listless and their vitality equally low. The effect of intense frost was similar in many ways to that of prolonged shelling. Both reduced men's energy and power of resistance to an incredible extent. Under prolonged shelling the bravest men often lost for a time control of their nerves, or used up reserves of strength, and only in rare cases were capable of supreme effort and heroism. Intense cold had a similar numbing, narcotic effect upon mind and body. Many a sentry on the firestep during those bitter nights opposite Ransart, when the thermometer registered twenty-eight degrees of frost and when the biting north easterly wind blew the sleet into his face, was almost as senseless and incapable as the frozen ground around him.

Working parties during this frost period were impracticable. Shovels were useless, and every blow of a pick on the iron ground could be heard by the enemy in his trenches. Moreover, shells bursting on such ground used to detonate magnificently, and were much more dangerous than when they buried themselves harmlessly in soft Flanders mud. The tracks across country from Bailleulmont to the trenches were simply long sheets of ice, and craved very wary walking. The nights were wonderfully clear and bright, whether the moon was out or not : and men going to the line by night could see the ruins of Gastineau several kilometres away, black against the snow-covered ground. To those permanently in reserve billets behind the line, the weather seemed glorious. What did it matter if before you began to boil an egg it was necessary to thaw it for ten minutes over the fire, or if your bath-water in the morning froze, and your sponge became a solid piece of ice ? It was healthy weather to healthy people, however merciless to all others !

During this period in the XVIIIth Corps great emphasis was laid on the importance of every man knowing exactly to which section and platoon he belonged, together with the number of his sentry or Lewis Gun Post. The moment the red tabs of a Staff Officer showed round the traverse the sentry broke out into a series of rapid ejaculations, " No. 3 Section," No. 2 Platoon, or " No. 4 Lewis Gun Post," etc., etc., and his description was still being continued by the time the said Staff Officer had passed the next traverse. Another form of what many people disparagingly called " eyewash " was the fixing against the trench wall at intervals along the front of pretty pictures of the enemy lines. These panoramas gave the names of prominent landmarks which could be seen from our trenches, and certainly did something to relieve the monotony of the front line trench.

Two of the outstanding events in the Ransart sector were the raid by the 1/8th Battalion West Yorkshire Regt. on a German Sap near Ransart, and a patrol on February 4th by the 1/6th Battalion Scouts. The raid was one of the first serious efforts at " winkling " undertaken by the Brigade, and was typical of many carried out later in the Laventie sector. The 1/6th Battalion spent much time and preparation for a similar raid, which would have been carried out if they had remained longer in the Ransart sector, and therefore some description of the 1/8th Battalion raid may be useful. The saps which the Germans had run out from their front line had been the object of much patrolling and reconnoitring by all the battalions in the Brigade. The information obtained as the result of these patrols was carefully handed over on relief by every battalion. Most of the enemy saps were found to be occupied at night, and they were all protected by very strong belts of wire, which surrounded the sap head, and ran along both sides of the sap up to the German front line wire. It was thus almost impossible to cut off the enemy garrison at the sap head. The 1/8th Battalion raiding party consisted of two officers and eighteen other ranks, who had been given extra rations and a rest out of the trenches. They had carefully practised the raid over ground which had been specially taped to represent the enemy sap. Every other man in the raiding party was given an aeroplane photo showing the sap, the position of the wire entanglements, the chalk thrown up during the construction of the enemy dugout, and above all, the thin white track through the wire used by the enemy when they left the sap head on patrol. Our raiding party intended to enter the sap by this narrow track through the enemy wire. In case the track was not found owing to the darkness, or any other cause, the raiding party took with them a " bangalore torpedo," or a charge of gun cotton in a long iron tube, which was to be placed under the wire and then exploded, clearing a path for the raiding party. In spite of these elaborate precautions, and a strong artillery barrage on the enemy front line near the sap, the raid was not a success. In the darkness and confusion of the attack, it was found impossible to find the narrow path through the wire to the sap head, and the bangalore torpedo did not penetrate deeply enough through the wire. The raiders thus spent several all important minutes in searching for a break through the enemy wire, and by the time our barrage lifted on to the enemy front line, the Germans in the sap head were on the alert, and firing their machine gun on to our raiding party. One month later, when the enemy evacuated his positions at Ransart, and retired to the Hindenburg Line, some of our men were able to walk across " No Man's Land," and inspect the enemy fortifications which they had gazed at and patrolled some weeks previously. They found ample excuse for the failure of the 1/8th Battalion raiding party on February 11th. There were three belts of wire round the sap which had been raided, each ten to eighteen yards deep, and the track through the wire, which showed clearly enough on the aeroplane photograph, was a mazy winding path a foot wide, which would have been difficult to use at leisure and in day time. The enemy trenches were deep and well constructed, with good dugouts and machine gun emplacements. Fortunately they had been given up, without assault, as a result of our advances in the closing battles of the Somme.

The 1/6th Battalion patrols were very active during this period, and there were several exciting encounters, not so much between patrols in No Man's Land as between our own patrols and fixed enemy posts. The Germans were on the defensive, and the initiative in No Man's Land belonged to us. Our best patrol leader throughout this period was Lance-Cpl. (after Corpl.) Silverwood, D.C.M., M.M. At 3-15 a.m. one winter's morning, in charge of a patrol of two other N. C. O.'s and three men, he proceeded down the slope of the L'Alouette-Ransart Road till within eighty yards of the enemy wire, where he established a listening post. The object of the patrol was the exact location of a strong enemy sentry post which our Brigadier wished the Battalion to raid. Silverwood and another scout, Ledgard, moved forward slowly to within twenty yards of the wire immediately in front of the enemy post. Unfortunately the enemy sentry was on the *qui vive*, and challenged suddenly, opening fire almost immediately with a machine gun on to our two scouts. Lance-Cpl. Ledgard was severely wounded. Silverwood went back to the remainder of his patrol, ordered them to return to our lines, as their "job was finished," and promptly turned himself towards the enemy. He found Ledgard still living. With great coolness Silverwood took off his comrade's equipment, and although only a few yards from the enemy wire, tried to bandage the wounds, and then dragged and carried Ledgard back to our lines. Enemy machine guns on right and left opened fire across No Man's Land during the whole episode, and wounded two of the four men whom Silverwood had ordered back to our line : Ledgard also was hit again two or three times, and died the following day. Silverwood was recommended for a bar to his D. C. M., but for some reason or other only received an M. M., for a deed which all those who knew the conditions realized was quite unique for its cool indifference to almost certain death, and which was performed under circumstances least likely to rouse excitement. The next night a party went out to try and find Ledgard's equipment, but the enemy had already taken it away, as the equipment had been left practically on their own parapet.

One or two minor events in this period may be mentioned. A German machine gunner in Ransart was in the habit of playing " tunes " in firing his machine gun, usually about midnight, and he kept up one particular rhythm for several nights in succession. He little knew what speculation his musical prowess called forth. As it happened, in August 1916, a German machine gunner had played exactly the same tune on his instrument in the trenches north of the Leipzig Salient, near Thiepval, and some Sherlock Holmes on our " Corps Intelligence " Staff tried to use the incident to prove that the 2nd Guard Reserve Division which had been in the Thiepval sector in August 1916, was opposite us in Ransart in February 1917. The theory seemed plausible, but unfortunately was proved to be false only a few days later.

In order to help in the identification of enemy regiments opposite the Division, an enthusiastic Staff Officer on Divisional Head Quarters obtained a very good telescope with a three-inch lens, and fixed it in an Observation Post, specially erected at the top of Lincoln Lane. The object was by the aid of a powerful telescope to distinguish the numerals on the shoulder straps of the enemy, or the colour of their forage cap bands, and thus identify the unit. But the telescope was unpopular with the Infantry in the line. In the first place, the construction of the Observation Post, and the constant succession of officers and orderlies near the place, attracted a certain amount of attention from enemy field guns, and Lincoln Lane at the best of times was the most unpleasant part of the Battalion front. The telescope was about the size and length of a machine gun, and possibly the sun in the east caught the lens at one time or another, and gave away to the enemy the position of the Observation Post. In any case Lincoln Lane began to be heavily shelled, and the Observation Post was blown in, although the telescope was rescued, and did good service in later days.

The last fortnight in the sector opposite Ransart was made more interesting than usual to most of the officers and men of the Battalion by the fact that the 2/2nd Battalion London Regt. was attached to the 1/6th Battalion for instruction, each of our companies receiving one platoon of the London Regiment. Our men enjoyed the privilege of initiating troops fresh from England into the mysteries of trench warfare. Other units of the 58th were attached to other battalions of the 49th Division. In order not to overcrowd the front line positions a 146 Inf. Brigade Composite Battalion, under Major Oddie of the 1/5th Bn. was formed by taking one platoon from each company in the Brigade. This composite Battalion marched to Ivergny, where they were attached to the 173rd Infantry Brigade of the 58th Division. On February 14th, the 58th relieved the 49th Division in the line, and the 49th Division moved back to the Le Souich area. The 1/6th Battalion after a few days in Humbercamp marched to Le Souich and occupied almost the same billets as in December, 1916. The stay in Le Souich was very brief. On February 24th, the Battalion began the long march north to the First Army Area. The weather was fine. The route lay through the Frévent, St. Pol, Pernes areas, on good roads, far from the traffic of the line, and surrounded by some of the pleasantest scenery in the north of France. On the whole the billets were good. The inhabitants in such quiet country villages as Bonnières, Siracourt, Floringhem, St. Floris, where the Battalion stayed overnight, had not often received English troops, and their welcome was sincere, and in many cases, cordial. The men marched splendidly, even on the fourth consecutive day from Floringhem to St. Floris, a march of about sixteen miles. Thus the Battalion left behind them the villages of Picardy and the Somme, never to return. The battlefields of the future, so far as the 49th Division was concerned, were to be north and east of Arras, at Nieuport, Passchendaele, Cambrai and Valenciennes.

CHAPTER VIII.

THE SCIENCE OF TRENCH WARFARE, MARCH–JULY, 1917.

WHEN the Battalion took over the line at Fauquissart on March 1st, 1917, trench warfare had become a matter of dull routine. One of the men, in April 1915, had remarked with surprise that the Border Regiment took their reliefs " as indifferently as woolcombers on the night shift at Isaac Holden's." Practically all our men had now reached the same stage of stolid indifference as the men of the Border Regiment in 1915. During the five months which had elapsed since the Battalion left Thiepval they had held the line in sectors opposite Gommecourt, Monchy-au-Bois and Ransart. They had thus gained considerable experience in trench warfare. Casualties, though constant, had not been so severe as to destroy continuity within the Battalion. After a review of his Brigade on February 23rd, 1917, Brigadier General Goring Jones expressed his certainty that his Battalions " would give a good account of themselves in the sector to which they were going." He was not mistaken. Soldiering had became a trade. The men had served their apprenticeship, and become proficient. Even in such a sector as Fauquissart, probably the quietest on the British front, there were enough excitements in a week to satisfy a normal man for the whole of his natural life. Yet these excitements were part of the routine, and men were accustomed to them. The prevailing atmosphere was one of boredom. As relief followed relief, and the dull iteration of the uncertainties of trench warfare numbed the sensation of the men, this spirit of boredom increased till it became almost intolerable. With some people foul language was a symptom of the malady ; with others, a craving for whisky or rum ; with many, the disease took the form of an utter incapacity to read or think. But everybody, at one time or another, muttered with extraordinary intensity, " Hell ! what a life ! "

Proficiency in trench warfare was not easily acquired. It was the boast of some battalions that they were " fighting " and not " trench holding " units : the inference being that " crack " battalions were allotted superior tasks to those of holding trench lines in comparatively stationary sectors of the front. The fact is that in both cases specialized training and preparation were equally necessary for success. In 1917 our Staff had realized that no battalion could be expected to advance many kilometres unless the " trench " tradition had been destroyed by a period of rest behind the line and continual manœuvres under " open warfare " conditions. For successful attack it was necessary to train men to think in kilometres, not in traverses. On the other hand, to hold trench positions with the minimum of exhaustion and casualties and at the same time inflict the maximum penalty upon the enemy, demanded equally specialized training and experience. At no time in the history of the 1/6th Battalion was this two-fold object of trench warfare so well fulfilled as in the four months spent near Fauquissart in 1917.

In the first place let us deal with the methods of holding the line so as to avoid unnecessary exhaustion and casualties. During most of this period, the Battalion occupied the left subsector, from Rue Masselot to New Bond Street—a frontage of 2400 yards. In 1915 a sector of this length would have been held by three battalions at full strength, with every man in the front line. In 1917 the frontage was held by three companies, with one company in reserve. Moreover behind the battalion in the line, there was a support battalion with Head Quarters at Red House and with two companies in Laventie (less one platoon at " Lonely Post "), and the remaining two companies in support positions in posts such as Wangerie, Hougoumont, Masselot, Dead End and Picantin. There was also another battalion in Brigade Reserve in Laventie. Thus the front line was thinly held, being treated as an outpost line. An enormous amount of labour was spent on const ucting strong points from 500 to 1,500 yards behind the front line, and the accompanying map (Map No. 10) shows a network of positions, with wire entanglements so arranged as to lead the attacking enemy into the zone of machine gun fire from cleverly hidden concrete emplacements. Given a resolute garrison, thoroughly trained in occupying prepared positions in case of attack, the Fauquissart sector when the 146th Infantry Brigade left it in July 1917 should have proved almost impregnable. Unfortunately during the German attack of April 1918 the 2nd Portuguese Division was holding the line, and full advantage of the positions so carefully prepared in 1917 was not taken.

The general aspect of the front line was just the same as in 1915. The breastworks and shelters were equally flimsy and unsubstantial, and could easily have been blown to pieces by a serious bombardment. The front line wire was good, and to a limited extent the dykes in No Man's Land and the " borrow pits " immediately in front of the fire trench, from which the material for the breastworks had been taken,

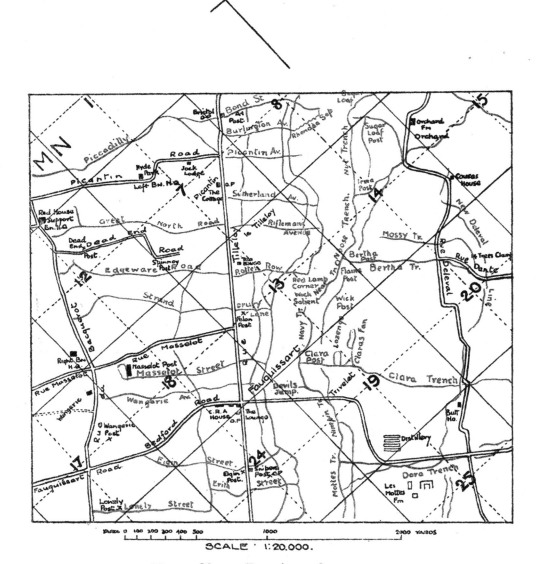

No. 10 Map. Fauquissart Sector, 1917.

were obstacles to an enemy attack. But the real defences of the sector lay in support and reserve positions behind the front line. Thanks chiefly to this method of holding the line, there were several days on which the Battalion suffered no casualties in spite of fairly frequent shelling.

Another point worth emphasizing is the elaborate precautions taken to avoid movement behind our lines being seen by the enemy. The bad tradition that it was good for morale to move about freely and despise enemy observation, was thoroughly discredited. Sentries stationed along the Tilleloy Road were pleased to have the opportunity of " putting the wind up " artillery and staff officers who wandered about in exposed positions and who rather admired their own reckless-ness. These people often escaped without casualties, but those who followed them received the full burst of enemy shelling. The careful use of camouflage on roads and trenches, and the avoidance of making tracks across country which could be seen in aeroplane photographs, were other methods in the technique of trench warfare. These efforts to deceive the enemy went so far as the construction across dykes and roads of bridges which were never intended to be used, but simply to attract enemy shelling. Dummy gun positions were also erected, but seem to have been usually ignored by the enemy.

During 1917 enormous developments took place in the use of codes and other Signal arrangements to prevent the enemy from understanding our telephone messages, and overhearing telephone conversations. Towards the close of the battle of the Somme in 1916, the importance of using Code terms for units was being realized by all ranks. The enemy had obtained far too much valuable information from his " listening sets " as to the dispositions of our units, and times of attack, etc. For some weeks the battalions in the Brigade were repre-sented by series of letters such as —I. K. (1/5th Battalion), I. J. (1/6th Battalion), I. M. (1/7th Battalion), I. G. (1/8th Battalion), I. L. (146th Brigade Machine Gun Coy.), I. P. (146th Brigade Trench Mortar Coy.), I. F. (146th Brigade Head Quarters). By this method, however, the enemy could easily infer with the aid of his " listening sets," when a relief had taken place owing to the changes in the code letters. Where-upon a code name was given to each subsector and the support and reserve positions, and these names were taken over by any battalion which entered the sector : and the whole system of names was changed fre-quently. Thus the right subsector of the Zillebeke sector in 1918 was called E Y 12, the left subsector E K 2 : the reserve position E Y 11 and so on. This system of " position calls " was applied to all parts of the stationary trench lines on the British front during 1918. In addition, all units in the Division during 1917 were given code names, such as Vacancy (49th Division Head Quarters), Valour, Vigilant, Valet, Victory, etc. These names gave place in 1918 to combinations of four letters, which were not so easy to remember, and which were frequently changed, such as Lemu, Doti, Dolu, Dohu, Higo, etc. The most trying and complicated development in the use of Codes came with the invention of the B. A. B. Code. Though as near being completely safe as a code used by several hundred formations can be, the " B. A. B." was a source of endless anxiety. The code was contained in a small yellow book of about fifty pages, very easily lost, and many adjutants had nightmare over it, as the Colonel was made to feel that the reputation of his battalion depended on its safe-keeping. The book consisted of hundreds of phrases, each represented by groups of figures, such as " Enemy about to attack "—4679, 8654, which could easily be mistaken for " Extra rum ration required "—4677, 8652. Every few days a new correction number was issued from " Intelligence General Head Quarters," which further complicated the B.A.B. Code. The ordinary field ciphers and Playfair Codes were also extensively used in 1917 and 1918, and untold hours were spent in trying to decipher impossible messages. At 3 a.m. in the morning some luckless adjutant would be roused by an orderly with an A. F. 2121 from a Company Head Quarters, with some such message as Mkeopr Ijmij, Ebfbn, Onalg, Hzdmy. After an hour and a half of painful effort, and with the aid of his Intelligence Officer, he would find out towards " stand to " that the message merely informed him " Officer Commanding B Company has nothing to report." Or the Transport Officer, on returning to his " bivvy " at 4 a.m. after a wild night taking up rations to his battalion in the front line, would find a message awaiting him, written in the all too familiar five letter groups of the Playfair code. The Transport Officer had probably forgotten or mislaid the key word of the day. After trying half a dozen key words in vain, he would return it to Battalion Head Quarters by orderly, with a polite request that it should be sent " in clear." Result—the message comes back to him translated. " Please send up to-night two large bottles Perrier, two tins sausage, one back collar stud." Whereupon the Transport Officer " goes off the deep end," and is unapproachable for an hour or two. If you had a bitter enemy in another company, and an hour's leisure, the approved plan was for you to sit down and write a long invitation to him in code to spend an evening with you out of the line : giving the signaller instructions to send it off in the middle of the night. But it was necessary to choose carefully the victim for this kind of practical joke, or the results were not pleasing.

In order to insure that no secrets were given away by incautious conversations on the telephone, an elaborate system of "listening sets" was set up along the whole British front, for the sole purpose of over-hearing and noting down any delinquencies on the part of everybody from Company signallers to Brigadier Generals who were in the "danger zone," and whose conversation could be picked up by the enemy listening sets. Naturally most of the above precautions were too elaborate for use in a battle sector, but they saved units from those enemy bombardments which used to coincide so frequently and so suspiciously with our reliefs, and also to some extent from the shelling of our Head Quarters positions, which had been too often in the past given away by careless telephone operators and indiscreet messages.

In quiet sectors the telephone communications between Company and Battalion Head Quarters were exceedingly good and reliable. Communications between units in a quiet trench sector were almost as secure as between city offices in England. Along the sides of some of the main communication trenches there was often a mass of telephone wires which would have done credit to a Fleet Street terminal. Many of these were artillery wires, or were obsolete or superfluous, and when a shell blew up wires and trench—as of course occasionally happened—the confusion of wires seemed past remedy. But the Signal Section was one of the most dependable units in the Battalion, and lines on such occasions were not often "dis" for more than a few minutes. The signallers were often cursed, however, for leaving tele-phone wires insecurely attached to the trench side, thus causing visiting generals, orderlies and men on ration fatigues to fall down and nearly break their necks. Most trench inhabitants will also remember times when they have been almost decapitated by a telephone wire which had been run across a trench just low enough to catch a short man on the forehead and a long man under the chin.

It was found eventually that far too much reliance was being placed upon the telephone, which after all was a most uncertain instrument under active fighting conditions. Hence frequent "Silent Days" were instituted, when the use of the telephone was forbidden, and battalions were compelled to employ all other means of communication, such as wireless, Lucas-lamps, power buzzers, pigeons, messenger dogs and even semaphore. On the whole the dogs were reliable and quick, and considerable use was made of them by the Battalion in the Ypres Salient in 1918. They had one serious fault—an ineradicable tendency to go "ratting," which sometimes resulted in their arriving an hour or two late at Battalion Head Quarters with a pleased expression on their faces, which did not come from a sense of duty quickly fulfilled. The number of rats near Ypres in 1918 was almost incredible! The pigeons were also useful. It was not always easy in a quiet sector to find sufficient messages for them worth sending back to Corps Head Quarters, and on many occasions they took back from the line such messages as " This pigeon has laid an egg. What shall we do about it ? "

The reader will have gathered that life in a calm sector such as Fauquissart cannot be compared in any respect with life in battle sectors such as those near Thiepval on the Somme. The difference could not be exaggerated. A good illustration of the two types of sector is given by the different method of " handing over " between companies during a battalion relief. In such a sector as the Leipzig Salient the " handing over " ceremony was of the briefest. The incoming company had probably been lost in the darkness amidst the debris of trenches, and arrived a few hours late. Shelling had been constant, and the temper of all ranks had become very frayed. Conversation between the relieving Company Commanders was usually very brief and not always bright or brotherly. " Where the hell have you been all this time ? " demands Officer Commanding outgoing Company of the incoming perspiring subaltern, who has informed him he is " the relief." " Heaven alone knows, ask your damned guide," says the latter, who has been wandering for hours with his platoons all over the front. Whereupon there is silence, apart from the shelling, and the noise of the men as they shuffle, cursing, into their positions. " Rotten line," says the subaltern. " Don't trouble to mention it," says Officer Commanding — Company, as bombing breaks out like a rash all over his company front. The Company Sergeant Major comes up with the message, " Relief Complete," whereupon Officer Commanding the relieved company adds " Think I'll be going....Bonne chance and best of luck !" Before he leaves the line, however, he adds grimly to the incoming Company Commander, " Mind you don't call on us for a blasted counter-attack. We've had enough of this line for a life time," and thereupon he cheerfully takes himself away. Apart from his " Bonne chance, best of luck," he has nothing to hand over, except a few hundred yards of ground which only human endurance and plenty of ammunition can hold.

Between this and " handing over " in stationary trench warfare such at Fauquissart there is a world of difference. Reliefs were carried out by daylight, and more easily than in any sector the Battalion occupied. Even when the Battalion was in reserve at Laventie, the distance to the line was only two miles, and the relief was begun after dinner and finished before tea. There is no comparison between relieving posts and Lewis Gun positions by daytime, and groping down narrow trenches for the same positions on a dark night. Moreover—lists of Trench Stores—bombs, S.A.A., rockets, maps, aeroplane photos, Klaxon horns, Verey lights, etc., were written on fairly clean paper, and were duly checked, and signed. Positions of dumps and dugouts were carefully explained : particulars of work done during the previous tour given : the state of wire, and the attitude of the enemy was a subject of detailed enquiry : and altogether the " handing over " had become quite an elaborate ceremony. There were many pitfalls for unwary Company and Platoon commanders. The outgoing unit could afford to be gaily indifferent as to the exact amount of S.A.A., bombs, and rifle grenades in the line, and unless the incoming unit knew its job thoroughly, and was very conscientious as to the position and number of boxes of ammunition, etc., there was the probability of a bad " strafe " next morning for the unfortunate Company Commander, when the Colonel or Brigadier made his round of inspection. Most trench systems were very complicated, and consisted of a labyrinth of disused communication and fire trenches, with sentry posts and dug-outs hidden in most unlikely corners. Woe to the Company Commander or Subaltern who was unable to explain his section of the line in detail, giving positions of his flanks and posts dugouts and bomb stores, etc., when his Colonel or Brigadier came round on a tour of inspection after " stand down " on the morning after relief !

It can easily be understood that in quiet sectors, such as Fauquissart, " paper " occupied a very important place, and in 1918 Battalion Head Quarters carried their own type-writers into the line, and made good use of them. The " Paper Merchant," otherwise an officer who retained a soft job by industriously writing " chits " all his days, became a fearful nuisance, especially on the staffs of higher formations. Appalling numbers of " soldiers " were really clerks, and even within fighting units officers spent hours over more or less frivolous and useless correspondence. The amount of paper which flowed into Battalion and Brigade Head Quarters was enormous, and a very ugly word was applied to most of it. Weekly " Work Reports " sent in by battalions to Brigade Head Quarters were often the result of great imagination and literary skill on the part of some adjutant or company commander, and bore little relation to the exact truth. But they filled many sheets of closely written foolscap, and looked very imposing. They were still further embellished by Brigade Head Quarters, till on paper, each battalion in the Brigade was credited with an amount of work in trenches and other positions which would have done honour to a dozen labour battalions. " Wire Reports " always looked well, as the state of our wire was given by different colours of pencil, according as to whether it was poor, fair, or strong, and the colour scheme looked pretty, especially when it was transferred to elaborate " Wire Defence Maps " at Corps Head Quarters. It is no exaggeration to say that these reports were often not even approximately true, but they satisfied Corps and Army Head Quarters and helped them in their pleasant convention that " all was well on the Western front." Paper was good currency. Many men gained their reputations as " soldiers " by clever and assiduous " pen-work." According to Lt. Alec. Johnston of " *Punch*," " there was once a very old-established Company Commander, who, having had to furnish the Brigade with lengthy reports on drainage, coke issue, sniperscopes, a wire-cutting patent, the health of his command, and a new anti-frostbite slush, and being asked, on the same day, to ' report on enemy's attitude ' sent in the following illuminating wire :—' Enemy's attitude hostile.' Anon came a brigade reply :—' Please amplify your report on enemy's attitude.' Whereupon the Company Commander amplified :— ' Enemy's attitude distinctly hostile.' This correspondence was then closed."

Battalion Head Quarters on the left subsector were at "Hyde Park," and consisted of a group of sandbagged elephant shelters pleasantly situated in an orchard. The dugouts were very comfortable, but the enemy had the place " taped," and although it was very rarely shelled, there was rather more than the usual sense of insecurity about the Head Quarters, as the dugouts were of the flimsiest description. Most of our casualties were caused by enemy machine gun bullets, which towards " stand to " in the evening made Picantin Road near Hyde Park extremely uncomfortable. Support Battalion Head Quarters was at " Red House," a two-storied red-roofed building within 1,600 yards of the front line, and untouched by a shell. The outside walls were pitted with machine gun bullets, but otherwise the house might have been near Boulogne. The walls of the mess room were decorated by some extremely well-drawn and witty charcoal sketches, illustrating types of soldiers and civilians with a finish and style equal to the best *Punch* cartoons. They were the pride and delight of scores of successive battalion messes, till an evil day in April 1918, when the house was gutted in the German advance. There were many rumours amongst the French population at Laventie as to why the Red House had remained untouched for two and a half years of war, but most of them were contradictory : the most popular rumour said that one of the Kaiser's sons had been well treated there by the owner in 1914, and had promised to spare the house from Hunnish " justice." The probable reason was that the house was hidden by trees from German observation, and that as the courtyard behind the house was of stone, and the front door opened almost directly on to the road, no tracks likely to give the house away as the centre of much movement could be seen on enemy aeroplane photographs. Near Red House there was a large farm called Harlech Castle, surrounded by a moat, which was very popular for bathing. Our second-in-command caused some amusement there one day by making a most magnificent dive—with his spectacles on. The right battalion Head Quarters at " Temple Bar " consisted of several camouflaged elephant shelters in the middle of a field. Shells rarely came near the place. The front line, apart from places such as Red Lamp Corner and near Bond Street, was quiet : and in the posts—Wangerie, Masselot, Houguemont, etc.—the men lived in dugouts, which, though small, were dry and warm.

There is little doubt that if the Division had decided to complete a rest cure in the Laventie sector, and had refrained from giving the enemy any sign of pugnacity, there would have been practically no casualties during the whole period. The British offensives of 1917 were in other sectors (Vimy-Arras, April 9th, and Messines, June 7th), and opposite us the enemy was on the defensive. But by offensive patrols, raids, and constant shelling of his reserve positions, we roused a certain amount of retaliation. The attachment of a Portuguese Division to the 49th Division in May also attracted enemy attention to the sector, which became more lively. For some months before the 49th Division had taken over the line there had been a tacit agreement between gunners on both sides that neither the town of Aubers nor Laventie was to be shelled. The Infantry in Laventie stood to gain by this arrangement, as there were many more troops there than Germans in Aubers : Laventie was also occupied by civilians, and accommodation in dugouts and cellars was very limited. About the end of June the enemy began to break this convention fairly frequently by shelling Laventie, probably in retaliation for our raids. After an advanced field battery near Red House and Dead End Post and one or two parts of the outskirts of the town had been heavily shelled, our Brigadier (Gen. Goring Jones), who took nothing " lying down," determined to strike back hard once and for all. A concentrated half hour's bombardment of Aubers was arranged, and guns of every calibre up to Corps 15 in. " Heavies " took part. All civilians in Laventie were ordered either to leave the town, or remain in their cellars, and the troops were moved out at dawn to the open country two or three miles away, as the enemy was expected to retaliate. The bombardment of Aubers was popular neither with civilians nor troops,

as everyone expected Laventie henceforth to become " impossible."
Our Artillery opened out at 6-30 a.m. and Aubers seemed to go up
in smoke. The half-hour passed. Everyone waited anxiously.
But the enemy did not fire a shell in retaliation. For the rest of the
period the Division remained in the sector there was no more shelling
of Laventie.

In dealing with developments in the technique of holding trenches,
the system of advanced Infantry Observation Posts should be mentioned. Infantry Commanders realized in 1917 that the development
of " barrage fire " deprived the front line sentry of one of his most
important functions. During the bombardment preliminary to an
attack it was impossible for the sentry either to observe what was happening in front or to send back information. In the majority of cases the
bombardment was so severe that the front line trenches and their garrison
were destroyed, and the enemy had reached our support or reserve
lines before any information could be sent back either to Battalion or
Brigade Head Quarters. In short, the front line sentry had become useful
simply for giving alarm in case of a gas attack, or watching for hostile
patrols in No Man's Land. Thus the duties of the sentry devolved
more and more upon the Battalion observers in concrete observation
posts a few hundred yards behind the front line. The observers were
connected with Battalion and Brigade Head Quarters by underground
telephones and occasionally by Lucas Lamps or " visual." There
were several such " Observation Posts " on the Tilleloy Road, which
had been constructed by Royal Engineers in ruined houses. After a time
the utmost importance was attached to these O.P.'s by Company and
Battalion Officers : a wide view of the enemy lines and No Man's Land
could be obtained from them : a log book was kept : and invariably
information could be got back from them to Head Quarters more
quickly than from the front line. The observation posts were often
the queerest and most uncomfortable places imaginable, and one
ran serious risk of concussion of the brain by striking one's
head against a concrete block in climbing the narrow stairs in the
darkness, or standing up incautiously near the loophole. There were
of course no outward signs that these ruined houses were used as
Observation Posts. The doorways gaped open, the windows were
innocent of frames, the roof was mostly gone, and the walls were often
more hole than wall. Very deftly had the R.E.'s concealed their work,
and the observers were equally keen that it should continue to escape
detection by the enemy. In some Observation Posts the battalion
observers had a " soft job " : in others such as the " Convent " or
" Tea House " Observation Posts, the enemy had located the loophole,

and sniped at it with whiz-bangs and 5·9's, and the observer's existence was sometimes uncomfortable.

There were many types of observers. Some were so imaginative that no reliance could be placed upon any report they made : frequently they deceived themselves, and were incapable of regarding anything critically or objectively. If, for instance, five Germans were seen repairing a trench, they probably reported that a platoon of the enemy had been observed fixing gas cylinders. Other observers could be relied upon to see nothing, and report nothing, unless the enemy began shelling their own Observation Post, when graphic details of the enemy shelling were sent in. Others again regarded their duties as undischarged unless at the close of the day they had filled their log books with such items as " four men seen carrying something heavy at N 26 d 6544 " or " one man seen ' chatting ' outside dugout in M 19 c 55, etc., etc." : such items being often pure shameless invention relieved occasionally by a sense of humour, and intended to impress the Scout Officer with a sense of the industry of his devoted band of observers. To find ideal observers, accurate, cool, conscientious, needed patience and judgment on the part of the Battalion Intelligence Officer, and only too often they were killed or wounded, and their place had to be taken by less experienced men.

The infantry observer not only became important as the sentry of his battalion, but was very necessary for the offensive part of trench warfare. Owing entirely to infantry observation, artillery fire was frequently brought to bear with excellent effect on places where enemy movement had been seen. The times of enemy reliefs were also ascertained by our observers, and systematic bombardments by artillery and machine guns were arranged on enemy tracks and roads behind his line during these reliefs. The method was simple. Through a gap in the enemy camouflage, all the movement in main communication trenches or on the Aubers-Fromelles Road could be seen, and a careful analysis made of the number of Germans who passed a certain point during every hour of daylight. Thus the observer quickly found whether the line was being held by increased numbers of troops, and occasionally he saw an enemy relief actually taking place. Such gaps served as a kind of barometer, and were invaluable. Instructions were given to the artillery not to fire on movement at such points. But the temptation to " strafe Germans " was often too great, and it was only realized slowly by both infantry and artillery that by observing the enemy carefully at a few selected points it was possible to put scores of Germans out of action, whereas the policy of firing at any and every movement seen would have only disturbed a few men, who would immediately have used other tracks, or repaired the gaps in their camouflage.

About five hundred yards behind the front line, where Rifleman's Avenue met the Tilleloy Road, there was a hollow " camouflage tree," cased inside with iron, and about twenty feet high. It was intended for use as an Observation Post and had a loophole near the top. It had been designed by an eminent Royal Academician employed at the Camouflage Works at Aire, and had been handed over, some months before the 49th Division arrived in the sector, to the Division then holding the line. The camouflage experts at Aire were very proud of it, and the tree must have cost several hundred pounds, and much labour in fixing. When the 1/6th Battalion took over the line the trench in which the tree stood was four feet deep in water, and any observer who desired to use it would have been drowned before he could have begun to crawl up the inside. It had been fixed so that an excellent view of our own front line could be obtained from it, but absolutely no part of the German trenches could be seen. And thus it remained, a monument of misguided effort. One of our subalterns went for a few days " course " to the Camouflage Works at Aire, and was surprised to hear the " Camouflage Tree at Fauquissart " spoken of as a " great success." He astonished and pained the camouflage experts by telling them the brutal truth. In true Army style they refused responsibility. They had handed " Alice " (the tree) to the Division : the Division to the Brigade : the Brigade to the Royal Engineers : and the Royal Engineers fixed it probably with no definite idea as to its use. Henceforth, everyone refused to have anything to do with it. Probably the tree is now being shown to American tourists as an essential property in scientific warfare.

More important than the Observation Posts was the work of the Reconnoitring and Fighting Patrols, which for over three months were active every night along the Brigade front, and established complete ascendancy over the enemy in No Man's Land. This work was not carried out only by the Battalion Scouts, but practically every man in the Battalion took his turn to go out on patrol. The situation was very peculiar. The enemy main line was the " New Deleval Line," which was about 1,500 yards behind the original front line. Several isolated posts, however, were held in his front line system, and after weeks of careful work these posts were located by our observers and patrols, and several efforts made to capture them. On one occasion, after failing for several nights to capture the garrison of an enemy post, some of our men carried out a 60-pound trench mortar shell across No Man's Land to the enemy parapet near the post. At " stand to " the next evening they fired at it with rifles and exploded it, completely wrecking the whole trench. Our observers noted some excitement in the enemy line : probably the garrison—if any were there—was puzzled with our invention of a " silent trench mortar ! " Every week our patrols encountered some of these posts, and inflicted casualties, but the good fortune to capture prisoners on these raids was reserved to one or two of the other Battalions in the Brigade. Our constant efforts at " winkling " these isolated posts alarmed the enemy, and he doubled his night garrisons, and took other precautions to avoid being surprised. One of the chief difficulties for our patrols in the Fauquissart sector was the network of dykes, many of them very deep, and too wide to jump. No Man's Land also was perfectly flat, and practically without cover. Thus in case the enemy were on the alert, and opened out on our patrols with machine gun and rifle fire at close quarters, it was almost impossible for our men to avoid casualties, or retire quickly. As the enemy never did any patrolling himself in No Man's Land in this sector, our risk of casualties was much g eater than his.

The following description of a patrol is typical of many scores in this sector :—

" *Composition of Patrol.* Two officers and thirty other ranks.

Object of Patrol. To find out if the enemy post at N19 a 32 (called the Devil's Wood, near Trivelet) is occupied, and to capture or kill any of the garrison.

Route Taken. Through gap in our wire at M 24 a 66, along dyke to N19 a 22 and thence to enemy parapet. Return, same way.

Description. Half moon : No Man's Land very muddy.

Advanced without incident for 300 yards to dyke running parallel to enemy front line and about sixty yards from enemy parapet, where covering party of one officer and twenty other ranks remained, lying out along bank of dyke. Remainder of party crept forward for about forty yards, where one N. C. O. and five other ranks were left. Enemy Verey Lights sent up immediately North and South of patrol, but no alarm given. Enemy posts seemed slightly (probably one hundred yards) behind their front line. Ground was one mass of shell holes filled with water and barbed wire. Progress difficult. Remainder of party took thirty minutes to reach enemy breastwork. Climbed into trench, which was waterlogged and unoccupied. Party advanced another 100 yards behind line to approximately N 19 c 3780 where enemy seem to have had a machine gun position. Stick bombs were found. Waited two hours in hope of meeting enemy post. Nothing happened. Returned to the section waiting near German parapet.

Whole patrol returned to our lines at 3-15 a.m., having been out from 11-30 p.m.

Observations. Impossible to move quickly over ground in front of Trivelet. Enemy posts at approximately N 19 a 48, and N 19 c 3780, latter unoccupied."

This report will convey nothing to the uninitiated, and will seem uninteresting. But such patrols demanded every ounce of soldierly courage and discipline. Both covering parties lay out in No Man's Land near the enemy parapet for over two hours, in mud and water, and in a position where, if the enemy had chanced to be on the alert immediately in front, they could not have escaped casualties. There was no shelter : the dykes behind them could only have been crossed in one or two places : and an enemy Verey Light accurately fired would have revealed the whole line extended in the open. As for the five men who advanced up to the enemy breastwork through the broken wire and shell-holes, where it took them half an hour to advance a few yards—they would not have had a dog's chance if the enemy post they were seeking had been occupied and alert. Sheltered behind his breastwork the enemy could have picked them off one by one with rifle fire. Such men, wet through and chilled to the bone after the night's exposure, returned to a cheerless dugout, without any reward except the consciousness that they had " finished the job," and conquered that nervous excitement and fearfulness which afflict most men under such circumstances.

The following is typical of the more eventful patrol, when our men encountered the enemy. Our Intelligence Officer at this time was 2nd Lieut. Harris, a boy about nineteen years of age, very keen and cheerful, who, like the rest of his scouts, had been bitterly disappointed with the Battalion's ill-luck in capturing prisoners. With two of his scouts he left our line at 1-10 a.m. on May 27th to reconnoitre the " Devil's Jump," a point in the enemy line immediately north of the wood mentioned previously. Before our patrol reached the enemy parapet several Germans were heard walking in their front line trench. Throwing caution to the winds and burning with desire to take a prisoner, our patrol moved forward to the enemy parapet, and from there saw a party of about fifteen Germans in the trench, about forty yards away from them. The enemy party advanced down the trench, and passed within a few yards of where our three scouts were lying. Several minutes passed. Then one of our men saw two of the enemy crawling towards them, and immediately warned 2nd Lieut. Harris. It was quickly arranged that if the two Germans discovered our patrol, Scout O'Donnell was to take on the left-hand man, and Harris the right-hand one. When the enemy had crawled to within a few yards of the shell hole where Harris was, he called upon the Germans to put up their hands. But the Germans shouted out, warning the rest of their group, whereupon both Harris and O'Donnell fired immediately, and both Germans dropped, one of them being killed. Harris and O'Donnell fired again, but one of the Germans was only wounded, and raising himself on his knees, he fired point blank just as Harris was in the act of throwing a bomb on the rest of the enemy patrol, who were approaching. Harris was killed, shot through the chest. The rest of the German party was now very near, and our two scouts, finding they were being surrounded, retired as quickly as they could. By great good fortune they got back to our lines. The body of Lt. Harris was not recovered. Corporal Silverwood and Private Martin (Battalion Scouts) crawled out in broad daylight the following morning to the enemy line in the hope of being able to find the body, but were not successful. His loss did not go unavenged. A large fighting patrol of two officers and seventy other ranks went out a few days later, and attacked an enemy post opposite Red Lamp Corner, killing several of the enemy.

The enemy tried to raid the Brigade front several times, but on no single occasion obtained either prisoners or identification. The most serious raid was on April 20th against our trenches at Red Lamp Corner. The enemy put down a heavy " box barrage " on Red Lamp Corner, i.e., enclosed the area he intended to attack by lines of fire which completely isolated it from the flanks and the support line. The enemy party consisted of about eighty men, and their object was probably not only to take prisoners, but to find out the reason for the extensive excavations which had been caused in that part of the line by sinking several mine shafts and constructing tunnels under No Man's Land. The enemy entirely failed in both objects. We had no casualties, and our Lewis guns opened out on the enemy party with such success that they were unable to get beyond our wire. They also gave us an identification—6th Bavarian Regiment.

In May and June elaborate preparations had been made to establish posts in the enemy front line system. There were two or three reasons for the establishment of these forward posts. A voluntary withdrawal of the enemy from the front of the XI. Corps had been expected for some time, and numerous instructions had been sent to battalions to keep closely in touch with the enemy, and to be prepared immediately to follow up the withdrawal. In accordance with Corps orders a special Battalion Patrol was organized to be ready to go out day or night, at ten minutes' notice, to find out if the enemy still held his positions up to the Deleval Line. Another reason for the project to establish posts in the enemy front line system was in order to give the enemy the impression that the British were going to attack on the XI. Corps front with the objective Aubers Ridge, instead of further north at Messines. For the purpose of such an attack, it would be necessary for us to advance our front line and get into closer touch with the main German positions on the "New Deleval Line." Map No. 10 gives the actual positions the battalions in the Brigade were detailed to attack and consolidate. For weeks the attention of patrols and observers was concentrated on these points. Small groups of our men established themselves by night at intervals in the German front line, and remained there hidden during the whole of the next day in order to observe the enemy movements behind the line near the positions it was intended to attack. The Battalion Operation orders issued in connection with this attack were the longest and most elaborate during the war, and Brigade Orders filled six typewritten sheets of foolscap. The minutiæ of the operation were prepared with a care only possible in a quiet sector, and many subalterns, after spending hours in mastering the details of the Operation Orders, felt that the actual " show " would be child's play in comparison. The following is an extract from only three out of twenty-five clauses in the document—

DRESS. (7) Shirt sleeves, box respirators, rifle with bayonet and scabbard attached, one bandolier S.A.A. (to be taut across the chest), belt with water bottle (full) attached.

ASSEMBLY POINTS. (8) Companies will march by Platoons at three minute intervals to their respective assembly points using Piccadilly and Bond Street Communication Trenches.

C, A and B Companies will assemble in Front Line between Exeter Avenue, N.8.d.42.97 on the Left and N.8.d.06.88. on the Right. The head of B. Company being at the latter.

Head Quarters behind mound at N.8.d.10.94, just behind the Front Line.

D. Company in old Support Line N. of Bond Street at N. 8.d.03.98.

The leading Company will not pass B. Line before 9-30 p.m.

Companies and Head Quarter Party will report when they have reached and are all present in their assembly positions to the Adjutant before 10-25 p.m. at dug-out at N.8.c.89.78.

TASK. (9) The task of digging the Communication Trench will be carried out as follows :—

FRONT LINE TRENCH—FAUQUISSART, 1915.

XXV.

TURCO FARM.

YPRES—ALGERIAN COTTAGE, 1915.

SCOUTS SECTION.
TOP ROW.—PTE. EAST, L/CPL. SILVERWOOD, PTES. ELLIS AND HELLEWELL.
SECOND ROW.—PTES. O'DONNELL, HELLEWELL, STEPHENSON, WOOLHAM, FISHER, STEWART,
SMITH AND MARTIN.
FRONT ROW.— PTE. BRUNTON, L/CPLS. SIMPSON AND SUTCLIFFE, CPL. FAIRBANK, LT. MITCHELL,
L/CPLS. AIREY AND BRUCE, PTES. HOLDSWORTH AND HOLLOWAY.

STRETCHER BEARERS.
TOP ROW.—S/BS. BUXTON, WALKER, WOOD AND WADDINGTON, L/CPL. COX, S/BS. GLEN AND COATES.
2ND ROW.—S/BS. LANGTON, WALWORTH, TERRY, —, —, GOTT, WOODCOCK AND TAYLOR.
FRONT ROW.—L/CPL. JONES, SERGT. UNDERWOOD, B/M KING, CAPT. A. HAMILTON, CPL. LUND, L/CPL. COOK,
S/BS. COOPLAND AND WILKINSON.

THE BAND.

BACK ROW.—MUS. OVERTON, JAMES, RAISTRICK, MANLEY, ROBINSON, L/CPL. H. M. KING, MUS. WARD.

SECOND ROW.—CPL. D. THOMAS, L/CPL. COOK, L/CPL. BERRY, MUS. GREEN, HAZELWOOD, MOORHOUSE, HAYES, L/CPL. BARTLETT AND L/CPL. HOYLE.

THIRD ROW—MUS. WINDLE, STEWART, BD/MR. G. M. KING, MUS. HACKETT, EDWARDS AND BRIGGS.

FRONT ROW.—MUS. HOLDEN AND L/CPL. FEARNLEY.

THE TRANSPORT.

BACK STANDING.—W. SYKES, F. DINSDALE, H. TOWNEND, C. DRACUP, J. WORSNOP, W. PICK, N. BEANLAND, W. SMITH AND T. BRITTON.

SECOND STANDING.—W. WILKINSON, J. W. BOYLE, W. CHARLES, W. WARD, RHODES, L. HALL, H. FIELD, E. MALTBY AND W. GOMERSAL.

THIRD STANDING.—B. BRADLEY, C. OUTHWAITE, W. WATSON, D. WHELAN, W. COY, E. ROBINSON, J. SOUTHERAN, R. ISLES, TIDSWELL, BASTOW AND BLACKBURN.

SITTING.—L/CPL. D. KEATING, CPL. W. WHITELEY, LT. F. W. MUSGRAVE, SERGT. S. CHAPMAN, L/CPLS. H. LONG, RUDDOCK AND H. CARTER.

FRONT.—W. TAYLOR, C. JONES, BURRON, A. GRIGGS, J. GOMERSAL, J. CLEGG AND J. C. WHITAKER.

On receipt of Orders from Commanding Officer, Companies will be marched out in single file (over the top) to their tasks in the following order :—

(i) *Trench*. B Company, who will dig the trench from E end of Rhondda Sap, men to be set out at two paces interval.

A Company will follow on B Company and will remain in Rhondda Sap until word is received from Officer Commanding B Company that all his men are paced out. Officer Commanding A Company will then lead his men to the point in No Man's Land where B Coy. end, and will pace his men out in the same way to Point in Bosch Parapet at N.8.d.35.15.

Dimensions of Trench will be depth three feet, width (at top) three feet, (at bottom) two feet, berm one foot.

(ii) *Borrow Pit (North)*. C Company will follow A Company and will dig Borrow Pit twelve feet from N. side of trench inclusive of Sap.

Men to be set out at intervals of five yards.

(iii) *Borrow Pit (South)*. D Company will follow C Company and will dig Borrow Pit on the South side of Communication Trench, inclusive of Sap.

Head Quarters will follow D Company and will clear Sap to a depth of three feet and grid same. Men to be set out at six paces interval.

When completed they will carry grids for B and A Companies in Communication Trench.

(iv.) *Rifles*. Rifles of A and B Companies will be laid on the berm.

According to the Operation Orders there were to be different S.O.S. rockets for every Post.

Sugar Loaf Post—White Rocket (Asteroid).

Irma Post—One white, one red rocket (Asteroid).

Flame Post—Red rocket (Asteroid).

Wick Post—One red, one green rocket (Asteroid).

Clara Post—Green rocket (Asteroid).

There were enough countersigns, station calls, and map references (all to the second place of decimals) to fill an A.B. 153 from end to end !

Fortunately however it was only a paper battle. On Zero day, when the last detail had been arranged, the whole scheme was cancelled. Even if the posts had been occupied without loss our casualties in trying to maintain the positions would certainly have been heavy, as the enemy trenches were known to be waterlogged, and were also directly under the fire of enemy artillery and machine guns on Aubers Ridge. During the months of April, May and June the enemy had been working incessantly on the New Deleval Line, constructing wire defences and concrete machine gun emplacements on the scale of the " Hindenburg Line." The network of dykes and elaborate wire entanglements had made the Aubers Ridge in 1917 one of the strongest fortifications on the Western front. Fortunately it was not necessary in 1918 to take it by direct assault.

Probably the chief event which led to the abandonment of the above scheme for occupying the " derelict " German front line system was the raid by B Company under Capt. W. L. Fawcett on June 12th. Two officers (Capt. W. L. Fawcett and 2nd Lieut. H. E. Jackson) and seventy O.R.'s, under cover of a heavy Stokes Mortar barrage, attacked the German positions near Bertha Post shortly after midnight, and in spite of much opposition, penetrated for some hundreds of yards behind the German line. The raid had only been definitely decided upon at 2 p.m. in the afternoon, but Capt. Fawcett worked out the details carefully, and in spite of the waterlogged condition of the ground and the extreme darkness of the night, there was no hitch in its execution. But our previous raids had put the enemy on the alert, and the advance party under Lieut. Jackson suffered several casualties, and Lieut. Jackson was killed. He was last seen chasing two Germans down a communication trench. This raid showed clearly that the enemy would not give up his advanced positions without a fight, and the advantages of forcing him out of them would not have been worth the inevitable cost.

The monotony of trench warfare in the Laventie sector was relieved by the arrival of the Portuguese Expeditionary Force. The 22nd, 23rd, 25th Regts., P. E. F., were attached to the 49th Division for instriction from May 3rd to July 9th. On July 9th the 1/6th Battalion was relieved by the 9th Battalion P. E. F. and the whole sector was taken over by the Portuguese Army. The Portuguese were a very mixed crowd, and could not by any stretch of the imagination be called popular. They suffered from all the disadvantages of being unaccustomed to trench warfare, but as all our own men had gone through the same experiences, the criticism on that score would have been very charitable. But the " Pork and Beans " were unusually filthy in their habits.* Now filthiness is a crime of no mean order in trench warfare, where thousands of men are crowded together in trenches

---

* The use of the nickname " Pork and Beans " was forbidden by an Army Order a few weeks after the arrival of the Portuguese Expeditionary Force in France, but this Order only increased the popularity of the nickname.

and dugouts with the scantiest sanitary arrangements. In 1918 at Kemmel our men came in contact with the French Infantry. The Frenchmen seemed to be always washing their shirts, and every time they came out of the line into reserve positions long rows of shirts could be seen drying on the grass or the hedges. The British Tommy concentrated attention on his equipment, buttons and boots. The Portuguese soldier never seemed to clean anything, least of all the dugout he had lived in for a week. One memorable morning the Portuguese Corps Commander spent several hours in the Fauquissart trenches pointing out to his junior officers and men the disgraceful state of their sanitary arrangements along the whole front. Followed by an amused crowd of interpreters, officers and orderlies, and by the perplexed Portuguese Colonel commanding the unit in the line, he visited almost every dugout and latrine on the Brigade front : and later on there was a slight, though very slight, improvement. The average Portuguese soldier thought nothing, if he was on sentry duty, of leaving his post because it was raining, or because he wanted a talk with his friends in the platoon dugout. Most extraordinary of all, he had no idea of cleaning his rifle, and hundreds of the Portuguese rifles had never been cleaned since they were issued from Ordnance. Individually the men seemed strong and intelligent, and would probably have made good soldiers if they had been trained and well-officered. But the average Portuguese officer seemed to take little interest in the comfort and well-being of his men. If the company rations were lost or late, the last man the Portuguese soldier would think of consulting was his officer ! There were, of course, many Portuguese officers who would have done credit to any Army, but they were exceptions. It was found necessary to attach two or three British " Interpreters " to every Portuguese Battalion, and some Portuguese units were in reality commanded by British Interpreters during the first few months in the Laventie sector.

Probably the funniest thing ever seen on the streets of France was the Portuguese Transport. Even French farmers were amused. The Portuguese mules seemed to walk at an angle of 45 degrees with the road, leaning against each other for support, and sliding on the cobbles in most erratic fashion. The Portuguese transport men seemed to care little about their horses, and were often deliberately cruel. The officers seemed to delight in cantering on the cobbles, a practice which generally made our transport men " see red." It must be admitted that some of the officers were magnificent horsemen, and came off victors in many of the Army racing and jumping competitions. But the average Portuguese battalion transport was a queer miscellany of half-starved mules with odd bits of harness patched up with string, ragged drivers, and a succession of broken-down old bone carts.

The enemy quickly found that the Portuguese were in the line, and seemed determined to give them a warm reception. Shelling increased, and on the morning of July 3rd a tremendous bombardment along the Brigade front began at 1 a.m.—far and away the heaviest bombardment the Battalion had known in the sector. The Portuguese were holding the line immediately on the right of the 146/7 Brigade, and received the heaviest shelling. The enemy came over and took about a hundred Portuguese prisoners. The reserve areas were full of Portuguese stragglers. At 6 a.m., five hours after the bombardment began, the Head Quarters of the Portuguese battalion in the line had no information as to the part of their line which had been attacked, the number of casualties, or the present position of their companies. Such a bombardment would have been a severe ordeal for the best troops, but the result on the Portuguese front hardly augured well for the future! When the battalions of the 49th Division handed over their fronts to the units of the Portuguese Expeditionary Force, they took consolation from the fact that the line was a quiet one, and that the British defences had been considerably strengthened and improved during their five months' occupation. The attention of the whole British Army was being concentrated on the northern portions of the line from Ypres to the sea. The offensive was in the hands of the Allies. The first two operations of 1917— Vimy and Messines—had been, within limits, entirely successful. The third offensive of the year would be—it was hoped—the final, culminating one of the war, and everything pointed to the 49th Division being chosen to take part in it. The Laventie sector was therefore regarded as being quite safely left in the keeping of the Portuguese Army.

On July 9th, the Battalion marched to Sailly-sur-la-Lys, and after four days there and at La Gorgue, the Battalion marched on July 13th to Lestrem, where they entrained, arriving at Loon Plage, about eleven kilometres west of Dunkerque, at midnight the same day. From Loon Plage the Battalion marched to a Camp at Mardyck, five miles away : the tents were few, and the men very crowded. But the Camp was on the Dunes, within a few hundred yards of the sea. The men examined the coast defences, and wished they could exchange places for a year or two with the French Territorials who were guarding the deep, dry and well revetted trench line along the coast. The weather was fine. Everybody was grateful for the prospect of a few days rest before entering the inevitable battle which was being so obviously prepared on the northernmost sectors of the Allied Line in France.

CHAPTER IX.

NIEUPORT.

THE period which the 49th Division spent in the Nieuport trenches in July, 1917, may reasonably be regarded as part of the great battle of the Northern Ridges which opened on July 31st. The 49th Division had been marked down to

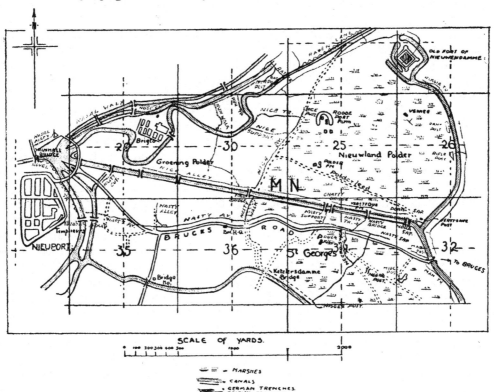

No. 11 Map.   Nieuport, 1917.

take part in a big attack in the Dunes Sector. There was a well-founded rumour that troops of two divisions had been specially trained for an attack on the Lombartzyde sector from the sea. Everyone in the Battalion was pleased with this idea: there seemed to be in it such possibilities of far-reaching success! But the first serious check which disturbed the fulfilment of this plan was on July 10th, when the Germans attacked on a narrow front north of Nieuport, and succeeded in wresting from us the more important half of the bridgehead north of the Yser, which was to have been used as an assembly and "kicking off" ground for the main attack. The second check was the lack of success which attended the great Flanders Offensive of July 31st, and which would have rendered abortive any partial success which might have been gained on the Lombartzyde-Nieuport front. As Sir Douglas Haig stated in his despatches, "If the weather had permitted the Ypres offensive to proceed more rapidly, it had been intended to develop offensive operations also along the coast. The Germans were not altogether wrong (by attacking on July 10th) in their appreciation of the situation." The phrase might have been made more emphatic by saying that the Germans were "altogether right" in their appreciation of the situation.

The German attack on July 10th was one of the neatest, and most successful operations of its kind made by any armies on the Western front. The first news of it received by troops of the 49th Division was when they were at Estaires and La Gorgue, before entraining for Dunkerque. A party of Brigadiers and the Divisional Staff had gone up to Nieuport to reconnoitre in advance the sectors the Division was going to take over. They brought back a most evil report of the land. In fact, from their description, Nieuport was the most unholy sector any troops could possibly enter. They described how enemy aeroplanes flew along the Dunkerque-Nieuport Road at a height of a hundred feet, and rained bullets on transport and men : how that nine miles behind the line the bombardment was terrific on all main roads and camps : and that neither our aeroplanes nor guns made any reply whatever. This advance party returned from Nieuport only an hour or two before the Germans attacked. They had thus received some of the preliminary bombardment. In fact the Brigadier of the 148th Brigade only just crossed the Yser half an hour before all the bridges had been blown up, and the enemy had captured nearly all the garrison (1st Battalion Northampton Regiment and 2nd Battalion K.R.R.C., 1st Division) on the north bank of the canal. Some of the 49th Division Engineers swam across the canal to Nieuport, and thus escaped capture. By concentrating a tremendous strength of artillery and a Naval Division of good and fresh troops, the Germans overran the north bank of the Yser from the sea for a distance of two kilometres to Nose Lane on the east of the Lombartzyde sector without much loss to themselves. The official report states that the "enemy's attack had failed to deprive us of a sufficient bridgehead," but no one who occupied the Lombartzyde sector believed in the possibility of a successful attack on our part after July 10th. There was neither room nor shelter in the ground which remained to us for more than a fraction of the men necessary for an attack. Troops assembling in that square kilometre of ground would have been swept out of existence by the enemy artillery. During the battle of July 10th our artillery was silent and our aeroplanes did not show themselves. After it was over the XV. Corps was not popular with any Divisions in the Nieuport sector. To some extent the confusion could be understood, as the line had only just been taken over by us from the French. After this battle our armaments increased hourly, and when the 146th Inf. Brigade moved up to Nieuport on July 18th, the concentration of artillery was greater than the Battalion had ever experienced in France, even on the Somme. Long lines of field guns were brought across the Yser to the narrow strip of ground south of Elizabeth Bridge, and lay out in the open in rows. Scores of batteries were massed in the fields south of Nieuport. Triangle Wood and the woods near the 146th Brigade Head Quarters and Rebaillet Camp near the Oost Dunkerque-Nieuport Road, bristled with "heavies" of all calibres. This show of artillery was all the more imposing as it was concentrated on a very narrow front of about four kilometres. The Belgian sector, immediately on our right, was a grateful abode of peace and quietness.

Needless to say, our concentration of guns was not overlooked by the enemy, who increased his own armament, and did his best to assist in making the Nieuport sector a veritable inferno. All his coast batteries as far north as Ostend, and the guns opposite the inundated Belgian sector, were switched on to the British lines near Nieuport, and our communications. Instead of knocking our destroyers about, his naval guns made holes as big as hotels in the Dunes from Nieuport to Oost-Dunkerque, and blew up enormous ammunition dumps. A "quiet" day at Nieuport would have been described as "very great artillery activity" in any other sector. Capt. P. G. Bales in his history of the 1/4th Battalion Duke of Wellington's Regiment reports that as many as 18,000 shells a day were fired in the Nieuport sector, and that when an S.O.S. was sent up, eighteen pounders alone fired over 8,500 rounds in about half-an-hour. And all this in an area so narrow and crowded that every shell seemed likely to hit a gun or an infantryman !

The Nieuport sector was a place of strange novelties and

contradictions. The fresh sea air of the Dunes will always be associated with the memory of an extremely dangerous form of poison gas. The long line of picturesque and irregular sea side resorts on the Dunes was being blown to pieces by artillery and aeroplanes. The communications of all the Infantry in the line depended on a few bridges which were being continually blown up. Patrols on the right of the sector punted across " No Man's Land," and rowing boats would have been most useful items in a battalion's equipment. The effect of 15 in. armour-piercing shells on dugouts constructed in sand was remarkable. The narrow water of the Dunkerque-Nieuport Canal divided the British sector and the extreme of noise and danger, from the Belgian sector, which was the last word in quietness and peace. The Belgian (Ramscapelle) trenches were an elysium where men fished from their advanced posts, were busy sniping duck instead of Germans, and kept pigs in the front line. In fact, a typical relief of a Belgian section has been described as follows :—First Belgian carried a basket of fish and a fishing rod : the second, a mattress from one of the villas in Coxyde or Nieuport : the third, two or three ducks and was followed by a dog : and the last man brought up the rear carrying the four rifles of the section. Their wives—and others—visited them in the trenches. When some of our batteries moved south of the Dunkerque canal and took up positions in old gunpits in the Belgian area, some of the Belgian gunners were annoyed because our guns persisted in firing, and reminding the enemy "there was a war on." Their annoyance was quite natural, as the enemy included them in his retaliation.

The Brigade first took over the sector on July 18th, with two battalions in the front line (1/5th Battalion on left and 1/6th Battalion on right), one in support (1/8th Battalion) at Nieuport, and the 1/7th Battalion in reserve in Rebaillet Camp, about one mile east of Oost-Dunkerque. The 1/6th Battalion relieved the 2nd Battalion Royal Inniskilling Fusiliers. On the right of the Battalion was the 1st Battalion of the 11th Regiment, Belgian Army. The Brigade sector (see Map No. 11) was divided by the canalized Yser River, a broad waterway about thirty-five yards wide. Another waterway, the Plasschendael Canal, formed the left of the Brigade front, and on the right was the Noord Vaart. All three waterways ran into a wide and deep canal which surrounded the town of Nieuport. Thus the communications of the front line depended on bridges. There was a very great contrast between the right and left subsectors of the Brigade front. On the right, in what was called the St. Georges Sector, a waste of water one kilometre in extent stretched between our own and the enemy line. Naturally this sector was very quiet. On the left the Brigade was holding about five hundred yards of the bridgehead on the north of the Yser which remained in British hands after the July 10th attack. This subsector was extremely unpleasant and noisy. It was therefore arranged that the 1/6th Battalion should remain in the St. Georges Sector during the whole time the Brigade was in the line, and that the other three battalions should relieve each other every four days in the left subsector. Thus the 1/6th Battalion was extremely fortunate, and our men were able every night to look northwards across the Yser to the lines on the left near the Plasschendael Canal and Lombartzyde, and from their comparatively quiet area regard the incessant fury of a constant battle, rather in the same way that men from Authuille Wood in 1916 looked across the valley to the fighting in the Leipzig Salient. No Battalion, however, in the Nieuport sector in July could escape heavy casualties, as all roads and trenches converged on to the Nieuport bridges. And it is no exaggeration to say that every man who lived in or walked through Nieuport from July 18th to July 29th was lucky if he escaped becoming a casualty.

When a man reached the outskirts of Nieuport, either on his way from the line or going up from Oost Dunkerque, there was usually a look of intense pre-occupation on his face. Nieuport was always being shelled, and at several points. But if he was alone he could choose which of two or three bridges he preferred to be shelled on in crossing the canal. Hence the look of intense pre-occupation ! Would it be safer for him to cross by the Elizabeth bridge, take the risk of houses falling on him in the town, and brave the main road past Triangle Wood ? If he crossed by one of the quieter bridges further south he would probably "get it in the neck" near the Railway embankment across the Dunkerque Canal south of Nieuport ! Moreover, if he walked on some of the tracks off the main thoroughfares south-east of Nieuport, he ran the risk of running into the mouth of one of our own field guns, which had been moved up during the night into an advanced and only too well camouflaged position. Nothing is so disconcerting as suddenly in a quiet lane finding yourself half-a-dozen yards from the gaping mouth of a field gun hidden in the hedge. Before you have time to fall down or run away the gun is fired and your eyes are blinded and ears deafened by a flash and a nerve shattering roar, which leave you for some seconds uncertain of your own existence. Many men would prefer to face an orthodox bombardment ! If a man was marching with his section or platoon his feelings were less complicated and more fatalistic. The danger was shared by several, and was therefore rather easier to bear. If the bridge was hit there would be at least ten or fifteen others who would be plunged with what was left of him in the water. Battalion,— and in the Nieuport sector especially,—Brigade runners, had a bad time, and suffered heavy casualties. Their heroism was of that common routine kind which is often overlooked. Shelling or no shelling their messages were delivered, though only too often the original messengers had been hit. On each of three consecutive days Brigade runners were blown to pieces by enemy shells within a few hundred yards of Brigade H.Q. on their return journey from the line ! Telephone communications were almost impossible and the best laid cables were continually broken by the shelling.

From the Battalion observer's point of view the ten days at Nieuport were exceptionally interesting. A concreted Observation Post had been built near Battalion Head Quarters at " White House," and a clear view of Westende and Ostende and the Dunes could be obtained. Under the incessant bombardments, Nieuport was rapidly disappearing, Lombardzyde had gone completely, and Westende was becoming a shambles. A cloud of smoke lay all day long over our trenches north of the Yser. In the midst of it new thick columns of shell smoke rose and remained stationary in the air like permanent black geysers. Scores of flashes of bursting shells could be seen every minute through the smoke-cloud. It appeared incredible that any human beings could exist in such a bombardment. The tall concrete enemy emplacement called " Rat Post," eighty yards from the extreme left of our Brigade front, stood out white and clear, and seemed to defy all the efforts of our " heavies " to knock it down. The XV. Corps 9-2's near La Panne fired several hundred rounds at it, without any visible effect. One day, orders were sent to the garrison in the front line near Rat Post to withdraw to the support line at Hun Walk, which was two hundred and fifty yards behind the front line, as the Corps " heavies " were going to demolish Rat Post. The precautions were necessary, as the Corps " heavies," after firing a whole day, demolished our own front line, but did not, so far as one could see, chip a splinter of concrete from Rat Post. After enquiries, it was found that the Corps artillery observer was observing from an Observation Post near La Panne, some eight or nine kilometres away, from which point he must have been fortunate even with a strong telescope to have been able to see Rat Post, quite apart from registering a shot on it.

An official war photographer reported to 146th Inf. Brigade Head Quarters about July 22nd, saying that he would like to take photographs of " bursting shells," and thought Nieuport would give him some " good effects." Army life breeds a wide charity, and he was shown much consideration. He was led by his guide, rather reluctantly, *via* Triangle Wood to the Five Lock Gates at Nieuport, where there was quite a good chance that if he was not hit with a 5·9, he would be blown by concussion from the narrow iron gangway into the canal sixty feet below. He stayed a few minutes, and though he experienced some hair-raising "effects," he probably did not obtain a photograph which satisfied him.

When the Battalion took over the St. Georges Sector, D and B Companies were in the front line, A and C in reserve in Nieuport. Inter-company reliefs took place every four days. The trenches were in bad repair, half breastwork, half trench, with very little parados, and were dirty. The 1/5th and 1/7th Battalions on the left carried out raids almost every night against posts in the enemy line, but without much success. The 1/6th Battalion carried out patrols on rafts and punts across the St. Georges marshes, also without much success, but with considerably more amusement than their less fortunate comrades north of the Yser. There were five posts on the Battalion front, called Nigger, Negro, Nasty, Nora and Doris (the last named was an isolated post on the north side of the Yser reached by bridge 53). As the tracks and roads from these posts across "No Man's Land" were sub-merged, it was easy to make a false step at night, and be plunged up to the neck in water. A knowledge of swimming was almost essential, and bathing suits would have been more useful than ordinary equipment. Scouts O'Donnell and Martin received the Military Medal for a patrol across the Nieuwland Polder, when they reconnoitred a "path," or rather a fairly shallow waterway, for 900 yards to the enemy wire in front of Venice Post. They swam across the Polderleed, and brought back planks from the enemy side, placing them in position for the rest of the patrol to get across. There was a certain amount of shelling near the Polderleed during the operation, and more than ordinary coolness and daring was needed to penetrate for nearly a kilometre right up to the enemy wire, across a swamp, the depth of which was unknown, and which was believed unfordable.

Our second-in-command, who was a member of the Bradford Rowing Club at Saltaire, had a brain wave one day when he discovered a boat near Brigade Head Quarters. He thought boating patrols would be a novelty, and accordingly sent two scouts to reconnoitre the route by canal from Brigade Head Quarters to the front line, telling them specially to take notice of any bridges or obstructions over which it would be necessary to lift the boat. There was considerable interest—even enthusiasm—in the scheme shown by everybody in the Battalion. The two scouts, appreciating a " cushy " job, made a very thorough reconnaissance, and reported that there was a clear passage for the boat—no bridges whatever. The same day, at dark, our second-in-command " proceeded " to Brigade Head Quarters accompanied by an imposing retinue of pioneers, scouts and kindred spirits, and manned the boat. The voyage was uneventful until suddenly about half-a-mile from the front line the boat collided against something with a fearful thump, and the black form of what seemed a bridge loomed up in the darkness. After some bitter and telling remarks on the utter uselessness of scouts, our gallant Major ordered the crew to disembark, and stepping first on to the " bridge which had not been reported," he was proceeding to drag the boat over the obstacle when—splash !—he disappeared into the canal ! The " bridge " turned out to be a short diving board, and the Major walked off the end ! It was so dark that there was some alarm, but he turned up all right and was pulled on board, and finished the cruise. But that little party will long remember the time when the Major " went off the deep end." He nearly " went off the deep end " again an hour or two later when Capt. W. N. Mossop, our adjutant, asked him how he had got on, and said it must have been an ideal night for a boating patrol !

Every night after " stand down " a patrol crossed the Noord Vaart Canal on the extreme right flank in order to keep liaison with the Belgians. This patrol was a fairly popular one, and frequently during the night there were volunteers—especially officers—for the liaison work with the right flank, and the punt was in great demand. One evening two officers were punting themselves across when the enemy opened on the boat with heavy and very accurate machine gun fire. One officer dived into the water, and the other overbalanced with the recoil, and fell in after him. They got ashore all right, but were, of course, wet through. One of them borrowed Capt. W. N. Mossop's spare change of clothes, and went down to the Base next day slightly wounded. Capt. Mossop's clothing was missing for some months. But sense of property was never a strong point in the Army.

The first night (July 18th) the Battalion spent in the St. Georges sector was a very disturbed one. The 148th Brigade had attacked in the Lombartzyde sector, and seemed to have wakened all the batteries for miles round. The enemy counter-attacked, and there was one long succession of bombardments, and S.O.S. signals, and streams of gas shells poured on to Nieuport and our battery areas. The 21/22nd July was the most awful night the 49th Division experienced in Nieuport, and for all those who were in the shelled areas it was one prolonged nightmare. From 11 p.m. on the 21st to 1 a.m. on the 22nd there was an unceasing bombardment of the whole Nieuport sector with the new "mustard gas" shells, which rained on the town in thousands. Our "Intelligence" had known for some time that the Germans were preparing a new gas, and our anti-gas box respirators when promptly used were an adequate protection. The enemy employed "mustard" gas simultaneously for the first time on Verdun, Armentières and Nieuport, and—it must be admitted—with considerable success. The 49th Division was practically put out of action. The 1/6th Battalion had only thirty-eight gas casualties, but the St. Georges Sector was outside the shelled area. The 1/5th and 1/7th Battalions each lost about 250 killed and wounded, and in the 1/8th Battalion, which was in reserve in Nieuport during the bombardment, there were over 400 casualties from gas alone. These numbers included several slightly gassed cases, but on the other hand there were hundreds of men left in the Brigade who remained in the line, but who were badly affected by the gas in the eyes or throat or in some other way, and who were really unfit for trench duties. A month after the Brigade left the Nieuport sector, men were compelled to "report sick" as the result of being gassed, and some of the men who went into the Passchendaele battle on October 9th were able to speak in little more than a whisper, and had not recovered from the shortness of breath and soreness of the eyes which were some of the effects of mustard gas.

This gas bombardment of Nieuport was one of the great and terrible experiences of the war. The gas shells came over with a peculiar scream quite unlike ordinary barrage fire, and the explosion was slight—merely a sharp "ping" as the glass nose of the shell was broken, and the gas poured out. Compared with the earth-shaking crashes of an ordinary bombardment this steady rain of thousands of "yellow cross*" gas shells seemed ominous, like silent death. Fear took hold of the bravest men as battery after battery of enemy guns poured more and more shells into the thickening gas cloud which lay over the town and all the approaches to the bridges. The gas was so deadly that if a man received the full force of the explosion, he was killed instantly. His comrades, not realizing that he had been gassed, in some cases delayed a few seconds before putting on their helmets. They could not see the gas fumes in the darkness, and the smell was novel, and not unpleasant—rather like burnt mustard. But even those few seconds delay were fatal. The gas produced irritation in their throats and lungs, especially as "Blue cross" shells were mixed with the "Yellow cross." The men gasped in their helmets and became

* Enemy gas shells were called "yellow cross" and "blue cross" from the markings on the shell which distinguished their properties.

intolerably hot, till at last, able to endure no longer, they pulled off their helmets for a few seconds "fresh air," and incapable of refixing them on again, died choking. Even the most cautious succumbed to this new danger. They wore their helmets throughout the bombardment, and then, when everything was over, carefully raised their masks, and sniffed the atmosphere. A sickly heavy smell was still in the air, but there seemed to be no great concentration of fumes, and arguing from past experience of gas, many men took off their helmets. They felt no bad effects for an hour or two. Then they began to cough, their eyes ran with water and their voices almost disappeared. Scores of them became completely blind and speechless. Before dawn, on the roads and tracks immediately south west of Nieuport, there were hundreds of men in every stage of the disease, lying down in exhaustion on the road side. Every few minutes their number was increased by small parties of blinded men, one man holding to the other, often led by a comrade who was coughing his lungs away, or who could not speak. These processions of "the gassed" were the last word in German "frightfulness." The danger was so mysterious and stealthy! After some slight exertion, a man who seemed to have hitherto escaped, would fall down fainting, or dead: the gas had a strange delayed action on the heart. It also raised blisters and ulcers on several parts of the body. As often seemed to happen on these mornings of supreme tragedy, the dawn on July 22nd was more than usually beautiful. The red rays of the sun gave a wonderful rose-coloured tint to the gas clouds and smoke which hung over Nieuport. To those standing amongst the gassed men in the fields south of the town, the ruins of Nieuport seemed invested with an unforgetable golden glory. The beauty and horror of the scene seemed inextricably mixed as in an amazing dream. This glamour of the rising sun quickly passed. The long line of gassed men groped wearily towards Oost Dunkerque. For days the gas lingered in shell holes and cellars of Nieuport, and anyone walking unwarily through the town ran the risk of becoming infected with some beastly ailment. Even men's clothing carried the fumes, and it was found necessary several days later to disinfect equipment and clothing.

A week after the gas bombardment, the 146th and 148th Brigades were relieved. The 1/6th Battalion was relieved by the 2nd Battalion Royal Inniskilling Fusiliers (32nd Division) and moved into billets at Coxyde, arriving there about 4 a.m. on August 2nd. From Coxyde the Battalion marched to Ghyvelde and Uxem, and remained in the latter place for nearly a month. The 1/7th and 1/8th Battalions with 146th Brigade Head Quarters were at Teteghem: 1/5th Battalion near

Leffrinckhoucke. The Brigade Training Area was on the Dunes between Rosendaël and Bray (Map No. 12). This training period at Uxem was thoroughly enjoyable. The weather was fine, and billets good. Leave to visit Rosendaël and Dunkerque was given fairly freely. The Dunes were within an hour's walk from Uxem and Teteghem, and the training was carried out on sound lines under good conditions. On several occasions the Battalion marched from Uxem in the morning, and after training and practising attacks on the Dunes, would eat their haversack rations, and then have a " bathing parade " before marching back in the late afternoon. On some parts of the coast a peculiarly obnoxious kind of jelly fish had caused several casualties to bathers and even to horses, and bathing had been forbidden. But the shore near Bray Dunes seemed safe. There were the usual inspections—one by the XV. Corps Commander (Lieut. Gen. W. P. du Cane) who rode up and down the ranks on horse back—and one by our Divisional General. These parades were held on the sands, and were thus more enjoyable than usual. The Battalion was complimented on its excellent discipline in the Nieuport trenches, which had been a means of preventing numerous gas casualties during the enemy bombardment on July 21-22nd.

August 25th was eventful. In the morning a Battalion practice attack took place on the Dunes with tapes, flags, etc., before the Divisional Commander. In the afternoon Battalion Sports were held in the grounds of the Mayor of Uxem's house (Battalion Head Quarters). The prizes were presented by Brigadier-General Goring Jones. In the evening a farewell concert and entertainment was given to Rev. Capt. R. Whincup, M.C., prior to his departure to England to be demobilized. The padre had a great send off, and every one was sorry to lose him. He had served with the Battalion from August, 1915, and by his unselfishness and constant anxiety to serve the best interests of officers and men, he had gained an unique influence in the Battalion. Frankly and unblushingly a civilian in outlook and sympathy, he helped to counteract some of the evil tendencies of military life—a narrow sympathy and a low moral standard,—but always without a trace of priggishness. Appreciation of his services was expressed during the concert by Lieut.-Colonel Wistance, Major Clough, and Rev. Major Sherwell, Chaplain to the Division.

This pleasant period of training was interrupted on August 27th. The Battalion left Uxem and marched to Zuydcote where it embarked on barges for Adinkerque. Two companies marched from Adinkerque to Nieuport, and were attached to the 257th Tunnelling Company, Royal Engineers. Battalion Head Quarters and the remaining two companies were attached to the 97th Infantry Brigade, and occupied dug-outs in the Sand Dunes north of the village of Oost Dunkerque. In addition to the ordinary routine of training, these two latter companies practised night attacks and " reliefs during gas bombardments." One of these night attack practices was made more realistic when the enemy supplied the barrage, which caused the " practice barrage " (consisting of men with flags under the command of our police corporal) to beat an undignified retreat ! Reliefs were arranged every few days

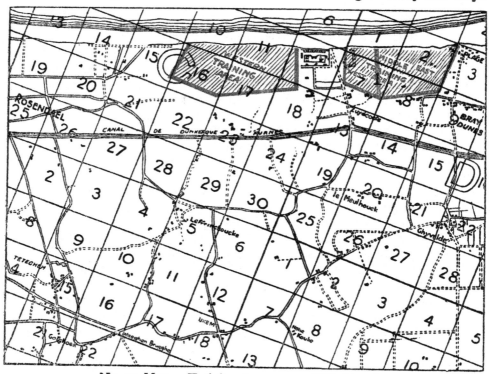

No. 12 Map. Training Areas, 1917 (XV. Corps).

between the two companies on working parties in Nieuport and the companies near Oost Dunkerque. The Oost Dunkerque Camp was frequently shelled, and the working parties in Nieuport also suffered a few casualties, but the sector had become much quieter than in July, as the enemy had transferred most of his guns to the battle further south in the Ypres Salient. On September 7th a football match took place between the Battalion and the 2/9th Battalion Manchester Regt.   The 2/9th Battalion was commanded by Lieut.-Col.

THE RAMPARTS, YPRES. 1918.

THE LILLE GATE, YPRES, 1917.

NO. 4 BRIDGE (YSER CANAL, YPRES), 1915.

MERVILLE CANAL, 1918.

xxix.

AEROPLANE PHOTO—GOMMECOURT WOOD.

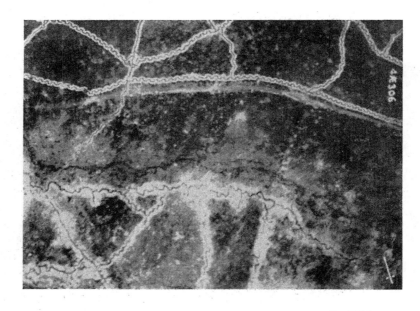

AEROPLANE PHOTO—TRENCHES, THIEPVAL, SEPT. 3, 1916.

XXX.

AFTER A PUSH (PASSCHENDAELE).

BY C. R. W. NEVINSON, FROM THE PICTURE IN THE POSSESSION OF THE IMPERIAL WAR MUSEUM.

xxxi.

THE TRENCHES N. OF YPRES, AUG., 1915.

xxxii.

J. L. Heselton who came out as a subaltern with the 1/6th Battalion in April, 1915, and went into action as Officer Commanding D Company on July 1st, 1916. Lt.-Col. H. L. Anderton was another of the original officers of the Battalion who was stationed near Oost Dunkerque at this time, in command of the 2/6 Bn. Lancashire Fusiliers. Col. Anderton commanded D Coy. in 1914 and 1915, and had a record at that time of fifteen years' service with the Battalion. He was one of the few officers of the 49th Division who was promoted from Captain to Lieut.-Colonel in 1916. He was wounded in February, 1916, whilst in command of the 11th Bn. West Yorkshire Regiment, and again in October, 1917, whilst serving with the 66th Division at Passchendaele. Few T.F. officers received such rapid promotion, and the Battalion has reason to be proud of the record of these two officers.

On September 13th the Battalion marched to Ghyvelde, where a further week's training was spent. The incessant practising of attacks over tapes on the sand hills close to the town was significant of the future. Brigade practice attacks were carried out before Lieut.-General Sir A. J. Godley (II. Anzac Corps) and Sir Herbert Plumer. At the close of these practice attacks a few words were addressed to all officers of the Brigade by Sir Herbert Plumer and Sir A. J. Godley. Both emphasized the fact that the 49th Division would soon be called on to take part in the battle for Passchendaele.

On September 24th the Battalion was transferred from the XVth Corps of the 4th Army to the II. Anzac Corps of the 2nd Army (Sir Herbert Plumer). The next day the Battalion began its march to the Ypres Salient. The distance from Uxem to Ypres is about twenty miles, a two days' march. But a very circuitous route was chosen, and the Battalion did not arrive in the Ypres Salient till a week later. The night of September 25th was spent at Wormhoudt, and other halting places were Noordpeene, Salperwick, St. Marie Capelle and Watou. The two days at Salperwick were spent in Divisional practice attacks on the Second Army Training area near St. Omer. During this period there was a very severe air raid on St. Omer. Over forty bombs were dropped and three hospitals were hit. Several men of the Brigade were able to assist in the evacuation of patients from the hospitals during the raid, but none of our men were injured. Everybody was expecting to make a more prolonged stay near St. Omer, but on the 1st October the Battalion marched to St. Marie Capelle, and the period of training for the battle was over. The weather was fine. The men were in splendid condition, after the month's training and the seven days of marching. Unfortunately, heavy rain began on October 5th and continued for some days. The Battalion was marching to a veritable sea of mud in the Ypres Salient. From Watou eastwards the roads were choked with traffic and men from almost every unit in the British Army. The Flanders battle was in full swing, and it was now the turn of the 49th Division to be thrown into the fray.

Up to this time a certain fatality seemed to have followed the 49th Division. They had been denied the opportunity of achieving any signal, outstanding victory. When the Division arrived in France in April, 1915, and had learnt the rudiments of trench warfare in the Fleurbaix and Neuve Chapelle sectors, it was sent for six months to the Ypres Salient, and in that dark winter had been condemned to slow attrition and exhaustion. Its work was magnificent : its spirit unbroken : but there was no opportunity for any great and inspiring feat of arms. Again on July 1st, when at the top of its form after a long rest, the Division was cut up into detachments, and given tasks which were admittedly impossible, and were only intended to create a diversion after the failure of the other divisions of the X. Corps. The same unfortunate destiny dogged the Division on September 3rd, when it may be said without fear of contradiction that no other division would have succeeded under the same circumstances. At Nieuport, without having had the remotest chance of success in attack, the Division lost approximately two-thirds of its infantry in maintaining difficult positions under heavy bombardments. A respite of nearly six weeks followed, during which units were re-formed and reinforced. Every old soldier who had passed through the somewhat bitter experiences of the past two years, believed that at last the Division would be able to crown the long list of minor actions with a great victory. The men felt they had a right to look forward to this, and that they had in fact deserved it. The Division was to attack in the first wave, the objective—Passchendaele ! At last the long score which had been totalled up against the enemy during two years' fighting was to be wiped out !

But the battles of October 9th and 10th were not to bring the kind of " glory " for which the battalions of the 49th Division hoped. Yet they were " glorious " days, though the victory was only partial. Human endurance and self sacrifice was never shown more widely and magnificently : the suffering of the men was more intense than even in the Ypres Salient in 1915, or Thiepval in 1916. The 1/6th Battalion formed up for the attack near a ruin called Calgary Grange. Calgary has a curious likeness to Calvary !—a place of skulls,—of human and divine suffering and conquest. The parallel is not far-fetched. To our own and many other units of the British Army, such was the kind of " glory that was Passchendaele."

CHAPTER X.

PASSCHENDAELE.

DURING the two days the Battalion was in Mill Camp, Watou, news was received that the British attack on October 4th had been a great success. The enemy had evidently planned a counter-attack, which was to have taken place a few minutes later than the hour fixed for zero by the British, and thus his troops had been caught in their assembly positions by our barrage fire. According to reports from the II. Army, three enemy divisions had been destroyed. Certain it is that the ridge from Gravenstafel and Korek to Boetleer and Aviatik Farm was covered with more dead Germans than British,—a rather unusual sight on the Flanders battle-fields. By this attack our line had been carried forward over a mile on a front of 9,000 yards. Molenaarelsthoek, Broodseinde, Abraham Heights, had been captured by New Zealanders and the 1st, 2nd and 3rd Australian Divisions, and our line brought to within a little over 2,000 yards of Passchendaele.

On October 9th the II. and V. Army again attacked on a front of over six miles from Zonnebeke to our junction with the French northwest of Langemarck. The general objective of the attack was the Passchendaele Ridge and Poelcappelle. The V. Army attacked on the left of the II. Army. The 49th Division was the left division of the II. Army, and the 66th Division operated on the right of the 49th Division. The attack was thus on the grand scale. The objective of the 49th Division was a frontage of about 1,300 yards on the Belle Vue Spur near Passchendaele (See Map No. 14). The 148th Infantry Brigade was on the right, the 146th Infantry Brigade on the left, and the 147th Infantry Brigade was in Divisional Reserve. The Passchendaele Ridge was the last obstacle which separated the British from the plains of Belgium, and the towns of Moorslede and Roulers. After nine weeks incessant fighting British Armies were at last about to drive the Germans from their last stronghold in the Flanders hills.

During 1917 there had been many changes in the tactics employed for attack. When Sir Herbert Plumer addressed the officers of the 146th Infantry Brigade after a practice attack near Ghyvelde he had emphasized some of these changes. He had pointed out that in the Third Battle of Ypres, which was then proceeding, there was approximation to the methods of " open warfare " fighting. The enemy was occupying, not trench positions, but defensive zones or areas. The old practice of " mopping up " trench lines had given way to mopping up areas of ground. In preparing for the July 1st battle, 1916, it had been possible to tape out the exact enemy lines it was intended to attack, and the training had been directed against clearly defined enemy positions. On the other hand, when the Division practised the October 9th attack on the II. Army Training area near St. Omer, the only things clearly defined were the formations in which battalions should move, the distance to which they should advance, and the lifts of the artillery barrage. It was only two days before the 49th Division attacked on October 9th that the " jumping off " ground could be given with any certainty. This was because on October 4th the attack mentioned above had been made by Australian and New Zealand Divisions, and had been a great success, with the result that the whole British line had been moving forward till on October 7th it had reached the last ridge before Passchendaele. It was from this line that the 49th Division attacked on October 9th.

During the Third Battle of Ypres the enemy had evolved a very successful and elaborate system of defence. He had organized a series of concrete emplacements or " pill boxes " in irregular groups throughout his " defensive zone," which was usually about 1,500 yards in depth. These "pill boxes" were built in order to give shelter to parties of the enemy until our barrage fire had passed over them, whereupon the enemy was able to rush out into the open, get his machine guns in position, and fire at our advancing waves, thus often holding up our attack. In the old days our barrage fire had been placed first on the enemy front line, and had then jumped some two hundred yards to the enemy support line : after which the enemy reserve lines had been bombarded. The enemy reply to this had been to place groups of men with machine guns between his lines of trenches, and our barrage fire having jumped over them, these groups were able to fire on our advancing infantry. Our gunners had then adopted a " creeping barrage," which swept gradually the whole of the ground between the enemy entrenchments. This " creeping barrage " had been brought to perfection during the Messines battle on June 7th, 1917, and had resulted in an almost bloodless victory. When the enemy adopted his " pill box " method of defence, he reduced very considerably the effect of our " creeping barrage," and caused us enormous casualties. Moreover, by the time our troops had fought through this " defensive zone," and captured the pill boxes in it, the impetus of our attack

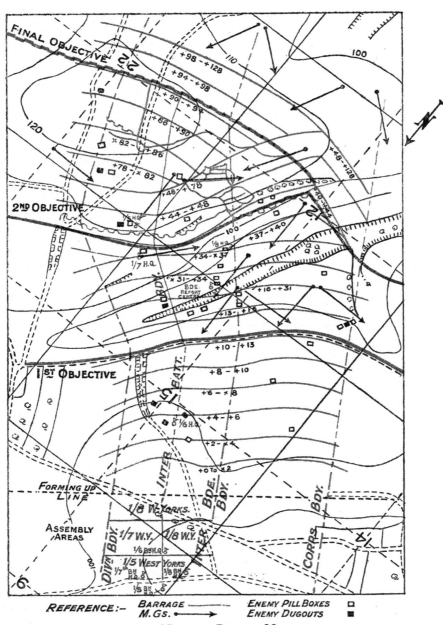

No. 13. Barrage Map.

had gone : our men were tired and scattered : and the enemy " local reserves " were able to launch very often a successful counter attack. Owing to these tactics, aided by Flanders mud, the tremendous battles from July 31st to the end of October, in which nearly the whole British Army was engaged, resulted in an advance of only twelve kilometres and casualties of approximately 600,000 men.

Such were the problems to be faced in the training of the Battalion for the October 9th battle. The following points were specially insisted upon during the practice attacks.

1   The line of advancing infantry must keep within a few yards of the " creeping barrage," so as to allow no time for the small machine gun groups in the enemy pill boxes to rush out when our barrage had passed over them.

2   The initiative of section commanders must be developed in dealing immediately with any such hostile posts, and in keeping their men under control. (During the practice attacks men with red flags representing active enemy " pill boxes " appeared at unexpected places, and our men were practised in dealing with them immediately.)

3   The use of the rifle was insisted upon, in preference to the bomb, which was regarded as principally a weapon of trench warfare.

4   The importance of keeping direction in the advance was emphasized on all occasions.

The reason for the last point is obvious. The fighting in Flanders was nearer open warfare than anything the British Army had known for years, and any loss of direction, resulting in an enemy defensive area being ignored, would have been fatal. Map No. 13 gives some idea of the methods adopted for the Divisional practice attacks on the 29th and 30th September. Few of the rank and file of the Division realized to what an extent such attacks were a colossal gamble till they saw the Division actually formed up for these practices. Everyone had heard how the Germans had attacked in massed formation at Ypres and Verdun, but the dense array of men at the " jumping off " positions near St. Omer convinced everybody that our tactics also were those of " massed battalions." The two assaulting Brigades of the Division, consisting approximately of 4,000 men, were drawn up on a front of 800 yards, with the support Brigade some 1,000 yards in rear. Everything therefore depended upon units being unobserved as they formed up for the actual attack, as an enemy barrage at " zero hour " on the " jumping off " ground would have meant irremediable disaster. This disaster actually had happened to some units in the course of the Passchendaele battle, but fortunately the 49th Division was spared from a repetition of it. The attack practices went well, but as usual the only people who were particularly interested in them were the officers, especially the Staff, who galloped about the enemy " pill box " positions with great éclat, and discussed the operations at length at the end of the day. In order to make the practices more realistic, casualty slips were handed round to great numbers of officers and men, directing them to " fall out " at specified points in the advance. Those who found themselves marked down as casualties at the jumping off tapes, counted themselves extremely fortunate, and commiserated with their comrades on the " privilege " of carrying through to the end of the day.

The last rest before the battle was in Mill Camp, No. 2 Area, Watou, where the Battalion arrived at 3-30 p.m. on October 3rd. In the afternoon of October 5th, a period of three hours " silence " was ordered throughout the units of the 146th Brigade. Men wrote letters home, read a little, or went asleep. It was a striking innovation, and not at all a bad preparation for battle. At 7-30 p.m. in the evening the Battalion marched two miles to the embussing point and was taken in buses to Vlamertinghe, arriving at 10-30 p.m. The night was very dark and quiet, with some rain. The roads were choked with traffic. Landmarks such as Vlamertinghe Church and the Old Mill, familiar to the Battalion in 1915, could dimly be made out in the darkness. Then began the march through Ypres on to the St. Jean-Wieltje Road, and for six kilometres over recently conquered ground to Spree Farm, one and a half miles north east of Wieltje, where the Battalion arrived at dawn on the 6th October. It was a miserable dawn ! The only landmarks in the grey waste all round the Battalion were a few pill boxes such as Gallipoli, Somme, and Schuler Fm., several derelict tanks, stumps of trees near St. Julien, and the duckboards of No. 6 track winding towards Kansas Cross. The billets were shell holes in familiar Flanders mud. The whole area was crowded with troops, and littered with the debris of battle. All trace of roads or houses east of Wieltje had entirely disappeared. Labour battalions were engaged in building a straight plank road across the mud, and thousands of men were making tracks to lead up to gun positions and dumps on either side of the main plank road, which was the only practicable method of communication on a front of nearly two kilometres. Hundreds of mules carrying ammunition and rations struggled forward on either side of the plank road. Transport wagons and lorries went forward as far as possible on the planks, but every half-hour there was some lorry or general service wagon which slipped into the mud, and caused an obstruction. If it was a G.S. wagon which had come to grief, it was lifted again on to the planks. In the case of a loaded motor lorry this could not be done, so the lorry was tipped off the planks into the mud, and the long line of traffic went on again. On either side of the plank road there were dozens of derelict motor lorries, thousands of shells, hundreds of dead horses and mules, all of them rapidly sinking in the mud. The enemy shelled the road constantly, and every hit—and there were many—resulted in casualties. But the road was quickly repaired and the traffic moved on. Near Kansas Cross there was a good landmark, which went by the name of the " Incinerated Man." A 5·9 shell had struck a lorry carrying petrol, and set it ablaze. The driver had been hit at the wheel, and had then been burnt to death. His skeleton remained, however, still sitting in the driving seat and leaning on the steering wheel of the lorry. The stream of traffic poured down the plank road past this ghastly landmark, and for two or three weeks no one troubled to remove it.

October 7th was spent at Spree Farm in making the final preparations for battle. There was a certain amount of enemy shelling, and a direct hit by a 5·9 on a dugout adjoining Battalion Head Quarters killed several men. The rain was incessant. By the morning of the 7th everybody was wet through, and remained so for four days, till the battle was over. A few shelters were built near Spree Farm, but they covered only a handful of the Battalion. The 8th October passed slowly with all ranks in the same positions. All units of the Brigade reconnoitred tracks up to the front line, and officers and platoon sergeants located their assembly positions. This was not easy, for it was extremely difficult to ascertain the exact position of the front line. It was not the slightest use reconnoitring by night, as it was impossible to see the way. An officers' party of the 1/7th Battalion who tried to find their way to the front line by night lost several precious hours the day before the attack in positions north-east of St. Julien, instead of in the Calgary Grange area. Thus our reconnoitring was carried out in daylight, from shell hole to shell hole, in view of the enemy. When the reconnoitring party had passed Kansas Cross, even the duckboards ceased, and the only landmarks were the German pill boxes captured three days earlier. On the Gravenstafel ridge, our reconnoitring party would come across isolated posts of three and four men in shell holes, who were naturally very annoyed if men lingered near their post to ask questions, as the ridge was in full view of the enemy from the Belle Vue Spur and Passchendaele. The only information these posts could usually give was that they were " in support," and there were " more fellows out there ! " So in full view of the enemy, with only a vague idea as to the line of shell holes which represented our front positions, the reconnoitring patrol would push on, very surprised that the enemy did not fire on them, but with an awkward feeling that he might do so any moment. The Brigade front for the attack extended for about 800 yards from east of Calgary Grange to Kronprinz Farm. These two pill boxes were advanced Company Head Quarters of the Battalion in the front line, and were a few hundred yards west of the Stroombeek River. One reconnoitring party of officers of the 1/5th and 1/8th Battalions had advanced beyond Korek, and were within about 400 yards of Calgary Grange, when the enemy put down a very heavy concentrated " area " bombardment for about five minutes between them and the Grange. Needless to say, they waited till it was over, and then " ran for it," so far as one could ever be said to run in such mud and water. The whole party would have been wiped out if they had been a matter of 150 yards nearer Calgary Grange, and two battalions of the Brigade would have attacked on October 9th with only a handful of officers. This " area " shelling was a feature of the Passchendaele battle, and anyone who happened to be in the area affected had little chance of coming out unscathed. There was practically no artillery " sniping," although all our movements on the Gravenstafel ridge were seen by the enemy.

The morning of October 8th was bright and sunny : the ground was drying up : and after two days in shell holes and rain, this change was more than welcome. But early in the afternoon the rain came on worse than ever, and continued without pause for nearly twelve hours. Everyone of the officers and men who had reconnoitred the forward positions felt late' on the afternoon of the 8th that the attack was doomed. Conditions near the Stroombeek were such that even without an enemy, men would have found it almost impossible to keep up to the creeping barrage. The state of the ground cannot have been understood by higher formations, or the attack would have been postponed. In official despatches there is the following :—" On the 8th October rain continued, and the slippery state of the ground, combined with an exceptionally dark night, made the assembling of our troops a matter of considerable difficulty." The " slippery nature of the ground" is, to say the least, an understatement. The 1/6th Battalion was fortunate. They had only 2,500 yards to march from Spree Farm to their assembly position west of Calgary Grange. As it was important not to arrive too early, the Battalion left Spree Farm at 2-30 a.m.. but instead of taking three-quarters of an hour over the journey, nearly three hours' hard work was needed, and it was zero hour, *viz.*, 5.20 a.m., when the Battalion reached the assembly positions. The other battalions of the Brigade had a much more difficult task. For instance the 1/7th Battalion marched off from La Brique (near Saint Jean) at 5 p.m. Their assembly positions were a few hundred yards east of Calgary Grange, and the distance from La Brique was eight or nine kilometres. The battalion marched by No. 6 track, which was fairly good as far as Kansas Cross. From this point a line of trench grids had been put down to within a thousand yards of Calgary Grange. After being seven hours on the way the battalion reached the Gravenstafel ridge

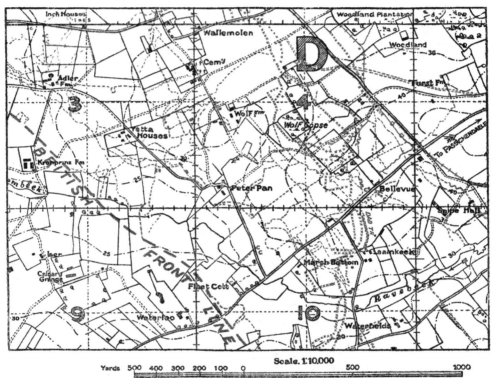

No. 14 Map. Operation Map. Passchendaele, Oct. 9th, 1917.

between Korek and Boetleer. But the worst part of the march was the last thousand yards, which took over two hours hard work to cover! Shells had ploughed up the ground a hundred times, and the rains had made it a quagmire. Woe to the man who slipped into a shell hole full of water! Loaded with equipment, exhausted with seven hours' marching after two days' exposure in the rain, and floundering in a shell hole a foot deep in mud and with water waist high, he was again and again compelled to stay there till some comrades had time to help him out at the risk of sharing his fate themselves. Many men were drowned, weighed down by their equipment, and exhaustion. Many men were stuck up to the thigh in liquid mud, and never reached the assembly positions : they were killed or wounded where they stood by the enemy barrage fire after zero. Feats of heroism and self sacrifice which are beyond praise were common that night. Men who could hardly stand themselves found fresh strength in helping a comrade. Fortunately there was practically no enemy shelling, and the few shells which came lost half their force by burying themselves deeply in the mud before exploding. In spite of the shouts and oaths and rattling equipment of thousands of our men, the enemy advanced posts east of the Stroombeek gave no sign that they were aware a division was massing against them on a 1,500 yard front for an attack at dawn. Notwithstanding the obstacles, the battalions of the 146th Brigade were in position before zero along the taped line from Fleet Cottage to Kronprinz Fm. They were thus more fortunate than some units of other divisions who were too late to take part in the battle. Official dispatches are often fallacious, as they are written in another world at the " back of the front," but they were rarely so misleading as when the Flanders battlefront of October 9th was described as " slippery."

The following are selections from Battalion Operation Orders for the battle.

1/6th BATTALION P. W. O. (WEST YORKSHIRE REGT.)
OPERATION ORDER No. 1.

Reference Maps. Special Operation Map.
Passchendaele, 1/10,000.
Zonnebeke, 1/10,000.
Polygon Wood, 1/20,000.

INFORMATION. 1. The 146th Infantry Brigade in conjunction with the 48th Division (V. Army) on Left and the 148th Brigade on Right, and 147th Brigade in Reserve, will attack, capture, and consolidate in depth the Red and Blue Lines—first and second objective as indicated in Special Operation Map. Compass Bearing of Advance 59° ;
1/5th Battalion West Yorks. Regiment on Right.
1/7th Battalion West Yorks. Regiment in Centre.
1/8th Battalion West Yorks. Regiment on Left.
1/6th Battalion West Yorks. Regiment in Reserve.

ARTILLERY. 2. Artillery Barrage as shewn on Special Operation Map.

As a signal to the infantry that the barrage has reached these lines, each 18-pdr. of barrage A will fire smoke shell for a period of one minute on arriving on the 22-25 lift, and on the 146-154 lift, and will also fire smoke shells for a period of five minutes on arriving on the Red and Blue protective barrage line.

TRENCH MORTARS. 3. Two guns of 146th Trench Mortar Battery will be attached to the Battalion.

AERIAL. 4. Contact Aeroplane will call for flares on the Red Line at Zero plus 80 minutes and on the Blue Line (Final objective) at Zero plus 170 minutes by sounding a series of 'A's' on Klaxon horn and by firing white Verey lights—The most advanced troops will be prepared to answer either of these signals—Flares No. 3 Red will be used. They are plainly visible and it is not necessary to light them in groups, as one is easily visible. They are most easily distinguishable when lit in the bottom of shell holes.

BRITISH MARKINGS ON AEROPLANES. 8. Black Streamer on each lower plane, large 'A' in white, dumb bell painted in white. These are on the fuselage working from the observers seat towards the rudder.

COMMUNICATIONS. 9. Communication will be maintained between Companies and Battalion Head Quarters by means of lamp, shutter and runner. Relay post will be established and indicated by lamps and discs.

BATTALION HEAD QUARTERS. 10. Will be in shell holes behind and between assembly positions of C and D Companies.

BRIGADE HEAD QUARTERS. 11. Brigade Head Quarters will be at Gallipoli.

MEDICAL. 12. Regimental Aid Post will be established near Battalion Head Quarters.

PRISONERS. 13. Prisoners will be sent down under escort (10%) to Battalion Head Quarters—The utmost care will be taken that prisoners do not destroy or get rid of any documents en route.

SYNCHRONIZATION. 14. Watches will be Synchronized at 8.0 p.m. to-night at Battalion Head Quarters by an Officer of each Coy. and again at Zero minus one hour.

INSTRUCTIONS

1. *DRESS.* Fighting order, entrenching tool to be worn sporran fashion.

2. *STORES*. All ranks will carry two sandbags, one flare, one bomb, Verey lights, an extra bandolier S. A. A.

The following also will be distributed and carried by Companies and Battalion Head Quarters :—

S.O.S. Grenades—10 each.
Shovels—10 each.
Tommies' Cookers.
Bottles of Tea.
Lamps, if available.

3. *PACKS AND SURPLUS STORES*. Packs and all surplus stores, dixies, etc. will be dumped near Spree Farm on the Right of ' A ' Coy's line by 6-30 p.m.

Officers Commanding Companies will detail one other rank per Company to report to Lance-Corporal Atkinson at The Dump and to remain in charge of their Company Stores.

4. *RATIONS*. The emergency ration and one day's rations will be carried on each man.

5. *ASSEMBLY*. It is of vital importance in occupying shell holes that men do not show themselves—especially in Assembly positions. One man on look out is all that is required.

6. *SILENCE*. Strictest silence must be maintained **In** and **Getting Into** Assembly Positions.

7. *MESSAGE MAPS AND CARDS*. Message Maps and Cards for distribution issued herewith.

LIST OF CODE CALLS.

Division	Y.D.I.
146th Brigade	B. J Z.
1/5th Battalion West Yorks. Regiment	B. J. A.
1/6th Battalion West Yorks. Regiment	B. J. B.
1/7th Battalion West Yorks. Regiment	B. J. C.
1/8th Battalion West Yorks. Regiment	B. J. D.
146th Machine Gun Coy.	B. J. M.
146th Trench Mortar Battery	B. J. T.
147th Brigade	N. B. Z.
1/4th Battalion West Riding Regiment	N. B. A.
1/5th Battalion West Riding Regiment	N. B. B.
1/6th Battalion West Riding Regiment	N. B. C.
1/7th Battalion West Riding Regiment	N. B. D.
147th Machine Gun Coy.	N. B. M.
147th Trench Mortar Battery	N. B. T.

148th Brigade	Q. K. Z.
1/4th Battalion King's Own Yorks. Light Infantry	Q. K. A.
1/5th Battalion King's Own Yorks. Light Infantry	Q. K. B.
1/4th Battalion York and Lancs. Regiment ..	Q. K. C.
1/5th Battalion York and Lancs. Regiment ..	Q. K. D.
148th Machine Gun Coy.	Q. K. N.
148th Trench Mortar Battery	Q. K. T.

The Fifth Army, 18th Corps are on our Left.

B. A. B. Code.   Correction of Fifth Army = S and B.

What happened on the six mile front of the attack is well known. The greatest progress was made on the extreme left, where French troops and the Guards advanced one and a half miles, and the 29th and 4th Divisions secured a line well to the east of the Poelcappelle-Houthulst Road.   From east of Zonnebeke to east of Gravenstafel our line was carried forward to an average depth of about 1000 to 1500 yards, and Nieuwemolen and Keerselaarhoek were captured.   Over 2,100 prisoners were taken and a few guns.   The 146th Infantry Brigade captured their first objective, except on the extreme left of the Brigade front, and advanced half way towards the second objective, which included the Belle Vue Spur, but the enemy positions were too strong, and the mud too great an obstacle for complete success.

When the barrage opened at 5-20 a.m. the Battalion was in shell holes on the hillside a few hundred yards west of Calgary Grange and Kronprinz Farm.   A and C Companies were on the right, B and D Companies on the left, and Battalion Head Quarters in a shell hole midway behind B and C Companies.   The 1/6th Battalion was in support to the other three battalions of the Brigade, and expected to be called on to help in consolidating the captured positions. " Support " in an attack was never an enviable position, and usually caused some grousing.   " Wish we wasn't in the damned supports," could be heard fairly often.   " Supports always get it worst ! "   And in such remarks there was a great deal of truth.   On this occasion the position the Battalion took up was in direct view of the enemy, and his barrage fire fell directly on the line of the Battalion shell holes. But for the number of " dud " enemy shells and the fact that the mud deadened the force of the explosions, half the Battalion would have been casualties during the first hour.

Our own artillery barrage was disappointing, and was never strong enough for its advance to be clearly defined by the infantry.   This was largely due to the comparatively small number of guns which, owing to the appalling difficulties of the ground, had been able to take up their firing positions. Several batteries which were supposed to have taken part in the barrage on the morning of October 9th, did not come into action till later in the same day. The front line troops on the right and centre of the Brigade front reached the Stroombeek without casualties, but were delayed in crossing it, as the ground was a morass. However, by superhuman exertions, most of them succeeded in again reaching the barrage by the time it was due to be on the first objective on the Red Line, east of Peter Pan and Yetta Houses. The 1/5th Battalion seem to have advanced furthest, and some of them reached the hedge near D4d13, 400 yards east of Peter Pan. A few also were seen within 200 yards of the Belle Vue pill-boxes at 9 a.m., but their position was hopeless. They were being killed off one after another by enemy snipers from Belle Vue and Wolf Copse, and their retreat was impossible owing to enemy machine gun fire from the direction of Wolf Farm. The 1/7th Battalion reached Yetta Houses, and joined up with the 1/8th Battalion on their left.

Casualties were very heavy. Lt. Colonel Bousfield (of the 1/5th Battalion) was wounded, and Lt. Colonel Hudson (of the 1/8th Battalion) was killed. Enemy sniping and machine gun fire was intense, and from all directions. Our barrage had not been sufficiently strong to give the infantry a chance against the enemy posts which remained in action, and although many of the enemy were killed by our rifle and Lewis gun fire, those who were left picked off our men with terrible precision as they stumbled slowly forward in the mud. Enemy machine guns were active even in the midst of our barrage ! At 6-40 a.m. German reinforcements were seen moving rapidly across the Passchendaele ridge to the dugouts near Belle Vue and Wolf Copse, and it was obvious to observers on the Korek ridge that our second objective could not be reached by the thinning line of exhausted men who were only half way up the Passchendaele slope. At 7-40 a.m. a gap was reported between the 1/5th Battalion W.Y. Regt. and the 1/4th Battalion York and Lancs. Regiment on the right, and A Company of the 1/6th Battalion was sent to fill it. At the same time B and C Companies moved forward to strengthen the line east of Peter Pan, and D Company (less two platoons which had been detailed to carry ammunition up to Peter Pan) moved forward to the old British front line near the Stroombeek. Battalion Head Quarters occupied a shell hole a few yards west of the Stroombeek. These movements were carried out under heavy artillery and Machine Gun fire, and casualties were heavy. The advance of A Company on the right of the Brigade front was held up by strong enemy posts at Belle

Vue, and shortly after 9 a.m. C Company was sent up the slope east of Peter Pan with instructions to attack the Belle Vue pill-boxes in conjunction with A Company. The attack was made, and considerable ground gained. Some men advanced within 150 yards of the pill-boxes, and reached the isolated posts of the 1/5th Battalion, but were unable to maintain their positions. The two companies therefore dug in half way up the slope of the hill between Peter Pan and Belle Vue. During this attack Capt. J. L. Speight, commanding C Company, was killed, and every second man in A and C Company became a casualty. Capt. Speight, though only nineteen years of age and with less than a year's service in France, had earned his rapid promotion by his steadiness and fearlessness. His death cut short a career of more than usual promise.

Morning passed almost imperceptibly into afternoon, and neither artillery nor rifle fire showed much sign of abating. Few men could have said whether it rained or not : fewer still had any definite idea of time. A thick cloud of smoke gathered over the valley : but frequent movement of enemy troops could be seen on the hill top, west of Passchendaele. Men were still stuck in the mud all over the battlefield, imploring help to lift them out : half crazy with the sense of their own impotence, and the enemy shelling. Round Calgary Grange the crowd of wounded grew every moment, till it had reached terrible proportions. By the afternoon of October 10th, there were over ninety stretcher cases round that single pill-box, practically every one of whom had been lying there for over twenty-four hours. The battalion medical officers did everything possible, but the arrangements for the evacuation of wounded had temporarily broken down. Calgary Grange was constantly being shelled, and the wounded were often put finally out of misery as they lay there on blankets in the mud. Calgary Grange was a typical pill-box of the smaller size, capable of holding about ten men, with two bunks on either side of the narrow entrance. The pill-box was about five feet high inside and the floor four or five steps below the level of the ground. There was about one and a half feet of water in the dugout. In this small confined space there were three Battalion Head Quarters on the night of October 9th (the 1/5th and 1/7th Battalion West Yorks. Regiment and the 1/6th Battalion West Riding Regiment). A silent crowd of orderlies gathered round the door, and sat on the steps. Stragglers and a constant stream of men who were lost crowded round the dugout and increased the confusion. The wounded lay in heaps on all sides. Every time a 5·9 came extremely near, there was a rush of orderlies down the steps of the dugout. The candles in the pill box were knocked down by the concussion, and the wounded began moaning afresh. As almost every shell in that crowded area claimed a victim, one was almost certain to hear the inevitable " stretcher bearer this way ! " shouted out with the same bored voice with which one might have demanded a small whisky and soda.

By the afternoon of the 9th October, the casualites in the Brigade had reached such proportions that the 1/4th Battalion and one company of the 1/6th Battalion West Riding Regiment (147th Infantry Brigade) were moved up to reinforce the line Peter Pan—Yetta Houses. By 5-30 p.m. two companies of the 1/4th Battalion West Riding Regiment were in position near Yetta Houses, and the other two companies near Peter Pan. The Company of the 1/6th Battalion West Riding Regiment arrived during the night of October 9/10th and took up a position midway between Peter Pan and Yetta Houses. The night passed quietly. There was little enemy shelling. The moon was clouded, there were practically no Verey lights, and men were wandering about, lost, in every part of the battlefield. " Where is Battalion Head Quarters ? " some one would ask hopelessly within five yards of the Head Quarters shell hole. After being out for hours with a message to a Company Head Quarters 800 yards away, an orderly would come back with the message undelivered, having been from one end of the line to the other. The wounded crawled in from advanced positions, and patrols moved forward to Belle Vue and Wolf Copse, and found the enemy very much on the alert, and strengthening his positions. The casualties for the day were two officers (Capt. J. L. Speight and 2nd/Lieut. H. Cheetham) and forty other ranks killed, and one officer and approximately 140 other ranks wounded.

During the night there was heavy rain. The crowd of stretcher cases round Calgary Grange increased every hour, and very few men were evacuated to the rear, owing to the appalling condition of the ground. Scores of seriously wounded men, who in ordinary circumstances would have found it impossible to walk many yards, seemed to have received an extraordinary hysterical energy, and staggered all night across the shell holes towards the First Aid Stations near Kansas Cross and Spree Farm. This break-down in the efforts to deal with the wounded was one of the worst features of the October 9th battle. When the New Zealand Division attacked the Belle Vue Spur three days later, special arrangements were made, and each battalion of the 147th Infantry Brigade provided 200 men to assist in evacuating the wounded. Captain Bales (History of 1/4th Battalion Duke of Wellington's Regiment) records that " volunteers were readily forthcoming from among men who had themselves learned the awful condition of

o   193

the ground." The 10th October passed drearily. The Battalion suffered several casualties from enemy sniping and artillery, but the positions reached the day before were maintained. About 4 p.m. our batteries opened heavy barrage fire on the enemy positions near Belle Vue, which provoked enemy retaliatory shelling along the Brigade front. Working parties were busy continuing the line of trench grids past Boetleer towards Calgary Grange. The Battalion was informed during the afternoon that they would be relieved at night by the 3rd Brigade New Zealand Division.

The New Zealanders began to arrive towards midnight. Never before or since in the history of the Battalion did a relief take place under such conditions. There was, of course, no organized system of shell holes, and sections and platoons of the New Zealanders simply moved forward till they reached approximately our front positions, and then settled down there in the mud and waited till morning, when they could obtain some idea as to their surroundings. There was heavy shelling during the relief. Our own men moved back in groups on the arrival of the New Zealanders, and after several hours wandering, found Calgary Grange, where they were given the direction to Kansas Cross and to Gravenstafel. Battalion Head Quarters was in a particularly " luxurious " shell hole near the Stroombeek. Two planks provided seating accommodation for officers and orderlies, and as the shell hole was deep, the enemy machine gun bullets whistled harmlessly over the heads of the Head Quarters Staff. Though wet through, caked with mud from head to foot, and so exhausted that the march back to Ypres seemed an almost impossible feat, everyone in the shell hole was cheery and undismayed. Colonel Wistance succeeded in infusing into those round him something of his own invincible optimism.

At dawn on October 11th the enemy bombarded violently the whole valley of the Stroombeek, Calgary Grange and Kronprinz Farm and the hill near Gravenstafel and Korek. The relief had not been completed. Parties of New Zealanders who had been lost were still trying to find their companies in the front line positions, and scores of men of the 146th Infantry Brigade, who had been too exhausted to move back after relief during the night, were struggling up the hillside at dawn. They were caught in this bombardment, and there were many casualties. At this time, remnants of the 1/6th Battalion were marching along the Wieltje-Ypres Road towards their rest billets, which were in Nissen Huts, near Vlamertinghe. An event which somewhat relieved the monotony of this eight miles' march happened in the early morning east of Ypres. The Battalion was staggering along in " column of lumps." Everyone was carrying at least a four days' beard, a week's accumulation of mud, and was minus many articles of clothing and equipment. Captain W. G. Tetley marched at the head of D Company, without steel helmet, but with a towel tied round his head, like a turban: with torn clothes and minus a puttee. An Army Service Corps driver on a passing wagon looked at him rather curiously, and said, " Has't ther bean 'oop in't loin, lad ? " The " column of lumps " marched on, and the Army Service Corps driver, by the time he had seen the last man march past, probably realized the answer to his question ! Colonel Wistance was so disguised in mud that he looked more like the Battalion pioneer than a colonel.

During the Passchendaele battle the Battalion Transport probably went through their most trying experiences in France. Few of the transport men will forget October 9th. In addition to the ordinary Transport duties there were several emergency calls on the battalion transports in the Brigade for the carrying of ammunition and water to the forward positions. All battalion transports were under the orders of Captain F. W. Musgrave, who was Brigade Transport Officer. (1/6th Battalion Transport Officer at this time was 2nd/Lieut. Dawson). Capt. Musgrave received orders at 4 p.m. on October 9th that 250 water tins were to be sent up to Spree Farm immediately: at 6 p.m. this order was cancelled and the instructions came that the water tins were to be taken to Wieltje, and filled there, when further orders would be given. Three hours later when the convoy succeeded in reaching Wieltje, it was found that there was no water available, as the Tank had run dry. What was to be done ? Everyone who wanted information of any kind in Wieltje went down into what was called " Admiral Dugout." This dugout was really an underground town, with scores of streets and offices. The dugout had twenty-nine entrances, which were generally crowded with " gas guards," orderlies and half the restless population of the place. Our Brigade Transport Officer fought his way down the steps, and found out that the above mentioned water tins could be filled at Ypres, and need not be up at Spree Farm before 8 a.m. next day. When the pack horses reached the Tank at Ypres next morning the water could not be made to run through the pipes, and some hours were spent in trying to coax it to fill the water tins ! Captain Musgrave also received on early morning of October 10th an order from 49th Division to send three officers and sixty men to report to the 1/2nd Field Ambulance in Ypres at 11 a.m.; a further order to send twenty men to the Town Major at Ypres for 6 a.m. as a ration party : and a few hours later a further order to send " all available men " to work for the A.P.M. in burying dead horses which were lying on the main road east of Wieltje. These orders came at a time when every available man was needed for the ordinary work of a battalion transport, and serve to illustrate the thousand and one demands made upon units immediately behind the firing line during these extraordinary days.

The following description by Captain Musgrave of the journey of a ration and ammunition convoy of pack horses up to Gravenstafel on October 10th gives a good idea of the difficulties of transport, not only during the Passchendaele battle, but throughout the 1917-1918 winter in the Ypres Salient. The convoy consisted of twenty-four pack horses from each battalion in the Brigade, and eight from the 146th Infantry Brigade Machine Gun Company, a total of 104 pack horses. The convoy was ordered to take rations and ammunition from Spree Farm to Gravenstafel, and was due to reach Spree Farm at 10 a.m.

"Prompt at 7 a.m. we got off, and made good time to one mile east of Ypres. No. 6 Track was between one and two feet deep in mud, and after crossing and re-crossing the trench grids, we eventually got back on to a road made by the Royal Engineers. My mare Sulky had already dropped me in the mud once, but no harm done ! Half a mile along this road we ran into a block. I went forward and told Dawson (Transport Officer of the 1/6th Battalion) to follow up, and said I would go on to Spree Farm. It was now well past ten a.m. and there were still two miles to do. I arranged matters at Spree Farm, and then started back for the convoy. I spent nearly two hours doing those two miles, riding between wagons and over shell holes, and found the convoy still blocked, and with no chance of getting forward for an hour or two. So we endeavoured to cut across country. It was the most awful mistake I could have made. We got on well for half a mile, Dawson leading, myself in rear. Then Dawson started winding in and out of shell holes. It was raining, and had been doing so for hours. The ground· was awful, and sodden past words. We went over trenches, barbed wire, dead horses, round tanks, guns and dead men. At one time I had as many as eight horses in shell holes. There was going to be disaster, unless the situation was handled firmly and quickly. I halted every man I could find, and took one man at a time back on to the main road. Five horses had been got out of the shell holes by N.C.O.'s and men, but three were still stuck. After a big fight two of them were got out, and Lieut. Harper (Transport Officer 1/5th Battalion), who was returning after having taken up his rations, went back nearly a mile to try and get the other out. At 2 p.m. we had loaded up at Spree Farm, and had started off for Gravenstafel. The track was about twelve feet wide, and made of tree trunks, hurdles and fascines, and was two feet deep in mud in some places. We had not been going five minutes before a pack horse was down with one foot caught between the poles of the track. We took off the load : pulled the poles apart : reloaded the animal, and started again. The same happened with another horse a few minutes later. Two more horses were down with absolute fatigue, and had to be beaten severely to get them on with the rest. How long would the horses last ? Shouts from behind came to the head of the column where I was, asking for a rest, as the men were also seemingly ' paid.' But the ammunition had to be got up, and we couldn't afford a voluntary halt for the men, as I was afraid the horses would drop if there was a halt. After a few hundred yards further we were blocked by a gun stuck in three feet of mud with ten horses nearly killing themselves to move it, but after some argument we got past all right. I had been told to dump the ammunition near a pile of biscuit tins at Gravenstafel, and eventually we got past all the guns to the place I imagined was correct. It was 3-30 p.m. Ten horses were unloaded and got away, when a few shells came over. One of them hit a gun which was being put into position about 700 yards away, and blew the gun and the artillery people near it to blazes. Then the enemy guns turned on us, so the order was given to dump where the horses stood. We got away without any worse disaster than one man hit. During the trip back, one man of the Machine Gun Company in his haste to mount his animal swung on to his horse's back and tumbled clean over—falling on his face and cutting it up somewhat ! The pony bolted and the fellow got up feeling very sorry for himself. He mounted an artillery horse later, and strange to say, his own pony was found and brought back to our lines."

The result of the October 9th battle on the front of the 146th Infantry Brigade was that our line was advanced across the obstacle of the Stroombeek, and continued for some hundreds of yards east of Peter Pan—an advance of nearly one kilometre. Some idea of the strength of the enemy positions near Belle Vue, where our attack was held up, may be gathered from the fact that the attack of October 12th, in which the New Zealand Division took part, failed altogether on this part of the front. The Belle Vue Spur was only captured nearly three weeks later, on October 26th, when the 3rd and 4th Canadian Divisions came up fresh for the attack, and after being checked early in the morning, succeeded in capturing the position by a second attack on the afternoon of the same day. In all these attacks the mud was the chief obstacle !

Appreciation of the work done by the 49th Division was expressed by the following message from the General Officer Commanding 2nd Anzac Corps :—

"Following message has been received by me, from Army Commander, begins :—

'Please accept and convey to all your troops engaged to-day my heartiest congratulations on success achieved.'"

General Plumer.

The Commander-in-Chief also called here to-day and wished specially to congratulate you and your Division.

I wish also to add my high appreciation and thanks to you personally and to all ranks of your Division on having done so much under such arduous and trying conditions.

General Godley.

Major General E. M. Perceval, C.B., D.S.O., General Officer Commanding 49th Division, issued a Special Order on October 19th which contained the following :—

"On giving up the Command of the Division which I have held since July, 1915, I wish to thank all ranks for their invariable loyal support, and to express my great admiration for their gallant conduct.....It will always be a special source of pleasure and pride to me that I was in Command of the Division in the recent action. Nothing could be finer than what the Division accomplished on that occasion....."

General Perceval's place in command of the 49th Division was taken by Major General N. J. G. Cameron, C.B., C.M.G., who had formerly commanded an Infantry Brigade of the 50th Division. General Godley still remained in command of the II. Anzac Corps.

After a night spent in Nissen Huts, near Vlamertinghe, the Battalion embussed on the afternoon of October 12th and moved west of Poperinghe to near Winnezeele, a village a few miles north of Cassel. For some reason or other the busses dumped the battalions of the 146th Infantry Brigade on the outskirts of Winnezeele, about five kilometres from their destination, which was Camp B, No. 3 area, and near Ouderzeele. The result of this mistake was that no guides were there to meet the 1/6th Battalion, which was compelled to wait over three hours in continuous heavy rain. The men had not been dry since October 7th, and this prolonged exposure, after the battle conditions of October 9th and 10th, all but "finished" every man in the Battalion! The last five kilometres march to Ouderzeele was a nightmare to all ranks. The men were so done up that many of them could not jump a small ditch into the Camp, and were helped across by some of the Transport men! The tents were in a very bad condition, and pitched in a sodden field which was several inches deep in mud and water. But everyone was too exhausted for anything but sleep.

PASSCHENDAELE

The next two days were spent in kit inspections, cleaning up sodden equipment, " baths," and all the other activities of a " rest " period.

A month passed before the Battalion again went up into the front line. During this period there was little opportunity for any training except that of specialists such as Lewis gunners, as the Battalion made several moves, and was engaged in working parties a good deal of the time. On October 16th the Battalion marched fourteen miles to Camp 29, on the south east outskirts of Poperinghe, and provided daily working parties under the supervision of the C. R. E. II. Anzac Corps on Oak Hangar Dump. Whilst working on this Dump the men paraded at 7-30 a.m. and worked till 4 p.m. in the afternoon. The Dump was occasionally shelled by a high velocity gun, which did not improve working conditions. After a week of this, the Battalion marched back to Winnezeele in heavy rain, and was billeted in the same camp. A further march of about eight miles took place five days later to the Steenvoorde area, where the Battalion remained doing company and specialist training till November 8th, when a move was made to Howe Camp near Ypres. The men were billeted in Nissen huts in a more than usually muddy camp.

During this month's respite after the Passchendaele attack news had been received that Lieut.-Colonel Wistance had been awarded the D.S.O., and Capt. Gordon and Lieut. Stansfield the M. C. for their services during the battle. Brigadier General M. D. Goring Jones, C.M.G., D.S.O., relinquished command of the 146th Infantry Brigade on proceeding to England, and the new Brigade Commander was Brigadier-General G. A. P. Rennie, D.S.O., of the King's Royal Rifle Corps, who had previously been in command of one of the battalions of the 14th Division. Brigadier-General Goring Jones was an officer of strong individuality, and had made his presence felt throughout the whole Brigade, of which he had been in command for nearly two years. He scorned compromise : was a stern disciplinarian : and during the battle of the Somme, in 1916, was unfortunate in showing the harsher side of his character to the officers and men of his battalions. When men saw him coming round the line, with his tall masterful figure, clean-cut jaw thrust forward, and sharp piercing eyes, they instinctively expected " strafing," and very often received it. Not until the last few months was he understood or appreciated by most officers and men of the Brigade. He loved his work passionately and never allowed himself or anyone else to shirk any part of it. He knew every trench in his Brigade sectors and had the soldier's love of detail and accuracy. He hated weakness or excuses, and was very sarcastic in his remarks on those whose motto was " I mean well." He died a few months after the armistice. His death was hastened by the tremendous energy he threw into all his work, whether in training or in front line conditions.

On November 11th the 146th Infantry Brigade took over the defence of the Broodseinde Sector, and the Battalion relieved the 21st Battalion Australian Infantry in Brigade left support at Garter Point, with one Company at Tokio, another on the Anzac Ridge and the remaining two Companies near Kit and Kat on the Westhoek Ridge. These support positions were about two thousands yards behind the front line. On November 15th the Battalion relieved the 1/5th Battalion West Yorkshire Regiment in the left sub-sector of the front line, and remained there for four days. The Brigade front extended slightly over two kilometres from immediately north of the Broodseinde-Zonnebeke Road to Molenaarelsthoek, and was held by two battalions. The 1/6th Battalion held the line with two companies in a series of shell holes on the forward slopes of the Broodseinde Ridge, and two companies in support about six hundred yards behind near the Cemetery. Battalion Head Quarters was in the pill box of Moulin Farm.

Those few unfortunate men who passed through both the winter of 1915 and the first six or seven weeks on the Broodseinde Ridge in the winter of 1917 are unanimous that in both cases the limits of physical misery and wretchedness were reached. The Broodseinde experiences were aggravated by the increased shelling and the extreme discomforts of " shell hole " existence in Flanders mud. In the " front line " small groups of four or five men lived in shell holes under the direct observation of the enemy from the Keiburg Spur opposite. Thus all movement was impossible except by night. It was useless digging the shell holes deeper, as they filled with water. If one tried to make them larger, they attracted the attention of the enemy. Almost every attempt at digging resulted in the disturbance of dead bodies, in every stage of decomposition. No fires could be lit; no hot food brought up from behind; water was very scarce owing to the extraordinary difficulties of the carrying parties in such a sea of mud, and the only chance of a hot drink depended on the inhabitants of the shell hole being in possession of Tommies' cookers.

When the Battalion took over the line in the Broodseinde Sector fighting was still going on three or four kilometres further north near Passchendaele. The collapse of Russia had released German Divisions and artillery for Flanders, and although the enemy had not been able to prevent us capturing the Passchendaele Ridge, he had made us pay an enormous price. The shelling on both sides was intense, and casualties were very great. The chief means of communication from

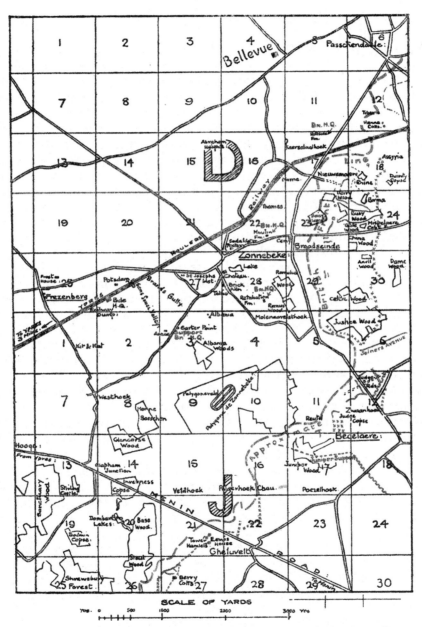

No. 15 Map. Zonnebeke-Passchendaele, Oct. 9th, 1917-1918.

Ypres to Zonnebeke were Mole Track and F. Track, and they were incessantly and accurately shelled. Zonnebeke and the Zonnebeke Road were places to avoid at all costs. The Gasometer east of Zonnebeke was a well-known and unhealthy rendezvous for guides to the front line posts. Reliefs were never accomplished without several casualties. Mole Track from Birr Cross Roads to Garter Point was a nightmare. The heaviest enemy fire was concentrated on to our support positions on the Anzac Ridge, and our companies suffered daily casualties when in support. The horrors of heavy gas shelling were added to everything else, and mustard gas claimed many victims. On the morning of November 11th, when moving up to Garter Point, the Battalion lost one of the best N. C. O.'s who ever served with the Battalion—Corporal Silverwood, D.C.M., M.M., one of the Battalion Scouts. A few days later Lieuts. Weighill, M.C., and W. McLean were wounded, Lieut. McLean fatally. Weighill was constantly being wounded, and succeeded in finishing the war alive with no less than five wound stripes. In the intervals when not in hospital, he was one of the best patrol leaders in the Brigade. He seemed indifferent to danger, and during the Somme battle made a very fine collection of " souvenirs,"—German helmets, bayonets, decorations, post-cards, etc., many of them gathered in No Man's Land. He was wounded in July, 1916, whilst souvenir hunting, and was extremely annoyed because other people made free with his collection whilst he was in hospital.

Few men had the honour—or misfortune— to experience both the winter of 1915 and of 1917-1918 in the Ypres Salient. The following description of conditions during November and December, 1917, is given by one of them (Lieut. C. G. Maufe), and the reader with any imagination will be able to appreciate, in this restrained summary, something of the long-drawn out suffering endured by infantry during these winter months.

"The tracks to the Broodseinde Ridge consisted of one single line of duckboards, and even these were limited—one only to the left battalion position, and one to the right battalion. These two tracks looped round and met each other, forming a sort of ' grand promenade ' along our side of Broodseinde Ridge, and out of sight of the enemy. The left track was F track and the right track to Molenaarelsthoek was Jabber track. Each track stretched back to Birr X Roads, about four miles away. These constituted the sole approaches for infantry—the ground being absolutely impossible for walking anywhere except on these duckboards. Transport used the Plank Road from Birr X Roads through Garter Point to Zonnebeke (' up traffic ' only being allowed), and thence came back from the line down the Zonnebeke-Ypres Road. This Plank Road had an even worse reputation for enemy shelling than the duckboard tracks —if that were possible ! Within a mile of Garter Point two hundred and fifty dead horses and mules could be counted in the mud on either side of the track—all of them killed by shell fire. Up to Westhoek Ridge a man was sportingly ' safe '—at least he had a fair chance ! But from the Westhoek Ridge all tracks and the Plank Road dipped into the Hannebeke valley—the worst spot of all, a perfect hell-hole...This valley was full of water-logged shell-holes, none of which seemed caused by a shell of less calibre than a 5·9. The enemy shelled the bottom of this valley incessantly day and night, and always had an 8-inch howitzer playing on it—the bursts from which exceeded anything I remember in the regular way of shelling. For a month the enemy also used an 11-inch armour-piercing gun on this valley, where the forward positions of our own guns were disposed. The main body of our artillery was in one line—wheel to wheel—on the west side of the Westhoek Ridge. Battalion relief nights were dreaded by everyone. It took many hours for a battalion to grope along the single duckboard tracks, and the man who took a false step in the dark was instantly immersed in seemingly bottomless liquid putrid mud. Once you reached the front line you were comparatively safe—provided you did not move ! The line consisted of rifle pits about four hundred yards down the slope of the Broodseinde Ridge. The supports on the top of the ridge had a rotten time, as they were continually being shelled by 5·9's. Ration parties and runners were always having heavy casualties. The feature of the German shelling was ' area ' strafes, when for about ten or fifteen minutes the enemy seemed to put a shell in every square foot of ground in the area affected, which was usually about two hundred yards square. Shelling with guns of less calibre than 5·9's was almost unknown, except when the enemy put a few 77 mm. into the front line rifle pits. As movement was so restricted it was difficult to visit these rifle pits except at dusk or dawn, and as a result hardly any work was done to improve the front positions.

Rations were brought up on pack animals for a long time, as it was found that, owing to enemy shelling on the roads and the frequent blocks which occurred when wagons and motor lorries were blown up, it was the only certain method of getting rations up to the line in time. As it was, animals and convoys were often separated, and arrived at intervals of hours. This description applies equally to December, 1917, when we held the line from Broodseinde Cross Roads to Passchendaele, only in this case the Ypres-Zonnebeke Road alone was used by the Brigade for both ' up ' and ' down ' traffic, thus making confusion worse confounded. In this sector the front line was more exposed to view, and the enemy snipers were busy, though their positions could not be found. The supports in this piece of line were even further behind the front line than they had been in the southern sector, and in case of attack it would have taken the supports about two hours to reach the front line! But the state of the ground precluded the possibility of successful attack by the enemy."

During the whole of the winter on the Broodseinde Ridge our patrols were very active. The enemy was content to be on the defensive, and his positions were on the average fully a kilometre distant from our own. On the second night in the line a patrol reconnoitred China Wood, which was six hundred yards from our own advanced shell holes, and on the same night another patrol advanced on the Broodseinde-Moorslede Road for over nine hundred yards without meeting

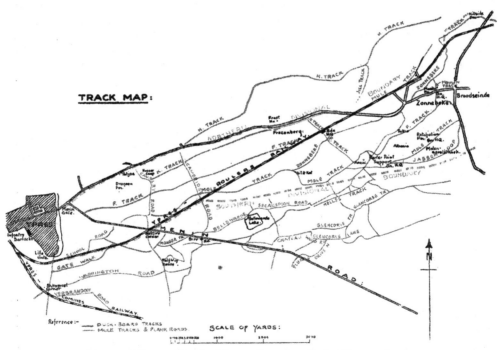

No. 16 Map. Track Map. Passchendaele-Ypres Sector.

the enemy. This patrol reported hearing sounds of enemy movement in Table Wood, immediately north of the road, but the main enemy positions had obviously been withdrawn to the line Droogenbroodhoek-

Keiberg, or over two kilometres from our own line. An enemy attack was not feared. No Man's Land was in the same fearful state of mud as the ground from Ypres to Passchendaele. Moreover, from the Broodseinde Ridge our men could see Moorslede and the other towns of the Belgian plain almost at their feet, and our commanding positions near Passchendaele gave every infantryman in the Ypres " Salient " a tremendous sense of superiority over the enemy. In spite of shell-hole conditions, and terrific artillery fire, the morale of the Battalion throughout the winter was excellent. During the first few weeks there were constant S.O.S. calls from the front line, owing to the heavy barrages the enemy put down, but no one doubted the ability of the Division to hold the Broodseinde Ridge.

On November 19th, the 146th Infantry Brigade was relieved by the 147th Infantry Brigade, and the Battalion moved on relief by the 1/7th Battalion West Riding Regt. to Half-Way House north of Zillebeke Lake, and thence to huts near Chateau Belge, south west of Ypres. After a few days spent in cleaning equipment, etc., the Battalion moved to Vancouver Camp, near Vlamertinghe, and on the 28th November to Infantry Barracks, Ypres. In spite of the artillery fire Ypres had suffered, the Infantry Barracks had been so solidly built that they still afforded excellent and ample shelter, and the wire beds were a great luxury. Working parties were supplied for salvage and for the construction of light tramways under the supervision of the 458th Field Company Royal Engineers, commanded by Major E. Jackson, D.S.O., a most capable and popular officer, and a worthy successor of Major A. F. Hobson, who had been killed near Hammerhead Sap when the Battalion was in line near Thiepval in August, 1916. On December 8th the Battalion again relieved the 1/5th Battalion West Yorks. Regt. in the Broodseinde Sector. Snow fell during this period, but thawed quickly, and made things even more miserable. The next period of rest was at Halifax Camp (adjoining Vancouver Camp near Vlamertinghe), where one or two strenuous games of Rugby formed a welcome diversion. The Sergeants beat the Officers by the narrow margin of eleven goals to nine, but the Battalion went down before the II. Anzac Cyclist Company. Christmas was spent in a new sector north of the Broodseinde-Moorslede Road and which extended to within 100 yards of the Ypres-Roulers Railway. This sector was immediately north of the one previously held by the Battalion. Battalion Head Quarters was in a pill-box near Daring Crossing, where one company of the 1/7th Battalion West Yorkshire Regiment was also attached as a tactical support. Conditions in this part of the line were even worse than those in the sector south of the Broodseinde Road. It was impossible to use the deep cutting of the Ypres-Roulers Railway, as it was covered with deep mud. From Seine to the front line near Nieuwemolen, trench grids were conspicuous by their absence, and reliefs and ration parties wallowed helplessly in and out of shell holes. Fortunately a hard frost about this time greatly improved conditions, and the ground became passable. The nights were fine and clear, and the earth was covered with snow. For the first and only time during the war, Christmas Day was spent by the Battalion in the front line. The enemy was more than usually unpleasant, and opened out an extremely heavy barrage at 5 p.m. on the whole Passchendaele sector. But there was no infantry activity. About the same time also on Boxing Day, the enemy sent up a single red light from his trenches opposite the Battalion front, and immediately heavy enemy barrage fire was opened on all the communications of the Passchendaele sector and on our front line positions, and continued for nearly three hours till 8-5 p.m. The division on our left and our own front line posts sent up the S.O.S. but again no infantry action followed. The Battalion remained two more days in the front line, during which the enemy artillery continued to be extremely active and our Transport suffered several casualties. Thus, so far as the Battalion was concerned, the last few days of 1917 passed noisily. The enormous strength of the enemy artillery, reinforced by batteries from the Russian front, was not an auspicious augury for the year 1918.

During the whole of the 1917-1918 winter a great deal of attention was concentrated on Salvage. A wave of economy swept over the Ypres Salient. Every stage of our advance during the battles of the late summer in 1917 had been marked by derelict tanks, rifles, equipment, gas helmets, shells, bandoliers and other war material of every description. A most praiseworthy, and owing to the shortage of supplies, necessary effort was made to collect this material into Brigade and Divisional dumps placed all over the battlefield. Everyone was ordered to carry something back to some of these dumps after every visit to the line. The saving thus effected must have been very great. For instance in the 146th Infantry Brigade area over three thousand shells were salvaged in one week! The Veterinary Officer of the Division was sent forward to skin the dead horses lying in hundreds round Garter Point, and the shoes of the horses were also salvaged. It is probably true to say that this salvage work was popular with all ranks. Men were tired of the waste and the reckless expenditure of war material, and units vied with each other on the amount of salvage they could save from the mud. But in spite of all these efforts the whole area still remained littered with an astonishing variety of war material.

PASSCHENDAELE

New Year's Day, 1918, was spent in rest in Infantry Barracks, Ypres. In the New Year's Honours our Quarter-Master, Major W. H. Hill, received the Military Cross, a richly deserved recognition of long and faithful service with the Battalion. On January 7th the Battalion again took over the left sub-sector south of the Broodseinde-Moorslede Road and after a comparatively uneventful four days in the line was relieved by the 2/5th Manchester Regiment of the 66th Division. This relief was part of the Divisional relief of the 49th by the 66th Division. Every unit in the 49th Division had endured nearly three months in the Passchendaele area, and urgently needed a rest or change. It was therefore arranged that two Brigades of the Division should go back for rest and training, and the remaining Brigade should continue to work on the new Corps Line which was being constructed on the Westhoek Ridge. From January 13th to February 10th the 146 Infantry Brigade was " out " for rest and training and was billeted near Cassel, the 1/6th Battalion being stationed at Bavinchove, a small village at the foot of Cassel Hill. A portentous programme of recreational training had been drawn up by the Division, and the weeks passed very pleasantly. This period at Bavinchove was interrupted by a visit of three days to the Second Army Rifle Ranges at Moulle, north-west of St. Omer. Every man was put through the usual musketry practices, and although the weather was broken, the men enjoyed the rifle practices, especially the last day, which was taken up with field firing. The Battalion won the Brigade Competition in the Assault Practice.

On January 31st a big reorganization of the Infantry Units in the British Expeditionary Force took place. Divisions were reduced from a thirteen battalion to a ten battalion basis. In the 146th Infantry Brigade the 1/8th Battalion West Yorkshire Regiment was broken up, and the officers, N. C. O.'s and men were divided among the other three battalions of the Brigade. The Head Quarters Staff of the 1/8 Battalion proceeded to join the 2/8th Battalion of the 62nd Division, and became the 8th Battalion West Yorkshire Regiment. In the 185th Brigade of the 62nd Division the 2/6th Battalion was disbanded. and a draft of four officers * and 100 other ranks were posted to the 1/6th Battalion whilst at Bavinchove. The next day (February 6th) another draft of two officers and forty-five other ranks arrived from the 18th Battalion West Yorks. Regiment. After the casualties at Passchendaele on October 9th, it had been found necessary to reduce Companies from four to two platoons per Company, but the arrival of these

---

* Lieuts. Beldon, F. C. Albiston, C. N. Pepper, W. Broadwith.

reinforcements resulted in the reorganization of the Battalion on a four platoon per Company basis. In his " Despatches " Sir Douglas Haig remarks as follows on the reduction in strength of divisions from thirteen to ten battalions. "Apart from the reduction in fighting strength involved by this reorganization, the fighting efficiency of units was to some extent affected. An unfamiliar grouping of units was introduced thereby, necessitating new methods of tactical handling of the troops and the discarding of old methods to which subordinate commanders had been accustomed." In the case of the 1/6th Battalion the reinforcements were all men of the same regiment and quickly settled down together.

On February 10th the Battalion began work on the Corps Line along the Westhoek Ridge. This line was over four kilometres west of the Broodseinde Ridge, and an enormous amount of work was being done to make it an almost impregnable inner defence of Ypres. The lessons of the Cambrai battles in November had impressed upon our General Head Quarters the importance of organized rear lines of defence. Unfortunately these rear lines on the greater part of the front were being constructed too near our original front line positions, and in the great German attack in March, it was found that our troops had not time to re-organize and occupy them, owing to the speed of the enemy advance. Whilst engaged on the working parties on the Corps Line, the Battalion was billeted in huts in Devonshire Camp, and moved later to Hussar Camp near Potijze. Like some other Camps in the Ypres district Devonshire Camp, although it had been condemned as being unfit for troops, was still being used owing to the lack of accommodation and billets in the Ypres Salient. The working parties marched from the Camp, which was near Ouderdom and Reninghelst, to Brandhoek, on the Poperinghe — Vlamertinghe Road, where the men entrained for Gordon House (near Halifax Corner) about two kilometres east of Ypres. The parties then marched up to their respective tasks near Frezenberg, or Kit and Kat, and after four hours work returned to Devonshire Camp.

During these weeks in February the storm was gathering on the Western Front, although our working parties in the Ypres Salient felt themselves comparatively secure, as they were defended by successive fortified ridges which would have proved a tremendous obstacle to an enemy advance. Yet the menace was great. The number of German Infantry Divisions in France and Belgium had risen to 192 on March 21st, 1918, an increase of 46 Divisions since the 1st November, 1917. The enemy infantry also became more aggressive. On March 11th, when the

GROUP OF OFFICERS TAKEN AT ESTAIRES, JUNE, 1917.

TOP ROW.—LIEUTS. R. D. MCLEAN, L. SPEIGHT, EMMISON, F. E. FAIRBANK, TALBOT, FRENCH INTERPRETER.

THIRD ROW.—LIEUT. TEMPEST, M.C., CAPT. DOUGLAS, R.A.M.C., LIEUTS. A. S. FAIRBANK, WEIGHILL, GOODALL, WALKER, DAWSON AND CHEETHAM.

SECOND ROW.—LIEUTS. SCALES, M.C., BRIGGS, DE GROOT, MILNER, ROBINSON, STANSFIELD, AMBLER AND S. GORDON.

FRONT ROW.—CAPTS. GRICE, HORNSHAW, LIEUT. AND ADJT. MOSSOP, LT.-COL. W. A. WISTANCE, M.C., MAJOR R. CLOUGH, M.C., CAPT. R. WHINCUP, M.C., C.F., AND CAPT. J. GORDON.

xxxiii.

AEROPLANE PHOTO—WYTSCHAETE, 1918.

GERMAN TRENCHES AND NO MAN'S LAND (NEAR " THE POPLAR ") N. OF
GOMMECOURT WOOD, 1916.

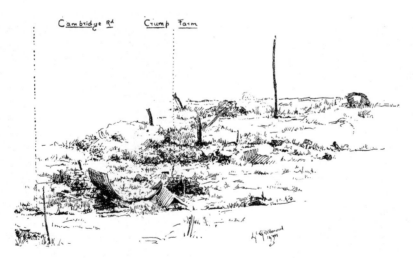

Mill Cot

Cambridge Rd End

SKETCH—" MILL COT," NR. YPRES, 1918.

Cambridge Rd   Crump Farm

SKETCH—" CRUMP FARM," NR. YPRES, 1918.

XXXV.

C.S.M. C. G. SIMPSON, D.C.M.

C.S.M. F. BAXTER.

SERGT. E. BUCKLEY.

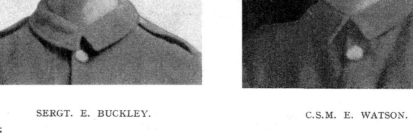

C.S.M. E. WATSON.

Battalion went into the line near Broodseinde for their four days " tour," the enemy raided an advanced post of C Company on the Broodseinde Road, and obtained an identification from us. This was the second time the enemy had tried to obtain an identification from the Brigade. The first occasion was on February 23rd when the 1/7th Battalion was occupying the same sector. The enemy raided the line of the 1/7th Battalion about midnight after a heavy barrage. He came over in two parties ; one of which was driven off, and the other party surrendered ! An officer (wounded) and thirteen other ranks (unwounded) were captured by the men of the 1/7th Battalion in this action. This increased activity on the part of the enemy was very marked and significant.

During 1917 he had been definitely on the defensive. Now the tables were turned, and the enemy was on the offensive. There was little artillery activity, however, as his guns were being massed further south near the Somme.

The morning of March 21st saw the opening of the great German Offensive on the Somme. It was a very beautiful spring morning in the Salient, though the beauty of it was marred by great enemy artillery activity. For some days previously the enemy artillery had been more active than during February and March, though it was still far from being as violent as during November and December, 1917. From 3 a.m. to 7-30 a.m. on the morning of March 21st, the enemy bombarded all the back area with gas shells, saturating the whole Salient. Fortunately during the winter every man in the Division had been practised frequently in wearing a gas mask for two hours and carrying on the ordinary routine at the same time. So this prolonged gas bombardment caused comparatively little inconvenience. At 7-30 a.m. the bombardment ceased, and all was quiet in the Ypres Salient! The storm had burst further south, far away ! From that day a remarkable change came over the Salient. It was dramatic in its suddenness. Instead of being one of the " high places of the field," upon which the attention of friend and foe had for so long been specially concentrated, the Salient became an abode of peace, an apparently forgotten corner of the battle line.

On March 29th battalions of the 16th Brigade (6th Division) relieved the 146th Infantry Brigade in the Broodseinde sector, and three days later the 1/6th Battalion took over a new sector astride the Menin Road in front of Gheluvelt. Battalion Head Quarters was in a pill-box near the remains of " Inverness Copse," and Brigade Head Quarters was in Jackdaw Tunnels. The enemy infantry was fairly active, though apart from light and medium trench mortars, there was no enemy shelling. After the Battalion had been in the line a week, one of A Company's posts, a few yards north of the Menin Road, was approached about midnight by an enemy patrol. Our sentry challenged, whereupon the enemy party attacked the post with bombs. The garrison opened out a heavy rifle fire which caused the enemy to withdraw and inflicted some casualties. A small party searched the ground immediately, and brought in one wounded German of the 24th Jäger Regiment. The next night the enemy made two more attempts to capture our posts, again without success. About 4-45 a.m. the garrison in a post on the left of the Battalion front near Polderhoek Chateau saw a party of about twenty Germans approaching. The enemy seemed in the darkness to have almost surrounded the position, and opened up a heavy fire with bombs. Our garrison replied immediately with their Lewis gun and rifles, and the enemy scattered. Several casualties must have been inflicted on the enemy, as cries and groans were heard. Simultaneously, another fight was going on about 500 yards further south. In this case the enemy had reached the wire surrounding our shell hole position before he was seen, and had begun throwing bombs, to which our men replied with rifle fire. In this case also the enemy was compelled to withdraw, without having caused us any casualties. A very smart piece of work was carried out on this occasion by two N.C.O's —Sergeants Cuthbert and Brookes (A Company). They left their post from a flank as the enemy party was retiring, made their way quickly round to the German line, and cut off part of the enemy patrol, capturing the German Officer who had been in charge of both the enemy raiding parties. This officer belonged to the 26th Jäger Regiment, and stated that the men he had brought with him were picked men, but they had lost their bearings in No Man's Land, and had attacked two of our posts, instead of one, as had been originally arranged. Again on the 13th April another of our posts on B Company's front succeeded in inflicting loss on the enemy, and brought in a wounded prisoner, who stated that he had been with a ration party which had lost the way to its own post, and wandered across No Man's Land. The above captures of prisoners were very useful, as they gave us important identifications of the enemy units opposite. On April 9th the enemy had begun his offensive near Armentières, and the necessity of identifying units in the Ypres Salient immediately after the battle began further south was urgent.

But these patrol encounters only accentuated the extreme quietness of the line. We will again quote from the experience of one who was in the Salient at this time.

" We lost all idea of war during these early days of April.

PASSCHENDAELE

A calm—most ominous and eerie—fell on the Salient. The sound of artillery was unknown. The Germans had removed their guns, and the sector became a rest camp. People indulged in walks from the support positions along Observatory Ridge to watch the sunsets, and spy on the Germans walking in the streets of Halluin and Wervicq. All the supporting troops were taken from us in early April after the Lys battle started. All battalions of the Brigade were in the line, and there was no one to relieve them. Our artillery consisted of eight 18-pounders and two 4·5 howitzers on a front of seven kilometres, stretching from the Railway Cutting near Hill 60, to Becelaere. Where we had once not dared to show our noses we now sat on the top of pill boxes and admired the view over the Moorslede Plain and southwards towards Lille. But day after day the sound of continuous terrific cannonading grew nearer and nearer from the South. Every night we went out to watch the flashes and the glare in the sky made by the intense artillery duels of the Lys battle. Every night the flashes seemed further west, until by April 14th, they appeared to be behind us, and we realized that the Ypres Salient was not likely to be a rest camp for many days longer. We realized the probability of being cut off where we stood. The only railway communication was now *via* Dunkerque and along the coast. The main line *via* Hazebrouck was no longer practicable, as in places the Germans were only four miles from it. We noted frenzied calls for Generals to conferences, and Colonels to meet Generals: an anxious look on the face of those in command: disappointment deep-seated, not to be spoken of, but more deeply felt because of necessary reticence. At last the command to retire to the old 1915 line close to Ypres was given, and we walked away from the enemy without firing a shot :—all the ground given up without a struggle, for which 250,000 men had given their lives in 1917. The feelings of all concerned cannot be portrayed in words. Only those who took part in its capture could realize what it meant to give it up. The work which had been put in to make the Ridges impregnable, was all left. It was hard not to lose one's pride, difficult to keep heart, to be cheerful.... We destroyed our concrete emplacements....It was a sad ending to the most self-sacrificing victory won by the British Army during the War."—(Lieut. C. G. Maufe).

Thus by the middle of April all ranks had begun to realize that their stay in the Ypres Salient was coming to an end. Nearly all Divisions in the British Army were being drawn into the battle further south, and our men were impatient to be playing their part in what clearly were decisive engagements of the war. The story of the last few days spent by the Battalion in the Ypres Salient in

April, 1918, is so inextricably bound up with the events happening further south near Vierstraat and Kemmel that we will deal with it in the next chapter. The withdrawal from the Broodseinde Ridge, which the Battalion was about to carry out and which is referred to above, seemed to many of the men almost an act of treachery towards comrades who had given their lives in capturing it in October and November, 1917. Certainly this withdrawal is one of the tragic episodes in the story of the second great German 1918 offensive on the Lys. Fortunately this "Great German Offensive" was itself only an episode, and was quickly followed by other more favourable battles which made possible our final victory.

CHAPTER XI.

THE GREAT GERMAN OFFENSIVE : APRIL, 1918.

TO the civilian in England the two German victories of March 21st and April 9th appeared to postpone indefinitely the end of the war. German strength seemed unimpaired, and further dark and terrible blows were awaited with sickening suspense and anxiety. On the other hand, to the infantryman in the Ypres Salient, the news of the battles further south brought a sense of relief. This may appear almost incredible till we understand the infantryman's point of view. For over three years the war had been an affair of trenches or " limited objectives." The man in the line knew that sooner or later he was bound to become a casualty. He could calculate his chances with almost mathematical accuracy. In spite of what he read in the papers or was told in official despatches, he knew that the allied offensive towards Passchendaele in 1917 had been too costly, and that with similar methods and sacrifices victory could never be won. Therefore when in April, 1918, the whole battle line seemed to be shaking, and armies were on the move, the infantryman felt that the long nightmare of " siege warfare " was over. The future was full of new excitements. Fighting in woods and villages and on highways, where advances or withdrawals were measured by kilometres, seemed more interesting, and could not be more deadly, than fighting in shell holes and trenches, and reckoning an advance in yards. The " war of attrition " had ended, and every man felt that the battles which remained to be fought would be decisive in history.

Before dealing with the battles of 1918, it may be well to state that as a general rule the morale of both British and German units was not so good as in 1915 or 1916. This fact will explain many of those strange " withdrawals " and rapid advances which became so common on both sides from March to November, 1918. Two or three determined groups of men again and again held up a battalion, and a rumour or false report often caused a whole line to disintegrate. Several officers and men became very cynical in their outlook, and gave endless variations on the theme that out of ten men in uniform only one or two could truly be called soldiers. Practically every battalion in the British Army had bathed in Ypres mud in the battles of the latter half of 1917, and the effect on morale had been lamentable. Officers and men, whether mistaken or not, felt a general lack of confidence in

British staff work and leadership, and this had an enormous influence on the behaviour of men during the perilous days of March and April, 1918. The Germans also, even during their advances on the Somme and the Lys, when they were heartened with success, rarely pushed an attack home if they met with determined opposition. The British line in 1918 was saved again and again, not so much by strategy or our artillery fire, as by the courage and self-sacrifice of small groups of men under junior officers or N. C. O's., who remained when others had surrendered or withdrawn, and who, by fighting to the last, checked the advance of the enemy, and gave time for units behind them to re-form. Fortunately such men were never lacking. In the darkest hours of the war they gave the brightest examples of heroism. The 1/6th Battalion had many such men, and though in several cases they were killed in the onrush of the enemy and their deeds are unrecorded and unknown, they accomplished their task, checked the enemy, and gave their comrades behind them time to " fill up the gaps."

There had been exceptionally little rain during the spring of 1918. This dry weather had considerably improved the ground in the Ypres Salient, and preparations for an attack by the enemy astride the Ypres-Menin Road were known to be in an advanced state in March. Moreover, before the battle of the Lys commenced on April 9th, no fewer than forty-six out of a total force of fifty-eight divisions under the command of Sir Douglas Haig had been engaged in the Somme battles. Owing to these facts arrangements were made for the evacuation of the Passchendaele Salient, as this would upset any preparations the enemy might have made for an attack there, and would also economize a few troops for use elsewhere. The opening of the German offensive on the Lys on April 9th, hastened this withdrawal. During the night April 12/13th the British line on the northern part of the Salient near Passchendaele was given up, and the Passchendaele Ridge held by a few outposts only. On the night April 15/16th a further withdrawal was carried out.

As we have seen in our last chapter the 1/6th Battalion was holding the line astride the Ypres-Menin Road. The 147th Infantry Brigade had been ordered to relieve the 146th Infantry Brigade in these positions on April 9th, but the German attack of the same day cancelled these arrangements. The 147th Infantry Brigade moved south to take part in the battle near Nieppe, and the 146th Infantry Brigade was left to carry out on the night April 15/16th the withdrawal from the line near Gheluvelt. The first stage of the operation was the withdrawal to an outpost line which approximately ran west of Langemarck, Korek, Gravenstafel, Anzac, Westhoek, Clapham

Junction and Klein Zillebeke. On the night of April 15/16th the section of this line from Clapham Junction to Klein Zillebeke (a frontage of about two miles) was held thinly by two companies of the 1/5th Battalion under Major Foxton. This force, as we shall see, was relieved on the night April 18th by two companies of the 1/6th Battalion under Major Hornshaw. The second stage of the operation was the withdrawal from the Corps posts to the main line of resistance, which was nearly five kilometres further west, and ran from Potijze to Zillebeke Lake and Bedford House. It was in order to give time for the strengthening and improvement of this main line that the Corps posts on "Observatory Ridge" were temporarily defended by a skeleton force.

This retirement, though undoubtedly wise from the point of view of the Higher Command, was a bitter disappointment to every man in the Battalion. In order to keep the withdrawal as secret as possible, the garrison of the front line was informed that an ordinary relief was taking place, but that the incoming units would occupy the posts after the Battalion had marched out. Thus the bitterness of the affair was not actually realized by the men till later in the day. It seemed a heavy blow. To give up positions which had cost thousands of lives to capture and a winter of misery to hold : and at the same time not to have the satisfaction of killing a single one of the enemy,—seemed worse than actual defeat. The men muttered and cursed, and were so exasperated that an enemy attack would have been welcomed !

But even more bitter was the retirement from the Corps posts on Observatory Ridge to Potijze and west of Zillebeke Lake, within barely a mile of Ypres and nearly a kilometre further west than the line originally held on July 31st, 1917. Our men had the mortification of seeing the enemy move freely on the famous Corps line near Kit and Kat and on the Westhoek Ridge, where some of the most elaborate fortifications and tunnelled dug-outs made by the British Army in France had been constructed during the 1917-1918 winter. On April 18th, Major F. G. Hornshaw, M.C., with A and B Companies and one platoon of D Company relieved two Companies of the 1/5th Battalion under Major Foxton in posts in front of Hooge, with Head Quarters at Jackdaw Tunnels. These Head Quarters were given up the next day, as they were in the front line, and heavily shelled. New Head Quarters were taken in Hooge Crater about a thousand yards further back. Till the preparations for occupying the main line of resistance from Potijze to Zillebeke Lake were complete, this half battalion under the command of Major Hornshaw (popularly known as " Hornshaw's Force ") was given the responsible task of holding for three days the whole Divisional outpost line of nearly two miles astride the Menin Road. All ranks moved about and showed themselves freely to the enemy in order to keep up the sham that we were still holding the line in normal strength. Verey lights and rifles were frequently fired during the night, and as a result of this activity it was forty-eight hours before the enemy suspected our retirement, and thus time was allowed for our men to consolidate the new-old line near Ypres, which had fallen into disrepair during the 1917-1918 winter. The only satisfaction which can be gained from this evacuation of the Ypres Salient is that our men inflicted severe casualties on parties

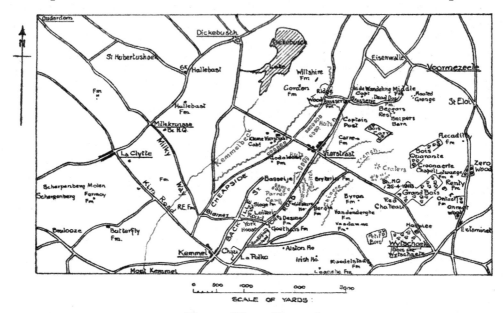

No. 17 Map. Kemmel.

of the enemy as they moved about our vacated positions and tried to get into touch with our line. The enemy gave splendid targets, and our rifles and Lewis guns were continuously active. On the night April 20th one of our patrols captured a German stretcher bearer of the 459 Res. Regt. who was looking for wounded in front of our line. The prisoner was brought to Battalion Head Quarters by one of our sergeants, whose brother had been killed a short time before, and who must have nearly scared the German to death by his ferocious attitude. In the darkness the entrance to Battalion Head Quarters looked more like the bottomless pit than an ordinary dug-out entrance, and when our Sergeant ordered his prisoner to get down first, the man set up a yell which roused everybody in the dug-out. Evidently the German thought he was being dropped into a well! He gave information that a raid was to be attempted the same night on one of our posts, but beyond some heavy shelling which blew up a section of our wire, the enemy took no action.

Whilst Major Hornshaw's force was in the line near Ypres, the rest of the Battalion (C Coy. and three platoons of D Coy. and Battalion Head Quarters) under Lieut.-Col. Wistance, had moved on April 19th to " Milky Farm " about five hundred yards south-east of the cross roads at Millekruisse, midway between Kemmel and Dickebusch. The Battalion Transport and rear echelon moved on April 21st from Dominion Camp near Vlamertinghe to Cornwall Camp near Ouderdom, about three kilometres from Bn. H. Q. at Milkruisse. The concentration of the Battalion in the Kemmel area was completed the same day by the arrival of Major Hornshaw's force from Ypres. They had been relieved by the 2nd Battalion Durham Light Infantry, and had been very heavily bombarded in Ypres by gas and high explosives after the relief, and were fortunate in only having a few casualties.

The time had now come when the Battalion was to write what is probably the most terrible and glorious chapter in its history. For over ten days the Battle of the Lys had continued with unabated intensity. The situation was changing every hour. In order to understand the part the Battalion played in the battle, it is necessary to describe briefly the course of events during the previous few days.

On April 9th the 2nd Portuguese and 40th Divisions were holding the line from Neuve Chapelle to Armentières. The Portuguese Division was to have been relieved on the 10th April, but the German attack began at 7 a.m. on the 9th, and was only too successful. By the evening of the following day the Germans had captured Lestrem, Estaires, Steenwerck, and were within two miles of Bailleul. Ploegsteert and Messines had been taken and our line pushed back to the crest of Wytschaete Ridge. Head Quarters 49th Division was at Chateau Ségard and the 148th Infantry Brigade was concentrated in the same area. But during the remainder of the battle the 49th was unable to act as a complete division, to the natural disappointment not only of the Divisional General but all ranks in the Division.

Not only did this dislocation of units apply to Brigades within the Division, but it also occurred within Brigades. Both the 1/5th and 1/6th Battalions West Yorkshire Regiment were detached during the whole of the April 25th battle from the 146th Infantry Brigade, and placed under the command of the G. O. C. 64th Infantry Brigade. Thus Brig. Gen. G. A. P. Rennie was in the unfortunate position of having only the equivalent of a weak company of the 1/7th Battalion under his direct command during the battle. From all points of view such a situation was regrettable, though probably could not be avoided in such a time of crisis.

Throughout the Lys battles units were flung into action the moment they reached the battle zone, and were attached to whichever formation happened to be holding the line. For instance, during the night of April 10/11th, the 147th Infantry Brigade took up positions near Nieppe, and rendered invaluable service in holding up the attack from Armentières. Then the 146th Infantry Brigade came into action near Wytschaete. The 1/7th Battalion West Yorkshire Regt. was the first unit of the 146th Infantry Brigade to enter the fight. On April 11th the 1/7th Battalion took up a position south of Wytschaete on the ridge near Bogaert Farm. The 1/7th Battalion was attached to the 62nd Infantry Brigade, which was also attached temporarily to the 9th Division. On the march to the Wytschaete area, orders had been given to the battalion to take every precaution against sudden attack, as the enemy was supposed to be in Vierstraat. This was untrue, as the enemy was not even in Wytschaete ! But the situation near Wytschaete was very obscure : there was heavy shelling : and the right flank of the battalion near Pickwood was " in the air." On April 15th the 1/7th Battalion took up new positions about a kilometre from Bogaert Farm, and on the eastern slopes of Spanbroekmolen. An hour after these new positions had been taken over, the enemy attacked at 4-50 a.m. in a thick mist. The S.O.S. signals could not be seen owing to the mist, and our artillery never opened fire. The enemy broke through, and captured the whole ridge from Spanbroek-molen to Wytschaete inclusive. Only about five officers and one hundred men of the 1/7th Battalion succeeded in avoiding being surrounded by the enemy, and these were chiefly from two platoons in reserve stationed west of Spanbroekmolen. On April 16th a counter-attack on the Spanbroekmolen Ridge was made by the 2nd Battalion Lincoln Regiment and battalions of the Gloucester and Sussex Regiments, but was unsuccessful. From April 17th to 25th the remnants of the 1/7th Battalion were in reserve positions near Millekruisse cross roads and west of Vierstraat.

With the exception of an attack by the enemy on Kemmel Hill on April 17th, which failed, these eight days passed fairly quietly. Fighting was incessant, but on a small scale. French troops came into the line near Meteren, and by the morning of April 21st had taken over the whole of the Kemmel sector, except Kemmel Hill itself, which was held by the 49th Division Trench Mortar Batteries and some Royal Engineers. The extreme right flank of the British line was the Messines-Kemmel road. The 1/5th and 1/6th Battalions West Yorkshire Regt. took up reserve positions near Vierstraat. 146th Infantry Brigade H. Q. was in a farm near Millekruisse. The situation was very tense. Reserve trench lines were being dug feverishly in the back areas. After the startling successes of the previous few days it was impossible to believe that the enemy would allow the remaining defences of the Wytschaete and Kemmel sectors to remain in our hands. Another great attack was expected daily.

On April 24th the 1/5th and 1/6th Battalions of the 146th Infantry Brigade moved into the front line immediately north of Wytschaete, and about two miles north-east of Kemmel. The 1/6th Battalion relieved the 15th Battalion Durham Light Infantry (64th Brigade attached 9th Division). The D. L. I.'s seemed to be mostly young lads, and they had had a bad time in the line and heavy casualties. The relief took place during a gas shell bombardment which lasted up to midnight. In spite of the gas shelling, however, the relief was carried out smoothly, and the positions were easily found. There was a very bright moon. The stumps of the trees in Wytschaete and Onraet Wood showed up clearly and mysteriously in the moonlight. The trenches seemed to have been dug in a bad position, as they were about fifty to one hundred yards below the crest of the hill, and in full view of the enemy. The line held by the Battalion was on the south-east outskirts of the Grand Bois, extending to Onraet Farm and Zero Wood, a frontage of approximately one thousand yards. On the left a similar frontage was held by the 1/5th Battalion West Yorkshire Regiment. Company dispositions of the 1/6th Battalion were as follows :—D Company on the right, B Company in the centre, A Company on the left, and C Company in support in the Grand Bois a few hundred yards east of Battalion Head Quarters. The Head Quarters of both 1/5th and 1/6th Battalions were close together in dug-outs on the western slope of the Grand Bois and about two hundred yards north of the Vierstraat-Kemmel Road.

The position held by the Battalion on the night 24/25th April was a very important one. The hill on which stood the Grand Bois was almost as high as Wytschaete, and formed the last natural barrier but one before the Ypres plain and an enemy advance towards Vlamertinghe and Poperinghe. The other barrier was the Vierstraat Ridge, along which " York Road " and " Cheapside " ran almost parallel to each other from Vierstraat to Kemmel. Both these roads were the scene of much fighting on the 25th and 26th April. Between the Grand Bois and Vierstraat there was a valley along which ran the Wytschaetebeek, a narrow unimportant stream. From the Vierstraat-Wytschaete Road near the Grand Bois a magnificent view could be obtained of the whole of the Kemmel defences, and with a pair of field glasses the traffic on the Ypres-Vlamertinghe road five or six miles away could be easily seen. The Vierstraat Ridge was nearly sixty feet lower than the Grand Bois, and as a distance of only two thousand yards separated the two crests, it can easily be imagined that when the enemy captured, on April 25th, the high ground of Kemmel and the Grand Bois, the garrison at Vierstraat and Ridge Wood was in a very uncomfortable position, and was completely dominated by the enemy.

Several lines of trenches had been dug along York Road and Cheapside, especially in the neighbourhood of Vierstraat. Unfortunately the whole of this area was littered with hutment camps and ruined shelters and houses, which gave excellent cover to the enemy, and broke up our field of fire. A maze of ditches and hedges near Vierstraat also enabled the small " infiltrating " groups of the enemy to work round our garrison on the afternoon of the 25th, and inflict heavy casualties. On the other hand the ground in the forward positions east of Grand Bois occupied by the 1/6th Battalion on the night April 24/25th was more open. It had been fought over many times, and a few concrete pill boxes and portions of trenches were the only cover. Grand Bois and Onraet Wood consisted merely of a few dozen stumps of trees. The most forward systematic trench line was " Chinese Trench " in the Valley behind Battalion Head Quarters, and from a defensive point of view this was useless, as it lay in the bottom of the valley.

What proved to be the most important physical feature of the sector was the valley between the Petit and Grand Bois, down which the stream of the Wytschaetebeek flowed from its source in Wytschaete Wood. It was down this fatal valley that the enemy advanced in the mist and smoke of the morning of April 25th, and cut off the garrisons of both Vandamne Hill and the Grand Bois, thus enabling him to reach our positions on the Vierstraat Ridge.

Nearly all ranks of the Battalion were familiar with most of the features of the countryside described above, as before they took over on the night 24/25th April the front line near Grand Bois, they had been for two or three days in the reserve trenches near Vierstraat. The men were in good spirits, and even the two Companies which had been in the retirement at Ypres had had two days' rest, and were well able to give a good account of themselves. The relief was completed about midnight. There was no regular trench line, and most of the men were in shell holes, with Company Head Quarters in concrete pill boxes or disused gun pits. There was practically no shelling till the enemy bombardment opened out at 2-30 a.m., but one or two of the older hands reported ominous signs of an attack. A continuous noise of transport, and shouting and the dumping of material was heard during the night behind the enemy lines. No Verey lights were sent up by the enemy, but his machine gun fire was heavy and incessant. This machine gun fire probably served the double purpose of keeping back our patrols, and covering the assembly of his troops for the attack.

At 2-30 a.m. a tremendous bombardment was opened by the enemy upon our positions from Bailleul to Voormezeele, near the Ypres-Comines Canal. The moment the first initial roar of the enemy artillery was heard everyone was on the alert. The Kemmel-Vierstraat area received the most intense concentration of fire. No one in those sectors had ever heard a bombardment which could be compared with it. Gas shells rained down in thousands, and in a few minutes a thick mist of gas covered the whole forward area. Telephone communications were broken instantly, and companies were cut off from battalions and battalions from Brigade Head Quarters. The impotence of Head-Quarter formations was never felt more keenly than in such terrific barrage fire. In the concrete dug-outs behind the Grand Bois our Battalion Head Quarters were cut off from the front line as completely as if they had been in Boulogne, instead of only a few hundred yards away from advanced Company Head Quarters. Brigade Head Quarters in a farm near Hubertushoek simply put on their gas masks, lit some candles, closed the doors to keep out as much of the gas as possible, and waited .... for the next shell. The night was lit up everywhere with burning farms and bursting shells. Under such a bombardment it seemed incredible that any human being in the forward area could survive to check the onrush of the German Infantry. Already batteries of heavy artillery began to move back into safer positions, expecting the worst. But they need never have moved. Thanks to British and French Infantry the German advance on the greater part of the front was checked in our forward infantry positions. So far as the 1/6th Battalion was concerned, Sir Douglas Haig's message of April 13th was obeyed—" With our backs to the wall, and believing in the justice of our cause, each of us must fight to the end."

This first bombardment lasted till about 4-30 a.m. By this time our front line had suffered severe casualties, but the losses had not been so heavy as to impair seriously the fighting strength of companies. In fact Capt. F. W. Whittaker, M.C. (D Company), reports that the enemy bombardment almost entirely missed his Company front, and gave his men the impression that the enemy attack was going to be made further south, on the right of the Battalion front. The enemy shelling was concentrated chiefly on back areas, and near Battalion Head Quarters and the valley of the Wytschaetebeek. All reports confirm the fact that our artillery support was very feeble on April 25th, and so far as the Grand Bois sector was concerned, caused no inconvenience to the enemy. For several days there had been unusually heavy morning mists, and at dawn on April 25th a dense fog lay over Grand Bois and Vierstraat. Gas shells and the smoke of the barrage fire did not improve visibility, and made it impossible for our men to see more than a few yards in front of their shell holes. They lost sight of comrades on either flank, and each group could only wait, with rifles ready, till the enemy was on top of them or the fog lifted.

Suddenly, about 4-30 a.m., the enemy barrage passed over the Grand Bois. A few minutes of almost uncanny quietness followed. Shells still passed overhead, but their bursts could be counted! Men in the front line positions came out of their pillboxes, and moved amongst the shell holes. The mist of gas and smoke cleared away slightly. When the enemy shelling began again about 5 a.m. with tremendous intensity, the shells burst far behind our men in the front line. But another even more terrible danger menaced them. German machine guns opened up a terrific fusillade, firing in enfilade along our lines on the eastern slopes of the wood. C Company sent back a runner to Battalion Head Quarters to ask for information, but he never returned. He was immediately lost to sight in the mist, and was killed by machine gun fire within a few yards of Company Head Quarters. About ten minutes later another runner was sent back by C Company. Battalion Head Quarters was only about five hundred yards away, and he was expected back with information in a few minutes. This second runner returned almost immediately, however, and with alarming news. He had run up against a large German party *marching in fours* down the Wytschaete-Vierstraat Road towards Wytschaete, " every one of 'em with a pair of new boots on his back." The significance of this last detail was not lost upon the men of C Company! Evidently the Germans had come to stay! This happened about 5-30 a.m., and so far as C Company at least was concerned the situation was clear. The enemy had broken through in force on the right of the Battalion, probably down the valley of the Wytschaetebeek, and our flank was " in the air."

This fact had been already realized by Battalion Head Quarters, as they appear to have been in contact with the enemy even earlier than C Company. When Lieut.-Col. Wistance had ascertained by runners the position on his right, he had withdrawn his Head Quarters *personnel* to a ridge near two large craters about one hundred and fifty yards west of the Battalion Head Quarters dug-outs. Lieut. F. E. Fairbank, Battalion Intelligence Officer, reconnoitred the Vierstraat Road, and quickly reported that he could see no enemy there, but the road was being swept by enemy machine gun fire from the south. In fact the whole valley between the Grand Bois and Vierstraat was under deadly enemy enfilade machine gun fire, and Lieut. Fairbank had been very fortunate in being able to get back alive with his message. By this time the fog was clearing, and Lieut.-Col. Wistance moved Head Quarters forward again to the old Battalion Head Quarters, where he believed a stand could be made. He was cheerful and resolute, and turning to his Adjutant (Captain W. N. Mossop) and others near him, said " We are in for it now. We must put up the best show we can." From this position the enemy could be seen advancing in force on the right. Our Battalion Head Quarters opened fire on them, and killed a great number. Lieut. Fairbank again reconnoitred to the front, where he found the enemy only two hundred yards away. Evidently C Company had been surrounded, and the natural inference was that the enemy had also over-run the three front Companies !

It was then about 7 a.m. There were very few survivors of Battalion Head Quarters. The Medical Officer (Captain H. E. Robinson) had been killed a short time previously. His Aid Post had been blown in, and as he could be of no further use there, and as few runners were left, he had volunteered to act as a runner. Whilst carrying a message from the Adjutant to the Colonel he was shot through the head and instantly killed. Men were falling every minute. There was no time to lose. Lieut.-Col. Wistance ordered those who were left of his Head Quarters *personnel* to withdraw again to the ridge one hundred and fifty yards behind, as otherwise they would have been almost immediately surrounded. The Colonel and Lieut. Fairbank remained behind till all Battalion Head Quarters had withdrawn. However, most of the men were hit before they had gone many yards. Captain W. N. Mossop was wounded and taken prisoner. The Regimental Sergeant-Major (H. Barker, M.C., D.C.M.) was killed. He was last seen surrounded by the enemy and firing his revolver at them till he fell. Almost immediately afterwards Lieut.-Col. Wistance was killed by a machine gun bullet as he was rejoining the remnant of his men on the ridge behind. No one saw him fall. His companion, Lieut. Fairbank, was seriously wounded by probably the same burst of enemy machine gun fire. He describes the event briefly as follows :—" I was shot before I had got many yards. I pitched into a shell hole full of water. My arm was useless, and my wound bleeding freely. It was impossible to get my field dressing on, and I fainted through loss of blood. The next thing I remember was seeing two Germans and one of my men bandaging me up, and four of our men carried me away."

It was nearly 7 a.m. when C Company were attacked. For some time previously they had been firing at parties of the enemy advancing near the Wystschaete Road. The mist had cleared and they had a good view of the enemy, but apart from causing a number of casualties, they were unable to hold up his advance. Suddenly strong enemy parties appeared on the Grand Bois ridge behind them, probably detachments of the same force which had been reported by Lieut. Fairbank a few minutes earlier, and which had attacked Battalion Head Quarters. The enemy attacked C Company in groups of six or eight men with a machine gun. Two Germans carrying the machine gun rushed forward a few yards in advance of their comrades and then opened fire, under cover of which the remainder of the enemy group was able to advance. A few of our men escaped by withdrawing to the north edge of the wood, but most of them were killed or captured. Captain Sanders, V.C., was last seen on the top of a pill box near his Company Head Quarters, firing his revolver at point blank range till he fell. When the men of C Company who had escaped capture reached the north edge of the wood, they saw the enemy was in possession of the Battalion Head Quarters dug-outs. A German waved a flag there for a few moments—probably a signal to others to consolidate the position—for almost immediately groups of Germans came up, and occupied positions near him. One of our Lewis Gunners—Pte. Harry King—immediately got to work, and caused the enemy heavy casualties. But retirement on our part was inevitable. By 8 a.m. all the survivors of C Company and Battalion Head Quarters were scattered in the trenches to the north of Vierstraat, and the three front Companies were completely cut off.

Practically no men came back from the three front Companies of the Battalion. Their fate remained a mystery till the end of the war, when prisoners came home and were able to tell their story. It was known that there were English troops still holding out on the eastern slopes of the Grand Bois up to 1 o'clock in the afternoon. But as they were completely surrounded, and small parties of the enemy were in positions near Vierstraat, it was impossible to get into touch with them. Messengers who were sent back were all either killed or captured. However, it was entirely owing to the way in which these three Companies, together with men of the 1/5th Battalion on their left,

AEROPLANE PHOTO—LOMBARDZYDE, 1917.

AEROPLANE PHOTO—BUSY WOOD, BROODSEINDE RIDGE, 1917-1918.

RANSART—SAP HEAD (AEROPLANE PHOTO).

xxxviii.

GROUP OF QUARTER-MASTER SERGTS.

GROUP OF SERGT. MAJORS.

xxxix.

CPL. A. SILVERWOOD, D.C.M., M.M.

BANDMASTER G. M. KING.

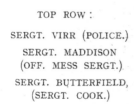

TOP ROW :

SERGT. VIRR (POLICE.)

SERGT. MADDISON
(OFF. MESS SERGT.)

SERGT. BUTTERFIELD,
(SERGT. COOK.)

BOTTOM ROW :

SERGT. HAWKINS
(PIONEER SERGT.)

SERGT. WARD, M.S.M.
(SIGNALS SERGT.)

H.Q. SERGEANTS.

stood their ground and held up the German advance, that our reserve positions immediately north of Vierstraat were not strongly attacked and captured on the afternoon of April 25th. The paragraph in Sir Douglas Haig's despatches which deals with this attack is worth quoting in full.

"The weight of the attack in the British sector fell on the 9th Division and attached troops of the 49th Division, who at 7 a.m. were still holding their positions about Wytschaete intact, though heavily engaged. Fierce fighting continued in this neighbourhood for some hours later, and great numbers of Germans were killed by rifle and machine gun fire at short range. Later in the morning the right of the 9th Division was forced to fall back fighting stubbornly to Vierstraat, but at 1 p.m. our troops still held the Grand Bois, north of Wytschaete." The men who "still held the Grand Bois" were A, B and D Companies of the 1/6th Battalion, and men of these Companies were not only holding it at 1 p.m., but actually remained in position till 7-30 p.m. of the same day!

In the early stages of the attack the enemy was completely checked on the front opposite A, B and D Companies. Men fired till their own ammunition was exhausted, and then they drew on the reserve stores at Company Head Quarters. About 6 a.m. the mist cleared. Shortly afterwards Germans were observed in the reserve lines near Battalion Head Quarters, and also on the right flank south of the Wytschaete Road. There was still a way of escape for our men to the north by Louwaege Farm and Bois Quarante. But very few tried to save themselves, and the fight went on. The Germans brought small field guns into their forward positions and fired point blank into our lines. Nothing has a more devastating effect on morale than a field gun firing from a distance of a few hundred yards on men extended in shell holes. The report and explosion are simultaneous, and the shell ploughs into the earth as though it had been fired from a 9-in. naval gun. Many casualties were also caused by an aeroplane which flew extremely low and fired belt after belt from its machine gun into our shell hole positions. The right Company (D Company) was the first front line Company to be surrounded by the enemy and compelled to surrender. It was, of course, the nearest company to the point in the British line where the enemy broke through, and for some hours it had been without support on its right flank. Moreover D Company was holding a line in the bottom of the valley with a sharp ridge immediately in front of it, and the result was that the position was untenable when the enemy began to attack directly from the rear. It was impossible for any of our men to move as the enemy could snipe at them with the greatest ease and accuracy.

Throughout the bombardment, and up to approximately 6-30 a.m., Capt. Whittaker (D Company) had been able to maintain telephone communication continuously with Capt. J. S. Gordon M.C. (B Company), but the communication was terminated very abruptly by the B Company operator shouting out " The Bosches are here." Whether the operator was killed by the enemy or the telephone line was broken, it is impossible to say, but half an hour later the enemy could be seen from D Company Head Quarters moving about near what had been B Company Head Quarters. D Company remained in their positions till approximately 10 a.m., when they were suddenly rushed from behind by large numbers of the enemy, and as they had used up their ammunition, our men were compelled to surrender.

In the meantime Capt. Gordon, with all available men of B Company, having lost his Company Head Quarters, had side slipped further north to positions on the left of A Company. Capt. Gordon sent runners to inform D Company Head Quarters of this move, but they never arrived with the message, and were either killed or captured. Towards noon the whole front still held by the Battalion was enfiladed by machine gun fire from both flanks. Men of A Company lined a light railway running in a south-east direction past Renty Farm, till they were surrounded by the enemy about 4-30 p.m. and the remnant were compelled to surrender. Capt. Gordon reports that the survivors of his Company Head Quarters, with his reserve platoon, occupied a strong point west of Onraet Farm with a number of men of A Company under Lieut. Warner. " Here we held out until about 7-30 in the evening, when we were finally surrounded, having used up all our ammunition. During the whole period we were unable to get into touch with the battalion on our left, and from all appearances we were the only people left on the right." Thus it was over twelve hours after the whole of our front line position had been surrounded that the fight ended. For twelve hours our men had held on to hopeless positions till all their ammunition was exhausted. No men could have done better. In no finer way could the resolution and tenacity of the British soldier have been vindicated. The history of the Battalion on April 25th gives many illustrations of how our line was steadied by the action of small groups of men who refused to retire, and who, in spite of inevitable cases of cowardice, incompetence and selfishness, saved the whole situation by their self-sacrifice. By the time the enemy infiltrating parties reached Vierstraat early in the afternoon of April 25th, they had lost the impetus of their advance, and the line east of Grand Bois, which throughout the afternoon was still being held by the three forward Companies of the 1/6th Battalion, effectively prevented Vierstraat being captured.

THE GREAT GERMAN OFFENSIVE, APRIL, 1918

The scenes immediately behind the firing line during this battle defy description. It would be untrue to say that the roads behind the line betrayed no signs of panic during the early hours from 5-30 to 9 a.m. on April 25th. Probably in every battle since the world began there have been many men who basely spread the wildest rumours of defeat, and took every opportunity to save their own skin. Men from the front line came past R. E. Farm down the "Milky Way" towards Mille-kruisse spreading tales of defeat which were only too infectious. There may not have been many of these men, compared with the number left in the line, but their influence was great. "The French have given way on the right." "Kemmel Hill and village is captured." "The enemy has broken through towards La Clytte." "No one left in the front line," etc., etc. And these hysterical falsehoods were being spread hours before Kemmel fell, and when the front line was fighting still! Thanks very largely to this kind of unfounded rumour, guns were being pulled out and moved back at an early hour of the morning when their assistance would have been invaluable to the infantry in the line. The work of some forward field guns was magnificent. One 18-pounder gun in a position near the Willebeek, a few yards behind the front line along Cheapside, remained in action the whole day. Even if it did not succeed in killing a single German, this gun near our front line was worth more than many massed batteries away back at Hoograaf, so far as the effect on our own infantry was concerned. About noon the situation on Cheapside was very tense. The enemy was in possession of Siege Farm, and was directly enfilading our line with deadly machine gun fire from the direction of Kemmel village. Cheapside Ridge was being shelled heavily. There was a gap in our line near R. E. Farm, and the situation was also very uncertain immediately south of Vierstraat. One incident amongst many will show the temper of the men who were fighting that stubborn battle. Four or five men reached the front line on the Cheapside Ridge carrying some boxes of S. A. ammunition. They had been heavily shelled on their way up to the line, and were swearing and cursing in a rather unusually profane fashion. Their Colonel happened to pass, and overheard them. He shouted out in a voice which could be heard clearly above the noise of the shelling, " If you fellows can't come into action without that kind of language, damn you, clear out, and leave the line for better men ! " It was good to see the way those four or five men quietly walked up to the fire trench, jumped in, and got their rifles ready. The same Colonel earlier in the morning had been wounded in the arm and the head, but was still "carrying on."

About 9 a.m. great numbers of the enemy could be seen from

Cheapside moving on York Road near Parret Farm and Camp, where a Brigade Observation Post had been established two or three days before the attack. About a kilometre further north small parties of the enemy began sniping about noon from ruined huts and houses in Vierstraat, and it was not before two or three o'clock in the afternoon that some reinforcements of the South African Cycle Corps and men of the 1/5th Battalion West Yorkshire Regt. came and established a line immediately west of the village. They were joined shortly afterwards by Lieut.-Col. W. Oddie, D.S.O., in command of about thirty men from the 1/5th and 1/6th Battalions West Yorkshire Regt. This party had succeeded, in spite of incessant sniping and machine gun fire which had caused heavy casualties, in withdrawing from the Battalion Head Quarters near Grand Bois, and reaching Vierstraat. They had put up a good fight the whole way, and were the last formed body of men to reach Vierstraat from the Grand Bois. Further north, a group of about twenty-five survivors of the 1/6th Battalion under Lieut. W. B. MacLusky, M.C., and another small party under Capt. B. E. Ablett, M.C. (of the 1/5th Battalion), succeeded in fighting through to Ridge Wood and our trenches near Voormezeele. These were practically the sole survivors from the two front line battalions!

Some idea of the difficulty of ascertaining the exact position of our front line on the afternoon of the 25th April may be obtained from the following incidents :—A sentry remained on duty in a wooden sentry-box within a few yards of Vierstraat cross roads up to 3 p.m., all the time being in blissful ignorance that enemy snipers were within a hundred yards of him. He admitted to someone who cautiously crept past his sentry box that he had not seen anyone on the road for a long time, and had become " rather uneasy ! " Needless to say, he quickly left his sentry box when he heard the situation. About half an hour later three mounted " Intelligence " men direct from Corps galloped up the main road to Vierstraat from Hallebast Corner. They had been sent to " find out the position of the front line." They would certainly have galloped towards Wytschaete if some one had not yelled out to them and stopped them just in time before they entered Vierstraat. When they heard that Vierstraat was in the front line they turned round and galloped back at such a speed that they probably never stopped till they reached Corps Head Quarters. A somewhat similar adventure befell the Transport Convoy bringing up rations the same night to the 1/5th Battalion Head Quarters, which was in a mined dug-out on the north side of the Hallebast-Vierstraat Road near Cheapside. The night was very dark, and Battalion Head Quarters was only about three hundred yards from the enemy line. The guide for the Transport lost his bearings, and a few wagons actually reached our sentry post on the Cheapside Cross Roads before they were turned back—just in time.

There was a large farm south-east of Millekruisse Cross Roads which a few days before the battle had been 146th Infantry Brigade Head Quarters. The enemy began shelling it too frequently, however, for the comfort of the Brigade Staff. The climax was reached one evening at dinner when a shell burst in the yard near the parlour window, and one of the splinters knocked a glass out of the hand of our Brigadier, who was sitting near the window. Thereupon 146th Infantry Brigade H. Q. decided they would remove. The old farmer was very distressed because the men were making free with his potatoes and sleeping on the straw in his barns. He became furious when one or two of his farm implements were found to be missing. But he might well have saved his breath and preserved his temper. The farm was not called " Bloody Farm " for nothing. Early on the morning of the 25th it was bombarded by the enemy, and burnt to the ground. A Brigade Head Quarters of the 9th Division saved a table and a few chairs from the flames, and placed them near one of the barn walls which was still standing. There the General and his Staff gathered, and tried to get some coherent idea of the situation in the line a thousand yards away. Their red tabs and bright equipment gave a rather picturesque splash of colour in the midst of smoke from shells and burning farms.

Towards evening on the 25th the order was given for all survivors of the 146th Infantry Brigade to concentrate in one of the Hutment Camps at Ouderdom. As units were scattered in all quarters of the battlefield from Voormezeele to south of Vierstraat, it was no easy task to inform them of the order. Messengers were sent out in every direction, and throughout the night and during the following day small parties of men were gathered in. The ground between La Clytte-Dickebusch-Ouderdom was lit up by burning farms, but the forward area was in darkness. There was little shelling, and the enemy transport could be heard very clearly on the Wytschaete-Vierstraat Road. A great ammunition dump at Hallebast Corner went up toward evening on the 25th. It had been burning during the afternoon, and no one had lingered near Hallebast, as men realized the ammunition dump was bound to go up sooner or later. The explosion was a magnificent and awe-inspiring spectacle, and seemed a fitting end to a long and dreadful day.

The casualties in the Brigade were as follows :—1/5th Battalion eighteen officers and 557 other ranks ; 1/6th Battalion twenty-two officers and 457 other ranks ; 1/7th Battalion, five officers and 139 other ranks. The Trench Mortar Battery of the Brigade was engaged on Kemmel Hill during the battle, and none of those in action returned.

The casualties of the 1/6th Battalion were not only very great in number, but unusually terrible because nearly all our best leaders had been taken. Capt. W. N. Mossop had been Adjutant of the Battalion for over two years, and had served with it in France since April, 1915. His conscientious work and steady devotion give him the right to be regarded as one of the most faithful servants the Battalion ever had. He died of wounds as a prisoner of war at Ghent, on May 8th, 1918. Company Sergeant-Major W. Walmsley was another very different type who also was taken prisoner during the battle of April 25th, and died as a prisoner of war, in Germany. During the whole war he had wielded a tremendous influence in the Battalion. As one of the Battalion " characters " it is impossible to do justice in a few words to his racy humour, picturesque language, unfailing cheerfulness and " grit." Off parade he was familiar with his men, and knew them by their Christian names. On parade and in action he was treated with a respect which spoke volumes as to his character and leadership. He refused several offers of a commission, as he preferred to stay with his Company and " take his luck with the boys ! " The death of Lieut.-Col. Wistance also meant far more than the loss of a mere " figure head " in the Battalion. During the whole period of his command he had shown a steady example of keenness and loyalty. He came to the Battalion from another unit, with all the disadvantages of being a stranger and knowing nothing of the Battalion traditions. His tact and unselfishness quickly made him " at home " with all ranks. He combined strict discipline with an unusual degree of " camaraderie," and there are many officers and men who have reason to be grateful for the sympathy and individual interest he always found time to show in the most difficult circumstances. As Capt. E. D. Stansfield, his Adjutant, declares, it was a " privilege " to work under him. Among others who were killed during the April 25th battle, special mention must be made of R.S.M. H. Barker. He combined nearly all the qualities which have made the British soldier formidable throughout history. A strict disciplinarian, untiring, capable and fearless :—these were four salient features of his character. And in addition he had a saving sense of humour, rare enough in a Regimental Sergeant-Major. Any battalion which can boast such a Sergeant Major has an invaluable asset. R.S.M. Barker had served with the Battalion for over twenty years. He was an A Company N.C.O. when Col. Hastings commanded the Company in 1900 : and the N.C.O.'s of A Company in those days were specially famous for their efficiency ! Thus he had grown up with the Battalion, and its welfare was his absorbing care. If he could have realized before his death how well the Battalion had fought, he would have been one of the proudest of men. But he was killed in a dark hour of the battle, when the Battalion seemed to have perished. He used often to declare that he would never be captured alive. And he was not. He died fighting, firing his revolver till the enemy were within a few yards of him.

The total strength of the 1/6th Battalion on April 27th, including the rear echelon, which had taken no part in the battle, consisted of seventeen officers and 210 other ranks. From these, three officers and 110 other ranks were withdrawn to make one company of a Brigade Composite Battalion, which was placed under the command of Major R. Clough, M.C. When the remainder of the Brigade moved back on April 28th to the Hutment Camp at Hoograaf, south of Poperinghe, this 146th Brigade Composite Battalion remained behind at Ouderdom, and was in reserve to the 147th Brigade during the great German attack on the 29th April. Fortunately the enemy was checked along the whole front, and the Composite Battalion was not called upon to take part in the battle. On May 2nd, Major Clough took over a series of irregular and isolated posts along Cheapside from the 6th Battalion Duke of Wellington's Regt., with two companies in front area, and two companies in support. (The 19th Battalion Lancashire Fusiliers, attached to the 49th Division as a pioneer battalion, had supplied the fourth company in the Composite Battalion.) The Composite Battalion Head Quarters was in a farm near Millekruisse Cross Roads. The night passed quietly. A gassed pig was taken down to the Transport lines, and provided a good meal for scores of the men. The Composite Battalion was relieved on the night May 3rd/4th by the 143rd French Regt. A heavy bombardment during the relief caused some anxiety, but the French troops seemed to know their business thoroughly, and were in fine fighting condition. The relief was carried out smoothly, and on May 5th, the Composite Battalion marched to School Camp, near St. Jan-ter-Biezen, where it was disbanded, and companies rejoined their respective battalions. The casualties in the Composite Battalion were comparatively slight, being about fifty altogether.

The battle of April 29th was the last German effort to exploit the initial success on the Lys on April 9th by capturing the chain of hills near Kemmel, and thus obtaining a clear road across the Ypres plain to the sea. The bombardment began at 3-10 a.m. From the hill near Hoograaf, the survivors of the 146th Infantry Brigade—about 300 men in all—had a magnificent view of Mont Vidaigne and Scherpenberg and the whole battle line to Voormezeele.

Hoograaf was only four kilometres from the French lines near Scherpenberg, and naturally all ranks " stood to " immediately the opening roar of the enemy bombardment was heard. The hills quickly disappeared in smoke, and the bombardment was of such intensity that no one would have been surprised if Mont Vidaigne and Scherpenberg had been moved from the face of the earth. The French artillery had been strongly reinforced, and put up a great show. The German Infantry attacked from 5 a.m. to 6 a.m., but did not advance at any point. The French infantry fought with the courage of desperation, and as the brunt of the attack was against their lines, they may be said to have retrieved magnificently the loss of Kemmel four days earlier, and to have fought what was one of the very greatest defensive battles of the war. Their stubborn resistance, combined with that of other troops of the 49th Division in the Cheapside—Vierstraat sector, saved the remnants of the 146th Infantry Brigade from being again called into the fighting. From the hill at Hoograaf, during the slow morning hours of April 29th, our men—exhausted, but not dispirited—waited anxiously for news. Men gathered in small groups and discussed the situation. Officers with the aid of field glasses tried to obtain information as to the position of affairs by observing the movement of men and transport immediately behind the firing line. There was a French Artillery Head Quarters in the Hoograaf Camp, and the anxious group of French officers round their artillery maps gave us what information they could as to the situation near Scherpenberg and Kemmel. Towards noon anxiety gave place to confidence, and in the afternoon, to the certainty of a great victory. As the cheering telegrams from the front line were received at Brigade Head Quarters, men felt a thankfulness beyond words. The enemy had failed. The great struggle on April 25th had not been in vain !

On the afternoon of April 29th, the Battalion moved back to Watou to be re-organized and to await drafts of reinforcements. The following day Brig.-General G. A. P. Rennie inspected the Battalion and expressed his admiration at the work of all units in his Brigade during the fighting. He read congratulatory messages from the Commander-in-chief, and from the Army Commander. The message from the Commander-in-Chief was as follows :—

" I desire to express my appreciation of the very valuable and gallant services performed by troops of the 49th Division....The courage and determination shown by this Division have played no small part in checking the enemy's advance, and I wish to convey to General Cameron and to all officers and men under his command my thanks for all they have done."

A few days after the battle General Cameron issued a confidential summary of operations, which was concluded with the following words :—

" The reputation which you have won for courage, determination and efficiency, during recent operations, has its very joyous aspect, and it is deeply precious to us all.

" It has also a serious aspect for us.

" It lays on each one of us a great responsibility—a personal responsibility for doing all he can to ensure that the next time the Division is engaged it will perform even better service than it has in the past.

" We shall shortly, we hope, be filling up with new men. Let every old hand put his shoulder to the wheel in the task of instilling into our new blood the spirit of courage, determination and efficiency which has carried you through your recent trial so successfully.

" Never fail to impress on all new hands what the rifle and bayonet can do in the hands of a determined British soldier who knows how to look after them and use them."

A characteristic message from the French Corps Commander will fittingly end this chapter :—

" The General Officer Commanding 2nd Cavalry Corps warmly congratulates the brave British troops who have heroically assisted in the defence of the chain of hills, and who, by their admirable resistance, have broken down the enemy's effort and barred the way to Dunkerque.

" Shelterless under a bombardment of the heaviest kind, surrounded by poisonous gas of various descriptions, stubbornly disputing every foot of ground, they have held their own against repeated attacks by greatly superior numbers, and though at first overwhelmed by weight of numbers they were obliged to give ground, they have inflicted such heavy losses on the enemy that his forces have been exhausted.

" Once more the Germans have seen their hopes dashed to the ground. France will remember that.—Robillot."

CHAPTER XII.

QUIET DAYS—THE LAST OF THE YPRES SALIENT.

AFTER the fevered days at Kemmel came a welcome period of rest which lasted for nearly six weeks. Five separate drafts of reinforcements increased the strength of the Battalion by sixteen officers* and 406 other ranks. Most of these drafts were composed of A IV. boys of eighteen and nineteen years of age, who had been sent out hurriedly to France to replace the enormous casualties caused during the German offensive. There was a certain natural anxiety as to how these boys would stand the strain of active operations. On the whole they made exceedingly good soldiers. They were brighter and showed more resiliency than many of the older men : were particularly good in raids and patrol work : and were smart and keen on parade. Fortunately their first experiences of warfare were in a quiet sector, and before they were called on to take part in any big operations they had learnt steadiness and self-reliance during several weeks of trench warfare. Under good officers and N. C. O.'s they did magnificently, but naturally they were more dependent on good leadership than their older comrades.

There were several changes amongst officers during this re-organization period. When the 146th Infantry Brigade Composite Battalion was disbanded at School Camp, near St. Jan-ter-Biezen, Lt. Col. R. Clough, M.C., took over command of the Battalion from Major F. G. Hornshaw, M.C., who became second-in-command. Throughout his long service with the Battalion in France, Lieut.-Col. Clough had been very popular with all ranks, and his promotion was felt to have been thoroughly deserved. Another well merited appointment made a few days later was that of Capt. E. D. Stansfield, M.C., as Adjutant, *vice* Capt. Mossop, who, as we have seen, had died as a result of wounds received on April 25th. Capt. Stansfield went out to France in 1915 with the Battalion as a private in A Coy., and rose gradually till during the action on Oct. 11/12th,1918, he took over for a short time the command of the Battalion. Such success not only implies merit on the part of the officer, but at the same time shows that a healthy democratic spirit pervaded

---

* The following officers joined during this period :—Lts. G. F. G. Rees, W. Rennison, C. Martin, 2/Lts. W. O. Alexander, W. N. Hamilton, S. Shoesmith, C. E. Richardson, H. Atkinson, V. J. W. Yorke, H. Carr, F. Kitching, R. Brown, — Simpson, Capt. H. T. Behrens ; Lt. H. Jowett (re-joined) ; Capt. J. S. James (R.A.M.C.), joined in place of Capt. Dobson (M.O.R.C., U.S.A,).

the Battalion. Before the Battalion moved to School Camp on May 5th, a most enjoyable rest of a few days was spent in farms between Abeele and Watou. The weather was fine and sunny, the billets were fairly good and were in the heart of a rich agricultural country. Battalion H.Q. was billeted in a farm several hundred yards from the main road and far from all signs of traffic and war. Every inch of ground was cultivated, and there were hundreds of acres of hop fields. An ideal rest area, but little use for training purposes! The noteworthy events of these few days were two football matches between the 1/6th Battalion and a French Battalion of the 32nd Division, the first of which was a draw, and the second lost by the 1/6th Battalion team. This lack of success was rather unusual, but the French put up a very fine team, as befitted the famous French " Verdun " Division. When the Battalion moved to School Camp training was carried on more strenuously. The men were billeted in huts and there were rifle ranges immediately outside the camp. Occasionally the Poperinghe-Watou Road was shelled by a German high velocity naval gun, and enemy aeroplanes came over and bombed the Camp, but there were no casualties in the Battalion. Sir Herbert Plumer (II. Army) inspected a representative company from the Battalion together with other units of the 49th Division, and congratulated the Division on its achievements in the recent fighting.

An enormous amount of work was begun about this time on reserve lines of trenches, especially east of Poperinghe. The principal systems were the West and East Poperinghe Line, the Brandhoek-Woesten Line, and the Vlamertinghe Switch. During the time the Battalion was re-organizing and training in School Camp parties of officers reconnoitred carefully the Corps Line from Brandhoek to Woesten, called the Yellow Line on the Defence Maps. An enemy attack was expected on the Ypres Sector, and naturally after the recent experiences on the Somme and the Lys, very elaborate defensive measures were being taken.

On May 25th, the Battalion moved to Cormette, near St. Omer, for a week's musketry practice. This was always a welcome change after the ordinary training. The weather was delightful. The Camp was on the hill top a few hundred yards from the rifle ranges. Permission was given freely for all ranks to visit St. Omer. During the three months which had elapsed since the Battalion was last in the St. Omer area, the war had been brought appreciably nearer to the pleasant old Artois town. Chinese labour battalions were constructing elaborate defensive lines east of the town, and enemy bombing squadrons visited it more frequently than ever. But life was still gay there: the shops were doing a roaring trade, and all the restaurants were full.

After a long morning on the rifle ranges, men streamed into the town, and returned in the evening, just in time before " turning in " to see the searchlights round St. Omer sweeping the sky, and hear the drone of the enemy bombing squadrons making their nightly visit.

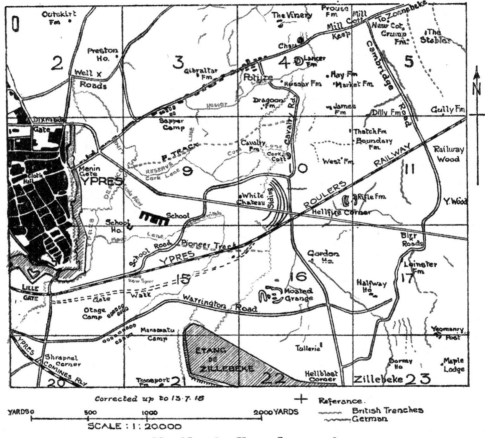

Corrected up to 13.7.18

SCALE : 1 : 20.000

Reference.
British Trenches
German

Map No. 18.   Ypres, June, 1918.

The musketry practices were finished only too quickly, and early in June the 49th Division took over the line east of Ypres.   The front line was divided into two Brigade sectors, and it was arranged that each Brigade should have sixteen days in the front line and eight days in reserve.   The 146th Infantry Brigade Brigade was at first in Reserve, with Brigade Head Quarters in Brake Camp, two kilometres north of Brandhoek.   The duty of the Reserve Brigade was to continue work on the Brandhoek Line and on the " Green Line " from Vlamertinghe to Elverdinghe. One battalion of the Reserve Brigade was billeted in Siege Camp, midway between Vlamertinghe and Elverdinghe, another in Orilla Camp, a little over a kilometre from Vlamertinghe Chateau, and the third in Brake Camp. During the first tour the 1/6th Battalion was billeted in Orilla Camp, probably the pleasantest of the three. The huts were large and well ventilated in a clear open space. For some reason difficult to understand, the Camp was seldom shelled by the enemy ; probably it was so conspicuous that he could not believe we should be so foolhardy as to occupy it with a full battalion. Several lines of Railway Sidings lay alongside the camp and a few hundred yards away a wide plank road carried continuous traffic from north of Poperinghe to Vlamertinghe and the front line.

Although Orilla Camp was 9 kilometres behind the line, the men had no opportunities of buying many of the luxuries usually associated with reserve billets. Poperinghe was deserted, and for 17 kilometres behind the front line there were neither shops nor civilians. During these early months of 1918 the "Battle Front" could no longer be regarded as stationary, and the days when a farmer ploughed within a few yards of our advanced gun positions seemed to have gone for ever. Everyone therefore depended upon the Divisional and Battalion Canteens for cigarettes, tobacco, etc. and any extra luxuries for the Mess. The whole area was filled with camps, dumps, trenches, transport lines, gun pits and the complex paraphernalia of modern armies. The events of the past few months had effectually frightened the civilians, and shown them the folly of living too near to that volcano—the battle line,—the eruptions of which were as unexpected as they were devastating. It was impossible not to regret that in many cases the civilians had cleared out of farms and villages before it was absolutely necessary. An empty house—even though occupied by fairly orderly and careful troops —quickly became dilapidated, and in a few months was hardly habitable.

The 49th Division was holding a front of about 3½ kilometres, extending from Potijze to a few hundred yards south of Zillebeke Lake. The Inter-Brigade boundary was approximately the Ypres—Menin Road. On June 11th, the 146th Infantry Brigade relieved the 148th Infantry Brigade in the northern sector, with two battalions in the front line and one in reserve. Brigade H.Q. was in dugouts near " Machine Gun Farm," a kilometre west of Ypres. The 1/6th Battalion relieved the 1/5th Battalion York & Lancaster Regt. in the left subsector, with A Coy. on the right, C Coy. in centre, D Coy. on left, and B Coy. in reserve. Company

Head Quarters of these front Companies were in Dragoon Farm, Hussar Farm and Potijze Chateau respectively. Battalion Head Quarters were in dugouts constructed in ruined houses about 500 yards from Ypres, on the Ypres—Potijze Road. After a very uneventful eleven days in the front line, the Battalion moved back to Brigade Reserve, with Battalion Head Quarters in the Ramparts in Ypres. When in Brigade Reserve the Battalion manned the Ypres defences from the Menin Gate to "Salvation Corner," north-west of the town. After four days in Brigade Reserve the Battalion was relieved and returned to Orilla Camp, having completed the quietest period in the trenches since the Laventie days of 1917.

The German Division holding the line opposite the Battalion was the 1st Landwehr Division, and appeared to be composed of troops of third-rate quality. They showed no initiative in patrolling : appeared to do no work on their trench lines : and neither by rifle fire nor artillery fire did they show during this first tour many signs of their existence. They were not holding a continuous front line, and their most advanced posts were on the "Cambridge Road," from 800 to 1,000 yards from our own front line. The Battalion sent out several patrols every night, and before the end of the first tour nearly all ranks were well acquainted with every corner of No Man's Land. The broken nature of the ground and the long grass aided our patrols, and every opportunity was taken by Company officers to practise the young reinforcements in patrol work. The enemy posts on the Cambridge Road were protected by the Bellewaardebeek, which had been dammed near some of the posts so as to form a dyke eight or ten feet wide. On several occasions our patrols reached this stream, but in attempting to put planks across it, were fired on by the enemy, and suffered casualties. It was necessary to maintain great patrol activity, in order that the enemy should not weaken his front. The position of our armies further south was of course still very critical. It was imperative that all ranks in the Battalion should be trained as quickly as possible in every duty of the soldier.

Men who had spent the winter of 1917-1918 on the Broodseinde Ridge found it very galling to see Germans moving freely on the Westhoek Ridge near Kit and Kat. Ten mtnutes' walk from the Menin Gate brought one to the British Front line ! The Ramparts of Ypres—the sacred city—were pitted with German machine gun bullets, and the ruins of the Cloth Hall were disturbed again, not by 15-in. shells, but by paltry whiz-bangs firing from positions near Birr X Roads! During May and June the men defending Ypres felt they were fighting with their backs to the wall. There was no room for further withdrawal. A spirit of dogged determination animated everyone. If the enemy had made a frontal attack on Ypres in May and June, 1918, it is highly improbable that he would have taken many prisoners, or that many of our men would have withdrawn across the Canal. If Ypres had been captured during those months it would have been over the dead bodies of almost every man of the 49th Division.

A factor which heartened and gave fresh determination to every British Soldier at this time was the arrival of American divisions in the Ypres Salient. The Camps round Poperinghe were full of them. Fresh battalions were arriving daily. The Americans were men of splendid physique, and it was easy to see they were of similar mental calibre to those Englishmen who joined our Army voluntarily in the early days of the war. The British soldier holding the line of the Salient knew that behind him an ever-increasing army of fresh and keen reinforcements was forming a tremendous barrier against the enemy. This knowledge doubled the morale of our men, and morale had been proved again and again to be the all-important factor in modern warfare. It would be safe to say that the moment our men realized the help America was giving, they never doubted their own capacity to win the war. All signs of pessimism and despondency disappeared. In one sense it is excusable to say that "America won the war." She gave such strength and confidence to the French and British soldier as nearly doubled the fighting value of the Allied Divisions. Compared with this moral accession of strength to the Allied troops already holding the line, the actual fighting aid of the American Army was almost negligible. This is a truth which no one would have agreed to more readily than the average infantryman in the Ypres Salient in June, 1918.

During the Battalion's first tour in the line at Ypres American Officers and N. C. Os'. were attached to Company and Battalion Head Quarters for instruction. These men were advance parties of the 30th Division American Expeditionary Force, and were almost all of them natives of North and South Carolina and Tennessee. Contrary to expectation, they were extremely modest and willing to learn. They took their duties very gravely, and seemed to some of our men rather too serious in their attitude toward military affairs. Where the British soldier often affected to treat warfare as a game and military orders as practical jokes, the American tackled Army life with tremendous seriousness and sobriety. A great number of them were idealists, and not afraid of confessing it ! On the whole the Americans were clean-living fellows, far removed from the hard drinking foul-mouthed type which, to some misguided people, was supposed to represent the ideal soldier. Their naiveté when in the line for the first time was amusing. They were fond of posting to their friends in America bits of shell or fragments of Ypres, and their Corps General returned from his first visit to the line with his pockets filled with bits of stone from the Cloth Hall. Their ignorance of the dangers of trench warfare also assisted them in one or two risky " coups " which would probably not have been undertaken by more experienced troops. For instance an enemy Machine Gun firing from Mill Cot had caused a good deal of trouble to our men. The first night the Americans took over the line, three or four of them thought they would go over and find this Machine Gun, and put it out of action. Without any preparation, they walked across No Man's Land, killed the enemy garrison, and brought back the gun. It was a fine piece of work, but they probably only realized some weeks later how lucky they had been in carrying it through successfully.

On the left flank at the " International Post " near the Vinery, the Battalion joined up with the Belgian Grenadier Guards Regiment. In this case also our men were compelled to alter any pre-conceived ideas they may have had which were detrimental to the fighting qualities of their Allies. The Belgians at Nieuport in 1917 had not impressed our men favourably—probably the Belgian troops holding the marshes near St. Georges were not a good sample of the Belgian Army. Certainly no one could have desired finer troops to be on the flank of a battalion than the Belgian Grenadier Guards. They were past masters in the art of capturing Germans, and their patrols must have struck terror into the enemy troops opposite the Belgian front. Their raiding patrols were carried out by a few specially trained men who were relieved of all trench duties in order to devote themselves exclusively to patrol work. They lived at Regimental (Brigade) Head Quarters, and were commanded by the Regimental " Intelligence " Officer, a certain " Sous-lieutenant Rousseaux," who was one of the most fearless and most decorated officers in the Belgian Army, and withal one of the most modest. Almost every week during the whole time the 1/6th Battalion was in the Ypres Salient in 1918 this officer led his raiding party to the enemy lines, and invariably brought back prisoners. Apart from this picked band of heroes, the Belgians sent out few patrols, and it was a question often discussed at the British Battalion and Brigade Head Quarters as to whether after all this highly specialized form of patrolling was better in the long run than the more haphazard but more general patrolling done by men of every platoon in a British battalion.

QUIET DAYS—THE LAST OF THE YPRES SALIENT

Thus the presence of fresh and keen American troops and of a first-class Belgian regiment assisted greatly, though perhaps unconsciously, in building up a good spirit in our own Battalion, which was composed chiefly at this time of young and immature soldiers.

As mentioned previously, an enemy attack was expected on the Ypres front. One of the measures taken to deal with this eventuality involved a good deal of hardship, though it was probably a wise precaution. All men holding the front line evacuated their trenches between the hours of 1 a.m. and 3 a.m., and lay out in the open about fifty yards in advance of the front line. Platoons in support also evacuated their trenches, and lay out about one hundred yards in rear of the support line. The object was of course to avoid casualties in the event of an enemy bombardment of our trench positions. For weeks this movement was carried out every morning, till the enemy must have discovered it, either from the numerous tracks leading through our wire, or from the movement of hundreds of men in No Man's Land being discovered by his patrols. In any case for several mornings in succession he shelled the ground in front of our trenches, and caused us many casualties, which eventually resulted in the practice of evacuating our trenches before dawn being discontinued. No one was more pleased than the infantryman, as it was a trying ordeal to lie out for hours in the long damp grass of No Man's Land without any protection from casual shelling or machine gun fire.

When the Battalion was in Brigade Reserve the Battalion H.Q. was in the Ramparts of Ypres, near St. Jacques' Church. The Battalion never had safer or more luxurious Head Quarters billets in the line. Every Battalion H.Q. officer had his own room, opening out from long corridors dug into the massive walls of the Ramparts. During the Third Battle of Ypres in 1917 these dug-outs had been used as Divisional H.Q., and they were well furnished—wire beds and tables, etc.—and lit with electric light. A narrow staircase from one of the dug-outs led to the top of the Ramparts, from which a magnificent view could be obtained of the whole Ypres Salient. There were over a dozen infantry and artillery observation posts on the Ramparts, and batteries of machine guns. A wide moat lay at the foot of the Ramparts and increased the sense of security.

The second tour of the Battalion in the Ypres Salient in 1918 was near Zillebeke Lake, on the extreme right of the 49th Division front. The 33rd Division was holding the line further to the south, and the Ypres — Comines Railway was the boundary between the two Divisions. The line was held very lightly. Early in July the Battalion had been re-organized into companies of three platoons with two Lewis Guns per platoon. When the Battalion took over the Zillebeke subsector five officers and one hundred men had been left behind in the " Details Camp " to continue their training, and in addition a platoon was detached from the Battalion for work under the supervision of the Divisional Royal Engineers. Thus the trench strength of the Battalion was low. The battalion front was over two kilometres in extent, being nearly twice as long as that previously occupied further north. However, as the Ypres sector continued to be very quiet, and the attack the enemy was preparing was expected further south on the Aisne, little uneasiness was felt. The front line was held by three companies as follows :—

Right :—D Company, from Zillebeke Lake to Warrington Road.

Centre :—B Company, from Warrington Road to immediately north-west of Moated Grange.

Left :—A Company, from the left of B Company to the Ypres-Roulers Railway.

Battalion H.Q. was in The Ramparts of Ypres, a few hundred yards from Lille Gate. The reason the right Company front was twice the extent of either of the others was owing to the embankment on the west side of Zillebeke Lake, which served as an excellent defence for about five hundred yards of the company front. The lake was dry, but the muddy bottom rendered it impassable, and the one or two sentry posts on duty on the high embankment had a " cushy " job, as the enemy was over a kilometre away and there was comparatively little shelling. Altogether the right Company in this Zillebeke subsector was very lucky, as the line was particularly quiet and there were numerous good dug-outs in the embankment—far more in fact than could be used by the garrison. Between the Lake and Ypres there were several Hutment Camps still in a good state but not occupied, as they were in full view of the enemy. To one walking through these deserted Camps, and across the wide plank " Warrington Road," it was impossible not to think of the time—only a few months previously—when the camps were filled by reserve troops and pioneer battalions, and when Warrington Road was congested with transport of all kinds.

The front line was very irregular, and several of the posts were completely isolated. If the enemy troops had been of first-class quality, they would probably have made the lives of our sentries much more unpleasant, as the enemy had many opportunities of playing against us the noble game of " winkling " with every prospect of success. But he made no such attempt, and the initiative in patrolling remained in our hands in the Zillebeke sector, as it had done some weeks previously near Potijze. In fact perhaps the most interesting daylight patrol in the history of the Battalion was carried out in this subsector, and the affair is worth describing in some detail.

From the Zillebeke Lake our front line rose gradually to the Ypres-Roulers Railway. The Moated Grange was a large ruined farm in No Man's Land situated within a hundred yards of the crest of Hill 40, which was the strongest enemy position opposite the Battalion. On the night June 19/20th the 1/4th Battalion Duke of Wellington's Regt. had organized a big raid on the whole of the Hill 40 area, and had captured eleven prisoners and inflicted severe casualties on the enemy. Up to the time of this raid the enemy had occasionally occupied the Moated Grange, but as a result of the success of the "Dukes" he was believed to be only holding positions on Hill 40. As "A" Company was on the left of the Battalion, Hill 40 was regarded as its special concern, and was carefully watched. On July 8th word was received by "A" Company from Battalion Head Quarters that an effort should be made at once to obtain an identification from the enemy. 2nd Lieut. R. B. Wright, of "A" Company, immediately volunteered for the task. He set to work in a daring fashion. At midday he crawled out from our front line and eventually reached a point which had been suspected as an enemy post, and which was about three hundred yards east of Moated Grange. No Germans could be seen, but there were several dug-outs about sixty yards away, from which Lieut. Wright heard sounds of the enemy. The long grass gave some protection, but as it was broad day-light, and he was over five hundred yards from our line, his task was one of extreme danger. However Lieut. Wright crept under the enemy wire surrounding the short trench and jumped into it. He found many signs of recent occupation, and some belts of machine gun ammunition. After de-detonating several stick bombs which he found on the parapet, Lieut. Wright crawled back to our lines.

He immediately called his platoon together, and asked for seven volunteers to go with him in daylight, and hold the enemy post until the Germans came to occupy it for the night. He quickly obtained his volunteers, and nearly all of them were eighteen year old boys! At 5 p.m. the party crept out to the German post, and occupied it safely. After waiting for some time our men found out that a dug-out or shelter about twenty yards from the post was occupied by Germans, who seemed to be asleep. Our men surrounded the enemy shelter, and Lieut. Wright entered and called on the occupants to "hands up." Everyone obeyed except the German N. C. O., who looked like giving trouble, whereupon Lieut. Wright fired on him with his revolver, but missed. The N. C. O. surrendered however, and our patrol rushed the Germans (nine altogether) out of the shelter, and made back with them towards our own line. Unfortunately these movements had caused a certain amount of noise, and though everything had been done very quickly, the enemy was on the alert, and two or three strong parties ran out of their dug-outs towards our patrol. Our men were hopelessly outnumbered. The German prisoners saw their chance and tried to escape. In the melée Lieut. Wright was shot through the head and killed by the German N.C.O., who must have succeeded in concealing his revolver. On the other hand, our men killed seven of the German prisoners, including the N.C.O., and returned the fire of the enemy parties who had run out of their dug-outs. Corporal A. P. Brown took command of our men, and ordered three of them to stay behind with the body of Lieut. Wright, whilst he himself with another N.C.O. brought back the remaining two German prisoners to our lines.

Perhaps the most commendable part of the story is the conduct of the three boys—for that is all they were—who remained to bring in Lieut. Wright's body. Although the enemy seemed to have had enough and did not molest them, their position in a shelterless part of No Man's Land within a few score yards of the enemy lines in broad daylight was very precarious, as the enemy was almost certain to be keeping a sharp look-out, and would search the ground at dusk for traces of his own men. If they had considered their own safety, they could certainly have crawled back to our lines, although, of course they would have had to leave the body behind. However the lads stayed, and several hours later brought back safely the body of their officer.

This exploit had a good effect on the Battalion, especially on the younger men, who felt that with ordinary luck they could meet the enemy in daylight on his own ground and take him prisoner.

Five days later Capt. N. A. Rymer, of " B " Company, with forty other ranks, tried to raid the enemy lines on a more ambitious scale, and he would have succeeded if the enemy, alarmed by our recent captures of prisoners along the Divisional front, had not doubled his posts by day and night. Another fact which told against the success of the raid was that the Landwehr Division had been relieved by the 6th Cavalry Division, which seemed to be of superior morale. Our party was divided into four detachments, which left our line south of Zillebeke Lake at 3 a.m. The object of these fighting patrols was to search the ground south of the lake very thoroughly, and to round up all the enemy posts in a limited area. The plan for each patrol was worked out in detail. Unfortunately the enemy had pushed very strong posts unusually far forward, and was on the alert. Each detachment ran into the enemy posts before it was expected, and from the beginning our men were completely outnumbered. If our raid did nothing else it proved conclusively that the offensive tactics of the Battalion were having their desired effect in compelling the enemy to hold the line with his full strength. Our first detachment under Sergt. Bolton had a lively fight with an enemy post immediately north of the Ypres— Comines Railway, and at least four of the enemy were killed by our rifle fire. A German who was attempting to surrender to our party was shot by his own men. The second detachment under 2nd Lieut. R. Brown also came almost immediately upon the enemy, and in the fighting 2nd. Lieut. Brown and three other ranks became separated from the remainder of their party, and were captured. The other two detachments were compelled to withdraw under heavy enemy machine gun and rifle fire, but they suffered no casualties. During the morning our snipers were active and killed two or three of the enemy as they were leaving their advanced posts, but our patrols which were sent out the following night could find no trace of Lieut. Brown and the three other men of his platoon.

After an uneventful week in Brigade Reserve, the Battalion was relieved by the 1/4th Battalion Duke of Wellington's Regt., and moved back to Brake Camp, north of Brandhoek. The relief of battalions in Brigade Reserve (Battalion Head Quarters in the Ramparts) was generally a dull affair, and was rarely interfered with in any way by the enemy. On this particular occasion however the relief was more than usually welcome, as the long deferred " Scheme B " was at last about to be put into operation. " Scheme B " referred to the discharge of cloud gas on to the enemy lines, and gas was always a rather uncertain weapon, which had a nasty habit of hurting ourselves as much as the enemy—at least so it was alleged by many of the men. According to Operation Orders, nine light railway trains, each consisting of seven trucks loaded with gas cylinders, were to be pushed on to the Railway Sidings in No Man's Land, east of White Chateau. At zero hour the cylinders were to be discharged electrically, and it was believed by " gas " enthusiasts that the extermination of the enemy front line garrison would be the inevitable result. A minor blessing would be the extermination also of millions of rats who were the curse of the whole area ! The thankless task of pushing the trucks on to No Man's Land, and then pulling them back again after the discharge, was entrusted to a battalion of the 147th Infantry Brigade, but our own men felt that it was a good thing to be relieved from their positions in reserve near the Ramparts before the discharge of gas took place. At zero hour the cylinders exploded with a tremendous noise and glare, and the wind was very favourable, so that none of the gas blew back into our lines. But nothing further happened. Not a shot or shell was fired by the enemy in retaliation. Capt. P. G. Bales in his history of the 1/4th Battalion Duke of Wellington's Regt. reports that " prisoners from the German 6th Cavalry Division, which relieved the 1st Landwehr Division, spoke vaguely of the latter having been withdrawn owing to the use of a new gas by the British. But nothing more definite was ever learned."

From the Battalion and Company Head Quarters point of view the most annoying feature of all operations such as " Scheme B " was the inevitable delay caused by the necessity of waiting for a favourable wind. Every night for weeks telegrams were sent to all units in the area containing mysterious code words which informed units if the gas discharge was to take place or not. The wind had a tantalizing way of changing direction an hour or two before a suitable zero hour, and after waiting up half the night in weary expectation that at last the " beastly stuff " would be let off on his Battalion front, the Adjutant would receive a code word signifying " postponed " ! Gas experts— like trench mortar enthusiasts—were not popular with companies in the line.

The week spent in Brake Camp at the end of July was very enjoyable. The weather was fine and warm, and the Camp was pleasantly situated in a wood. Occasionally the enemy shelled our batteries in the vicinity with an 8-in. gun, and once or twice enemy aeroplanes dropped bombs in the camp which caused heavy casualties. But the news further south was much brighter. On the 15th July the enemy had launched his expected attack east and south west of Reims, but the great allied counter-offensive of July 18th had met with extraordinary success, and men felt that the nightmare was over. The initiative was in the hands of the Allies. In every Head Quarters there was a great demand for Maps showing the Allied progress to the Aisne, and men gathered round the notice boards in the Camp to read the daily telegrams giving details of continued victories. Several battalions were billeted in and near the Camp, and the battalion bands played on these summer evenings under the trees to an audience which was more appreciative and free from care than any crowd gathered on the promenades of English parks. Few men are so sentimental as the average British soldier on such an occasion. None of the men who were in Brake Camp during this period will forget those evenings when Pte. Moyes sang " Roses of Picardy " (one of the most popular songs in his repertoire) to the accompaniment of the band. The Battalion was very proud of Moyes' singing, and was not altogether pleased when " The Tykes " enticed him away to become the " principal lady " in the Divisional Concert Party.

On August 1st, the Battalion took over the line in the Ypres Salient for the last time, and relieved the 2nd Battalion of the 118th Regt. American Expeditionary Force in the right subsector of the left Brigade. The front was nearly one kilometre in extent, from the Menin Road to north-east of Cavalry Farm, and there were three companies in the line and one in reserve. Battalion Head Quarters was in the Ramparts. During this tour every man in the Battalion became personally acquainted with men of the American Army. The 1st Battalion 118th Regt. A.E.F. was attached to the 1/6th Battalion for instruction, and the system adopted was a very good one. Each American company spent three days in the line. During the first day the Americans were attached individually to our men; on the second day one of our platoons was relieved by an American platoon, and on the third day the relief was carried out between an American and a British company. On August 7th the whole of the 1st Battalion 118th Regt. relieved the 1/6th Battalion for forty-eight hours, and the Battalion took up positions in the Green Line, near Vlamertinghe. On August 15th the method of holding the 49th Divisional front in the Salient was changed. Each Brigade front was held by one battalion only. The 1/5th Battalion West Yorkshire Regt. took over the 146th Infantry Brigade sector, and the 1/6th Battalion moved back to the " Brown Line," about 1,200 yards west of Ypres. Battalion H.Q. was in Compass Farm. The next day the Battalion moved to Orilla Camp. The 49th Division was being relieved by the 34th Division, and on August 18th the Battalion entrained on the light Railway at Orilla Camp for Proven.

Few of the men realized that they were leaving the Ypres Salient for ever. During the morning the enemy had been shelling the massive pile of Vlamertinghe Chateau, and there was quite a possibility that he would detect the entraining of a full Infantry Brigade barely five miles from his own front line. But the Brigade was allowed to depart in peace. Everyone was very cheerful as they crowded into the open railway trucks and proceeded on their leisurely way to Penton Camp, near Proven. The great Allied attack on August 8th on the Amiens—Montdidier front had opened out tremendous possibilities in the near future. The enemy strength was waning, and it seemed more than probable that the 49th Division—after the quiet days in the Ypres Salient—would be called upon to take part in the next attack.

Thus the Battalion bade adieu to the Ypres Salient in a very light-hearted and optimistic mood.

Ypres will always occupy a great place in the Battalion story. It had been a training ground and testing place for soldiers, and an opportunity for heroes. Men who played their part in defending Ypres will for ever feel bound together in an unforgettable brotherhood. And in this " happy band of brothers " the dead also have their place. Though their bodies are buried in the mud of the battlefield, their souls still owe allegiance to the regiment, and the ideals for which the regiment fought. Ypres will remain a " name to conjure with " to soldiers of the 1/6th Battalion West Yorkshire Regiment ! We have seen how well the original Territorial Battalion emerged after its five months' ordeal in the Salient in 1915, and we have also seen against what odds the Battalion fought and conquered near Passchendaele in 1917. In the final chapter of our story we shall also see how the experience gained in front of the Ramparts of Ypres by the youths who joined the Battalion in 1918, was turned to good account and resulted in the victories near Cambrai and Valenciennes.

An interval of six weeks lapsed, however, before the Battalion took part in the battles near Cambrai. This period may be divided into two parts : the first of which was spent in rest and training north-west of St. Omer ; and the second in holding the line near Plouvain, east of Arras.

It was impossible not to enjoy a rest period near St. Omer. The very name had a kind of magic in it. And the Battalion was never billeted in a more pleasant district than that midway between St. Omer and Calais. The 146th Infantry Brigade was concentrated in villages near Audruicq. Brigade Head Quarters was billeted in Tournehem, and the battalions in Zutkerque, Nortkerque and Nordausques, the 1/6th Battalion being stationed in the last-named village. Billets were good, and the weather was very fine. Everyone expected a fairly long rest, but just when the Battalion had settled down comfortably, and had arranged training tables for a long time ahead, an order to move came suddenly and caused great disgust. After spending several days in choosing the most comfortable billets possible and making elaborate arrangements for Company and Battalion messes, it was extremely annoying to have to come back with a jerk to the unpleasant realities of warfare. Although the order to move came as a surprise to most of the men, those who observed the signs of the times had realized for some days previously that the 49th Division would not be allowed to stay for long in a rest area. The Allied offensive of August 8th had been continued relentlessly by the Third and

Fourth Armies, and towards the end of August our line had been advanced an average depth of over fifteen miles on the front from Amiens to Arras. The result of this advance had been to leave a sharp German Salient near Arras, which would have imperilled any further success of our Armies south of the Scarpe. So far the First Army (Sir Henry Horne) had not taken part in the fighting, but on August 26th the Battle of the Scarpe opened, and the southern Corps of the First Army was quickly engaged. The day before the Battalion left Nordausques the news had been received that Wancourt and Guémappe and the famous hill of Monchy-le-Preux had been captured by the 2nd and 3rd Canadian Divisions, and that north of the Scarpe the 51st Division had taken Greenland Hill, and was pushing towards Roeux and Gavrelle. The Battalion entrained at Audruicq at noon on August 28th for the St. Pol area. On the same day the 51st Division reached Plouvain, and south of the Scarpe the Third Army advanced up to the famous enemy defences called the " Quéant-Drocourt Line." Thus no one was surprised when the destination of the 49th Division was found to be near Arras.

On the way to the line the Battalion remained for four days in Ostreville, near St. Pol. The billets were good, but a great change had come over the whole St. Pol area since the Battalion had passed through it on the march from Le Souich to Laventie in 1917. At that time the district was far removed from all sound and sight of war, and troops were only rarely billeted in the area. In August, 1918, however, half the shops in St. Pol were closed, hundreds of windows broken, and great numbers of the inhabitants had fled, as the town had been continually bombed and shelled, especially during the German offensive early in the year. The villages near St. Pol, however, had not suffered much, except from being constantly used as billets for reserve troops. During the stay at Ostreville, an opportunity was given for Officers and N. C. O.'s to watch Tanks practising their evolutions in the training ground near Wavrans. The moral effect upon infantrymen of seeing Tanks knocking down walls, wobbling up embankments and crashing through hedges, was very great, and during these Tank practices all ranks realized how powerful was the new weapon which had played such a great part in the recent battles.

From St. Pol the Battalion marched to a Hutment Camp near St. Eloi, where a week was spent in training, and waiting events. In the morning, Brigade Attack Schemes were practised near the Bois de Berthonval, and in the afternoon the men played football or walked to such places as Carency or Neuville St. Vaast. In football the Battalion played two games with the 2nd Battalion West Yorkshire Regt., the honours being equal, both teams winning one game. From St. Eloi many of the men walked to Maroeuil, where the beer was very good, or to a wood near St. Eloi, which was popular because it was full of blackberry bushes. Many walked further afield over the old French trenches near Souchez, and looked with a certain awe on those scenes of tremendous bygone battles—the great ridges of Notre Dame de Lorette and Vimy. On the hillside near Carency, the French had made a great cemetery of their dead. From this point a wonderful view of Lens and the other cities of the plain could be obtained, and it seemed an act of poetic justice that the French soldiers who died in the fighting for Lens in 1915 should be buried within sight of the goal, to reach which they gave their lives.

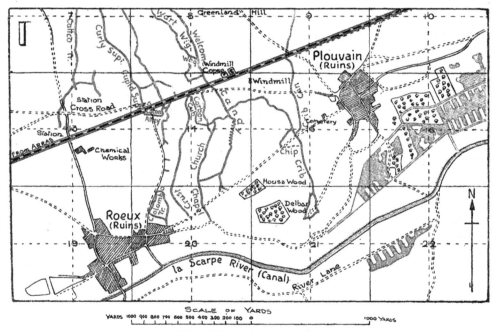

Map No. 19. Plouvain.

On September 12th, the 49th Division relieved the 51st Division in the sector immediately north of the Scarpe. The Division took over a frontage of approximately three kilometres, and the front line was held by the 146th and 148th Infantry Brigades, the 147th Infantry Brigade being throughout the period in Divisional reserve near Feuchy. The 146th Infantry Brigade took over the right sector of the

Divisional front, with one battalion in the line (1/7th Battalion), one in support (1/6th Battalion), and one in reserve (1/5th Battalion). On the right, the Brigade boundary was the marshes of the Scarpe valley, and on the left the cutting of the Biaches Railway. The Battalion moved from St. Eloi on September 11th, and after spending one day in Roclincourt West Camp, relieved the 6th Battalion Seaforth Highlanders in Brigade support near Roeux and the Chemical Works. After four days in support and four days in the line, the Battalion moved back to the Railway Embankment, west of Athies.

Many of those who look back on this period will be surprised to learn the Battalion only spent eight days in the Plouvain sector. The time passed very slowly. The line was not a pleasant one, and there was a good deal of enemy shelling. The situation was tense and uncertain. The whole enemy front seemed on the point of breaking up. The day after the Battalion came into the line, our comrades of the 62nd Division attacked and captured Havrincourt, and the enemy obviously was expecting the attack to be continued north of the Scarpe. Every morning during the eight days the Battalion was in the line, the enemy artillery put down a heavy " counter preparation " barrage about dawn, and the companies on the left of the Battalion front near the Biaches Railway Embankment suffered many casualties. The 148th Infantry Brigade also carried out a few raids, which somewhat " livened up " the sector.

The position of our front line was peculiar. Except on the extreme left, the front line trench had practically no field of fire, being blocked by trees, ruins of houses, or rising ground, and it was moreover nearly a mile from the German trenches. The ruins of the village of Plouvain were really in No Man's Land, although the Battalion pushed out four or five advanced posts into the village in order to keep close touch with the enemy. An enemy attack was not feared, and there was practically no wire in front of our trenches. It was strange to occupy a trench line in which some of the ordinary precautions of trench warfare were not considered necessary ! Still more extraordinary was a front line to which it was possible to ride on horseback, and then tether the horses to a tree and leave them for a few hours in charge of a groom. This was possible owing to the fact that south of the Scarpe River our troops had reached the Canal du Nord, and a horseman could ride beyond Pelves along the south bank, and after leaving his horse in the thick bushes near the river, he could walk over a narrow bridge into our front line on the north bank. Probably the most isolated post the Battalion ever held was one on the north bank of the Scarpe, south-east of Plouvain and within a thousand yards of Biaches.

This Post was relieved every forty-eight hours. It was eight hundred yards from our front line, and seemed lost in thick undergrowth and the trees of the Biaches marshes. The two sentries were in an advanced cutting about sixty yards in front of the remainder of the garrison of the post. Early one morning the Brigadier (Gen. G. A. P. Rennie) on one of his tours in the line found both of these sentries asleep. They were boys, and were dealt with leniently, but they might have fallen an easy prey to an enemy patrol. There were one or two other such cases of sleeping on duty in the Plouvain sector. The men were excessively tired, and the younger lads in the Battalion had not yet become thoroughly " seasoned " to trench warfare. During the eight days in the line at Plouvain the working parties were very heavy, as the trenches were neither continuous nor in a good state of repair. The front line was only held by two companies with two in support, and thus Company frontages were unusually long. The weather also was very hot, and men in the line near the River Scarpe were probably lulled to a false sense of security by the closed-in nature of the ground, and the distance which separated our lines from those of the enemy. Both Officers and N. C. O.'s were particularly glad when the Battalion was relieved on September 23rd, as it was felt to be a heavy responsibility to hold such an extended front with thoroughly exhausted men. Often before " stand to " in the morning an officer on duty would jump on to the fire step alongside a sentry who seemed to be gazing intently into No Man's Land, and would ask as usual if the sentry had noticed " anything unusual." After a moment's silence, the sentry would say " No, sir," and if the officer was new to his job he would pass on, satisfied. Otherwise, he would ask one or two more questions, and would often find that, in reality, the sentry was asleep. The burst of a 5·9 a few yards away would have been needed to waken him! It is a strange fact, which often occurred however after long exhausting spells in trenches, that a man sometimes appeared able to reply sensibly to questions, and yet remain in a fast sleep. Many an N. C. O. found that it was not sufficient to waken a man and tell him he was " next for duty," but that it was necessary to take him to the firestep, and remain with him some minutes talking and asking questions in order to be quite sure that the sentry was capable of fulfilling his duties.

The Plouvain sector was littered with interesting souvenirs of the German occupation a week or two before. There was a great system of underground tunnels and caves near Roeux, such as Indian Caves in I 19 b 28 (see Map No. 19) near Battalion Head Quarters. These caves were filled with thousands of boxes of German S.A.

Ammunition, bombs, Verey lights, shells, etc., etc. All kinds of German trench guns and mortars were dumped near Battalion Head Quarters in Cabbage Trench, and alongside the river south of Delbar Wood there were long lines of German shell cases and baskets, near former enemy battery positions. There was a well-constructed German observation post in Delbar Wood, which must have given the enemy a magnificent view of our lines from Fampoux to Arras. Our own Brigade observation post was in Windmill Copse, and commanded an excellent view of the strong enemy entrenchments known as the Fresnes—Rouvroy Line. Unfortunately this observation post was in the most heavily shelled section of the Brigade front. Before the war the valley of the Scarpe must have been beautiful. In September, 1918, it looked as if it had been shaken by an earthquake. Everyone in the Battalion had an unique opportunity of examining the effect of artillery fire on villages ! Plouvain and Roeux were heaps of bricks, and Roeux Church simply a red mound. The Chemical Works was a pile of broken iron twisted into a thousand fantastic shapes. From Monchy Hill looking northwards one saw nothing but a vast desolation. To the south of Monchy the roads were black with traffic moving for the most part eastwards towards the Canal du Nord and Cambrai. On September 23rd, the 51st Division relieved the 49th Division in the Plouvain sector, and the 1/6th Battalion moved back from the Railway Embankment near Athies to billets in Arras. Four days later the Battle of Cambrai opened, the Canal du Nord was crossed, and the Hindenburg Line broken. The 49th Division was about to take part in its last battles

CHAPTER XIII.

CAMBRAI—VALENCIENNES.

IN 1917 the Battalion had held the line near Ransart, a few miles south of Arras, and in 1918 the men had been able to see the ruins of the Cathedral and the Hotel de Ville from the trenches near Plouvain. Naturally everyone was pleased when at last in September, 1918, the Battalion was actually billeted in the City. It was said that not a single house had escaped some destruction from enemy bombardments. Considering, however, that for over a year of the war the enemy lines had been on the eastern outskirts, and that throughout the war the enemy had never been more than six miles away till September, 1918, it seemed remarkable that the town was not more seriously damaged. The Battalion was billeted in Arras for twelve days, and everyone enjoyed a complete rest. Permission was obtained for the re-opening of the Salle des Concerts, and " The Tykes " gave several performances. They never had more appreciative audiences. Training was carried on near Agny, and the valley of the river Crinchon. Every night enemy aeroplanes bombed the town, and a high velocity gun fired on the Railway Station for an hour each evening with great regularity. But these discomforts were negligible. Day and night long columns of troops and transport passed through Arras towards Cambrai, and every day brought news of fresh victories. Maps of Valenciennes were issued to all units, and the burning questions on everybody's lips were " When will Cambrai fall ? " and " When will the 49th Division take its part in the great adventure ? "

At last on October 7th orders came for the Battalion to move. The Brigade marched out at dusk on to the Cambrai Road, and after waiting for an hour or two, was taken by a great convoy of buses to Inchy. Few will forget the journey. No lights were allowed, the night was cold, and when the battalion debussed at Inchy, rain was falling. Guides led the Battalion to some old German positions near Cagnicourt, and at dawn everybody had settled down for a few hours sleep in more or less comfortless trenches. The rest of the day was spent in souvenir hunting in German dug-outs and trenches. During the day the weather was fine and sunny. The next day came further orders for an immediate move. Dinner had just been served, and the orders came at an inopportune moment. But in a few minutes blankets were being rolled up in the usual bundles of ten, and dumped in accordance with Brigade Operation Orders, and at 1 p.m. every one was on the march eastwards to Haynecourt, north-west of Cambrai. It was dark when the Battalion arrived at their destination, and bivouaced in a field near the village of Haynecourt. Some of the men slept in Tanks which were drawn up alongside the Cambrai Road near the camp. The traffic on the main road was incessant. Night was everywhere being turned into day, and the whole British Expeditionary Force seemed on the move.

The battle for Le Cateau had begun the day before, and the boom of guns continued throughout the night. Cambrai and the villages round it were burning, and the glare lit up the long lines of bivouacs and the piles of stacked rifles. There was an air of unreality about the whole scene. It seemed a different kind of war, much more pleasurable and exciting. Whilst the Battalion was sleeping in bivouacs near Haynecourt on October 9th, the Canadian Corps was engaged in the capture of Ramillies and the crossing of the Canal de l'Escaut at Pont d'Aire, nearly four miles away. At dawn the next day Canadian patrols entered Cambrai from the north, and joined hands with patrols of the 57th Division working through the southern portions of the town. By this time the Canadians had suffered enormous casualties and were thoroughly exhausted. They had been in continuous action for nearly a week. But relief was very near.

At 3 p.m. on October 10th the 1/6th Battalion moved off down the Cambrai Road, through Sailly to the railway embankment near Tilloy. On all sides there were many signs of heavy fighting, especially near the embankment, which the enemy had defended strongly the day before. On the high ground west of Tilloy the enemy had arranged a system of extremely well-sited " shell hole " positions, with a field of fire to the front of nearly 500 yards. These " shell holes " had been dug flat with the ground, the spoil had been carefully removed, and twenty or thirty yards away they were invisible. Enemy machine guns firing from these positions must have caused the Canadians heavy casualties, and scores of their dead were lying in the open 300 and 400 yards from the fortified shell holes. From the Tilloy railway embankment our men could see the ruins of Sancourt Chateau. In the grounds of the Chateau was the emplacement of the 15-in. naval gun which fired on St. Pol, and in the German artillery dug-outs near the emplacement were boxes of foodstuffs which had been sent by the American Relief Commission for the French people, but which obviously had been providing the German gunners with more variety in their diet! In the Chateau itself everything was destroyed except a grand piano!

Whilst the Battalion was waiting near the Tilloy Railway Embankment, Lt.-Col. Clough was at 146th Inf. Brigade Head Quarters receiving details for the attack of the following day. It was dusk when he returned. All Company Commanders and Specialist Officers were immediately called to a conference which was held in the nearest house to the Railway Embankment. The situation and plan of attack was quickly explained. The 4th Canadian Brigade had reached the line of the River Erclin, south of Inchy, during the day, and had reported that the enemy was retiring opposite their front. The Canadians were going to make an effort during the night to advance further and occupy the high ground east of the River. After this operation the 146th Infantry Brigade was to relieve the 4th Canadian Brigade and continue the attack.

The following were some of the instructions for the operation given by Lieut-Col. Clough in the brief conference with his officers :—

1. The Battalion was to be in the assembly positions on the Rieux—Iwuy Road by 6 a.m. the following morning (October 11th).

2. The 146th Infantry Brigade was to attack on a frontage of 400 yards, with the 1/6th Battalion on the right, the 1/7th Battalion on the left, and the 1/5th Battalion in Brigade Reserve.

3. The 147th Infantry Brigade was attacking on a similar frontage on the right of the 146th Infantry Brigade. The Inter-Brigade boundary was the Sugar Factory on the Iwuy—Rieux Road. On the left the 28th Battalion Canadian Light Infantry was to attack immediately south of Iwuy.

4. The first objective of the Battalion was the Railway Cutting and Station south of Avesnes-Le-Sec, and the second objective the village of Haspres—a total advance of 10,000 yards approximately.

5. The Battalion was to attack with " A " Company on the right, " B " Company on the left, " C " Company in support, and " D " Company in reserve. By 6 a.m. all companies were to be east of the River Erclin with the exception of " D " Company, which was to take up its position with Battalion Head Quarters in the bed of the river Erclin.

6. Zero hour—9 a.m.

Information was received later that the night attack of the 4th Canadian Brigade on the high ground east of the River Erclin had been unsuccessful. A heavy artillery barrage was therefore arranged to begin at 9 a.m. and to cover the advance of the 146th and 147th Infantry Brigades up to the crest of the hill. This artillery barrage, after remaining for half-an-hour on the ridge, would move forward 100 yards every three minutes for a further half hour. Lieut.-Col. Clough

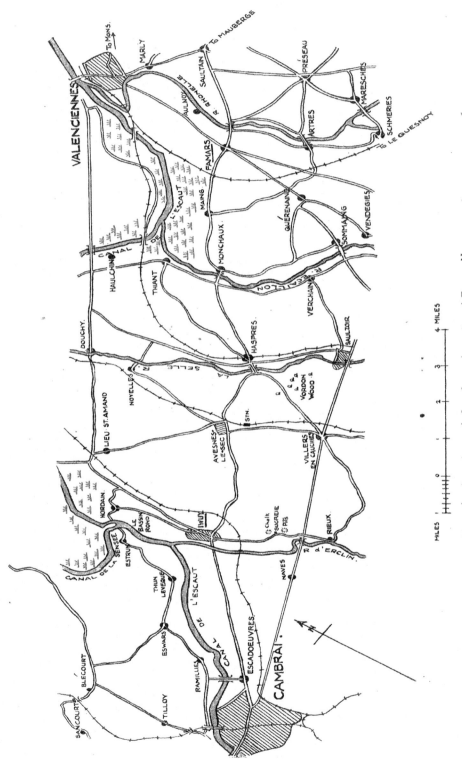

MILES

|————|————|————|————|
0   1   2   3   4 MILES

No. 20 Map.   Attack on Avesnes-le-Sec, Oct. 11th, 1918, and Famars, Nov. 1st, 1918.

explained to his officers the extreme importance of pushing forward quickly beyond the ridge south-east of Iwuy *at all costs*. A rapid advance was the most certain method of keeping down the number of casualties. Stretchers were not to be carried into action. Everything depended on rapidity of movement.

Thus the Operation Orders were very simple, and easily understood. The day when a battalion carried a typewriter into action, and Operation Orders for a small attack occupied several foolscap sheets of typewriting, had gone for ever. On this occasion the Adjutant (Capt. E. D. Stansfield, M.C.) wrote out Operation Orders in pencil on two small sheets of A. B. 153. During the brief Battalion Officers' conference in the cottage near the Tilloy Railway Embankment the enemy began shelling, and the Colonel's instructions were interrupted frequently by shells bursting a few yards from the cottage. The conference was not therefore very prolonged, and officers were soon back with their companies !

At 11 p.m. the Battalion moved off into the night with intervals of fifty yards between companies. The blackness was so intense that no landmarks could be discerned. The roads were crowded with transport of all kinds, and as the 147th Infantry Brigade was using the same route, a certain amount of confusion was unavoidable. There had been, of course, no opportunity to reconnoitre the ground beforehand, so the march offered a severe test to knowledge of map reading, and the compass was invaluable. However, no time was lost. The Canal de l'Escaut was crossed at Morenchies by a bridge which the enemy had not had time to demolish. The Battalion marched safely through Escadœuvres : the 49th Divisional Artillery was not so fortunate, as several guns were put out of action and a score of horses killed by heavy enemy shelling of Escadœuvres, which took place in the early hours of the morning.

Naves was reached about 3 a.m. The village had been heavily shelled with mustard gas a few hours earlier, and the streets reeked with it, and were littered with bricks and broken glass and the mess of a bombardment. After a brief halt in Naves, the Battalion left the main road, and crossed the fields to their assembly positions. The Canadian Battalion Commander informed the officer in charge of our Battalion guides that as the enemy was now retiring on the whole front, he had withdrawn his men without waiting for the usual relief. Fortunately this rather unusual course of action did not prevent our companies getting quickly into their correct assembly positions, though it made the work of the Battalion Intelligence Officer (2nd Lieut. B. Hick) rather more difficult. Towards 5 a.m. there was considerable enemy shelling of our assembly positions, and of the area between the Erclin River and Naves. The front companies were lined up in a ditch along the Iwuy—Rieux Road, and were thus somewhat protected, but " C " Company was compelled to lie out in the open, and suffered several casualties from enemy shell-fire, their Company Commander, Capt. H. A. Jowett, being wounded. Lt. C. E. Richardson (killed a few hours later) then took command of " C " Company, which withdrew to the bed of the Erclin. " D " Company and Battalion Head Quarters also did not escape without several casualties, although the bed of the river in which they were assembled was quite dry, and gave fairly good shelter. Transport on the Naves Road was shelled, and some mules bringing up the Battalion S.A.A. were hit. In addition to the enemy shelling, there was a considerable amount of machine gun fire. The enemy was obviously holding the ridge in some strength, as his machine guns were firing from immediately in front of the Battalion. It was known that the enemy was occupying Iwuy, but fortunately his machine guns there did not open fire on our lines. If they had done so our assembly positions would have been almost untenable, as enemy machine guns could have raked them with enfilade fire.

A light mist covered the ground, and must have assisted in concealing our men from the enemy. On both sides of the Erclin River the ground was open and under cultivation : there were no hedges or ditches on the slope east of the river, and as the ridge rose gradually from the Iwuy—Rieux Road, the enemy had an excellent field of fire. It was impossible not to feel somewhat anxious as to the result of the battle, and a great deal depended on the strength and accuracy of our Artillery barrage. The three hours of waiting from 6 a.m. to 9 a.m. passed very slowly, and were very trying to all ranks.

At 9 a.m. prompt our artillery barrage began. It was magnificent. The ridge quickly seemed to disappear in smoke and bursting shells. One felt instantly that the attack would be successful, as our men were thoroughly rested, and in splendid form. The whole British line advanced steadily across the Iwuy Road. Enemy machine guns opened out, but our men were on them before they had time to hold up the advance. In several cases the Germans were shot or bayoneted before they were able to get their machine guns into action. The Canadians on the left flank of the 1/7th Battalion had not succeeded in silencing the machine guns in Iwuy, and the direct enfilade fire of these guns caused the 1/7th Battalion a good many casualties in the early stages of the attack, among them being Lieut.-Col. Pinwell, D.S.O. But the attack was not held up for a moment. The advance of our troops was so steady along the whole Brigade front that the enemy must have been thoroughly intimidated, and Germans came running forward with their hands up when our front wave was nearly a hundred yards away from them. In half an hour our front line had disappeared over the ridge, and the barrage was thundering on towards Avesnes-le-Sec. Apart from streams of German prisoners running across country towards Naves, and our support troops advancing towards the sky line, the whole valley of the Erclin seemed empty. Battalion Head Quarters moved forward to a position on the ridge, from which a view could be obtained of the progress of the battle in the forward area. "D" Company took up positions in reserve along a light railway a few hundred yards from Battalion H.Q. The Battalion Aid Post was established in the Sugar Factory on the Iwuy Road. Scores of wounded were coming in from all directions. The enemy barrage had been prompt and heavy, and it was easy to see that he had intended making a determined stand on the ridge south-east of Iwuy. But by this time our front line, though broken and thinned by casualties, was advancing steadily towards Avesnes-le-Sec.

About five hundred yards beyond the ridge a slightly sunken road ran across the front from Iwuy towards Villers-en-Cauchies. There the enemy resistance stiffened. Parties of Germans lined the road and caused heavy casualties. But they could not prevent our men from working round their flanks, and the Germans either surrendered or were killed. A line of telegraph posts ran towards Avesnes-le-Sec two or three hundred yards south of the Iwuy—Avesnes Road; the ground was somewhat broken and undulating, and the enemy had prepared hastily two or three machine gun positions, one behind the other, near these telegraph posts. Here also small groups of Germans tried to put up a stand for some minutes till they were surrounded. A few of our men had advanced to within a mile of Avesnes-le-Sec shortly after 10 a.m. On the right some of our men had come upon enemy field guns firing at point blank range from positions west of Villers-en-Cauchies. Sergt. Ernest Franks, seeing that his platoon was being held up by these guns, which were firing over open sights, worked his way forward with one of his men, shot four of the German gunners, and took the remainder prisoners. Further on the right of the Battalion the advance was continued to within a few hundred yards of Villers-en-Cauchies. Everything appeared to be going according to time table !

The news of the success of the attack was quickly carried back. All kinds of transport, artillery and ammunition limbers were moving forward. The Naves—Villers-en-Cauchies Road was thick with traffic two kilometres east of Naves. Guns were being moved to advanced positions. Motor ambulances were arriving at Rieux Cross Roads to evacuate wounded. Success was taken for granted. Then the unexpected happened! Observers on the ridge south-east of Iwuy saw men retiring from the direction of Avesnes-le-Sec. For a few minutes it was believed they were manœuvring for another position, or were some of our own men who had been slightly wounded—they came back so slowly and steadily. But the retirement was spreading along the whole front! At the same time, the enemy artillery fire increased, and the ridge was plastered with bursting shells. Enemy machine guns opened out from the Railway embankment near Avesnes-le-Sec, and bullets skimmed along the ridge with unmistakable viciousness. Suddenly this distant machine gun fire was supported by other machine guns firing at comparatively close quarters from German tanks, which were advancing from Avesnes-le-Sec, and driving our infantry before them. There were about four tanks altogether, small in size and able to manœuvre rapidly : they fired their machine guns incessantly, and expended a prodigious amount of six pounder ammunition.

No German counter-attack could have been delivered at a more critical—and from the German point of view—more opportune moment. Our front line had advanced nearly four kilometres, and had naturally become somewhat disorganized. Our men were moving forward in small parties, on a comparatively wide front, and across strange ground, which was open and gave no cover of any kind. Our artillery fire had entirely ceased, and our guns were moving forward. Moreover, our men had had no previous experience of enemy tanks, and the brunt of the counter attack fell on the troops of the 146th Infantry Brigade. Some of the men made determined efforts to put the tanks out of action with rifle fire, but without success : they were shot down. The enemy on the Avesnes Railway embankment had splendid observation of the whole area, and his machine guns worked considerable execution. The German counter-attack must have been timed for 10-45 a.m., and half-an-hour later the whole of our front line was retiring across the ridge which had been captured—apparently so successfully—two hours earlier. It would be impossible to describe the dull rage and disappointment with which men saw themselves thus cheated of victory.

But it was not the enemy who spoke the last word on October 11th. Fortunately there is a spirit in the average Englishman which refuses to accept defeat. On the western slope of the ridge the whole line rallied. Some Canadians who had retired from the left on to the 146th Infantry Brigade front, together with details from the reserve companies of the 1/5th and 1/7th battalions, moved forward to reinforce the remnants of the front wave. Men from all four companies and Battalion H.Q. of the 1/6th made a stand along the light railway and on the sunken road near the ridge top. The recovery was made just in time to save the situation, and to prevent our line from being pushed back into the Erclin valley from which it had started. Already the news of the retirement had thrown the traffic immediately behind the line into confusion. But by the time men in reserve in Naves were expecting to see the enemy on top of them, our front line was advancing again across the ridge in an irresistible determination to re-capture it at all costs. The second advance was more desperate, but more magnificent than the first. If the troops of the 146th Infantry Brigade were the first to retire, as they certainly were the first to receive the brunt of the enemy attack, they were also the first to rally and advance anew against the enemy.

It was about 11-30 a.m. when the enemy tanks reached the western summit of the ridge. Battalion Head Quarters was in position in the sunken road previously mentioned, and their situation was very precarious. A great number of the front line troops had retired behind them, and the *personnel* of Battalion Head Quarters were thus suddenly thrown into the front of the battle. Capt. N. A. Rymer reported from A Company to Bn. H. Q. that the German tanks were still advancing, and would arrive in sight any moment. He was ordered by Lieut.-Col. Clough to take all available men and hold a position on the right of D Company on the light railway. Capt. Rymer was wounded within a few minutes of receiving the order, and about the same time one of the German tanks appeared on the ridge top within three hundred yards of Battalion Head Quarters. The tank kept up an incessant fire, and several Head Quarters men were wounded. A party of Germans with two machine guns also opened fire from the ridge. Lieut.-Col. Clough ordered his men to extend along the sunken road, and open fire immediately on the enemy. He sent a party under Regt. Sergt-Major Arthur Sugden to creep up the sunken road to try and outflank the enemy machine gunners. The sunken road gave a certain amount of shelter, and the steady fire which was kept up by our men helped to restore the situation. Lieut.-Col. R. Clough personally organized his men into a firing line, and with his Intelligence Officer (Lieut. B. Hick) arranged for forward posts to be held in advance of the main line. By his coolness and indifference to danger Lieut.-Col. Clough heartened his men, and helped to save the situation at the critical moment, when the enemy advance had reached the top of the ridge. Unfortunately, Lieut.-Col. Clough was wounded, but his place in command of the Battalion was taken by the Adjutant, Capt. E. D. Stansfield, M.C. Thus in spite of casualties, the enemy advance was stopped, and our line was able to move forward again.

Before Lieut.-Col. Clough was wounded a composite company of about one hundred men had been rapidly organized under the command of Capt. G. F. G. Rees, and had dug in on the ridge top. Other Officers and N. C. O.'s with the spirit of leadership gathered men round them, and slowly advanced in spite of a murderous hail of machine gun bullets. One officer, whose energy and fearlessness had been conspicuous, was leading his men by about twenty yards over the ridge, when he suddenly fell, riddled with machine gun bullets: but those behind him advanced over his body as steadily as if on parade. That critical moment in an action—when the line is wavering and everything depends on the action of one or two individuals—had finally passed. The men were thoroughly roused. The reorganization of the Battalion was done in full view of the enemy, and a continuous barrage of high explosives and gas shells was put down on our forward posts east of the Iwuy-Cauchies Road, making it extremely difficult to hold them. But the enemy infantry did not continue the attack. There is not the slightest doubt that the sight of what must have appeared to be a fresh army of reinforcements advancing over the ridge completely demoralized him. By the time the Battalion had again reached the Iwuy—Villers-en-Cauchies Road, the Canadian on the left and the 147th Infantry Brigade on the right had also begun to advance, and the ridge remained firmly in our possession. After patrolling uselessly in front of Avesnes-le-Sec for nearly an hour, the enemy tanks withdrew. The 146th Infantry Brigade consolidated a position nearly three kilometres in front of the original starting point, and thus succeeded in retaining the high ground which, according to 49th Divisional orders, was to be captured *at all costs*.

In the evening the 1/5th Battalion West Yorkshire Regt. took over the front line from the 1/6th and 1/7th Battalions, and the first stage of the battle was over. The 1/6th and 1/7th Battalions withdrew to their original positions on the Iwuy—Rieux Road. Some hours were spent in strenuous efforts to reorganize companies, to gather in stragglers who had become attached to other units during the battle, and to estimate casualties. The remnants of the Battalion were organized into two companies, with a skeleton Battalion Head Quarters, which took up its position at the Sugar Factory. Lieut. A. M. Thomas and Capt. Duprez, Medical Officers of the 1/6th and 1/7th Battalions respectively, and both belonging to the American Expeditionary Force, were still hard at work on the wounded, who seemed to fill every corner of the factory buildings. During the afternoon the enemy had shelled the factory heavily, and caused several casualties. But the medical staff continued their work without interruption, and the evacuation of wounded was carried out more quickly and efficiently than in any battle in which the Battalion had previously taken part.

During the night of October 11/12th there was little rest for any-one in the Battalion. At midnight Brig.-Gen. G. A. P. Rennie called his Battalion Commanders together, and informed them that the attack was to be continued in the morning, with the same objectives. Zero hour was to be 12 noon, and the advance was to be made under cover of a heavy artillery barrage : the 1/5th Battalion being in the front wave, the 1/6th in support, and the 1/7th in reserve. On the right, units of the 147th Infantry Brigade were also to attack, and the 51st Division was coming up during the night to relieve the Canadians on the left, and would take part in the next day's battle. The 1/5th Battalion Head Quarters was in a red brick house on the Iwuy Road about five hundred yards from the Sugar Factory, and after the information regarding the advance for next day was received, the road became busy with runners and orderlies and troops reorganizing for the attack.

The night passed without much enemy shelling, except a few whiz-bangs at dawn on the ridge top. It was very cold, and no one was tempted to indulge in a long sleep. During the night our patrols were not able to get into touch with the enemy, and at dawn the situation in the front line was very peculiar. As far as the eye could see there was no enemy in sight. By ones and twos, and then by groups, our men got up out of their hastily dug trenches, and moved freely in the open. Not a shot was fired, and the enemy artillery was quiet. The silence was uncanny, and made many men uneasy and suspicious. For an hour or two after dawn there was a thick morning mist on the ground, and nearly everyone expected there would be some unpleasant developments when it lifted. By 8 a.m. the mist had cleared, the sun shone brightly, and the railway embankment near Avesnes-le-Sec could be clearly seen from our positions on the top of the ridge. But there was no sign or sound of the enemy. Everyone realized what had happened. Our possession of the ridge had compelled the enemy to retire beyond Avesnes to the high ground east of the village. The original orders for the attack at noon were cancelled on the 49th Divisional front, and battalions prepared to advance immediately.

In the meantime the 49th Divisional Artillery was moving guns forward in a most daring manner. Before the infantry began their advance, Lieut.-Col. H. D. Stanley (246th West Riding Brigade, R. F. A.) had established his Head Quarters on the ridge top, and was watching his guns moving forward across country to positions a few hundred yards west of Avesnes-le-Sec. The Brigadier of the 147th Infantry Brigade had ridden nearly to Villers-en-Cauchies without being fired on by the enemy. The situation reminded one of comic opera. Two hours before so-called zero hour men were moving about " No Man's Land " very cheerfully, smoking cigarettes, and watching that most inspiring sight—guns being taken into action at the gallop across the open country of " No Man's Land."

The advance began irregularly. On the right, the 147th Infantry Brigade moved forward at 10-15 a.m. The 146th Infantry Brigade followed at 11-10 a.m., units advancing in artillery formation. By this time troops of the 51st Division (the 5th Battalion Seaforth Highlanders were on the left of the 1/5th Battalion West Yorkshire Regt.) had come up, and were waiting on the ridge top for zero hour, twelve noon, before beginning to advance. Their orders had not been cancelled, and at noon the front wave of the 51st Division advanced under cover of a magnificent barrage. Some of their shells fell perilously near the advance guard of the 1/5th Battalion, which had then arrived within a few hundred yards of Avesnes-le-Sec. This tremendous barrage on the 51st Divisional front, rolling over country which had been clear of the enemy for several hours, increased the " comic opera effect " of the whole scene, and the gallant Scotsmen advanced rather self-consciously and seemed somewhat embarrassed by their own barrage.

After noon, however, the enemy began to waken up, and to disturb the peaceful promenade of our troops. By the time the 1/5th Battalion had established their H.Q. in the cellar of a house near the railway station at Avesnes-le-Sec, the enemy was putting a very heavy barrage round Avesnes, and on the area across which the 1/6th Battalion was advancing in support, south-west of the village. The volume and intensity of the enemy shelling was much greater than it had been on the previous day, and it was obvious that the enemy had determined to make a stand along the line of the Selle River, and that he was being supported by a considerable strength of artillery. Till noon on October 12th Avesnes-le-Sec appeared to have been practically untouched by shell-fire, and the red roofs of the houses seemed to promise very good billets to any troops fortunate enough to occupy them. But a few hours of enemy bombardment changed everything. The village reeked with gas : the houses were falling like packs of cards : and a more unhealthy-looking place for billets could not be imagined. Fortunately, the village was empty of civilians.

About 1 p.m. the advance of the 1/5th Battalion was held up by machine gun fire from positions on the high ground east of Avesnes-le-Sec. The advance of the 147th Inf. Brigade was also stopped by strong opposition from near Vordon Wood, north-west of Saulzoir. Also on the left of the 146th Inf. Brigade front the enemy was making a stand against the 51st Division from a copse about two kilometres north of Avesnes-le-Sec. Thus the afternoon passed without much further progress on the part of our troops. News that the 1/5th Battalion was being counter-attacked was received about 5 p.m. by the 1/6th Battalion, which had dug into a position in support south of Avesnes. Capt Stansfield ordered one of his companies to move forward to support the 1/5th Battalion, and with the remainder of his men he took up positions along the Railway Embankment. The enemy counter-attack—if there was one—did not fully develop, and local troops were able to deal with the situation. About this time troops of the 147th Infantry Brigade obtained possession of the southern part of Vordon Wood, and during the darkness, patrols pushed forward to the Selle River, without meeting the enemy. The night passed uncomfortably on the 146th Infantry Brigade front. The enemy bombardment with high explosives and gas was continuous, and everyone was compelled for long intervals to wear gas masks. Fortunately the Battalion transport worked with customary smoothness and efficiency. Rations were plentiful, and " Jim " the Postman turned up with his usual cheerful countenance, and a heavy mail.

The 13th October passed quietly on the Battalion front, though further south the 148th Infantry Brigade with the 19th Battalion Lancashire Fusiliers had come into action, and had attacked through the 147th Infantry Brigade in an effort to secure the crossings of the Selle River. Unfortunately the attack did not succeed, as the enemy was holding the east bank stubbornly, and was in a very strong natural position. On the following night the 146th Infantry Brigade relieved the 147th Infantry Brigade in the Vordon Wood—Saulzoir sector, the relief being completed about 9 p.m.

Saulzoir was built on the two banks of the River Selle, which was in reality merely a stream about twenty feet wide. There were three bridges in the village, all of which had been destroyed by the enemy. The village was in a deep valley, and the eastern slopes, which were in the possession of the enemy, were higher than those on the western bank, and commanded nearly all our positions from Saulzoir to Villers-en-Cauchies. The greater part of the village was situated on the eastern bank, and was held by the enemy. " A " and " D " Companies took over five or six posts on the western bank amongst the houses. These posts commanded the three broken bridges and the north and south edge of Saulzoir. The posts were under cover and the men were fairly comfortable, with the exception of those holding the post commanding the cross roads at the south entrance to the village : they were dug in under a bank on the road side, and could not move, as they were under the direct observation of the enemy, who periodically shelled the cross roads. Naturally, these posts in the village could only be visited at night. The remainder of the Battalion was extended in shallow trenches on the slope west of Saulzoir. Here also every movement was under enemy observation, and several casualties were caused by enemy shell fire and sniping. The situation was so peculiar that there was considerable temptation to be incautious and move about too freely. For instance, the day before the Battalion entered the line near Saulzoir, Major-General Lipsett, General Officer Commanding 4th Division, whilst reconnoitring near Vordon Wood in full view of the enemy lines east of the Selle, was shot through the mouth and killed instantly. Enemy snipers did not often take such advantage of their opportunities, and there would have been many more casualties if the Germans had been more alert.

The same night on which the Battalion took over the Saulzoir sector, a Royal Engineers' patrol of an officer and six sappers reconnoitred the bridges in Saulzoir. The patrol was guided through the village by Lieut. B. Hick, the 1/6th Battalion Intelligence Officer. The party succeeded in getting half-way across one of the bridges, apparently unobserved, when suddenly an enemy machine gun opened out on them from the opposite bank at about fifteen yards range. The sapper officer (Lieut. R. B. Paul, M.C.) was seriously wounded, but the rest of the party made an almost miraculous escape, thanks to the wild shooting of the German machine gunners. The next night a small patrol of three men of the 1/6th Battalion was surprised to see a hostile patrol of between twenty and thirty Germans *on the west side of the river*. The Germans appeared to know the village well, and our men did not take any action against such overwhelming odds.

The situation in Saulzoir was further complicated by the presence of great numbers of civilians, who had been concentrated in the area by the Germans, probably in order to impede our advance at a point of considerable tactical importance. Before he retreated from the line of the Selle River, the enemy deluged the village with gas shells, and caused unspeakable suffering to the unprotected civilians who had not been evacuated. Nothing could have so effectively inspired our men with the lust for killing Germans as the sight of these wretched civilians. After four years of misery, they had been crowded together in cellars at the most vital points of the German defensive system. Our first patrols who entered Saulzoir certainly felt that the welcome given to them by these French villagers more than repaid the hardships endured during the previous fighting. By this time, most of the civilians were suffering from the effects of gas shelling : many of them were ill through sheer fright ; and numbers also had been killed or wounded.

On the night of October 15th a praiseworthy effort was made to evacuate the civilians. Major-General N. J. G. Cameron, the Divisional Commander, believed that from a humane as well as from a military point of view, risks taken in evacuating these people were warranted. Two motor lorries and several motor ambulances were ordered during the night to load up with civilians on the main road five or six hundred yards from Saulzoir. There was some difficulty in persuading the civilians to leave their cellars, and a number of the women were naturally terror-struck with the idea of walking on the roads within rifle shot of the enemy. However, everything was carried out successfully. There was no enemy shelling or machine gun fire during the time the refugees were being collected. The people behaved splendidly, and the evacuation was carried out in a very orderly manner. Although they were very calm and undemonstrative, it was easy to see that the spirits of these old men and women and children were not broken, in spite of incredible hardships. Our men were rather astonished at the fierce passion and intensity with which some of the French folk spoke of the Germans. Not many will forget the look of concentrated hatred with which one or two of the old men shook their fists towards the enemy lines before they crowded into the lorry and were driven towards Villers-en-Cauchies.

The Battalion held the line near Saulzoir for two days. Battalion H.Q. was in the cellar of a house within a hundred yards of the Railway Station near Villers-en-Cauchies, and received a great deal of enemy shelling. The men were cheerful — unusually so ! They had tasted victory, and had deserved it. But all ranks were thoroughly exhausted after being continuously in action for nearly six days. On the night of the 16th October the Battalion was relieved by the 6th Battalion Duke of Wellington's (West Riding) Regt. The relief was carried out under a heavy high explosive and gas bombardment of Villers-en-Cauchies, and the 1/6th Battalion was fortunate in escaping with only a few casualties. The night after the relief the whole of the Head Quarters of the 6th Battalion Duke of Wellington's (West Riding) Regt. was gassed in the cellar which our own Battalion H.Q. had occupied the day before in Villers-en-Cauchies. During the same bombardment over forty men of the 4th Battalion Duke of Wellington's (West Riding) Regt. were also gassed. Thus the 1/6th Battalion West Yorkshire Regt. was fortunate in the date of its relief.

After spending a night at the Sugar Factory, the Battalion

marched back to Escadœuvres, where a very welcome period of three days was spent in billets. Major F. G. Hornshaw, M.C., took over the command of the Battalion from Capt. E. D. Stansfield, M.C., and the Battalion was also reinforced by the rear echelon which had been kept out of action. During this brief rest period the Battalion was reviewed by the Divisional General, and congratulated on its achievements. The following is a message sent, along with the congratulations of the Corps Commander, by Major General N. J. G. Cameron to all units in his Division :—

" It is with feelings of great pride and pleasure that I forward to you the attached copy of a message received from the XXII. Corps Commander. Evidence accumulates to show that your attack on the 11th October was a very real success. It cost the enemy heavily, and dealt him a severe and much needed blow. It entirely turned the enemy's position at Iwuy, the possession of which was necessary to the further advance of the right wing of the First Army in the required direction. My heartiest congratulations to you all.

N. G. Cameron, *Major General*,
Commanding 49th (West Riding) Division."

By the night of October 19th, the 4th Division had taken over from the 49th Division the whole of the Haspres—Saulzoir front. During the same night the enemy withdrew from the Selle River. The withdrawal had been anticipated for some days, and was quickly followed up by the 4th Division, which established itself by nightfall on the line of the River Ecaillon, an advance of nearly 4 kilometres. It would hardly be true to say that most men in the Division would like to have had the opportunity of following up this further withdrawal of the enemy. But in so far as the enemy's retreat was caused by the fighting on October 11th and October 13th, it is only natural that the 49th Division should claim some considerable share in the success.

On October 20th the 1/6th Battalion marched to Ramillies and thence to Iwuy. On leaving Ramillies word was received that H.R.H. The Prince of Wales was waiting to see the Battalion march past. The weather had been very unsettled, and as the Prince came in sight, the rain fell down in torrents. However, the weather did not damp anyone's enthusiasm, and cheer after cheer was raised as the different companies passed the saluting point. It is not often that one hears such lusty unrehearsed cheering on a ceremonial parade. The strength of the Battalion was reduced at this time to nine officers and one hundred and twenty men. No volume of shouting on a ceremonial parade could disguise the fact that nearly four hundred men were missing from the ranks, and that the Battalion had paid a heavy price for victory.

The state of the billets which the Battalion occupied in Iwuy was appalling. The Germans as usual had wantonly destroyed every piece of furniture, broken all the crockery, defaced the walls and torn the books in almost every cottage. There were many signs that the enemy had intended to set the village on fire before he evacuated it, as the floors of several houses were covered with piles of shavings soaked in petrol. Fortunately the enemy had left an enormous dump of soda-water, which was a priceless boon for weeks to nearly every mess within a few kilometres of Iwuy. There were also fairly large stocks of potatoes and carrots in some of the cellars, and industrious " scrounging " brought in good hauls of fresh vegetables which gladdened the heart of many a worried Mess President. The chaplain attached to the Battalion at this time was Capt. K. S. Whitehead, who earned a great name for himself a few days later by the energy and persistence with which he raided a large field of carrots near Battalion Head Quarters. For many days carrots were the " plat de résistance " at every meal in the Battalion Mess.

Although the strength of the whole 146th Infantry Brigade was hardly that of half a normal sized battalion, it was realized towards the end of October that the Brigade would be called upon to take part in another battle. Reinforcements were not expected, and the Battalions were each re-organized into two companies on a two-platoon per company basis. As far as possible everything was done to make each battalion in the Brigade an efficient and complete fighting unit. The entry of the 49th Division into battle was delayed day after day. For instance, on the morning of October 27th, the 146th Infantry Brigade marched to Noyelles, south of Denain, with orders to attack the following morning at 5-30, and capture the village of Aulnoy. The attack was postponed for twenty-four hours; then it was again twice deferred for a further twenty-four hours, until eventually some people thought it would never take place. These postponements of the attack were due to the situation further south, and to the preparations which Sir Douglas Haig was making for a great final effort to capture Mormal Wood and cross the Sambre. The general plan is given in the following selection from Sir Douglas Haig's despatches.

" The principal British attack was to take place at the beginning of November, as soon as possible after the capture of Valenciennes, which I regarded as a necessary preliminary (to the Battle of the Sambre). In view of the likelihood of fresh withdrawals, time was of importance. Accordingly, at 5-15 a.m. on the 1st November, the XVII. Corps of the Third Army and the XXII. and Canadian Corps of the First Army attacked on a front of about six miles south of Valenciennes, and in the course of two days of heavy fighting inflicted a severe defeat on the enemy. During these two days the 61st Division (Major General F. J. Duncan), 49th Division (Major General N. J. G. Cameron) and 4th Division (Major General C. H. T. Lucas) crossed the Rhonelle River, capturing Mareshes and Préseau after a stubborn struggle, and established themselves on the high ground two miles east of it. On their left the 4th Canadian Division captured Valenciennes and made progress beyond the town. As a consequence of this preliminary battle....our principal attack was ready." Thus the fighting round Valenciennes in which the 49th Division was about to take a part, was a necessary preliminary to the last great battle of the War.

On the morning of the 28th October, the 1/6th Battalion took up a position in the sunken road south-east of Maing, four miles south of Valenciennes. The 1/5th Battalion West Yorkshire Regiment was holding an outpost line on the eastern edge of Famars, with the 1/7th Battalion in close support, the 1/6th Battalion being in Brigade Reserve. The 4th Division was on the right and the 4th Canadian Division on the left of the 49th Division. The 147th Infantry Brigade was holding the line immediately south of Famars with the 6th Battalion West Riding Regt. in the front line, and the other battalions of the Brigade disposed in depth in the same way as those of the 146th Infantry Brigade. As we have seen, the attack was originally planned for October 28th, but was postponed three times for twenty-four hours, and came off eventually on November 1st.

The general plan of the attack was as follows :—

1.   The 4th, 49th and 4th (Canadian) Divisions were to attack towards Saultain, force the passage of the La Rhonelle River, and endeavour to turn the defences of Valenciennes from the south.

2.   The 146th Infantry Brigade was to advance through Aulnoy to the Valenciennes—Préseau Road, and to consolidate positions on a front of about one kilometre along the road, the left flank of the Brigade objective being the point where the Railway crosses the Rhonelle River, one mile south-east of Valenciennes.

3.   Zero hour was 5-15 a.m.

According to the original Operation Orders, the 1/6th Battalion was to provide stretcher parties, prisoners' escorts and ammunition carriers to the 1/5th and 1/7th Battalions. Everyone was pleased when this arrangement was dropped. On the morning of the battle the Battalion remained in Brigade Reserve, waiting till called on to exploit the situation in case the attack was successful.

Promptly at 5-15 a.m. the artillery opened out. Our men could not have advanced under the protection of a more splendid barrage. It was feared the crossing of the Rhonelle would be a matter of considerable difficulty. The attack began just before dawn, in order to allow the leading wave to carry footbridges down to the Rhonelle, place them in position, and get across before daybreak. On the 146th Infantry Brigade front the advance was at first more in the nature of a promenade than a battle. Our attack was particularly well-timed, as it caught the 20th (German) Division in the midst of relief by the 6th (German) Division. The Germans at first put up no resistance, and prisoners came through our lines in hundreds. The first news the 6th Battalion received, waiting in reserve in the sunken road south of Maing, was from two of the Battalion scouts who brought back with them the first batch of prisoners—four German officers and fifty-five other ranks ! These scouts reported that the Rhonelle River had been easily crossed, and that Famars was full of German prisoners. Lieut. G. N. Bisatt, the Battalion Intelligence Officer, describes the scene in Famars as follows. " About 9-30 a.m. I got a horse and went up to Famars. I'll swear for every Englishman I saw there were at least five Germans. I was honestly alarmed. So I told all our men who were collecting prisoners to hurry down all the able-bodied Germans as fast as possible, and not to worry about those who were wounded. So many Germans between the front line and the supports were an obvious source of danger. I met two men in Famars with a party of eighty-one Germans, and hardly an Englishman in sight ! The village at this time (11 a.m.) was getting it hot and heavy with stuff even as big as eight-inch shells." On the whole the prisoners were men of poor physique, and were obviously pleased to be captured, their morale being thoroughly broken. The 6th (German) Division was one of the active Divisions which had invaded Belgium at the beginning of August, 1914, and it had a famous record during the war ; the poor quality of the troops which composed it during this battle was therefore very significant.

At 9 a.m. the 1/5th Battalion was within 200 or 300 yards of the final objective. An hour later the 1/7th Battalion had moved up to the eastern outskirts of Aulnoy, and the 1/6th Battalion was in position on the eastern outskirts of Famars. On both flanks of the 146th Infantry Brigade the situation was not quite so favourable, as the enemy had offered more resistance. The 4th Division had entered the village of Préseau, but had been heavily counter-attacked by two regiments of a fresh enemy division from reserve, and was driven out again. The 147th Infantry Brigade, which was immediately on the left of the 4th Division, had therefore dug in on the Aulnoy-Préseau Road, which was the intermediate objective. As the right of the 146th Infantry Brigade was over a mile in advance of this road, it will be seen that the Brigade right flank was very much exposed. Moreover on the left the 4th Canadian Division had not been able to cross the Rhonelle immediately south of Valenciennes, and thus the left flank also of the 1/5th Battalion West Yorkshire Regt. was " in the air."

At noon the situation on the Brigade front was becoming rather serious. The 1/5th Battalion sent up the S. O. S., as the enemy was believed to be counter-attacking on their front. Lieut. E. C. Gregory (1/6th Battalion), who was acting as Brigade Mounted Orderly Officer, rode out with instructions from Brigade H.Q. to the 1/6th Battalion to send an officer to the 1/5th and 1/7th Battalions to find out the exact position of affairs. Whereupon Lieut. Bisatt (1/6th Battalion) went forward and found 1/5th Battalion H.Q. in the cellar of a house in the sunken road south-east of Aulnoy. He received there instructions to return immediately to the 1/6th Battalion and ask for it to be sent up at once to reinforce the 1/5th Battalion in the front line. The request was quickly submitted to Brigade H.Q. and instructions issued for the 1/6th Battalion to move forward. At this time the enemy was shelling heavily the front between Aulnoy and Famars, and there were several casualties before the Battalion reached Aulnoy. When Lieut.-Col. Hornshaw arrived at the 1/5th Battalion Head Quarters he found Lieut.-Col. Foxton of the 1/7th Battalion there also; but no one had satisfactory information with regard to the position of the front line and the units on either flank.

Lieut.-Col. Hornshaw thereupon sent one company under Capt. W. B. MacLusky to the left and the other under Capt. N. Grice to the right of the Brigade front, with instructions to reinforce the front line, and take up positions on the final objective. On the left Capt. MacLusky had no difficulty in reaching the final objective, and found men of the 1/5th Battalion already there in position. It was the 1/6th Battalion which sent back to Brigade H.Q. the first message of the day, stating that on the left of the Brigade front the final objective had been reached. Another party of the 1/6th Battalion under 2nd Lieut. J. Hamilton reinforced the front line in the centre of the Brigade front, and was able to push forward several hundred yards and reach the final objective, capturing several prisoners. On the right, the reinforcement company of the 1/6th Battalion met with considerable resistance. There was a good deal of rifle and machine gun fire, and the enemy had several trench mortars in action. However, here also by dusk our line had been pushed forward to the final objective, and was being firmly consolidated.

At 7 p.m. the situation on the whole front was clear. Our patrols were able to reconnoitre several hundred yards east of the final objectives, and found that on the left of the Brigade front the Canadians had succeeded in reaching the suburbs of Valenciennes. On the right, our flank was somewhat exposed, but at 5-30 a.m. on November 2nd, the 7th Battalion Duke of Wellington's (West Riding) Regt. attacked, and easily reached the objective of the day before, capturing over one hundred prisoners. During the night of November 1st/2nd the 1/6th Battalion was relieved, and marched back to the reserve positions south of Maing.

Thus ended a very satisfactory piece of work, in which the Battalion may be said, without any exaggeration, to have played a most important part at a critical moment. Owing to the fact that the Battalion was by far the weakest in the Brigade, consisting of only nine officers and 107 other ranks, it was put in reserve for the battle, but as we have seen its arrival towards the end of the day enabled the whole line to advance and consolidate on the final objective. Over 600 prisoners were captured by the 146th Infantry Brigade, though the total strength of the Brigade was only slightly over 400 men. The casualties of the Battalion were very slight—being two other ranks killed and one officer and fourteen men wounded. Aulnoy was full of civilians when our troops entered it. These civilians had been told by the Germans that the British had all been killed. They asked our men what States in America they had come from, and could hardly believe the reply that they were " English." " But the brave English are all killed : the ' Boches' told us so ! " Our men quickly proved to them that the English were still very much alive, and could appreciate " café noir " and good cognac.

By a somewhat romantic coincidence, this last attack in which the Battalion took part started from Famars, the village which was captured in 1793, during the war with revolutionary France, by the Fourteenth Regiment of Foot, or the old West Yorkshire Regiment. It was on this occasion that the " Ça Ira " was first adopted as the regimental march. In the Historical Records of the Regiment, the grandson of Colonel W. E. Doyle, who commanded the Regiment during the battle, thus relates the family tradition as to how the famous French quickstep was adopted by a British Regiment. " At the battle of Famars, the French attacked so fiercely that the Fourteenth Foot wavered for a moment. The revolutionary fever, in truth, blazed out as a new element in war, and everywhere the discipline learned under average drill-sergeants was at a loss how to meet it. Colonel Doyle, however, was not at a loss, for, dashing to the front, he called out in a loud voice, ' Come along, my lads ; let's break the scoundrels to their own damned tune. Drummers, strike up 'Ça Ira' ! The effect was irresistible, and the enemy found themselves running away (it was an Irish exploit and a bull is permissible) before they could turn round!"

On the night of the 2nd November, the 56th Division relieved the 49th Division in the Valenciennes area, and after two or three days in the villages near Lieu St. Amand, the 49th Division moved to the Douai area. All three battalions of the 146th Infantry Brigade were billeted in the village of Evin Malmaison, about five miles north of Douai. The 147th Infantry Brigade was billeted in Auby and the 148th Infantry Brigade in Leforest. Divisional Head Quarters was in Douai. Few men realized on October 5th when they entered the Douai area, that, so far as the 49th Division was concerned, the war was over.

About 10 p.m. on November 10th, 146th Infantry Brigade Head Quarters in Evin received a wire from 49th Division stating that hostilities were to cease at 11 a.m. the following morning. The news of the armistice was immediately telephoned to all units in the Brigade. It would be quite impossible to describe the emotions with which men heard of this "miracle." For some hours the intelligence was barely credible : it seemed part of a pleasant dream, and men were afraid of waking up to the bitter reality of continued war! But on the morning of the 11th November, all parades were cancelled : men gathered together in groups in the billets and on the village streets, or discussed the great event with "madame" in the farm kitchen.

The French civilians seemed rather stunned, and unable to appreciate the news for some time. There was an isolated cottage on the Evin-Blanche Maison Road where an old woman lived. She was digging in her small garden when a group of our men passed, and shouted out to her carelessly "Bon jour, Madame....Guerre finie!" She thought they were joking, and smiled feebly, but when someone coming behind assured her the news was true at last, [the old woman broke down. She sobbed painfully, and ran into the house. A few days later men noticed that the cottage seemed to be transformed, the windows had been cleaned, new curtains put up, and the garden looked trim and tidy. "Madame" herself was brighter and seemed years younger. When she was asked the reason for the transformation she said she was making everything ready for the return of her family! But she did not know then that two of her sons were killed, and the one who eventually came back nearly three months later was a cripple.

On the afternoon of Armistice Day the Brigade paraded in a field outside the village. The Mayor and the venerable old priest of the village were present. The Battalion Orders for the Parade were brief, and the matter was cheerful.

CAMBRAI—VALENCIENNES

" 146th Infantry Brigade will parade at 13-30 (1-30 pm.) in the field about R12d15 (on the eastern outskirts of the village). Company markers will report to R. S. M. at Orderly Room at 13.00. Procedure will be as follows :—

The Brigadier will address the Brigade.

The Band of the 1/5th Battalion West Yorkshire Regt. will play the ' Marseillaise.'

The Band of the 1/6th Battalion West Yorkshire Regt. will play ' God Save the King.'

Short Thanksgiving Service.

Brigade will march past in column of fours.

Dress :—Belts and sidearms with Service Dress Caps.

While the ' Marseillaise ' and the ' National Anthem ' are being played Officers will salute, other ranks will stand to attention. Parade will be strong as possible."

This parade may well be regarded as the last event in the war history of the Battalion. In a few words Brigadier General G. A. P. Rennie expressed the thankfulness of all ranks that victory had crowned the efforts of over four years' fighting. The privilege of being present on the parade, he said, was reserved to only a very few out of those many thousands who had served in the Brigade in almost every corner of the northern battlefields. He closed a brief but very telling speech with a reference to the responsibilities of peace, and the need in the future for the same endurance and discipline which had been shown in the difficult situations of the past.

The Battalion spent nearly four months in Evin-Malmaison. The time was marked by few events of importance. Early in December all units in the Brigade began salvage work in the Evin-Malmaison area. The German defences on the east bank of the Canal de la Haute Deule were very elaborate, and miles of barbed wire entanglements were taken up by the Battalion salvage parties. Shells were collected into dumps : and German camps dismantled. On December 16th the 49th Division was inspected by the General Officer Commanding XXII. Corps, under whom it had served so long. This was the first and only time the whole Division paraded together in France. Several Divisional Competitions were held about this time, and on the whole the Battalion did very well. On December 20th, the Battalion Band won the first prize in the Divisional Band Competition. In January the Battalion also won the Divisional Cross Country Run at Leforest. Approximately over 180 runners started, ten entries being allowed for each battalion or battalion equivalent. In the Final for the VIII. Corps Football Competition on February 19th, 1919, the Battalion team represented the 49th Division, and played the Drake Battalion of the 63rd (Naval) Division, winning the match by one goal to nil. As a result of all-round excellence in sport, the Battalion was awarded by Major-General Cameron the 49th Divisional Shield, in January, 1919. All kinds of schemes were inaugurated to keep everybody actively employed and in good humour, and the weeks spent in Evin before demobilization are full of many pleasant memories.

Dancing was very popular, and during the Christmas Festivities everybody from the Colonel to the newest lance-corporal danced together with an abandon and enjoyment which would have astonished any of the opposite sex if they had been present. The most popular sport with the officers was probably the "Paper Chases" which were held every week. Fifty or sixty horsemen usually turned out, and on the whole it was surprising that some subalterns and company commanders, who had escaped being killed during the war, were able to escape breaking their necks in trying to jump the dykes on the flat country round Evin.

Early in December it was decided to bring the Battalion Colours out to France, and a colour party was sent to England to fetch them. The Colour party consisted of Lieuts. E. C. Gregory, G. N. Bissatt, Coy. Sergt.-Major Banks, D.C.M., Coy. Sergt.-Major E. Bradley, D.C.M., Coy. Sergt.-Major G. Humphries, D.C.M., Sergt. Hird, M.M. The Colours had been placed in the Parish Church at Bradford since May, 1918, and were handed over to the Battalion Colour Party on January 5th, 1919. An escort of fifty men was provided under the command of Capt. W. G. Tetley and Lieut. F. E. Fairbank, M.M. The Parish Church was crowded, and large crowds also assembled in Forster Square to do honour to the Colours of the Battalion.

There were only about 300 civilians in Evin, and for the first few weeks the men made themselves very comfortable in empty houses, and transferred tables and chairs and crockery from one house to another with great impartiality. When the civilians began to come back to their village in greater numbers during January, 1919, the problem of billeting the men became rather acute, but the difficulty was usually settled in an amicable way, and was quickly lessened by the increasing numbers of men who were demobilized early in the year.

A great number of Concert Parties performed in the village, a popular troupe being formed by the 1/1st West Riding Field Ambulance, who were also billeted in Evin. Head Quarters 146th Infantry Brigade also raised a Concert Party, which gave its performances in a large hut in a Prisoners of War Camp built by the Germans. In this hut an interesting series of lectures on all kinds of topics was also arranged by the Division. An elaborate system of Educational Training was inaugurated immediately after the Armistice throughout the British Army, and morning parades in the Battalion consisted largely of classes in "Reading, Writing and Arithmetic," elementary French, or any other subject on which any officer or N. C. O. was proficient and capable of giving useful instruction. An Educational Officer was appointed in each Battalion, and apart from the Adjutant and Demobilization Officer, he was probably the busiest man in the unit. This Educational Training was taken very seriously, and was undoubtedly useful in preparing men for the routine work of civilian life. Battalion and Brigade Reading Rooms were formed in the village : each Battalion ran a small circulating library : and in the evening debates were held in the Brigade Reading Room in the village. The Brigade Major, Capt. C. F. Witts, D.S.O., M.C., threw himself keenly into this Educational work, and by giving lectures and taking charge of debates and supervising the classes he helped to make the Educational work a live and useful part of the Brigade Training.

One novel form of this Educational Training deserves special mention. Major General N. J. G. Cameron bought a carefully selected number of Medici Prints of Old Masters, and arranged for them to be carried about from village to village throughout the Divisional Area, and to be hung up in suitable rooms in each village for a day or two, so that every man in the Division could have the opportunity of inspecting this "travelling picture gallery." A showman (one of the Brigade Educational Officers) went round and "explained" the pictures to an amused, but on the whole interested and appreciative audience. Thus during the four months' stay at Evin the energy and spirits of the Battalion did not slacken or grow stale, and it was a remarkable fact that after the Armistice men worked almost as many hours and were quite as active as they had been during the war—but the work was pleasant and to a large extent self-imposed.

On February 24th, 1919, the remnant of the Battalion entrained at Douai to join the 3rd Northern Division of the Army of Occupation on the Rhine. Apart from an interval of a fortnight in June, the Battalion remained in Cologne from February 26th to November 13th 1919. On April 18th, Lieut.-Col. T. M. S. N. Howard, D.S.O., took over command of the Battalion from Lieut.-Col. F. G. Hornshaw, M.C. Five months later on August 22nd Lieut.-Col. N. F. Barwell, M.C., assumed command of the Battalion on the appointment of Lieut.-Col. Howard to be General Officer Commanding 3rd London Brigade. On May 1st the Battalion furnished a guard of honour of two officers and fifty other ranks for the visit of General Pétain to the Commander-in-Chief of the British Army of Occupation. A few days later the Battalion was reviewed by Field Marshal H.R.H. The Duke of Connaught and General Sir Wm. Robertson. Guards of Honour were also provided by the Battalion for the Commander-in-Chief of the American Army and General Fayolles on their visits to Cologne on July 26th and July 30th. The Battalion was frequently complimented on its very smart appearance, and its frequent selection to provide Guards of Honour in the 3rd Northern Division of the Rhine Army was a well-merited compliment. In Sports also the Battalion continued its extremely good record. On October 8th the Battalion Football Team won the Kalk Shield, open to all units of the Rhine Army, by defeating the 23rd Battalion Royal Fusiliers. The Battalion also won easily the Northern Divisional Athletic Competition, gaining eighteen points to the three points of the battalion in the second place. The list of trophies won by the Battalion from December, 1918, to November, 1919, is imposing :—

49th Divisional Shield, presented by Major General Cameron to the best all-round battalion in the Division (Drill, Scouting and Sniping, Football—Rugby and Association, Cross Country Run, Band).
Association Football VIII. Corps Cup.
Basket Ball Competition. VI. Corps.
Musketry Competition. Drove. Rhine Army
Rhine Army Cup for advancing in sections. Fire and Cover.
Shell Case for highest total in War Savings in the Rhine Army.

On November 11th, 1919, the first Anniversary of Armistice Day, the Battalion paraded at 11 a.m. and the Last Post was sounded. All traffic in Cologne was suspended from 11.00 to 11.02. Officers saluted, and the men stood to attention. The next day the Battalion with the Colours paraded in the Dom Platz in Cologne as Guard of Honour to General Degoutte. And on November 13th, the Battalion left Cologne *en route* for Calais. The Battalion reached Dover on November 17th, 1919, after an absence of four years and eight months abroad.

Instead of immediately entraining for Bradford, the Battalion spent four months in Kinmel Park Camp, North Wales, where it was gradually demobilized. On March 30th, 1920, at 5-30 p.m., the Cadre of the 1/6th Battalion, consisting of forty-five officers and men, arrived at the Exchange Station, Bradford. Lieut.-Col. N. F. Barwell, M.C. was in command, and other officers with the Cadre were Lieut.-Col. and Quartermaster W. H. Hill, M.C., Capt. and Adjutant G. N. Bissat, Lieut. R. A. Russell. Lieut. W. Rumney and 2nd Lieut. J. A. Hunter were Colour Bearers. The Cadre was met at the station by several officers who had served overseas with the Battalion, amongst whom were Col. H. O. Wade, D.S.O., Major H. W. Barker, Rev. R. Whincup, M.C., Capt. A. Hamilton. The Lord Mayor of Bradford (Alderman W. Wade) was also present. In spite of heavy rain large crowds of people lined the streets from the station to Town Hall Square. The Band of the 2nd Volunteer Battalion (augmented by several bandsmen of the 6th Battalion) struck up as the Cadre moved out of the Station, and hundreds of demobilized men marched, once again, in fours behind the Colours.

At noon on the following day the Cadre was officially welcomed home by the Lord Mayor in the Town Hall Square, Bradford. The Guard of the new 6th Battalion West Yorkshire Regiment received the Colours from the Cadre of the 1/6th Battalion with the customary ceremonial. The scene was brief, but impressive. A large proportion of the great crowd which witnessed the ceremony consisted of demobilized men, who watched the familiar movements of the ceremonial drill with a keen and critical interest. Long after the parade was dismissed, groups of demobilized men remained on the Town Hall Square discussing with comrades their Army experiences, when they too had served with the 1/6th Battalion, which had now finished its task, and had ceased to exist as a separate unit.

Officers and men of the Cadre were entertained to luncheon in the Town Hall by the Lord Mayor. Lieut.-Col. N. F. Barwell, M.C., replied to the toast of the 1/6th Battalion, which was proposed by the Lord Mayor. Other speakers at the luncheon were Col. H. O. Wade, D.S.O., Lieut.-Col. W. H. Hill, M.C., and Rev. R. Whincup, M.C. Lieut.-Col. H. L. Anderton, now commanding the 6th Battalion West Yorkshire Regiment, and one of the original Company Commanders who crossed over to France with the Battalion in April, 1915, read a greeting from Lieut.-Col. R. Clough, M.C., who was unable to be present. Col. Anderton then expressed the general feeling of all members of the Battalion when he said—" The comradeship which existed at Ypres, on the Somme, at Arras, at Kemmel, and at other places where this Battalion fought, will never be forgotten by officers or men, and we in Bradford know it. That comradeship will never die so long as there is a single man of the old 1/6th Battalion living amongst us."

The assembly rose and stood in silence for a few moments in memory of the dead.

CHAPTER XIV.

NEC ASPERA TERRENT.

SUCH a story as the one given in the foregoing pages may seem to many readers to lack unity, and to be the history, not of one, but of many battalions. And to some extent such a criticism would be just. The Battalion was changing continually. Again and again it was scattered and destroyed, and nothing seemed left but a name. Hospitals and depots in England and cemeteries in France seemed to be the places where the majority of the men of the 1/6th Battalion were gathered together. When men rejoined from England, after an absence of a few months, they found themselves strangers in a strange unit. Reinforcements who knew nothing of the old traditions had filled up the ranks.

Not including cases of sickness, there were 139 battle casualties amongst officers alone during the three and a half years' active service in France and Flanders. Thus the entire establishment of officers was put out of action over five times during the war. There were 2,038 casualties to other ranks during the same period, or nearly four times the average strength of the Battalion. And when it is remembered that in addition to battle casualties there were 1,092 cases of sickness, some idea can be obtained of the wastage continually taking place in an infantry battalion.* For a few weeks or months men lived an intense vivid life in the Battalion, and then passed on. Their deeds seemed forgotten. Experiences which to them as individuals appeared of tremendous importance were really transitory episodes in the story of the Battalion.

However, even in this ever changing organism it is possible to single out periods when there was a very obvious unity within the Battalion. For instance from April to December, 1915, the Battalion was a self-conscious Territorial unit. Pre-war intimacy, and the knowledge born of months of training together, had produced a feeling of confidence between officers and men. The effect on morale was magnificent. The story of Ypres in 1915 proves how well the Battalion stood the bitterest tests. On the other hand, during these months the Battalion was probably too much of a " closed corporation." There

---

* The casualties in the 1/6 Battalion during the war were as follows;—Officers, 38 killed, 96 wounded, 5 missing. Other Ranks, 374 killed, 1,488 wounded, 196 missing.

BELGIAN BATTERY CORNER. NR. YPRES.

" THE TYKES,"
DIVISIONAL CONCERT PARTY.

SGT. COOK T. GARRETT.

L/CPL. J. WALKER,
" JIM THE POSTMAN."

L/CPL. J. ROSCOE.
" POET, POLITICIAN AND PIONEER."

PTE. T. BRITTON.

LOOKING TOWARDS KEMMEL FROM THE VIERSTRAAT-
HALLEBAST RD. (NEAR BARDENBRUG), 1918.

DICKEBUSCH-YPRES ROAD, ONE MILE FROM DICKEBUSCH, 1918.

XMAS CARD, 1916.

XMAS CARD, 1918
49TH (WEST RIDING) DIVISION.

THE BOMBERS.

BACK ROW. - METCALFE, JONES, WILSON, HUDSON, FISHBURN, JEFFERSON, PRITCHARD, FOX, REECE.
3RD ROW.—PARKINSON, DUCKETT, COYNE, THISTLEWAITE, ROBINSON, ROOME.
2ND ROW.—CAWTHRA, L/CPL. ANDREWS, L/CPL. BUTTERFIELD, SERGT. MᶜIVOR, LT. H. A. JOWETT,
L/CPL. FOULDING, L/CPL. FOSTER, BROWN, HAIGH, BRADY.
1ST ROW.—SWITHENBANK, WATERWORTH, HANSON, WARD, BROWN, HALL, BANNISTER, MORRIS.
(All privates unless where otherwise stated).

THE SIGNALLERS.
STANDING.—PTES. BINKS, ROLFE, SMETHURST, WICKS, ROBINSON, RILEY AND PRATT.
CENTRE ROW.—L/C FOSTER, SERGT. WARD, L/C CLARK.
FRONT ROW.—PTES. EDMONDSON AND WOLSTENHOLME.

xlv.

THE G.O.C. VI. CORPS (LT.-GEN. SIR A. L. HALDANE) ACCOMPANYING MR. WINSTON CHURCHILL (SECRETARY OF STATE FOR WAR), PASSING THE REGIMENTAL COLOURS OF THE 1/6TH BATT. PRINCE OF WALES'S OWN WEST YORKSHIRE REGIMENT, COLOGNE, 1919.

xlvi.

THE RETURN OF THE CADRE, MARCH 30TH, 1920.

HANDING OVER THE COLOURS OF THE 1/6 BATTALION TO THE NEW 6TH
BATTALION WEST YORKSHIRE REGIMENT, MARCH, 31ST, 1920.

MEMORIAL WINDOW, BRADFORD CATHEDRAL.
(See Appendix vi.

xlviii.

was a tendency in 1915 to regard reinforcements as interlopers. New comers were ragged unmercifully, or, worse still, left severely alone. When the reinforcements had " made good " their claim to belong to the fellowship, their path was easy—but not till then ! There was some justification for much of this apparent intolerance and aloofness. The T. F. Battalion had reached in 1915 a high level of excellence, and officers and men were jealous for the reputation of their unit.

The battles of the Somme in 1916 smashed up a good deal of this " Territorial " influence. Only a handful of the original Territorial officers and men survived. Reinforcements from all parts of England served in the Battalion. The enthusiasm and keenness of the " amateur " soldier gave place to a spirit more akin to the prosaic efficiency of the professional. War was no longer a patriotic game for a few willing spirits, but a grim routine in which everyone was compelled to take a more or less satisfactory part. Thus what was narrow and " local " in the Battalion died out in the " blood bath " on the Somme. At the same time some of the intense enthusiasm and splendid pugnacity of 1915 died out too !

More important than these changes within the Battalion is the fact that the same will and the same incentive distinguished the unit throughout the war. Men forgot themselves in the common effort. Every week tremendous tasks, which would never have been attempted for any private or personal ends, were cheerfully and triumphantly accomplished. Many illustrations of this have already been given. One more however is worthy of record, especially as it is an incident which in all its details may seem at first somewhat trivial and commonplace. Yet such incidents are remarkable precisely because they were of such frequent occurrence.

Near Calgary Grange on the morning of October 9th, 1917, and a few minutes before the battle opened, there were several men still helplessly stuck in the mud. A small party of scouts came across one of these men who had been in his shell hole for nearly eight hours, and who was in the last stages of exhaustion. His struggles only seemed to have fixed him more deeply in the mud. It was about a quarter of an hour before zero. The whole area was in the line of the enemy barrage fire. Our attacking waves were in position. The scouts had little time to lose, but after struggling hard for some minutes they succeeded in extricating the man from the shell hole. There was a concrete shelter about two hundred yards away. They tried to get the man there in safety. But he would not move. " I must have my rifle," he said, pointing to his weapon, half buried in the mud. It was ridiculous ! He could hardly stand, quite apart from using his rifle, and delay was dangerous. Still the man would not move. " I must ' go over ' with B. Company," he said obstinately. By dint of curses, and after carrying him most of the way, the scouts got the exhausted and half-delirious private of B. Company under cover in the German pill box a few minutes before the enemy barrage came down. But his comrades will not forget the momentary fire and resolution with which the man said, " I must ' go over ' with B. Company." There seemed to be no limit to the self-sacrifice of many of the men. Nor did they seem to understand why such a spirit should be worthy of special praise.

A few months in an infantry battalion on active service was a liberal education. The artificial distinctions of civilian life were broken down, and a man lived in intimacy with different types and classes. Preconceived ideas as to the kind of man likely to be a good soldier or comrade were often falsified. The foul-mouthed heavy drinking libertine whom one thought " just the man for a scrap," in a crisis was almost invariably either a coward or a failure. On the other hand the so-called " religious " man often lacked every element of good comradeship. Everyone who has served for however short a period in the Battalion must have preserved the memory of some comrade who had many of the qualities of the ideal soldier. Hero-worship was strong in the Battalion, as in every healthy community. Yet if the ideals which appealed to men could be compared, how great a diversity of type there would be, and what a revelation of unexpected heroic qualities. The writer remembers two men, who, though contrasted in many ways, were akin in most of the essential qualities of leadership. They were both killed, but fortunately men of their type were never lacking in all ranks of the Battalion throughout the war.

The first, Lieut. X——, was huge and muscular, a man of strong will and vehement passions. His enemies said he was obstinate, even brutal. His friends sometimes feared the results of his wilfulness and self-indulgence. If he had a sense of religion it was not developed. The world and the flesh figured prominently in his actions and thoughts. Thus he challenged criticism and the criticism was not always favourable. Yet responsibility transformed him. In a time of crisis—that is, throughout the whole period of his service with the Battalion—he showed such courage and self-sacrifice, and even discipline, as in the last resort can only belong to strong moral character. Moreover, he had the instinct of leadership. His men would have followed him anywhere without misgiving. They knew that in the biggest emergency he would think coherently, and act quickly : and that his last thought would be about himself. His faults seemed personal and limited. His virtues had a wide scope, and the whole strength of his character seemed concentrated in them. Altogether, Lieut. X——— was one of the queer and startling contradictions of army life. A short time ago the writer heard the following story about him. The enemy was bombarding heavily a short section of our line immediately after stand down one morning. A new recruit was ordered to report immediately to the platoon which was holding the bombarded trenches. It was not a pleasant errand for an untried youngster, and would have made a veteran hesitate. Lieut. X——— was quick to notice the thinly disguised fear in the mind of the recruit. Although Lieut. X——— was about to " turn in " after a long spell of duty, he changed his mind after he had looked at the trembling youngster. " I am going your way," he said indifferently. The two set off down the trench together. The bombardment continued, but they got safely through.

Lieut. Y——— was a complete contrast. He was rather thin and short, and not particularly athletic. He had a peculiarly long straight back, and walked stiffly, with his head very erect, as though he was always on parade. His eyes were usually so gentle, and his smile so ingenuous that his men at first believed they could take liberties with him : he was a " soft-un." But they forgot his lips were very firm, and his chin squarely set : and no one took liberties with him twice. However he remained, to many officers and men, something of a problem. He did not drink much, or smoke, was not fond of horseplay, seemed to like reading rather heavy literature, and enjoyed talking French to old women and French peasants. He was rather too much of a student, and in the general opinion it was easier for a camel to go through the eye of a needle than for a student to be a soldier.

Yet any prejudices against him disappeared entirely when the Battalion was in the line. If his trench section was being shelled he was rarely in his dug out, but nearly always in his trench, either alongside a sentry, or, with a strange aloofness, yet without affectation, reading a book on the firestep. He lived even more simply than his men and entirely on Army rations. He was always busy, and seemed to sleep less than anyone else in the line. He used often to say he was afraid, but he never showed it. In a few weeks he had earned the reputation of being one of the most reliable men in the Battalion.

Undoubtedly his strength came from his religion. Few men ever heard him mention the name of Christ, or heard him talk for five minutes about religion. No one ever heard him criticize a living soul. He did not object openly to dirty stories or filthy language. But it must be admitted that one rarely heard dirty stories in his presence, and his men used to refrain from foul language if he was near. One felt instinctively that he never acquiesced in anything likely to lower a man's estimate of himself: that he could not understand the bad side of a man: and that his own character was a perpetual and quiet protest against evil. He was mortally wounded during an attack. Though he must have been in great pain, he was quite calm, even cheerful. One of the stretcher bearers who attended him for a few moments could hardly believe he was mortally wounded, and within a few minutes of death. He smiled cheerfully as he told the stretcher bearer " not to waste any more time over him," but to look after the others, who were lying around. The stretcher bearer went away, and when he returned a few minutes later was astonished to find that Lieut. Y—— was dead.

Probably never before in any war were men called on to pass through such a succession of sordid, nerve-racking and perilous experiences as from 1915 to 1918. Human endurance was tried to the uttermost, yet human endurance triumphed. " *Nec aspera terrent.*" The proud motto of the West Yorkshire Regiment was not an empty boast. Hardships did not terrify. The spirit of a man again and again proved invincible.

THE END.

APPENDIX I.

Officers and O.R's. (of the 1/6 Battalion West Yorkshire Regiment) who went abroad on April 15th, 1915.

OFFICERS.

Lieut.-Col. H. O. Wade, Commanding Officer.
Major C. E. Scott, second in command.
Major R. Clough.
Captain and Adjutant G. R. Sandeman.
Captain and Quarter-Master W. H. Hill.
Captain H. L. Anderton.
Captain R. A. Fawcett.
Captain A. C. C. Walker.
Captain H. W. Barker.
Captain N. Muller.
Captain R. G. Fell.
Lieutenant J. L. Heselton.
Lieutenant J. L. Oddy.
Lieutenant W. G. Tetley.
Lieutenant E. W. Knowles.
Lieutenant F. W. Musgrave.
Lieutenant N. Grice.
Lieutenant S. C. Savill.
Second-Lieutenant R. G. Dobson.
Second-Lieutenant J. M. McLaren.
Second Lieutenant W. L. Fawcett.
Second-Lieutenant F. G. Hornshaw.
Second-Lieutenant T. E. Armistead.
Second-Lieutenant W. N. Mossop.
Second-Lieutenant J. C. Watson.
Second-Lieutenant E. Myers.
Second-Lieutenant W. L. Birch.
Lieutenant A. Hamilton, R.A.M.C. (attached).
Captain J. Muller (Brigade Machine Gun Officer).
Lieutenant S. J. Gordon (Brigade Transport Officer).
Captain L. S. Middleton (left behind temporarily, sick).*

*Rejoined later.

HISTORY OF THE 1/6TH BN. WEST YORKSHIRE REGT.

"A" COMPANY.

Sgt.-Major Freeman, C. L.
Coy. Sgt.-Major Pottage, J.
Coy. Q.M.S. Dawson, H.
Sgt. Griffiths, I. E.
Sgt. Simpson, C. G.
Sgt. Rhodes, H. E.
Sgt. Overton, G. F.
Sgt. Banks, H.
Sgt. Riley, B. M.
Sgt. Rhodes, H. H.
Sgt. Hamilton, R.
Sgt. Hammond, J.
Sgt. Abott, A.
Lc.-Sgt. Lunn, H.
Lc.-Sgt. Stanton, W. E.
Cpl. Sharkey, T.
Cpl. Kelly, J. W.
Cpl. Cusworth, W.
Cpl. Kennedy, F.
Cpl. Rawlings, C.
Cpl. Constable, J.
Cpl. Hutchinson, J. B.
Cpl. Murphy, J.
Lc.-Cpl. Foster, J.
Lc.-Cpl. Firth, H.
Lc.-Cpl. Ambler, P.
Lc.-Cpl. Thompson, T.
Lc.-Cpl. Nally, W.
Lc.-Cpl. Bairstow, J.
Lc.-Cpl. Baker, H.
Lc.-Cpl. Poole, A.
Lc.-Cpl. Moulson, F.
Lc.-Cpl. Mulley, F.
Lc.-Cpl. Walker, J.
Lc.-Cpl. Cresswell, J. W.
Lc.-Cpl. King, G. M.
Lc.-Cpl. Newhall, J.
Lc.-Cpl. Bentley, J. S.
Lc.-Cpl. Ellison, W.
Lc.-Cpl. Wells, C. H.
Lc.-Cpl. Lennon, C. B.

Dr. Bussey, T.
Dr. Jenkinson, E.
Dr. Frost, F.
Dr. Fryer, J.

PRIVATES.

Abbott, J.
Atkinson, R.
Ayrton, J.
Atkinson, T.
Allan, W.
Bloomfield, T.
Bell, A.
Bailey, A.
Brear, W.
Brearley, P.
Barker, E.
Brooks, F.
Brunton, G.
Benson, E.
Braithwaite, F.
Bannister, J. W.
Burgess, J. H.
Bownas, C.
Baxter, W.
Britton, T.
Boyle, E.
Brooks, F.
Bullock, R. V.
Backhouse, A. D.
Bird, J.
Barker, H.
Carter, H.
Cuthbert, H.
Cohen, G.
Cannon, E.
Clegg, H.
Cordingley, E.
Creyke, R.
Clayton, A.
Coultas, M.

Coopland, A.	Hall, W. F.
Clark, J. W.	Harvey, A.
Coleman, J.	Helliwell, A.
Dooley, J.	Hirst, H.
Duckett, H.	Hardcastle, H.
Dracup, C.	Hammerton, J.
Drake, W. V.	Hanson, C.
Devanney, J.	Howard, E.
Dakin, A.	Irvine, I.
Dossett, H.	Ibbotson, W.
Dracup, J.	Johnson, E.
Dinsdale, F.	Jones, W. H.
Earle, W.	Jarvis, I.
Elliott, J.	Jefferson, T.
Edmondson, G.	Kermode, E. M.
Elliott, F. A.	Kettlewell, H. W.
Francis, W.	Kinsley, J.
Fynn, T.	Knowd, H.
Freeman, S.	King, J.
Florence, G.	Kershaw, T.
Farley, T.	Kay, H.
Fitzgerald, J.	Lacey, E. H.
Fearnley, L.	Lennon, A. E.
Foulds, F.	Lee, S.
Farrelly, G.	Lee, F.
Forbes, R.	Lister, E.
Grey, J. T.	Laycock, A.
Grant, L.	Lambert, A.
Grant, C. E.	Macmaster, J. K.
Greenwood, F. C.	Mitchell, R.
Garnett, T.	McGrath, J. W.
Ginn, G.	Miller, J. W.
Grimshaw, P.	Moore, N.
Greenwood, L.	Mason, A. W.
Gordon, B.	Moss, E. S.
Heseltine, L.	Mason, A. V.
Hutchinson, F.	Marvel, A.
Hulligan, W.	Morris, W.
Horn, F.	Narey, S.
Hammond, H.	Ormondroyd, P.
Hensby, W.	Overton, J. W.
Hird, C.	Pyrah, H.

Pemberton, J.

Priestley, R. H.

Petcher, R.

Paley, B. J.

Prime, A.

Pearson, H.

Redhead, W.

Ryan, T.

Ramsbottom, R.

Robinson, T.

Raistrick, W.

Rudolph, G.

Ramsbottom, E.

Robertshaw, F.

Roberts, C. H.

Roe, J. A.

Reece, H.

Rushforth, H.

Robinson, F.

Ross, E.

Redburn, J.

Robinson, E.

Smith, A.

Sugden, R. C.

Swire, W.

Sharper, J. W.

Smith, A.

Speight, H.

Sunderland, J. L.

Sharp, B.

Stansfield, E.

Sunderland, A.

Styles, C.

Shearer, J.

Swann, E.

Slater, W.

Spencer, H.

Shaw, H. G.

Sykes, W. E.

Shaw, A.

Small, A.

Sargent, P.

Shone, H.

Stansfield, J.

Smith, R.

Simpson, J.

Sadler, A.

Simpson, W. W.

Sutcliffe, W.

Swithenbank, W.

Smith, J.

Taylor, J. H.

Thompson, W.

Thompson, J.

Tong, E.

Tynan, T.

Taylor, J.

Townend, H.

Tattersall. W.

Tetley, J. W.

Wilson, W.

Watmough, H. R.

Warrener, G.

Worsnop, T.

Walker, M.

Wilkinson, H.

Wilkinson, W.

Wilkinson, A. R.

Worsnop, J.

Wainwright, A.

Whittam, H.

West, R. A.

Whitfield, W.

Wood, J.

Waters, J.

Waterworth, W.

Wilkinson, P.

Weatherill, T.

Wild, G. F.

Wilkinson, W.

Watson, A.

Watson, T.

Yeoward, D.

APPENDIX

" B " COMPANY.

Coy. Sgt.-Major Mackay, T.
Coy. Q. M. S. Woodhead, C.
Sgt. Hardaker, B.
Sgt. Dalgleish, J.
Sgt. Middleton, H.
Sgt. Clark, H.
Sgt. Servant, W.
Sgt. Smith, S. V.
Sgt. Howard, F.
Sgt. Hughes, H. M.
Sgt. Chapman, S.
Sgt. Garrett, T. W.
Lc.-Sgt. Kellett, J.
Lc.-Sgt. Wood, A.
Cpl. Taylor, A.
Cpl. Ross, A. A.
Cpl. Marchant, H.
Cpl. Vickerman, H. L.
Cpl. Baxter, F. C.
Cpl. Badland, S. H.
Cpl. Meekosha, S.
Cpl. Whitehead, H.
Lc.-Cpl. Balmforth, F.
Lc.-Cpl. Fenton, A.
Lc.-Cpl. Johnston, S.
Lc.-Cpl. Watson, J.
Lc.-Cpl. Whiteley, W.
Lc.-Cpl. Sharp, J. W.
Lc.-Cpl. Smithies, T.
Lc.-Cpl. Chapman, F.
Lc.-Cpl. Scarfe, E.
Lc.-Cpl. Foster, H.
Lc.-Cpl. Hutchinson, W.
Lc.-Cpl. Scully, J.
Lc.-Cpl. Yarker, J.
Lc.-Cpl. Powell, R.
Lc.-Cpl. Bartlett, C.
Lc.-Cpl. Ratcliffe, T.
Lc.-Cpl. Turner, G.
Lc.-Cpl. Haigh, H.
Lc.-Cpl. Foster, J. W.

Drummer Midgley, W.
Drummer Sutcliffe, R.
Drummer Holmes, J.
Drummer Ledgard, H.

PRIVATES.

Adcock, A.
Adcock, H.
Allan, A. G.
Avison, W.
Andrews, S. J. D.
Allan, H.
Alston, R.
Barnard, H.
Bowers, S.
Bateson, T.
Bentley, D.
Butler, H.
Brown, A.
Boldy, H.
Bottomley, H. C.
Buckroyd, C.
Brown, E.
Brewer, T. H.
Broadhead, M.
Burgess, C.
Blaydes, C. H.
Brown, H.
Brown, W.
Clarke, E.
Coghlan, D.
Cook, B.
Carter, J. W.
Corke, C. A.
Coe, G. R.
Cutler, J.
Cadamateri, W.
Clayton, A. E.
Carrol, H.
Cunningham, T.
Cole, A.

Cahill, E.
Crabtree, R.
Delaney, T.
Dickinson, A.
Dickson, E. T.
Dodson, F.
Driver, H.
Derry, A.
Dixon, T.
Davis, H.
Doherty, E.
Dooley, E. P.
Dean, J.
Davy, S.
Duffy, R.
Excell, J.
Emmott, A.
Easton, J. H.
Firth, J.
Fuller, R.
Foster, J. W.
Ferrand, H.
Fitton, R.
Garrett, A. K.
Gomersal, J.
Gaunt, H.
Goldsborough, J.
Greenwood, J. A.
Galtress, F.
Holroyd, E.
Hepworth, E.
Halmshaw, H.
Haigh, H.
Harrison, V.
House, W.
Hainsworth, H.
Harrison, R.
Hardcastle, H.
Harvey, P.
Helliwell, A.
Higgins, E.
Hoyle, N.

Holdsworth, W.
Holt, J.
Holyday, T. E.
Hustwick, P.
Hird, E.
Hodgson, A. L.
Hodgson, W.
Hindle, W.
Horrocks, E.
Hewitt, H.
Hollingworth, G. H.
Harrison, B.
Ingleson, R.
Ingham, J.
Ibbetson, J.
Jackson, W.
Johnson, E.
Jones, E. M.
Johnson, H.
James, P.
Johnson, C.
Jordan, F.
Kershaw, E.
Kilkenny, J.
Keeley, G. P.
Kilner, E. S.
Lythe, H.
Laycock, H.
Loftus, M.
Laycock, W.
Mercer, S.
McLennon, U.
Morton, J.
Metcalfe, W.
Myers, W.
Meehan, J.
Mann, H.
McCarthy, J.
Mitchell, J.
Morton, B.
Manson, C.
Myers, J.

APPENDIX

Mawson, R.
Naismith, J. W.
Naismith, R.
Nixon, J. T.
Norton, W. H.
Needham, J.
Needham, R.
Nicholson, A.
Noble, H.
O'Grady, E.
O'Donnell, G.
Orwin, J.
Pratt, A.
Pearson, W.
Proctor, A.
Petty, F.
Pullinger, A.
Patefield, E. E.
Pottage, F.
Parker, G.
Peekstone, J. M.
Padgett, C.
Ross, G.
Ray, A.
Ray, B.
Rowlandson, E.
Ratcliffe, J. H.
Spencer, G.
Scott, W.
Simpson, J.
Sibson, W.
Southeran, J.
Stott, A.
Stokoe, W. L.
Smith, S.
Stanton, J.
Sargeant, J.
Scott, C.
Scott, W.
Settle, H.
Shaw, L.
Shields, F.

Simpson, A.
Spirrits, H.
Sutcliffe, J.
Swithenbank, G.
Sayers, J.
Smith, C.
Stott, W.
Theakston, S.
Toft, C.
Tippett, R.
Thorp, G. E.
Tindall, F.
Turton, H.
Tidswell, J.
Tomlinson, J.
Varley, H.
Waterhouse, H.
Walsh, S.
Williams, L.
Wilson, H.
Waller, H.
Williams, J.
Wilkinson, H.
Whalley, F.
Wilkinson, E. J.
Whelan, D.
Wolfe, J. H.
Wood, W.
Wraith, F.
Wilman, S. O.
Ward, T. R.
Walker, F.
Walker, N.
Wilkinson, H.
Wrigley, J.
Walker, A.
Walker, G.
Wood, J. M.
Whitaker, M.
Yeadon, B.
Yates, J.

"C" COMPANY.

Coy. Sgt.-Major Barker, H.
Reg. Q.M.S. Welch, G.
Coy. Q.M.S. Packett, E. A.
Sgt. Buckley, E.
Sgt. Stevenson, H.
Sgt. Rendall, L. P.
Sgt. Moorhouse, A.
Sgt. Atwell, R.
Sgt. Walmsley, W.
Sgt. Jowett, H. A.
Sgt. Derwent, R. I.
Sgt. Sandbach, F.
Sgt. Martin, J. R.
Lc.-Sgt. Cordingley, L.
Lc.-Sgt. Hawkins, G. W.
Cpl. Beldon, E.
Cpl. Maddison, W.
Cpl. Emmison, P. C.
Cpl. Ward, W.
Cpl. Baxter, A. C.
Cpl. Ellis, W.
Cpl. Humphreys, G.
Cpl. Sellars, S.
Cpl. Ingham, N.
Lc.-Cpl. Sunter, T.
Lc.-Cpl. Norton, H.
Lc.-Cpl. Beckett, J.
Lc.-Cpl. Thompson, A.
Lc.-Cpl. Brown, J. P.
Lc.-Cpl. Ward, J.
Lc.-Cpl. Thompson, J. H.
Lc.-Cpl. Alvey, B.
Lc.-Cpl. Foster, R. J.
Lc.-Cpl. Pollard, J.
Lc.-Cpl. Howard, C.
Lc.-Cpl. Parker, W.
Lc.-Cpl. Haley, T.
Lc.-Cpl. Capstick, W.
Lc.-Cpl. Wasteney, W.
Lc.-Cpl. Underwood, S.
Lc.-Cpl. White, J.

Lc.-Cpl. Humphries, W.
Lc.-Cpl. Speight, H.
Lc.-Cpl. Hindle, E.
Lc.-Cpl. Mitchell, H.
Lc.-Cpl. Dennis, W.
Lc.-Cpl. Cockburn, F. T.
Drummer Cates, H.
Drummer Hawley, A.
Drummer Kemp, D.
Drummer Sprint, W.

PRIVATES.
Ackroyd, W.
Attenborough, J.
Allum, W. H.
Allum, C. E.
Atkinson, J. W.
Arnold, N. A.
Booth, H.
Bray, C.
Barker, S.
Bower, J. E.
Brown, J.
Bradley, T.
Brooke, J. W.
Binks, W.
Burke, T.
Balmforth, F.
Boyes, A.
Bentley, C.
Birkenshaw, J. W.
Brocklehurst, F. T.
Best, A. J.
Butterfield, T.
Bloomer, A. H.
Bradley, E.
Benson, G. L.
Butterfield, A.
Binns, J.
Bolton, G. P.
Chattaway, R.

APPENDIX

Craven, C.
Clark, H. C.
Clarke, F.
Craven, T.
Cure, C.
Cassarley, V.
Chippendale, S.
Cole, E.
Carter, H. W.
Condor, G. E. W.
Cutcliffe, J. H.
Cryer, H.
Carter, E. C.
Craven, J.
Collins, N. P.
Crowther, P. M.
Clough, H.
Davies, A.
Dowling, J.
Douglas, F.
Douglas, H.
Docker, W.
Dyer, F.
D'Andria, L. P.
Dennison, L.
Dyson, F.
Evans, H.
Edmondson, P.
Foster, H.
Fox, J. W.
Fairbank, A. S.
Field, H. W.
Fairbank, F. E.
Foster, F. L.
Featherstone, S.
Firth, J.
Field, J. B.
Gough, P. J.
Gill, J.
Greensmith, G. B.
Green, A.
Griffin, J.

Green, E.
Gibson, G. E.
Gill, A.
Gellert, E.
Garbutt, W.
Gawthorpe, A.
Gillson, S.
Henderson, H.
Holmes, R. H.
Helliwell, R.
Hall, E.
Hindley, H.
Healey, H.
Harrison, J. W.
Hall, L.
Hollings, W.
Howitt, A.
Haigh, W.
Howlett, T. E.
Hodgson, G. K.
Hodgson, J. J.
Horseman, S. J.
Harrison, L.
Holdsworth, C.
Holloway, F. G.
Hill, P. A.
Holmes, F.
Hampshire, R.
Humphries, T.
Jefferson, F.
Jackson, V.
Jennings, G. T.
Jones, C.
Jennings, J. C.
King, F.
Kellett, G.
Kennedy, J. T.
Kenefick, T. E.
Keighley, P.
Long, H.
Lord, A. C.
Lawrence, J.

Lonsdale, G.
Lister, J.
Lustig, H.
Lumby, S. H.
Miller, G. H.
Mills, J.
Martin, H.
Moore, A.
McPhail, W.
Mee, R.
Metcalf, W.
Marsden, W.
Myers, W.
Maufe, C. G.
McDonnell, G.
Maltby, A. E.
Morton, C.
Massey, P.
Matthewman, F.
Mitchell, G. O.
Matthewman, C.
Melhuish, H.
Mossop, V.
Milnes, E.
Margerison, A.
Narey, B. P.
New, D. W.
Nightingale, A.
Newby, C. A.
Pattinson, S.
Parker, G.
Poole, G. R.
Parsey, R.
Parsey, N. E.
Parsey, W. R.
Rhodes, F. W.
Ruffe, E.
Ruddock, A.
Robinson, A.
Roome, F.
Riley, M. W.

Rhodes, J. A.
Robinson, C.
Schofield, W.
Smith, E.
Storrs, J.
Sykes, W.
Smith, A.
Schofield, C.
Smith, H.
Smith, G. H.
Smith, H.
Simpson, G. V.
Sellers, G. N.
Slimming, G.
Stanley, J. L.
Scaife, G.
Tomlinson, J.
Taylor, W.
Turpin, N.
Turner, A.
Thackeray, E. A.
Terry, W.
Townson, A. J.
Todd, J.
Unwin, W.
Unna, H. G.
Vitty, E.
Wilcock, H. E.
Webb, W.
Wright, J.
Westerman, H.
Woolham, H.
Waterhouse, D. W.
Watkins, W.
Wilson, A.
Wright, H. R.
Whitaker, J. C.
Whitaker, F. W.
Wilkinson, J. E.
Wilson, V.
Woodiwiss, E. B.

APPENDIX

" D." COMPANY.

Coy. Sgt.-Major Hanson, A.
Coy. Q.M.S. Vaughan, C. St. John.
Sgt. Finney, C. G.
Sgt. Watson, E. T.
Sgt. Pullan, W.
Sgt. Hetthen, F.
Sgt. King, H. R.
Sgt. Virr, R.
Sgt. Virr, W.
Sgt. Parsey, J. L.
Sgt. Ward, P. G.
Sgt. Matthews, H.
Sgt. Butterfield, H.
Lc.-Sgt. Byatt, S.
Lc.-Sgt. Kelly, W.
Cpl. Comerford, A. J.
Cpl. Cawthron, G.
Cpl. Cordingley, W.
Cpl. Flatley, W.
Cpl. Beanland, F. D.
Cpl. Gill, N.
Cpl. Kellett, E.
Cpl. Goodwin, E.
Cpl. Jennings, W.
Lc.-Cpl. Roscoe, J.
Lc.-Cpl. Ward, W. W.
Lc.-Cpl. Clarke, R.
Lc.-Cpl. Davis, R.
Lc.-Cpl. Grace, F.
Lc.-Cpl. Garbutt, D. G.
Lc.-Cpl. Rhodes, C.
Lc.-Cpl. Wood, E. H.
Lc.-Cpl. Pemberton, B.
Lc.-Cpl. Wallace, G.
Lc.-Cpl. Muscroft, H.
Lc.-Cpl. Jennings, W.
Lc.-Cpl. Kinsey, H.
Lc.-Cpl. Onion, W.
Lc.-Cpl. Moorhouse, W.
Drummer Molloy, J.

Drummer Balm, V.
Drummer Longbottom, W. I.
Drummer Roper, J.

PRIVATES.

Aldersley, A.
Avis, P.
Andrews, F.
Anderson, J.
Austerberry, H.
Ambler, A.
Arnott, J.
Berry, J. W.
Brown, J. E.
Bentley, J.
Bottomley, J.
Bailey, J.
Belcher, J.
Barnett, W.
Bell, J.
Burke, M.
Brearton, H.
Bard, A. H.
Barker, F.
Bruce, H.
Brown, J. L.
Boldy, J.
Beanland, N.
Brakes, A.
Beck, D.
Baker, W.
Bell, W.
Blackburn, P.
Blackburn, F.
Blaire, J.
Croft, W.
Crowther, T.
Chaffer, G.
Coates, A.
Coy, W.
Cawthra, M.

Coates, G. H.
Conroy, F.
Connell, F.
Crawt, F.
Crossley, C.
Collins, E.
Calvert, P.
Carr, J. A.
Coe, F.
Cahalan, T.
Cordingley, A.
Dewhirst, C.
Drewitt, A.
Donald, W.
Dawson, J. H.
Denison, A.
Dyson, F.
Donovan, J.
Deegan, J.
Dunn, J.
Dinsdale, J. W.
Elliott, G.
Elliott, A.
Eaton, C. H.
Ellis, F.
Ellerton, J.
Edmondson, A.
Ellison, J. S.
Emmott, G.
Ellse, A.
Eccles, G.
Fishburn, A.
Firth, C.
Firth, T.
Firth, L.
Fell, J.
Faulding, J.
Flesher, E.
Furness, G.
Fearnley, G.
Firth, G.
Farrar, T.

Fawcett, C. E.
Frank, A.
Ferrigan, W.
Galloway, A.
Gant, W. T.
Greening, J.
Gibson, H.
Gallagher, J.
Gomersall, W.
Gill, E.
Howker, J.
Hudson, E.
Hoyle, H.
Holland, W. C.
Hind, L.
Helmsley, A.
Hewitt, A.
Hewes, C.
Holden, C.
Horne, J.
Holdsworth, W.
Hudson, W.
Heseltine, V. W.
Heap, L.
Hardman, H.
Helliwell, H.
Hargreaves, A.
Huggans, N.
Iles, R.
Johnson, J.
Jackson, A.
James, E.
Jones, W.
Jenkins, E. F.
Keatings, D.
Law, J. H.
Lawrence, H.
Laycock, H.
Lord, R.
Myers, A.
Mayes, A.
McIver, R. E.

APPENDIX

Morton, T.
Mallinson, R.
McDermott, T.
Merrall, H.
Metcalfe, J. B.
McDonnell, M.
Metcalfe, M.
Miller, W. E.
Neale, W. H.
Normington, F.
Nicholson, S.
Northrop, H.
Neale, G.
Neaves, B. A.
Noble, E.
Newton, J.
Outhwaite, C.
Onion, J.
Ogden, S.
Overton, G.
Petty, C. W.
Penrose, R.
Preston, E.
Powell, F.
Payton, T.
Pickard, W.
Pickard, L.
Page, M.
Payton, J.
Parkinson, H.
Rolfe, G.
Rose, H.
Rose, A.
Rushton, E.
Raistrick, G.
Ryan, J. W.
Sellars, A.
Shindler, W. R.
Scott, S.
Sutcliffe, J.
Skinner, W.
Stamper, W. H.

Stansfield, W.
Sutcliffe, H.
Sutcliffe, A.
Swire, N.
Smith, J. T.
Sellars, T.
Smethurst, F.
Sowden, W.
Thornton, S.
Taylor, G.
Turpin, W.
Tetley, A.
Tunnicliffe, E.
Turner, G.
Tomlinson, G.
Uttley, T.
Wilman, H.
White, H.
Wallace, A.
Watling, C. W.
Webster, J.
Wicks, C.
Wolstenholme, E.
Wood, J. J. D.
Wall, O.
Watson, F.
Walton, H.
Wild, A.
Wood, A.
Wormald, J.
Waller, J.
Ward, W.
Walton, E.
Walker, W.
Wade, H.
Windle, H.
Ward, F. C.
Watts, C. R.
Woodhouse, J.
West, J. H.
Whitehead, A. G.
Young, J.

LIST OF R.A.M.C. MEN ATTACHED TO THE BATTALION.

Cpl. D. Normington.

Peckett, L.
Smith, P. L.

PRIVATES.

Taylor, A. V.

Watson, W. R.

APPENDIX II.

Itinerary of the 1/6th Battalion West Yorkshire Regiment, 1914-1920.

Date of move.

1914.

5/8/14	Bradford—Belle Vue Barracks. Mobilization.
11/8/14	Selby—Billets. By rail.
19/8/14	Selby—Tents.
24/8/14	York—Knavesmire. By rail and route march.
31/8/14	Strensall Common. By route march.
28/10/14	York—Billets. By route march.
22/11/14	Redcar—Half Battalion consisting of E, F, G, H Companies. By rail.
2/12/14	Redcar—Machine Gun detachment.
10/12/14	York—Half Battalion rejoined from Redcar. By rail.

1915.

26/2/15	Gainsborough—Lincolnshire. By rail.
14/4/15	Boulogne, *via* Southampton and Havre (Battalion Transport and Machine Gun Detachment only), crossing on s.s. *Archimides*.
15/4/15	Boulogne—St. Martin's Rest Camp. By train to Folkestone, by s.s. *Victoria* to Boulogne.
16/4/15	Merville (Le Sart)—IV. Corps., 1st Army. By march route.
22/4/15	Estaires. By march route.
24/4/15	Trenches—East of Neuve Chapelle and Laventie. Platoons attached to Staffordshire and Border Regts. for training.
25/4/15	
27/4/15	Battalion took over trenches east of Laventie from 2nd Border Regt. for 24 hours.
28/4/15	Estaires.
2/5/15	Bac St. Maur. By march route.
5/5/15	Laventie and trenches at Neuve Chapelle.
15/5/15	Battalion relieved by Worcester Regiment.
16/5/15	Laventie—Billets.
18/5/15	Front line, Le Trou—Fleurbaix trenches.
25/5/15	Reserve billets, Rue Duquesne and Rue du Bois, relieved by 1/5th Battalion West Yorks. Regt.
29/5/15	Front line, Rue Petillon—Fleurbaix trenches, relieved 1/7th Battalion West Yorks. Regt.

Date of move.

1915.

4/6/15	Reserve billets—Rue Duquesne and Rue du Bois. Relieved by 1/7th Battalion West Yorks. Regt.
9/6/15	Front line—Rue Petillon. Relieved 1/7th Battalion West Yorks. Regt.
16/6/15	Reserve billets—Rue Duquesne. Relieved by 1/7th Battalion West Yorks. Regt.
22/6/15	Front line—Rue Petillon. Relieved 1/7th Battalion West Yorks. Regt.
25/6/15	Sailly-sur-la-Lys. Relieved in Fleurbaix sector by 2nd Battalion Northampton Regt.
26/6/15	Doulieu. By march route.
28/6/15	Near Flatre—Billets.
29/6/15	Proven—Billets, VI. Corps, 2nd Army. By march route.
4/7/15	Canal Bank—one mile north of Ypres. By bus to Vlamertinghe ; by march to Canal Bank.
13/7/15	Ypres—Front line—Turco Farm and Morteldje Estaminet. Relieved 1/5th Battalion West Yorks. Regt.
19/7/15	Chateau des Trois Tours. Relieved by 1/5th Battalion West Yorks. Regt.
25/7/15	Trenches—Turco Farm. Relieved 1/5th Battalion West Yorks. Regt.
31/7/15	Canal Bank. Relieved by 1/5th Battalion West Yorks Regt.
5/8/15	Trenches—Turco Farm. Relieved 1/5th Battalion West Yorks. Regt.
12/8/15	Chateau des Trois Tours. Relieved by 1/5th Battalion West Yorks. Regt.
14/8/15	Canal Bank. Relieved 1/8th Battalion West Yorks. Regt.
18/8/15	Trenches—Turco Farm. Relieved 1/5th Battalion West Yorks. Regt.
24/8/15	Canal Bank. Relieved by 1st Battalion K. S. L. I., 16th Brigade, 6th Division.
30/8/15	Trenches on left of Turco Farm. Relieved 1/7th Battalion West Yorks. Regt.
9/9/15	Rest Bivouacs—Copernolle Wood, north east of Poperinghe. Relieved by 1/4th Battalion West Riding Regt.
20/9/15	On the Yser Canal—In support of 1/7th Battalion in the Pilkem Trenches.
23/9/15	Pilkem Trenches. Relieved 1/7 Battalion West Yorks. Regt.

APPENDIX

Date of move.

1915.

27/9/15   In support Canal Bank.   Relieved by 1/7th Battalion West Yorks. Regt.

1/10/15   Pilkem Trenches.   Relieved 1/7th Battalion West Yorks. Regt.

5/10/15   In Support.   Relieved by 1/7th Battalion West Yorks. Regt.

9/10/15   Pilkem Trenches.   Relieved 1/7th Battalion West Yorks. Regt.

13/10/15   Copernolle Wood—Divisional Reserve near Poperinghe. Relieved by 1/7th Battalion West Riding Regt.

2/11/15   Trenches—Ypres.   Relieved 1/8th Battalion West Yorks. Regt.

7/11/15   Right support.   Relieved by 1/7th Battalion West Yorks. Regt.

9/11/15   Trenches—Relieved 1/8th Battalion West Yorks. Regt.

13/11/15   Brielen and District.   Relieved by 1/5th Battalion West Yorks. Regt.

15/11/15   Trenches.   Relieved 1/8th Battalion West Yorks. Regt.

19/11/15   Divisional reserve near Poperinghe.   Relieved by 1/5th West Yorks. Regt.

27/11/15   Trenches—Turco Farm.   By motor lorries.   Relieved 1/7th Battalion West Yorks. Regt.

1/12/15   Right Support Elverdinghe Chateau and Canal Bank.

3/12/15   Trenches.   Relieved 1/8th Battalion West Yorks. Regt.

7/12/15   Right support at Elverdinghe Chateau.   Relieved by 1/7th Battalion West Yorks. Regt.

9/12/15   Trenches, D19, D20—Belle-Alliance.   Relieved 1/8th Battalion West Yorks. Regt.

13/12/15   Right support.   Relieved by 1/7th Battalion West Yorks. Regt.

15/12/15   Trenches, D21, D22.   Relieved 1/5th Battalion West Yorks. Regt.

19/12/15   German Gas Attack.   Canal Bank.   Relieved by 1/7th Battalion West Yorks. Regt.

20/12/15   Right support, Elverdinghe Chateau.

21/12/15   No. 4 Camp, near Poperinghe.   Relieved by 1/5th Battalion West Yorks. Regt.

29/12/15   Poperinghe—Billets.   By route march.

30/12/15   St. Jan-ter-Biezen—Tents.   By route march.

31/12/15   Houtkerque.   By route march.

Date of move.

1916.

1/1/16	Wormhoudt. By route march.
15/1/16	Bollezeele. By route march.
16/1/16	Zutkerque. By route march.
17/1/16	Calais—Tents. By route march.
1/2/16	Ailly-sur-Somme. By train to Amiens, and route march to Ailly.
10/2/16	Rubempré. By route march.
11/2/16	Bouzincourt. By route march.
12/2/16	Thiepval Trenches. Relieving 16th Battalion Lancashire Fusiliers.
20/2/16	Martinsart—Reserve. Relieved by 1/5th Battalion West Yorks. Regt.
24/2/16	Trenches—Thiepval. Relieving 1/5th Battalion West Yorks. Regt.
29/2/16	Authuille—Support. Relieved by 1/5th Battalion West Yorks. Regt.
3/3/16	Bouzincourt. Relieved by 9th Battalion Inniskilling Fusiliers.
4/3/16	Varennes. By route march.
14/3/16	Half Battalion, Bouzincourt. Half Battalion, Senlis.
3/4/16	Molliens au Bois. By motor lorries.
5/4/16	Vignacourt. By route march.
16/6/16	Puchevillers. By route march.
27/6/16	Varennes.
30/6/16	Assembly Trenches—Aveluy Wood.
1/7/16	Thiepval Wood. Attack on Thiepval.
2/7/16	Trenches near Thiepval—At 11 p.m. to trenches in Aveluy Wood. Relieved by 7th Battalion West Riding Regt.
3/7/16	Martinsart—Divisional reserve.
5/7/16	Hedauville—Billets. By route march.
7/7/16	Martinsart Wood and Aveluy-Hamel Road.
8/7/16	Dug-outs near Aveluy.
9/7/16	Liepzig Salient. Relieving 1/7th Battalion West Yorks. Regt.
12/7/16	Dug-outs—" South Bluff " Authuille. Relieved by 1/7th Battalion West Yorks. Regt.
13/7/16	Liepzig Salient. Relieving 1/7th Battalion West Yorks. Regt.
15/7/16	Liepzig Salient. Relieved by 1/8th Battalion West Yorks. Regt., and moved to Trenches—Authuille Wood.

APPENDIX

Date of move.

1916.

27/7/16	Forceville—Billets. Relieved by 1/5th Battalion West Yorks. Regt.
1/8/16	Hedauville.
3/8/16	Trenches—Thiepval Avenue to Oban Avenue.
18/8/16	Lealvillers. Relieved by 3rd Battalion Worcester Regt., 29th Division.
26/8/16	Hedauville and North Bluff, Authuille. Relieving 2nd Battalion Royal Irish Rifles.
2/9/16	Aveluy Wood.
3/9/16	Attack on St. Pierre Divion Trenches.
4/9/16	Forceville after attack. By march route.
18/9/16	Hedauville.
20/9/16	Trenches—Thiepval. Relieving 5th Battalion York and Lanc. Regt.
25/9/16	Englebelmer. (C & D Coys.). Trenches—Thiepval Wood (A & B Coys.)
26/9/16	Attack on Thiepval—Battalion at Macmahon's Post.
27/9/16	Battalion less B Coy. Englebelmer. By route march.
28/9/16	B Coy. rejoined at Englebelmer.
29/9/16	Arquèves.
30/9/16	Mondicourt. By route march
1/10/16	Sombrin.
10/10/16	Pommier.
18/10/16	Trenches—Fonquevillers. Relieving 1/5th Battalion West Riding Regt.
24/10/16	St. Amand—Billets. Relieved by 1/4th West Riding Regt.
27/10/16	Trenches—Hannescamps. Relieving 1/5th Battalion West Yorks. Regt.
2/11/16	Bienvillers—Billets. Relieved by 1/5th Battalion West Yorks. Regt.
8/11/16	Trenches—Hannescamps. Relieving 1/5th Batallion West Yorks. Regt.
14/11/16	St. Amand. Relieved by 1/5th Battalion West Yorks. Regt.
20/11/16	Trenches—Hannescamps. Relieving 1/5th Battalion West Yorks. Regt.
26/11/16	Bienvillers—Billets. Relieved by 1/5th Battalion West Yorks. Regt.
2/12/16	Trenches—Hannescamps. Relieving 1/5th Battalion West Yorks. Regt.
6/12/16	Pas. Relieved by 4th Battalion Leicester Regt.
7/12/16	Le Souich. By route march.

Date of move.

1917.

7/1/17 Bailleulval. Relieved the 2nd Battalion Yorks. **Regt.** (30th Division). By route march.

11/1/17 Trenches—Opposite Ransart. Relieving 1/5th Battalion West Yorks. Regt.

15/1/17 Bailleulval—Divisional reserve. Relieved by 1/5th West Yorks. Regt.

19/1/17 Trenches—Opposite Ransart. Relieving 1/5th Battalion West Yorks. Regt.

23/1/17 Bailleulval. Inter-relief with 1/5th Battalion.

27/1/17 Trenches—Opposite Ransart. Inter-relief with 1/5th Battalion West Yorks. Regt.

31/1/17 Bailleulmont—Divisional Reserve. Inter-relief with 1/5th Battalion West Yorks. Regt.

3/2/17 Trenches—Opposite Ransart. Inter-relief with 1/5th Battalion West Yorks. Regt.

7/2/17. Bailleulmont. Inter-relief with 1/5th Battalion West Yorks. Regt.

11/2/17 Trenches—Opposite Ransart. Inter-relief with 1/5th Battalion West Yorks. Regt.

15/2/17 Humbercamp—Divisional Reserve. By route march.

23/2/17 Le Souich. By route march.

24/2/17 Bonnières. By route march.

25/2/17 Siracourt. By route march.

26/2/17 Floringhem. By route march.

27/2/17 St. Floris. By route march.

28/2/17 La Gorgue.

1/3/17 Trenches—Picantin (left sub-sector). Relieving 9th Battalion London Regt.

7/3/17 Laventie—Brigade reserve.

13/3/17 Trenches—Picantin. Relieving 1/5th Battalion West Yorks Regt.

20/3/17 Laventie—Brigade reserve. Inter-relief with 1/5th Battalion West Yorks. Regt.

1/4/17 Laventie—Brigade reserve. Inter-relief with 1/5th Battalion West Yorks. Regt.

5/4/17. Trenches—Picantin. Inter-relief with 1/5th Battalion West Yorks. Regt.

12/4/17 Laventie. Inter-relief with 1/5th Battalion West Yorks. Regt.

APPENDIX

Date of move.

1917.

19/4/17	Trenches—Picantin. Inter-relief with 1/5th Battalion West Yorks. Regt.
24/4/17	Laventie—Inter-relief with 1/5th Battalion West Yorks. Regt.
30/4/17	Trenches—Fauquissart. Inter-relief with 1/5th Battalion West Yorks. Regt.
7/5/17	Laventie—Reserve. Inter-relief with 1/5th Battalion West Yorks. Regt.
12/5/17	Rue du Bacquerot—Support. Relieving 1/8th Battalion West Yorks. Regt.
18/5/17	La Gorgue—Divisional reserve. Relieved by 1/7th Battalion West Yorks, Regt.
23/5/17	Trenches—Fauquissart. Relieving 22nd Regt. Portuguese Expeditionary Force.
30/5/17	La Gorgue. Relieved by 1/7th Battalion West Yorks. Regt.
5/6/17	Posts rue du Bacquerot. Relieving 1/5th Battalion West Yorks. Regt.
10/6/17	Trenches—Fauquissart. Relieving 14th Regt. Portuguese Expeditionary Force.
13/6/17	Rue du Bacquerot. Relieved by 1/5th Battalion West Yorks. Regt.
17/6/17	Trenches—Fauquissart. Inter-relief with 1/5th Battalion West Yorks. Regt.
23/6/17	Laventie—Reserve. Inter-relief with 1/5th Battalion West Yorks. Regt.
29/6/17	Trenches—Fauquissart. Inter-relief with 1/5th West Yorks. Regt.
5/7/17	Rue du Bacquerot. Inter-relief with 1/5th Battalion West Yorks Regt.
9/7/17	Sailly-sur-la-Lys. Relieved by 9th Battalion Portuguese Expeditionary Force.
11/7/17	La Gorgue. By route march.
14/7/17	Sand Dunes east of Fort Mardick between Dunkerque and Gravelines. March to Lestrem Station, train to Loon Plage, thence by route march to Fort Mardick.
16/7/17	Bray-Dunes—Billets and camp east of town. By route march.
17/7/17	Camp east of Oost-Dunkerque.
18/7/17	Nieuport Trenches—St. Georges Sector. Relieving 2nd Battalion Royal Inniskilling Fusiliers.

Date of move.

1917.

1/8/17   Coxyde—Billets, Divisional reserve. Relieved by 2nd Battalion Royal Inniskilling Fusiliers.

2/8/17   Ghyvelde. By march route.

3/8/17   Uxem. By march route.

27/8/17   Two Coys. to La Panne, *via* Pont de Zuydcoote and Adinkerke, thence by bus to Nieuport, attached to 257th Tunnelling Coy.

Battalion Head Quarters and two Coys. to Oost-Dunkerque, attached to 97th Infantry Brigade.

13/9/17   Ghyvelde—Training. By route march.

24/9/17   Uxem.

25/9/17   Wormhoudt.

26/9/17   Noordpeene.

28/9/17   Salperwick.

1/10/17   St. Marie Capelle—Tents. By route march.

3/10/17   Mill Camp, No. 2 area, Watou.

5/10/17   Spree Farm $1\frac{1}{2}$ miles north east of Wieltje. Bus to Vlamertinghe and route march through Ypres.

9/10/17   Attack—Passchendaele.

10/10/17   Vlamertinghe. By route march, relieved by 3rd Brigade New Zealand Division.

12/10/17   Ouderzeele—Camp. Bus to near Winnezeele, and route march to camp.

16/10/17   Poperinghe—Camp 29.

23/10/17   Winnezeele—B Camp, No. 3 area. By route march.

28/10/17   Steenvoorde. By march route.

8/11/17   Howe Camp, near Ypres. By bus.

11/11/17   Garter Point, E. N. E. of Ypres, left support. Relieving 21st Battalion Australian Infantry.

15/11/17   Front Line—Left subsector south of Broodseinde-Moorslede Road. Relieving 1/5th Battalion West Yorks. Regt.

19/11/17   Half Way House—Support. Relieved by 1/7th Battalion Duke of Wellington's West Riding Regt.

20/11/17   Canal area—Huts near Chateau Belge.

24/11/17   Vancouver Camp, near Vlamertinghe.

28/11/17   Infantry Barracks, Ypres.

5/12/17   Anzac House—Left support. Relieving 1/5th Battalion York. & Lancaster Regt.

8/12/17   Moulin Farm—Front line. Relieved 1/5th Battalion West Yorks. Regt.

APPENDIX

Date of move.

11/12/17   Hussar Camp. Relieved by 1/4th Battalion King's Own Yorkshire Light Infantry.

12/12/17   Halifax Camp, near Vlamertinghe—Huts.

17/12/17   Anzac House—Right support. Relieved 1/7th West Riding Regt.

23/12/17   Front line Right sub-sector—Broodseinde Ridge. Relieving the Battalion West Yorks. Regt.

29/12/17   Infantry Barracks, Ypres—Divisional Reserve. Relieved by 1/5th King's Own Yorks. Light Infantry.

1918.

3/1/18   Dragoon Camp, Potijze. Relieving 1/7th Battalion Duke of Wellington's (West Riding) Regt.

7/1/18   Trenches, Zonnebeke—Left sub-sector. Relieving 1/5th Battalion West Yorks. Regt.

12/1/18   Argyle Camp, Potijze. Relieved by 2/5th Battalion Manchester Regt., 66th Division.

13/1/18   Bavinchove, *via* Cassel. By march route to Asylum, Ypres, and bus to Bavinchove.

1/2/18   Moulle area—Training. By rail to Watten, and by march route to Moulle.

5/2/18   Bavinchove. By route march.

10/2/18   Devonshire Camp, near Reninghelst. March to Caestre, train to Brandhoek, march to Devonshire Camp.

23/2/18   Hussar Camp, east of Potijze—In Brigade reserve. March to Brandhoek, train to Gordon House, march to Hussar Camp.

29/2/18   Front line—Zonnebeke. Relieving 1st Battalion New Zealand Rifle Brigade.

3/3/18   Garter Point—Brigade support. Inter-relief with 1/7th Battalion West Yorks. Regt.

7/3/18   Hussar Camp—Brigade Reserve.

11/3/18   Front line—Zonnebeke. Inter-relief with 1/7th Battalion West Yorks. Regt.

15/3/18   Brigade support—Garter Point. Inter-relief with 1/7th Battalion West Yorks. Regt.

19/3/18   Brigade reserve—Hussar Camp.

23/3/18   Front line—Zonnebeke. Inter-relief with 1/7th Battalion West Yorks. Regt.

27/3/18   Garter Point—Brigade support. Inter-relief with 1/7th Battalion West Yorks. Regt.

Date of move.

1918.

28/3/18   Hussar Camp. Relieved by 1/7th Battalion West Yorks. Regt.

30/3/18   Maida Camp. Relieved by 2nd Battalion York. & Lancs. Regt. (16th Brigade).

1/4/18   Front line—Menin Road, west of Gheluvelt. Relieving 1/4th Battalion King's Own Yorkshire Light Infantry.

10/4/18   Rear Echelon to Ontario Camp—Reninghelst-Vlamertinghe Road.

16/4/18   Dominion Camp.

18/4/18   Jackdaw Tunnels, near Hooge. A and B Companies.

19/4/18   Milky Farm, south-east of Dickebush. C and D Companies and Battalion Head Quarters.

21/4/18   A and B Companies rejoin Battalion at Milky Farm.

22/4/18   Support trenches, Vierstraat and Grand Bois.

24/4/18   Front line—Grand Bois. Relieving 15th Battalion Durham Light Infantry (64th Brigade).

25/4/18   German Attack—Grand Bois.

26/4/18   Ouderdom.

28/4/18   Hoograaf. By march route. 146th Inf. Brigade Composite Battalion remained at Ouderdom.

29/4/18   Watou.

4/5/18   School Camp—St. Jan-ter-Biezen.

25/5/18   Cormette—Training Camp. By train to St. Omer, by march route to camp.

31/5/18   Proven. Pekin Camp. March to St. Omer, train to Proven, march to Pekin Camp.

3/6/18   Orilla Camp. March route to Proven, light railway to Orilla Camp.

11/6/18   Front line east of Potijze—Left sub-sector. Relieving 1/5th Battalion York & Lancs. Regt.

22/6/18   Ramparts, Ypres.—Brigade reserve. Relieved by 1/5th Battalion West Yorks. Regt.

29/6/18   Orilla Camp—Divisional reserve. Relieved by 1/6th Battalion Duke of Wellington's (West Riding) Regt.

7/7/18   Trenches, near Zillebeke Lake—Right sub-sector. Relieving 1/5th Battalion West Yorks. Regt.

15/7/18   Ypres—Brigade reserve.

23/7/18   Brake Camp, north of Brandhoek—Relieved by 1/4th Duke of Wellington's (West Riding) Regt.

APPENDIX

Date of move.

   1918.

1/8/18   Zillebeke Lake—Right sub-sector. Relieving 2nd Battalion 118th Regt., American Expeditionary Force.

16/8/18   Orilla Camp. Relieved by 1/5th Battalion West Yorks. Regt.

18/8/18   Penton Camp, near Proven. To Proven by light railway, to Camp by march route. Relieved by 10th Highland Light Infantry (34th Division).

19/8/18   Herzeele. By march route.

22/8/18   Nielles. Train and march route.

23/8/18   Nordausques. By march route.

28/8/18   Ostreville—St. Pol Area. Train to Bryas, route march to Ostraville.

1/9/18   Fraser Camp—Mont St. Eloi. Route march and bus to Mont St. Eloi.

11/9/18   Roclincourt—West Camp. Relieving 4th Battalion Gordon Highlanders.

16/9/18   Trenches—West of Plouvain. Relieving 1/7th Battalion West Yorks Regt.

20/9/18   Railway Enbankment, near Athies. Relieved by 1/5th Battalion West Yorks. Regt.

23/9/18   Rue d'Amiens, Arras—Brigade Reserve. By March route.

7/10/18   Bus to Inchy, march to Cagnicourt.

9/10/18   Haynecourt—West of Cambrai.

10/10/18   Tilloy. Outskirts of Cambrai.

11/10/18   Naves—Assembly position. Attack 9 a.m.

12/10/18   Avesnes-le-Sec. Advance continued.

14/10/18   Saulzoir.

15/10/18   Villers-en-Cauchies.

16/10/18   Sugar Factory, north-east of Naves.

17/10/18   Escadœuvres. By march route.

20/10/18   Ramillies-Iwuy—Billets.

27/10/18   Noyelles.

28/10/18   Reserve Position—South of Maing.

1/11/18   Sunken Road, S.E. of Maing. Attack beyond Famars.

2/11/18   Lieu-St.-Amand. By march route.

5/11/18   Evin Malmaison. By march route.

   1919.

9/1/19   Battalion Colours arrive from England.

24/2/19   Battalion entrained at Douai to join Army of Occupation in Germany.

HISTORY OF THE 1/6TH BN. WEST YORKSHIRE REGT.

Date of move.

1919.

26/2/19	Cologne.
18/6/19	Dunwald.
20/6/19	Hilgen.
1/7/19	Cologne.
13/11/19	Cologne to Calais *via* Charleroi. By train.
15/11/19	Calais—No. 5 Rest Camp.
17/11/19	Dover by s.s. *Arundel*.

1920

29/3/20	Cadre of Battalion arrive at Bradford.
30/3/20	Colours handed over to 6th Battalion West Yorkshire Regiment, Town Hall Square, Bradford.

APPENDIX III.

1/6th BN. WEST YORKSHIRE REGIMENT—CASUALTIES.

Roll I.—Officers.

Rank.	Name.	Details.
2nd Lieut.	Backhouse, W. H	Killed in Action, 13/3/18
2nd Lieut.	Cheetham, H.	Killed in Action, 9/10/17
2nd Lieut.	Dodd, N.	Killed in Action, 1/7/16
Capt. acting Major	Dobson, R. G.	Died, 4/1/19
2nd Lieut.	Fisher, J. H.	Died of Wounds, 7/9/18
2nd Lieut.	Higgins, C. G.	Died of Wounds, 1/7/16
2nd Lieut.	Harper, C. R.	Killed in Action, 15/7/16
2nd Lieut.	Heaton, S. T.	Killed in Action, 27/9/16
2nd Lieut.	Hesketh, J...	Killed in Action, 14/10/18
2nd Lieut. acting Captain	Hepburn, D. L. I.	Killed in Action, 25/4/18
2nd Lieut.	Illingworth, J.	Killed in Action, 1/1/18
2nd Lieut.	Jackson, H. E.	Killed in Action, 12/6/17
Lieut. acting Capt.	McLean, W.	Died of Wounds, 17/11/17
2nd Lieut.	Matthews, G.	Died of Wounds, 2/7/18
Captain	Muller, N.	Killed in Action, 28/7/18
2nd Lieut.	Moore, R.	Killed in Action, 15/7/16
2nd Lieut.	Mitchell, C. H.	Killed in Action, 3/9/16
Capt. and Adjut.	Mossop, W. N.	Died of Wounds, 8/5/18
Lieut. temp. Capt.	Oddy, J. L.	Died of Wounds, 3/9/16
Lieut.	Richardson, C. E.	Killed in Action, 11/10/18
Captain	Robinson, H. E., R.A.M.C.	Killed in Action, 25/4/18
Lieut. Colonel	Scott, C. E.	Died of Wounds, 9/8/16
Captain	Speight, J. L.	Died of Wounds, 9/10/17
Lieut. temp. Capt.	Scales, W. A.	Killed in Action, 6/1/18
2nd Lieut.	Senior, W. T.	Killed in Action, 3/9/16
2nd Lieut.	Storey, H. L.	Died of Wounds, 12/9/16
Captain	Strachan, D. L.	Died, 29/12/16
Lieut.	Straker, H...	Died of Wounds, 9/11/18
2nd Lieut	Treleavan, N. H.	Killed in Action, 23/11/16
2nd Lieut.	Turner, E. A.	Killed in Action, 3/9/16
2nd Lieut.	Worrall, H.	Killed in Action, 25/4/18
2nd Lieut.	Whitteron, C.	Killed in Action, 25/4/18

Rank.		Name.		Details.
2nd Lieut.	..	Williams, A.	..	Killed in Action, 25/4/18
Lieut. Colonel	..	Wistance, W. A.	..	Killed in Action, 25/4/18
Lieut.	..	Ward, E. A. H.	..	Killed in Action, 11/8/17
2nd Lieut.	..	Wood, J. A. S.	..	Killed in Action, 12/6/17
2nd Lieut.	..	Wright, R. B.	..	Killed in Action, 8/7/18

Name, *b.* Place Born, *e.* Place of enlistment, Number, Rank, *K. in A.* Killed in Action, *F. & F.* France and Flanders, 9/10/17 Date of Death, *Formerly,* Previously served in other Corps.

Roll II.—Warrant Officers, N.C.O's. and Men.

ABBOTT, Richard Fred., *b.* West Hartlepool, *e.* Stanley, Durham, 42705, Pte., *k. in a., F. & F.,* 9/10/17, *formerly* 40130 Durham Light Infantry.

ABRAMS, Solly, *b.* Leeds, *e.* Leeds, 242689, Pte., *k. in a., F. & F.,* 9/10/17.

ACKROYD, Arthur, *b.* Bradford, *e.* Bradford, Yorks., 5481, L./Cpl. *k. in a., F. & F.,* 3/9/16.

AIKMAN, William, *b.* Bradford, Yorks. (Bradford), 240797, Pte., *k. in a., F. & F.,* 1/7/16.

ALDIS, Harry, *e.* Green Hammerton, Yorks (Allerton, Yorks.), 201315, Pte., *d., F. & F.,* 19/10/18.

ALLAN, Harry, *e.* Bradford (Bradford, Yorks.), 3267, Pte., *d. of w., F. & F.,* 15/7/15.

ALLEN, Harry Charles, *e.* Ipswich (Hadleigh, Suffolk), 63665, Pte., *d.,* home, 30/10/18.

ALLEN, Thomas Treeth, *b.* Mexbro', *e.* Mexbro', Yorks., 7000., Pte., *d. of w., F. & F.,* 9/1/17.

ALLUM, William Hylbert, *b.* Stanningley, Yorks., *e.* Bradford, Yorks. (Leeds), 2426, L./Cpl., *k. in a., F. & F.,* 1/7/16.

ALSTON, Robert, *e.* Bradford (Allerton), Yorks., 3313, Cpl., *k. in a., F. & F.,* 19/12/15.

ANDERTON, Tobias Copley, *b.* Bradford, *e.* Bradford, Yorks., 4156, Pte., *k. in a., F. & F.,* 19/12/15.

ANDREWS, Fred, *b.* Undercliffe, Yorks., *e.* Bradford, 1874, Pte., *d. of w., F. & F.,* 7/7/16.

ANGUS, John Crosby, *b.* Choppington, Northumberland, *e.* Blyth, Northumberland, 58858, Pte., *k. in a., F. & F.,* 1/11/18.

ANKERS, Bertram, *b.* Hanworth, Durham, *e.* Darlington (Darlington), 7155, Pte., *k. in a., F. & F.,* 3/9/16.

APPENDIX

APPLEBY, John Thomas, *b.* Bank Head, Durham, *e.* Houghton le Spring, Durham, 242819, Pte., *d.*, F. & F., 4/11/18, *formerly* 18/1211 Durham Light Infantry.

APPLEYARD, Harry, *e.* Leeds (Marsh, Huddersfield), 242661. Pte., *k. in a.*, F. & F., 9/10/17.

ARROWSMITH, Robert Chandler, *b.* Sedgefield, Durham, West Hartlepool, 7040, Pte., *k. in a.*, F. & F., 23/11/16, *formerly* 30678 Durham light Infantry.

ASHLEY, Clarence, *b.* Bradford, *e.* Bradford, Yorks., 1226, Pte., *k. in a,* F. & F., 12/7/16.

ATKINS, Alfred, *b.* Elvington, Yorks., *e.* York, 242640, Pte., *d. of w.*, F. & F., 21/12/17.

ATKINSON, Charles, *b.* Leeds, *e.* Leeds, 260036, Pte., *k. in a.*, F. & F., 11/10/18.

ATTWOOD, Jesse, *e.* Bradford (Bradford, Yorks.), 4677, Pte., *k. in a.*, F. & F., 7/7/16.

AUSTERBERRY, Harry, *b.* Sheffield, *e.* Bradford, Yorks., 240429, L./Cpl., *k. in a.*, F. & F., 25/4/18.

BAILES, Thomas, *b.* Leeds, *e.* Harrogate, 242626, Cpl., *k. in a.*, F. & F., 10/10/17.

BAILEY, Arthur, *b.* Bradford, *e.* Bradford, Yorks., 2104, Pte., *k. in a,* F. & F., 31/5/15.

BAILEY, Frank, *b.* Pontefract, *e.* Bradford, Yorks., 4491, Pte., *k. in a.*, F. & F., 14/8/16.

BAIRSTOW, James, *b.* Bradford, *e.* Bradford, Yorks., 1934, L./Cpl., *k. in a.*, F. & F., 9/5/15.

BAIRSTOW, Stead, *b.* West Ardsley, Yorks., *e.* Wakefield, 260092, Pte., *k. in a.*, F. & F., 25/4/18, *formerly* 205194 K. O. Y. L I.

BANKS, John William, *b.* Bradford, *e.* Bradford, Yorks., 1751, Pte., *k. in a.*, F. & F., 1/7/16.

BANNISTER, John William, *b.* Otley, *e.* Bradford, Yorks., 1126, Pte., *k. in a.*, F. & F., 3/9/16.

BANTICK, John, William, *b.* Leeds, *e.* Leeds, 49550, Pte., *d.*, F. & F., 7/6/18.

BARBER, Walter, *e.* Bradford, Yorks. (Bradford), 3560, Pte., *k. in a.*, F. & .F, 19/12/15.

BARKBY, Henry, Thomas, *b.* Leeds, *e.* Leeds, 263034, Pte., *k. in a.*, F. & F., 25/4/18.

BARKER, Bert., *b.* Newport Pagnall, Bucks., *e.* Wolverton, Bucks., 72597, Pte., *k. in a.*, F. & F., 11/10/18, *formerly* 6/16649 Oxford and Bucks. Light Infantry.

BARKER, Henry, *b.* Bradford, *e.* Bradford, Yorks., 240002, Regt. Sergt.-Major, *k. in a.*, F. & F., 25/4/18, M.C., D.C.M.

BARKER, Stephen, *b.* Bradford, *e.* Bradford, Yorks., 1483, L./Cpl., *k. in a.*, F. & F., 1/7/16.

BARKER, T. C., 3560., *k. in a.*, 19/12/15.

BARNETT, William, *e.* Bradford, Yorks. (Thornbury, Yorks.), 2789, L./Cpl., *k. in a.*, F. & F., 3/9/16.

BARRACLOUGH, Fred, *b.* Bradford, Yorks., *e.* Bradford, 241606, Pte., *k. in a.*, F. & F., 3/9/16.

BARRACLOUGH, Hirst, *b.* Bradford, *e.* Bradford, Yorks., 202476, Cpl., *d.*, F. & F., 26/4/18.

BARRETT, Alfred Cecil, *e.* Bradford (Leeds), 3398, Pte., *k. in a.*, F. & F., 24/8/15.

BARRY, Jack, *b.* Bradford, *e.*, Bradford, Yorks., 241806, L./Cpl., *d.*, F. & F., 16/10/18.

BARRY, Joseph Vincent, *b.* Sheffield, *e.* Leeds, 305517. Pte., *k. in a.*, F. & F., 11/10/18.

BAXTER, Ernest, *b.* Bradford, Yorks. (Windhill), 2990, Pte., *d. of w.*, F. & F., 5/9/16.

BAXTER, William, *b.* Liverpool, *e.* Bradford, Yorks., 834, Cpl., *k. in a.*, F. & F., 1/7/16.

BEAL, Frederick, *b.* Leeds, *e.* York, 307707, Pte., *d. of w.*, F. & F., 14/3/18.

BEALE, Harry, *e.* Bradford (Bradford, Yorks), 241003, Pte., *k. in a.*, F. & F., 9/10/17.

BECKETT, John, *b.* Bradford, Yorks. (Tong, Bradford), 4937, Pte., *k. in a.*, F. & F., 11/7/16.

BEECROFT, Thomas, *b.* Bradford, *e.* Bradford, Yorks., 4239, Pte., *k. in a.*, F. & F., 17/2/16.

BELL, Frederick, *b.* Bradford, *e.* Bradford, Yorks., 241236, Pte., *k. in a.*, F. & F., 3/9/16.

BELL, Henry, *b.* Tam Hill, Durham, *e.* Chester-le-Street, 42708, Pte., *k. in a.*, F. & F., 9/10/17, *formerly* 40106 Durham Light Infantry.

BENNETT, Willie, *b.* Bradford, *e.* Bradford, Yorks, 263027, Pte., *d. of w.*, F. & F., 19/11/17.

BENSON, Arthur, *b.* Stockton-on-Tees, *e.* Stockton-on-Tees, 242852, L./Cpl., *k. in a.*, F. & F., 25/4/18.

BENTON, Willie, *b.* Rothwell, Yorks., *e.* Leeds, 306485, Pte., *k. in a.*, F. & F., 11/10/18.

BICKERDIKE, Walter, *b.* Driffield, *e.* Bradford, Yorks., 18/91., Pte., *d. of w.*, F. & F., 28/4/18.

APPENDIX

BIRCH, Ernest, *b.* Bradford, *e.* Bradford, Yorks., 4775, Pte., *k. in a.,* F. & F., 9/8/16.

BIRD, John, *b.* Bradford, *e.* Bradford, Yorks., 1567, Pte., *d. of w.,* F. & F., 27/10/15.

BIRKETT, John, *e.* Bradford (Bradford), 3422, Pte., *d.* home, 9/2/17.

BLACKBURN, Percy, *e.* Bradford (Bradford), 2944, Pte., *k. in a.,* F. & F., 20/12/15.

BLAKEY, Frederick, *e.* Bradford, Yorks., 4481, Pte., *k. in a.,* F. & F., 20/7/16.

BLANSHARD, Ernest, *e.* Leeds, (Leeds) 242551, L./Cpl., *d.,* F. & F., 29/10/18.

BLAYDES, Charles Henry, *e.* Bradford (Leeds), 3479, *k. in a.,* F. & F., 3/11/15.

BLENKINSOPP, Cecil William, *b.* Barnard Castle, *e.* Bishop Auckland, 63668, Pte., *k. in a.,* F. & F., 11/10/18.

BLOOD, Joseph, *b.* Burton-on-Trent, Staffs., *e.* Bradford, Yorks., 241812, Pte., *k. in a.,* F. & F., 25/4/18.

BLOOMER, Arthur Kenneth, *b.* Eccleshill, Yorks., *e.* Bradford, 2070, Pte., *k. in a.,* F. & F., 1/7/16.

BOND, Thomas, *e.* Scunthorpe (Scunthorpe), 202333, Pte., *d.,* F. & F., 23/10/18.

BONNER, George William, *b.* Jarrow, *e.* Jarrow, 42710, Pte., *k. in a.,* F. & F., 26/4/18.

BOOTH, Haydon, *e.* Bradford (Bradford), 3936, Pte., *d. of w.,* F. & F., 21/8/15.

BOOTH, Herbert, *e.* Bradford (Bradford), 3048, Pte., *k. in a.,* F. & F., 2/7/16.

BOTTOMLEY, Fred., *b.* Kildwick, Yorks., *e.* Keighley, 18/1513, Pte., *k. in a.,* F. & F., 12/10/18.

BOTTOMLEY, Herbert Cecil, *e.* Bradford (Bradford), 2660, Pte., *k. in a.,* F. & F., 19/12/15.

BOUCHER, Fred., *b.* Leeds, *e.* Leeds, 3/9024, Pte., *k. in a.,* F. & F., 10/8/18.

BOWERS, Stanley, *e.* Bradford (Idle), Yorks., 3475, Pte., *d. of w.,* F. & F., 2/8/15.

BOYLE, Edgar, *b.* Bradford, *e.* Bradford, 526, Pte., *d. of w.,* F. & F., 5/9/16.

BRACEWELL, John William, *e.* Bradford (Bradford), 2585, Pte., *k. in a.,* F. & F., 10/8/16.

BRADLEY, Greenwood, *b.* Windhill, Yorks., *e.* Bradford, 241764, Cpl., *k. in a.,* K. & F., 25/4/18, M.M.

BRADLEY, Thomas, *b.* Bradford, *e.* Bradford, Yorks., 1756, Pte., *k. in a.,* *F. & F.,* 3/9/16, M.M.

BRAWN, Cyril Frederick, *b.* Earls Barton, Northants., *e.* Kettering, 62613, Pte., *d. of w., F. & F.,* 12/10/18, *formerly* 168097 Middlesex Regt.

BRAYSHAW, William Wright, *b.* Leeds, *e.* Leeds, 28878, Cpl., *k. in a., F. & F.,* 11/10/18.

BREARTON, Michael, *e,* Bradford (Cullingworth, Yorks.), 263025, Pte., *F. & F.,* 25/4/18.

BRECKONS, James, *e.* Newcastle-on-Tyne, 46315, Pte., *k. in a., F. & F.,* 11/10/18, *formerly* 45388 King's Own Yorks. Light Infantry.

BREWER, Thomas Henry, *e.* Bradford (Bradford), 2514, Cpl., *d. of w., F. & F.,* 8/1/17.

BREWIN, William, *b.* Burton-on-Trent, Staffs., *e.* Burton-on-Trent, 263028, Pte., *k. in a., F. & F.,* 18/10/18.

BRIGGS, William Arthur, *b.* Bradford, *e.* Bradford, Yorks., 241586, Pte., *k. in a., F. & F.,* 25/4/18.

BROADBENT, Gibson, *b.* Cragg Vale, Yorks., *e.* Halifax (Todmordon), 242651, Pte., *k. in a., F. & F.,* 25/4/18.

BROADBENT, John Thomas, *b.* Bradford, *e.* Bradford, Yorks., 263017, Pte., *k. in a., F. & F.,* 25/4/18.

BROADBENT, William Edward, *b.* Bradford, *e.* Bradford, 240288, L./Cpl., *d. of w., F. & F.,* 26/4/18.

BROADLEY, John Henry, *e.* Bradford, Yorks. (Manningham, Yorks.), 2733, Cpl., *k. in a., F. & F.,* 9/8/16.

BROGDEN, Albert Percy, *e.* Bradford (Bradford, Yorks.), 240732, Pte., *k. in a., F. & F.,* 3/9/16.

BROOK, Arnold, *e.* Bradford (Bradford, Yorks), 3071, Pte., *k. in a., F. & F.,* 17/2/16.

BROOKES, Frank, *b.* Bradford, *e.* Bradford, Yorks., 240502, Pte., *k. in a., F. & F.,* 3/9/16.

BROOKES, Frederick, *e.* Bradford (West Bowling, Yorks), 240798, Sergt., *k. in a., F. & F.,* 25/4/18.

BROWN, Harry, *e.* Bradford, Yorks. (Bradford), 4265, Pte., *k. in a., F. & F.,* 13/8/16.

BROWN, John, *b.* Bradford, *e.* Bradford, Yorks., 241598, Pte., *k. in a., F. & F.,* 25/4/18.

BROWN, Robert Henry, *b.* Salford, *e.* Newcastle-on-Tyne, 63000, Pte., *k. in a., F. & F.,* 11/10/18, *formerly* 3/66369 Lancashire Fusiliers.

BUCKLEY, Edward, *b.* Bradford, *e.* Bradford, Yorks., 61, Sergt., *k. in a., F. & F.,* 21/12/15.

APPENDIX

BUCKLEY, Frank, *b.* Bradford, *e.* Bradford, Yorks. (Idle, Yorks.), 3441, Pte., *k. in a.*, F. & F., 1/7/16.

BUCKROYD, John Willie, *b.* Leeds, *e.* Bradford, Yorks., 18/329, Pte., *d.*, F. & F., 19/10/18.

BUDDLE, Heze., *b.* Beverley, *e.* Beverley, Yorks., 57010, Pte., *k. in a.*, F. & F., 14/4/18.

BULMAN, William, *b.* Newcastle-on-Tyne, *e.* Newcastle-on-Tyne, 63660, Pte., *k. in a.*, F. & F., 11/10/18.

BUNDELL, Frederick, *e.* Hertford (Rickmansworth, Herts.), 236194, L./Cpl., *d.*, F. & F., 7/11/18, *formerly* 5806 Herts. Regt.

BURD, Albert Harry, *e.* Bradford, Yorks (Bradford), 2793, L./Cpl., *k. in a.*, F. & F., 3/9/16.

BURGESS, Harold, *e.* Bradford, Yorks. (Bradford), 2735, Pte., *k. in a.*, F. & F., 30/4/15.

BURGESS, John Henry, *b.* Bradford, *e.* Bradford, Yorks., 1846, Pte., *k. in a.*, F. & F., 25/5/15.

BURNELL, Charles Henry, *b.* Bradford, *e.* Halifax, Yorks., 242197, Pte., *k. in a.*, F. & F., 8/10/17.

BURKE, T., 3081, *k. in a.*, 15/12/15.

BUTLER, Henry, *b.* Shipley, Yorks., *e.* Bradford, Yorks., 240147, Pte., *k. in a.*, F. & F., 3/9/16.

BUTTERFIELD, Alfred, *e.* Bradford (Manningham, Yorks.), 241355, Pte., *k. in a.*, F. & F., 26/4/18.

CAFFERTY, James, *b.* Bradford, *e.* Bradford, Yorks., 4524, Pte., *d. of w.*, F. & F., 10/7/16.

CAINE, Frederick, *e.* Bradford, Yorks., 4405, Pte., *k. in a.*, F. & F., 1/7/16.

CAPPS, Arthur, *b.* Sheffield, *e.* Sheffield, 13375, Pte., *k. in a.*, F. & F., 11/10/18.

CARR, James, *b.* Newcastle-on-Tyne, *e.* Newcastle-on-Tyne, 114077, Pte., *k. in a.*, F. & F., 12/10/18.

CARR, William Benjamin, *b.* Spennymoor, Durham, *e.* Bradford, Yorks. (Bradford), 4251, Pte., *k. in a.*, F. & F., 3/9/16.

CARRADICE, Ramsey, *b.* Bradford, *e.* Bradford, Yorks., 743, L./Cpl., *k. in a.*, F. & F., 1/7/16.

CARROL, Hugh, *b.* Bradford, *e.* Bradford, Yorks., 240264, Pte., *d. of w.*, F. & F., 9/9/17.

CARTER, Charles Henry, *b.* Harrogate, *e.* Harrogate, 201096, Pte., *d. of w.*, F. & F., 2/8/17.

CARTER, Gilbert Norton, *b.* Harrogate, *e.* Leeds, 242518, Pte., *d.*, F. & F., 5/11/18.

CAWTHRON, George, *b.* Bowling, Yorks., *e.* Bradford, Yorks., 1282, Cpl., *d. of w., F. & F.,* 19/1/16.

CHADD, Leslie Francis, *b.* Camberwell, Surrey, *e.* Camberwell, 62614, Pte., *d., F. & F.,* 2/11/18, *formerly* 129291 Middlesex Regt.

CHAFFER, George, *e.* Bradford, Yorks. (Manchester), 12431, Pte., *k. in a., F. & F.,* 23/11/15.

CHILD, John, *b.* Bradford, *e.* Bradford, Yorks., 4217, Pte., *k. in a., F. & F.,* 25/7/16.

CHIPPENDALE, Samuel, *e.* Bradford, Yorks., 240564, Pte., *d., F. & F.,* 19/4/17.

CHRISTIAN, John William, *b.* Spennymoor, Durham, *e.* Consett, Durham (Annfield Plain), 42712, Pte., *k. in a., F. & F.,* 25/4/18.

CHRISTIE, Colin, *b.* Chelsea, *e.* Chelsea, London, 62619, Pte., *d. of w., F. & F.,* 12/10/18, *formerly* 168081 Middlesex Regt.

CLACY, Ernest Edward, *b.* Little Sandhurst, Berks., *e.* Camberley, Berks. (Ash Vale), 72577, Pte., *k. in a., F. & F.,* 11/10/18, *formerly* 20733 Oxford & Bucks. Light Infantry.

CLAREY, William, *b.* Bradford, *e.* Bradford, Yorks., 4215, Pte., *d. of w., F. & F.,* 25/7/16.

CLARK, Edward, *b.* Bradford, *e.* Bradford, Yorks., 1613, Pte., *k. in a., F. & F.,* 1/7/16.

CLARKE, John Willie, *b.* Bradford, *e.* Bradford, Yorks., 240361, Pte., *k. in a., F. & F.,* 1/3/18.

CLARK, Samuel, *b.* Bradford, *e.* Bradford, Yorks., 241162, Pte., *k. in a., F. & F.,* 3/9/16.

CLAVEN, John, *b.* Bradford, *e.* Bradford, Yorks., 4575, Pte., *k. in a., F. & F.,* 7/7/16.

CLAYTON, Arthur, *b.* Bradford, *e.* Bradford, Yorks., 2172, Pte., *k. in a., F. & F.,* 24/9/15.

CLEALL, Ernest William, *b.* Dorchester, Dorset, *e.* York (West Lulworth, Dorset), 22106, Pte., *d. of w., F. & F.,* 18/10/18.

CLOSE, Harold, *b.* Bradford, *e.* Bradford, Yorks., 4734, Pte., *k. in a., F. & F.,* 3/9/16.

CLOUGH, Herbert, *e.* Bradford, Yorks., 3396, Pte., *k. in a., F. & F.,* 9/8/15.

COBURN, Gilbert, *b.* Dewsbury, Yorks., *e.* Dewsbury, Yorks., 19906, Sergt., *k. in a., F. & F.,* 12/10/18.

COHEN, Arthur Gordon, *b.* Bradford, *e.* Bradford, Yorks., 2338, Sergt., *k. in a., F. & F.,* 19/12/15.

COLLINGHAM, Joseph, *b.* Whitwell, Derbyshire, *e.* Derby, 46213, Pte., *d. of w., F. & F.,* 12/2/18, *formerly* 68206 King's Own Yorks. Light Infantry.

APPENDIX

COLLINS, Walter, *b.* Stainland, Yorks., *e.* York (York), 49611, Pte., *k. in a.*, F. & F., 11/10/18.

CONDER, George William, *b.* Lancaster, *e.* Bradford, Yorks., 2006, L./Cpl., *k. in a.*, F. & F., 11/10/15.

CONLIN, James, *b.* Sunderland, *e.* Sunderland, 242867, Pte., *k. in a.*, F. & F., 8/10/17, *formerly* 21/100 Durham Light Infantry.

COOK, Harry, *b.* Cleckheaton, Yorks., *e.* Bradford (Bradford, Yorks.), 4286, Pte., *k. in a.*, F. & F., 20/12/15.

COOPE, William, *b.* Bradford, *e.* Bradford, Yorks., 4499, Pte., *d. of w.*, F. & F., 7/7/16.

COULTAS, Walter, *e.* Leeds (Leeds), 242516, Pte., *k. in a.*, F. & F., 25/4/18.

COULTON, Willie, *b.* Bradford, *e.* Bradford, Yorks., 18/98, Pte., *k. in a.*, F. & F., 25/4/18.

COUSINS, Frederick, *e.* York (Ripon, Yorks.), 6545, Pte., *k. in a.*, F. & F., 22/10/16.

COUSINS, Stanley, *e.* Bradford (Bradford, Yorks.), 3004, Dmr., *d. of w.*, F. & F., 2/7/16.

COWEN, Joseph, *b.* Newcastle-on-Tyne, *e.* Gateshead, 63679, Pte., *d.*, F. & F., 30/10/18.

COYNE, Bernard, *b.* Ballen Lough, Roscommon, Ireland, *e.* Bradford, Yorks., 4592, Pte., *k. in a.*, F. & F., 1/7/16.

COYNE, William, *e.* Leeds (Leeds), 307491, *k. in a.*, F. & F., 25/4/18.

CRABTREE, Ede., *e.* Bradford (Bradford, Yorks.), 4931, Pte., *k. in a.*, F. & F., 3/9/16.

CRAVEN, William, *b.* Girlington, Yorks., *e.* Bradford, Yorks., 1651, Pte., *k. in a.*, F. & F., 3/9/16.

CROSSLEY, Lewis, *e.* Halifax (Sowerby Bridge), 242602, Pte., *d.*, F. & F., 17/10/18.

CRYER, Harry, *b.* Muswell Hill, London, *e.* Bradford, Yorks. (Westcliffe-on-Sea, Essex), 1962, L./Cpl., *k. in a.*, F. & F., 19/8/15.

CURE, George, *b.* Manninhgam, Yorks., *e.* Bradford, Yorks., 1543, Pte., *k. in a.*, F. & F., 29/7/15.

CURTIS, Asa, *e.* Bradford, Yorks. (Ambler Thorn, near Queensbury, Yorks.), 4946, Pte., *k. in a.*, F. & F., 14/7/16.

DALE, Frank, *e.* Bradford, Yorks., 2647, Pte., *k. in a.*, F. & F., 25/7/16.

DAWSON, Henry, *b.* Marylebone, Middlesex, *e.* Bradford, Yorks., 1516, Coy. Quarter Master Sergt., *d. of w.*, F. & F., 3/6/15.

DAWSON, John Edward, *b.* Fleckney, Leicestershire, *e.* Coalville (Desford, Leicestershire), 42835, Pte., *k. in a.*, F. & F., 25/4/18, formerly 28028 Leicestershire Regt.

DEACON, Ernest, *e.* Bradford (Bradford, Yorks.), 241045, Pte., *k. in a.*, F. & F., 25/4/18.

DEAN, Joseph Gledhill, *e.* Leeds (Armley, Leeds), 306597, Rfm., *k. in a.*, F. & F., 25/4/18.

DEANS, Percival, *b.* Leeds, *e.* Leeds, 260043, Pte., *d.*, F. & F., 30/10/18, *formerly* 269019, 3/6th Duke of Wellington's (West Riding) Regt.

DENISON, Lawrence, *b.* Calverley, Yorks., *e.* Bradford (Shipley, Yorks), 2428, Pte., *d. of w.*, F. & F., 18/12/15.

DENNIS, George Herbert, *b.* Ilkley, Yorks., *e.* Harrogate, 242938, L./Cpl., *k. in a.*, F. & F., 25/4/18.

DIXON, John, *b.* Gateshead, *e.* Chester le Street, Durham, 42715, Pte., *k. in a.*, F. & F., 25/4/18, *formerly* 40104 Durham Light Infantry.

DIXON, Robert, *b.* Leeds, *e.* Leeds, 23913, L./Cpl., *k. in a.*, F. & F., 9/12/17.

DIXON, Thomas, *b.* Bradford, *e.* Bradford, Yorks., 240426, Cpl., *k. in a.*, F. & F., 25/4/18.

DOBSON, Stephen, *b.* Bradford, *e.* Bradford, Yorks. (Windhill, Yorks.), 3804, Pte., *d. of w.*, F. & F., 5/7/16.

DOHERTY, William, *b.* Leeds, *e.* Leeds, 242913, Pte., *k. in a.*, F. & F., 25/4/18.

DOOLEY, Edward Patrick, *e.* Bradford (Bradford, Yorks.), 2329, Pte., *k. in a.*, F. & F., 4/8/16.

DUCKETT, Harry, *b.* Bradford, *e.* Bradford, Yorks., 240588, Cpl., *d.*, F. & F., 16/10/18.

DUCKWORTH, James, *b.* Bradford, *e.* Bradford, Yorks., 4427, Pte., *d. of w.*, F. & F., 4/9/16.

DUFFY, Thomas, *b.* Leeds, *e.* York, 46217, Pte., *k. in a.*, F. & F., 25/4/18, *formerly* 388275 York. & Lancaster Regt.

DUNN, Frank, *b.* Trimdon, Durham, *e.* Bradford, Yorks., 4546, Pte., *k. in a.*, F. & F., 9/8/16.

DUNN, Joseph, *e.* Bradford, Yorks. (Bradford, Yorks.), 2853, Pte., *k. in a.*, F. & F., 1/7/16.

DUTHOIT, John Albert, *b.* Leeds, *e.* Leeds, 263020, Pte., *d.*, F. & F., 27/10/18.

DYSON, Frederick Selby, *e.* Bradford, Yorks. (Baildon, Yorks.), 2589, *k. in a.*, Pte., F. & F., 25/7/16.

EARNSHAW, William, *e.* Bradford, Yorks. (Bradford), 3325, Pte., *d. of w.*, F. & F., 23/9/16.

EASTON, James Henry, *e.* Bradford, Yorks., 3594, Pte., *k. in a.*, F. & F., 19/12/15.

EDEN, Horace, *b.* Pickering, Yorks., *e.* York, 42840, L./Cpl., *d.*, F. and F., 13/8/18.

APPENDIX

EDMONDSON, George, *b.* Bradford, *e.* Bradford, Yorks., 2532, L./Cpl. *k. in a.,* F. & F., 1/7/16.

EDMONDSON, Joseph Bernard, *e.* Bradford, Yorks. (Mansfield, Notts.), 3221, Pte., *k. in a.,* F. & F., 1/7/16.

ELLERTON, John Willie, *b.* Bradford, *e.* Bradford, Yorks., 1755, Pte., *k. in a.,* F. & F., 16/5/15.

EMMOTT, Gilbert, *b.* Bolton Wood, Yorks., *e.* Bradford, Yorks., 240554, Sergt., *k. in a.,* F. & F., 9/10/17.

EVANS, Ernest George, *b.* Southwark, Surrey, *c.* Camberwell, (Walworth, S.E.), 62630, Pte., *k. in a.,* F. & F., 12/10/18, *formerly* T2/10/129324 33rd Battalion Middlesex Regt.

FALLON, John, *e.* Bradford, Yorks. (Bradford), 4735, Pte., *k. in a.,* F. & F., 13/2/17.

FARMERY, Clive, *b.* Halifax, *e.* Bradford, Yorks., 240447, Pte., *d. of w.,* F. & F., 11/3/18.

FARNISH, Leonard, *b.* Bradford, *e.* Bradford, Yorks., 241648, Pte., *k. in a.,* F. & F., 3/9/16.

FARRAR, Thomas, *e.* Bradford, Yorks. (Bradford), 3307, Pte., *k. in a.,* F. & F., 2/7/16.

FARRUGIA, Publio, *b.* Whisidia, Malta, *e.* Malta, 46245, Pte., *k. in a.,* F. & F., 25/4/18.

FAULDING, John, *e.* Bradford, Yorks. (West Bowling, Yorks.), 240549, Sergt., *k. in a.,* F. & F., 28/4/18.

FAWTHORPE, Bertram, *e.* Halifax, Yorks. (Bradford, Yorks.), 41629, Pte., *k. in a.;* F. & F., 11/10/18.

FEATHER, Ernest, *b.* Bradford, *e.* Bradford, Yorks., 242181, Pte., *k. in a.,* F. & F., 3/9/16.

FEATHERSTONE, Sidney Watson, *b.* Castleford, Yorks., *e,* Bradford, Yorks., 2403, Sergt., *k. in a.,* F. & F., 3/9/16.

FELL, Thomas, *e.* Bradford, Yorks. (Bradford), 3508, Pte., *k. in a.,* F. & F., 1/7/16.

FELLOWS, Frank, *b.* Coseley, Staffs., *e.* Tipton, Staffs., 41963, Pte., *k. in a.,* F. & F., 11/10/18.

FENDER, David Richardson, *b.* North Shields, *e.* Southampton, 40102, Pte., *k. in a.,* F. & F., 25/4/18.

FENWICK, Edward, *b.* Stamford, Alnwick, *e.* Newcastle-on-Tyne, 267534, Pte., *k. in a.,* F. & F., 25/4/18.

FERRIGAN, William, *e.* Bradford, Yorks. (Bradford), 3094, Pte., *d. of w.,* F. & F., 20/12/15.

FIELDHOUSE, Robert, *b.* Windhill, Yorks., *e.* Bradford, Yorks., 241516, Pte., *k. in a.,* F. & F., 2/7/16.

FIELDHOUSE, Rufus, *b.* Bradford, *e.* Bradford, Yorks., 241658, L./Cpl., *k. in a., F. & F.,* 9/10/17.

FIRTH, Charles, *e.* Bradford (Bradford, Yorks), 3143, Pte., *k. in a., F. & F.,* 15/6/15.

FIRTH, Gilbert, *b.* Bradford, *e.* Bradford, Yorks., 1833, Pte., *d. of w., F. & F.,* 12/5/15.

FIRTH, Joel, *b.* Horton, Yorks., *e.* Bradford, Yorks., 1379, Pte., *d.,* 23/3/16, *F. & F.*

FLETCHER, James William, *b.* York, *e.* Leeds (Hunslet, Leeds), 18911, *Pte., k. in a., F. & F.,* 11/10/18.

FLINT, Herbert, *b.* Sheffield, *e.* Sheffield, 50573, Pte., *d. of w., F. & F.,* 12/10/18.

FLOWER, Percy Preston, *b.* Leamington, Warwick, *e.* Rugby, 51164, Pte., *k. in a., F. & F.,* 12/2/18.

FORBES, Robert, *e.* Bradford, Yorks., 2691, L./Cpl., *k. in a., F. & F.,* 12/7/16.

Foster, Harold, *b.* Shipley, Yorks., *e.* Bradford (Bradford), 1744, Cpl., *k. in a., F. & F.,* 19/11/15.

FOSTER, George Douglas, *b.* Southwark, *e.* Southwark (Walworth), 62601, Pte., *k. in a., F. & F.,* 11/10/18, *formerly* 129292 Middlesex Regiment.

FOSTER, John Bryden, *b.* Sunderland, *e.* Sunderland, 242794, Pte., *k. in a., F. & F.,* 9/10/17, *formerly* 3/12643 Durham Light Infantry.

FOUNTAIN, Ernest, *b.* Leeds, *e.* Leeds, 49654, Pte., *d., F. & F.,* 30/8/18.

Fox, Walter James, *b.* Faversham, Kent., *e.* High Wycombe (High Wycombe), 80030, Pte., *k. in a., F. & F.,* 11/10/18.

FRANKLIN, William, *b.* Leeds, *e.* Leeds, 49629, Pte., *k. in a., F. & F.,* 25/4/18.

FRETWELL, John, *e.* Leeds, 242546, Pte., *k. in a., F. & F.,* 9/10/17.

FRIEDLANDER, David, *b.* Hackney, E., *e.* London, 20418, Pte., *k. in a., F. & F.,* 11/10/18.

FROST, Frederick Daniel, *b.* Northampton, *e.* Bradford, Yorks., 1430, Pte., *d. of w., F. & F.,* 21/12/15.

FRYER, James Mitchell, *b.* Bradford, *e.* Bradford, Yorks., 240123, L./Cpl., *k. in a., F. & F.,* 3/9/16.

FULLER, Raistrick, *b.* Bradford, *e.* Bradford, Yorks., 4047, L./Cpl., *k. in a., F. & F.,* 14/8/16.

FURNISS, George, *b.* Sheffield, *e.* Bradford, Yorks. (Bradford), 2125, Pte., *k. in a., F. & F.,* 10/5/15.

GARDNER, Edward, *b.* Islington, London, *e.* Holloway, London, 62620, Pte., *k. in a., F. & F.,* 11/10/18, *formerly* 129347 Middlesex Regt.

APPENDIX

GAUNT, Stanley, *b.* Leeds, *e.* Leeds, 307077, Pte., *k. in a., F. & F.,* 25/4/18.

GAWTHORPE, Alfred, *e.* Bradford, Yorks. (Otley), 3176, Pte., *k. in a., F. & F.,* 1/7/16.

GELLERT, Edward, *b.* Bradford, *e.* Bradford, Yorks., 2353, Pte., *k. in a., F. & F.,* 19/12/15.

GIBBON, John George, *b.* Shildon, *e.* Shildon, Durham, 242787, Pte., *k. in a., F. & F.,* 25/4/18, *formerly* 30566, Durham Light Infantry.

GIBSON, William Wilke, *b.* Newcastle-on-Tyne, *e.* Newcastle-on-Tyne, 63684, Pte., *k. in a., F. & F.,* 11/10/18.

GILBERT, Patrick, *b.* Bradford, Yorks. (Manningham, Yorks.), 2975, Pte., *k. in a., F. & F.,* 12/11/15.

GILES, Sidney John, *b.* Hammersmith, *e.* West London (Fulham), 54261, Pte., *k. in a., F. & F.,* 29/9/18.

GILL, Arthur, *b.* Bradford, *e.* Bradford, Yorks. (Saltaire, Yorks.), 4564, Pte., *k. in a., F. & F.,* 3/9/16.

GILL, John, *b.* Bradford, *e.* Bradford, Yorks., 1877, Pte., *k. in a., F. & F.,* 24/9/15.

GILL, Norman, *e.* Bradford, Yorks. (West Bowling, Yorks.), 240067, Sergt. *k. in a., F. & F.,* 3/9/16.

GLEDHILL, Ben, *b.* Bradford, *e.* Bradford, Yorks., 263055, Pte., *k. in a., F. & F.,* 25/4/18.

GODSON, Arthur, *b.* Beeston, Leeds, *e.* Leeds, 15/381, Pte., *d. of w.,* home, 4/11/18.

GOODCHILD, George Henry, *b.* South Moor, Durham, *e.* Stanley, Durham, 242856, Pte., *k. in a. F. & F.,* 25/4/18.

GOODRICK, Stephen, *b.* Huntington, Yorks., *e.* York, 7312, Pte., *d. of w.,* home, 12/10/16.

GOODWIN, Ernest, *b.* Manningham, Yorks., *e.* Bradford, Yorks., 1274, Sergt., *d. of w., F. & F.,* 16/12/15.

GRAINGER, Alfred, *b.* Consett, Durham, *e.* Gateshead (Swallwell), Durham, 42719, Pte., *k. in a., F. & F.,* 25/4/18, *formerly* 40083 Durham Light Infantry.

GRAINGER, Arthur, *e.* Ripon (Ripon, Yorks.), 260012, Pte., *d. of w., F. & F.,* 19/6/18.

GREEN, Frederick, *b.* Stockton-on-Tees, *e.* York, 242632, Pte., *k. in a., F. & F.,* 25/4/18.

GREEN, John, *b.* Lawton, Lancashire, *e.* Wombwell, Yorks., 29707, Pte., *k. in a., F. & F.,* 11/4/18.

GREENBERG, Phillip, *b.* Leeds, *e.* Leeds, 242578, Pte., *d. of w., F. & F.,* 13/3/18.

GREENWOOD, Fred Clarkson, e. Bradford (Bradford, Yorks.), 3136, Pte., k. in a., F. & F., 19/12/15.

GREENWOOD, Henry, b. Leeds, e. Leeds, 307448, Pte., k. in a., F. & F., 25/4/18.

GREENWOOD, Lancelot, b. Thornton, Yorks., e., Bradford, Yorks., 2305, Cpl., k. in a., F. & F., 14/7/16.

GRIFFITHS, Arthur, e. Bradford, (Bradford, Yorks.), 307584, Pte., d. F. & F., 28/10/18.

GUEST, Frank, b. Leigh, Lancs., e. Blackpool, 51900, Pte., k. in a., F. & F., 25/4/18, formerly M/287447 A.S.C. (M.T.)

HAIGH, Ernest, b. Bradford, e. Bradford, Yorks., 4235, Pte., k. in a., F. & F., 14/8/16.

HAIGH, James William, b. Meltham, Yorks., e. Halifax (Meltham, Yorks.), 30753, Pte., k. in a., F. & F., 25/4/18.

HAIGH, Robert Firth, b. Huddersfield, e. Huddersfield, 21/709, Pte., k. in a., F. & F., 25/4/18.

HAIGH, William, e. Bradford, Yorks. (Shipley, Yorks.), 3344, Pte. k. in a., F. & F., 4/8/16.

HAINSWORTH, William, b. Leeds, e. Leeds, 32400, Pte., d. of w., F. & F., 11/10/17.

HALEY, Edmund, e. Bradford (Bradford, Yorks.), 3796, Pte., d. of w., F. & F., 18/8/16.

HALL, Arthur, e. York (Borobridge, Yorks.), 3627, L/Cpl., k. in a., F. & F., 23/11/16.

HALL, Charles Hicks, b. Kenowyn Tours, Cornwall, e. Bradford, Yorks., 240043, Pte., d. of w., F. & F., 26/5/18.

HALL, Harry, b. Bradford, e. Bradford, Yorks., 4310, Pte., k. in a., F. & F., 20/12/15.

HALL, John William, b. Sunderland, e. Sunderland, 242749, Pte., d. of w., F. & F., 7/5/17, formerly 30201, 17th Durham Light Infantry.

HALL, William Frederick, e. Bradford (Bradford, Yorks.), 2844, Cpl., k. in a., F. & F., 26/8/16.

HALLIDAY, Joseph, e. Bradford, Yorks. (Saltaire, Yorks.), 3562, Pte., k. in a., F. & F., 22/10/16.

HAMILTON, Richard John, b. Brighton, e. Brighton, Sussex, 62622, Pte., d. of w., F. & F., 15/9/18, formerly 168067, 53rd Middlesex Regt.

HAMMOND, John, b. Houghton, Durham, e. Bradford, Yorks.(Darlington), 264, Sergt., k. in a., F. & F., 16/5/15.

HARDY, David, b. Bedlington, e. Bedlington, 63690, Pte., d. of w., F. & F., 3/11/18., M.M.

APPENDIX

HARE, John Albert, *b.* Kitton, Rutland, *e.* Stamford (Stamford, Leicestershire), 242242, Pte., *d., F. & F.,* 27/4/18.

HARPER, Miles, *b.* Garsdale, Yorks., *e.* Kirkby Stephen, Westmoreland (Sedbergh, Yorks.), 242184, Pte., *k. in a., F. & F.,* 3/9/16.

HART, Charles, *e.* Stockton-on-Tees (Norton-on-Tees), 325063, Rfm., *k. in a., F. & F.,* 11/10/18, *formerly* 22788, 4th Res. Yorks. Regt.

HARTLEY, Bernard North, *b.* Bradford, Yorks., *e.* Halifax, 46227, Pte., *d. of w., F. & F.,* 11/4/18, *formerly* 42861 King's Own Yorkshire Light Infantry.

HARTLEY, John William, *b.* Halifax, Yorks., Bradford (Bradford, Yorks.), 4715, Pte., *k. in a., F. & F.,* 26/8/16.

HARTLEY, Thomas Herbert, *b.* West Moor, Northumberland, *e.* Newcastle-on-Tyne, 63691, Pte., *k. in a., F. & F.,* 11/10/18.

HARVEY, Percy, *b.* Wyke, Yorks., *e.* Bradford, Yorks., 240253, Sergt., *k. in a., F. & F.,* 18/6/17.

HARVEY, Willie, *b.* Bradford, *e.* Bradford, Yorks., 5611, Pte., *k. in a., F. & F.,* 8/9/16.

HASTE, Walter Bottomley, *b.* Idle, Yorks., *e.* Bradford, 4884, Pte., *k. in a., F. & F.,* 3/9/16.

HAYDEN, John Henry, *b.* Poplar, London, *e.* Poplar, 204102, Pte., *d. of w., F. & F.,* 12/10/18.

HEARN, Donald Henry, *b.* Norwich, *e.* Bradford (Bradford, Yorks.), 1399, Pte., *k. in a., F. & F.,* 25/7/16.

HEELEY, Lawrie, *b.* Liversedge, Yorks., *e.* Heckmondwike, Yorks. (Millbridge, Yorks)., 805996, Pte., *k. in a., F. & F.,* 1/11/18.

HELLIWELL, Alfred, *b.* Bowling, Yorks., *e.* Bradford, Yorks., 1752, L./Cpl., *k. in a., F. & F.,* 14/8/16.

HELLIWELL, Robert, *b.* West Bowling, Yorks., *e.* Bradford, Yorks., 1158, L./Cpl., *k. in a., F. & F.,* 1/7/16.

HEMSLEY, Arthur, *e.* Bradford, Yorks·, 2584, Cpl., *d. of w., F. & F.,* 8/9/16.

HENDERSON, Thomas William, *b.* Gateshead, *e.* Gateshead, Durham, 242791, Pte., *k. in a., F. & F.,* 11/10/18.

HESELTINE, Harry, *e.* Bradford (Bradford, Yorks.), 241116, Pte., *k. in a., F. & F.,* 9/10/17.

HEWITT, Arthur, *e.* Bradford, Yorks., 240688, Pte., *k. in a., F. & F.,* 11/10/18.

HEWITT, Henry Bastow, *e.* Bradford, Yorks., 241109, L./Cpl., *d. of w., F. & F.,* 11/10/17.

HIGGINS, Edward, *b.* Bradford, *e.* Bradford, Yorks., 1876, Pte., *k. in a., F. & F.,* 12/7/16.

HIGGINSON, Thomas, *b.* Felton Downs, *e.* Houghton le Spring, Durham, 59031, Pte., *k. in a.*, F. & F., 11/10/18.

HILL, William, *b.* Bradford, *e.* Bradford, Yorks., 240451, Pte., *d.*, F. & F., 13/11/18.

HILLMAN, John, *e.* Bradford (Bradford, Yorks.), 241062, Cpl., *k. in a.*, F. & F., 11/6/17.

HINDLEY, George, *b.* Bradford, *e.* Bradford, Yorks., 263001, Pte., *d. of w.*, F. & F., 9/10/17.

HIRD, Ernest, *b.* Shipley, Yorks., *e.* Bradford, 240334, Pte., *d. of w.*, F. & F., 19/4/18.

HIRST, Harold, *b.* Cleckheaton, *e.* Cleckheaton, Yorks., 260053, Pte., *k. in a.*, F. & F., 3/7/17.

HITCHEN, Edmund, *b.* Liverpool, *e.* Bradford, Yorks., 18/641, Pte., *k. in a.*, F. & F., 25/4/18.

HOLGATE, Harry, *e.* Bradford, Yorks., 2858, Pte., *k. in a.*, F. & F., 1/7/16.

HOLGATE, Richard, *b.* Bradford, *e.* Bradford, Yorks., 1471, Pte., *k. in a.*, F. & F., 29/8/16.

HOLMES, Edgar Stephenson, *e.* Bradford, Yorks. (Bradford), 3940, Pte., *k. in a.*, F. & F., 30/8/16.

HOLMES, Harry, *b.* Horton, Yorks., *e.* Bradford, Yorks., 4226, Pte., *k. in a.*, F. & F., 26/9/16.

HOLMES, Joseph, *b.* Bradford, *e.* Bradford, Yorks., 1321, Pte., *d. of w.*, F. & F., 14/7/15.

HOLT, Joseph Alfred, *b.* Bradford, *e.* Bradford, Yorks., 1727, L./Cpl., *k. in a.*, F. & F., 31/10/15.

HOPWOOD, Arthur, *e.* Bradford, Yorks. (Bradford), 4201, Pte., *k. in a.*, F. & F., 28/8/16.

HORGAN, William, *e.* Bradford, Yorks. (Thornbury, Yorks.), 241841, Pte., *k. in a.*, F. & F., 3/9/16.

HORNE, Fred, *b.* Daisy Hill, Bradford, *e.* Bradford, Yorks., 1530, Pte., *d. of w.*, F. & F., 22/7/16.

HORNER, Alfred, *b.* West Hartlepool, *e.* Bishop Auckland, 242878, Pte., *k. in a.*, F. & F., 25/4/18., M.M.

HORNSBY, Charlie, *e.* Bradford, Yorks. (Bradford), 4754, Pte., *k. in a.*, F. & F., 1/7/16.

HORSFIELD, Harry, *b.* Bradford, *e.* Bradford, Yorks., 4615, Pte., *k. in a.*, F. & F., 3/9/16.

HORSMAN, William, *b.* Keighley, *e.* Keighley, Yorks., 18/586, Sergt., *k. in a.*, F. & F., 25/4/18.

APPENDIX

HOWARD, George Bagnall, *b.* Dovercourt, Essex, *e.* Colchester, 62632, Pte., *k. in a., F. & F.*, 11/10/18, *formerly* 129304, 53rd Middlesex Regt.

HOWARTH, James, *b.* Morley, Yorks., *e.* Bradford, Yorks., 16/1525, Pte., *k. in a., F. & F.*, 8/9/17.

HOWKER, Joseph William, *e.* Bradford, Yorks., 2618, Pte., *k. in a., F. & F.*, 10/9/16.

HOWLETT, Thomas Edward, *b.* Bradford, *e.* Bradford, Yorks., 185, Cpl., *k. in a., F. & F.*, 27/9/15.

HUBBARD, Clifford, *b.* Chesterfield, *e.* Sheffield (Sheffield), 57258, Pte., *k. in a., F. & F.*, 11/10/18.

HUDSON, James Henry, *b.* Sheffield., *e.* Bradford, Yorks., 4408, Pte., *k. in a., F. & F.*, 3/9/16.

HUDSON, John, *e.* Bradford, Yorks., 240558, Cpl., *k. in a., F. & F.*, 25/4/18.

HUMPHREYS, Sydney, *e.* Bradford, Yorks., 3461, Pte., *k. in a., F. & F.*, 2/10/15.

HUMPLEBY, Thomas, *b.* Undercliffe, Yorks., *e.* Bradford, Yorks., 4252, Pte., *d. of w., F. & F.*, 13/7/16.

HUNTINGTON, George Edward, *e.* Framewellgate, Durham (Durham), 7121, Pte., *k. in a., F. & F.*, 22/10/16, *formerly* 31590 3rd Durham Light Infantry.

HURDLE, Cyrus George, *b.* Headley, Surrey, *e.* Guilford, Surrey, 62604, Pte., *k. in a., F. & F.*, 11/10/18.

HUSTWICK, Percy, *b.* Ilkley, Yorks., *e.* Bradford, Yorks. (Bradford), 1155, Pte., *k. in a., F. & F.*, 1/7/16.

HUTCHINSON, Horace, *b.* Bradford, *e.* Bradford, Yorks., 4285, Pte., *d. of w., F. & F.*, 11/7/16.

HUTCHINSON, James William, *b.* Horsforth, Yorks., *e.* Horsforth, Yorks., 242511, Pte., *k. in a., F. & F.*, 9/10/17.

ILLINGWORTH, James Albert, *e.* Bradford, Yorks. (Bradford), 240441, Pte., *d., F. & F.*, 9/11/18.

INGHAM, Jack, *e.* Bradford, Yorks. (Shipley, Yorks.), 3005, Sergt., *k. in a., F. & F.*, 18/7/16.

INGLESON, Ronald, *b.* Harrogate, *e.* Bradford, Yorks. (Bradford), 1623, Pte., *k. ib a., F. & F.*, 24/9/15.

INNS, John Frederick Rawlins, *b.* Cowley, Oxon, *e.* Oxford, 56737, Pte., *d., F. & F.*, 21/6/18, *formerly* 234138 R.F.A.

IMESON, Albert, *b.* Bradford, *e.* Bradford, Yorks., 4470, Pte., *k. in a., F. & F.*, 14/8/16.

JACKSON, Arthur, *e.* Bradford, Yorks. (Bradford), 240552, Pte., *k. in a., F. & F.*, 1/7/16.

JACKSON, Charles Wallace, *b.* Bradford, Yorks., *e.* Salford (Bramley, Yorks.), 23843, Cpl., *d. of w.*, F. & F., 12/10/18.

JACKSON, Tom, *e.* Leeds (Leeds), 306463, Pte., *k. in a.*, F. & F., 11/10/18.

JACKSON, Vernon, *b.* Leeds, *e.* Bradford, Yorks., 240182, Pte., *k. in a.*, F. & F., 3/9/16.

JAGGER, Sylvester, *b.* Shelf, Bradford, *e.* Bradford, Yorks., 241732, Pte., *k. in a.*, F. & F., 2/7/16.

JAMESON, Fred, *b.* Leeds, *e.* Leeds, 267681, Pte., *k. in a.*, F. & F., 9/10/17.

JARVIS, Isaac, *e.* Bradford, Yorks. (Laisterdyke, Yorks.), 3424, Pte., *k. in a*, F. & F., 9/10/15.

JENKINS, George, *b.* Burton, Staffs, *e.* Lichfield, 5523, Pte., *k. in a.*, F. & F., 3/9/16.

JENKINS, William, *b.* Gloucester, *e.* Bradford, Yorks., 240100, Sgt., *k. in a.*, F. & F., 10/10/17.

JENNINGS, William, *e.* Bradford, Yorks. (Bradford), 98, Cpl., *k. in a.*, F. & F., 3/6/15.

JOHNSON, Alfred, *e.* Bradford, 4505, Pte., *k. in a.*, F. & F., 9/7/16.

JOHNSON, Edward, *b.* Bradford, *e.* Bradford, Yorks., 2240, Pte., *k. in a.*, F. & F., 1/7/16.

JOHNSON, Leslie Richard, *b.* Bromley, Kent, *e.* Whitehall, S.W., 62623, Pte., *k. in a.*, F. & F., 11/10/18, *formerly* 168005, 53rd Middlesex Regt.

JONES, Ernest William, *e.* Bradford, Yorks. (Bradford), 241304, Pte., *k. in a.*, F. & F., 25/4/18.

JONES, John, *e.* Bradford, Yorks. (Bradford), 242606, Pte., *k. in a.*, F. & F., 25/4/18.

JONES, Robert, *b.* New Brighton, Derbyshire, *e.* Abercynon, 72593, Pte., *d. of w.*, F. & F., 30/9/18, *formerly* 15065, Oxford Light Infantry.

JONES, William Henry, *b.* Bradford, *e.* Bradford, Yorks., 1866, L./Cpl., *k. in a.*, F. & F., 9/7/16.

JORDON, Frank, *b.* Bradford, *e.* Bradford, Yorks., 1473, Pte., *k. in a.*, F. & F., 1/7/16.

KALAHER, Daniel, *e.* Bradford, Yorks. (Bradford), 2693, Pte., *k. in a.*, F. & F., 15/7/16.

KAY, Fred, *b.* Burley, Yorks., *e.* Leeds, 242541, Pte., *k. in a.*, F. & F., 7/10/17.

KAY, Harry, *e.* Bradford, Yorks., 241123, Cpl., *k. in a.*, F. & F., 10/8/18.

KAYE, George, *e.* Bradford, Yorks., 3933, Pte., *k. in a.*, F. & F., 2/7/16.

APPENDIX

KAYE, John, *b.* Liversedge, Yorks., *e.* Bradford, Yorks., 4183, Pte., *k. in a., F. & F.*, 9/7/16.

KEELTY, James, *b.* Hull, *e.* Leeds, 37370, Pte., *k. in a., F. & F.*, 25/4/18.

KEIGHLEY, Philip, *e.* Bradford, Yorks. (Esholt, Shipley, Yorks.), 2469, Pte., *d. of w., F. & F.*, 24/12/15.

KELLETT, Ernest, *b.* Leeds, *e.* Leeds, 77775, Pte., *d., F. & F.*, 22/8/18.

KELLETT, George, *b.* Bradford, *e.* Bradford, Yorks., 240291, Pte., *k. in a., F. & F.*, 9/10/17.

KELLETT, William, *b.* Bradford, *e.* Bradford, Yorks. (Bowling, Yorks.), 41745, L./Cpl., *k. in a., F. & F.*, 25/4/18.

KEMP, Joseph Albert, *e.* Leeds (Leeds), 268016, Pte., *k. in a., F. & F.*, 25/4/18.

KENWORTHY, Fred, *b.* Wakefield, Yorks., *e.* Bradford, Yorks., 4789, Pte., *k. in a., F. & F.*, 2/7/16.

KETTLEWELL, Albert, *b.* Bradford, *e.* Bradford, Yorks., 1980, Pte., *d.* home, 20/10/14.

KILNER, Henry, *b.* Sunderland, *e.* Sundarland, 242880, Pte., *k. in a., F. & F.*, 9/10/17, *formerly* 23/10 23rd Durham Light Infantry.

KING, James, *e.* Bradford, Yorks. (Bradford), 2300, Pte., *k. in a., F. & F.*, 3/9/16.

KING, Walter, *b.* Bradford, *e.* Bradford, Yorks., 4526, Pte., *d. of w., F. & F.*, 7/8/16.

KIRK, Samuel, *b.* Leicester, *e.* Leicester, 7174, Cpl., *d. of w., F. & F.*, 29/1/17.

KITCHINGMAN, Simeon, *b.* Bradford, *e.* Bradford, Yorks., 18/1339, Pte., *d. of w., F. & F.*, 2/11/18.

KNIGHT, Reginald Herbert John, *b.* Acton, Middlesex, *e.* Walthamstow, 62594, Pte., *d., F. & F.*, 30/10/18, *formerly* 68075 Middlesex Regiment.

KNOWLES, Jarvill, *e.* Bradford, Yorks. (Bradford), 3948, L./Cpl., *k. in a., F. & F.*, 1/10/15.

LALLY, James Edward, *b.* Howden, Yorks., *e.* Leeds, 263039, Pte., *d. of w., F. & F.*, 20/10/18.

LAMBERT, Percy, *b.* Manningham, Yorks., *e.* Bradford, Yorks., 1672, Pte., *k. in a., F. & F.*, 7/7/16.

LAMBERT, Willie, *b.* Bradford, *e.* Bradford, Yorks., 235126, Pte., *d. of w. F. & F.*, 26/7/17.

LANCASTER, Horace, *b.* Baildon, Yorks., *e.* Bradford, Yorks., 241261, Pte., *k. in a., F. & F.*, 25/4/18.

LANGLEY, Arthur, *b.* Leeds, *e.* York (Leeds), 37536, Pte., *d. of w., F. & F.*, 11/10/17.

LAWRENCE, Henry, *b.* Bradford, *e.* Bradford, Yorks., 240106, Sergt., *d. of w.*, F. & F., 29/4/18.

LAYCOCK, Alfred, *b.* Bradford, *e.* Bradford, Yorks., 2668, L/Cpl., *k. in a.*, F. & F., 16/8/16.

LAYCOCK, Harry, *b.* Bradford, *e.* Bradford, Yorks., 1453, Pte., *k. in a.*, F. & F., 11/8/15.

LEDGARD, Harrison, *b.* Manningham, Yorks., *e.* Bradford, Yorks., 1307, L./Cpl., *d. of w.*, F. & F., 5/2/17.

LEE, Anthony, *e.* Bradford, Yorks. (Bradford), 2763, Pte., *k. in a.*, F. & F., 1/7/16.

LEE, Fred, *b.* Bradford, *e.* Bradford, Yorks., 241799, Pte., *k. in a.*, F. & F., 25/4/18.

LEE, Fred, *b.* Garforth, Leeds, *e.* Leeds, 33366, Pte., *k. in a.*, F. & F., 11/10/18.

LEE, Harry, *b.* Leeds, *e.* Leeds, 242555, Pte., *k. in a.*, F. & F., 8/10/17.

LEE, Samuel, *e.* Bradford, Yorks., 2281, L./Cpl., *d. of w.*, F. & F., 8/9/16.

LENNON, Albert, Edward, *b.* Thackley, Bradford, Yorks., *e.* Bradford, Yorks., 2468, Cpl., *k. in a.*, F. & F., 26/8/16.

LEVI, Dan, *e.* Leeds, 242685, Pte., *k. in a.*, F. & F., 25/4/18.

LIGHTOWLER, Allen, *e.* Bradford, Yorks. (Bradford), 3323, Pte., *d. of w.*, F. & F., 14/9/16.

LINFOOT, Jim, *b.* Leeds, *e.* Leeds, 23638, Pte., *k. in a.*, F. & F., 25/4/18.

LINNEY, Harry, *b.* Normanby, Yorks., *e.* West Hartlepool (West Hartlepool), 63697, Pte., *k. in a.*, F. & F., 11/10/18.

LISTER, John, *b.* Bradford, *e.* Bradford, Yorks., 1429, Pte., *k. in a.*, F. & F., 11/8/15.

LISTER, Reginald, *b.* Malta, *e.* Bradford, Yorks., 240163, Pte., *k. in a.*, F. & F., 25/4/18.

LLOYD, John, *e.* Seaham Harbour, Durham, 307333, Pte., *d.*, F. & F., 14/5/18, *formerly* 282 N. D. Cyclist Corps.

LOFTUS, Mark, *b.* Bradford, *e.* Bradford, Yorks., 1700, Pte., *k. in a.*, F. & F., 13/10/15.

LONG, Horace, *b.* Bradford, *e.* Bradford, Yorks., 240306, L./Cpl., *d. of w.*, F. & F., 29/12/17.

LONG, John James, *b.* Wapping, London, *e.* London (Stepney), 242943, Pte., *k. in a.*, F. & F., 7/4/17.

LONGSTAFF, Fred, *e.* Bradford, Yorks. (Bradford), 4940, Pte., *k. in a.*, F. & F., 21/7/16.

LORD, Alfred Clifford, *e.* Bradford, Yorks. (Leeds), 2384, Pte., *d. of w.*, F. & F., 21/10/15.

APPENDIX

LORD, Richard, *b.* Gt. Horton, Yorks., *e.* Bradford, Yorks., 1697, Pte., *k. in a.*, F. & F., 16/5/15.

LOVE, John, *b.* Kirkconnell, Dumfrieshire, *e.* Dumfries, 30434, Pte., *k. in a.*, F. & F., 20/9/18, *formerly* 21621 West Riding Regt.

LOWE, Alfred, *b.* Salford, Lancs., 62900, Pte., *k. in a.*, F. & F., 26/6/18, *formerly* 3/59822 Lancs. Fusiliers.

LUMBY, Stanley, Haigh, *e.* Bradford, Yorks. (Baildon, Yorks.), 240612, Sergt., *k. in a.*, F. & F., 25/4/18.

LUND, Harold, *e.* Harrogate, 43847, Pte., *k. in a.*, F. & F., 9/9/17.

LUND, Ernest, *b.* Leeds, *e.* Bradford, Yorks., 241456, Pte., *k. in a.*, F. & F., 25/4/18.

LUSCOMBE, Fred, *b.* Bingley, Yorks., *e.* Halifax, Yorks., 263040, Pte., *k. in a.*, F. & F., 9/10/17.

MAJOR, Nathaniel, *b.* Gateshead, *e.* Newcastle-on-Tyne (Gateshead), 242757, L./Cpl., *d. of w.*, F. & F., 12/6/17, *formerly* 28815 Durham Light Infantry.

MAKEPEACE, Thomas Frederick, *e.* Bletchley (Buckingham), 51123, Pte., *k. in a.*, F. & F., 11/10/18, *formerly* 38486 Worcester Regt.

MANSFIELD, William, *e.* London (Brixton), 51296, Pte., *k. in a.*, F. & F., 11/10/18, *formerly* 48813, Suffolk Regt.

MANSON, Charles, *e.* Bradford, Yorks. (Shipley, Yorks.), 240748, Pte., *k. in a.*, F. & F., 9/9/17.

MARCHAM, William, *b.* Chesham, *e.* Oxford, 72573, Pte., *d. of w.*, F. & F., 13/8/18, *formerly* 1599 Oxford & Bucks. Light Infantry.

MARGERISON, Albert, *b.* Thornbury, Yorks., *e.* Bradford, Yorks., 2437, Pte., *d. of w.*, F. & F., 17/7/15.

MARGETTS, John, T. C., *b.* Bradford, Yorks. (Baildon, Yorks.), 2220, Pte., *d. of w.*, F. & F., 14/12/15.

MARSHALL, Thomas Crossley, *b.* Halifax, *e.* Huddersfield, Yorks., 260058, Pte., *k. in a.*, F. & F., 3/7/17, *formerly* 268332 West Riding Regt.

MARTIN, Edward, *b.* Bradford, *e.* Bradford, Yorks., 241548, L./Cpl., *d. of w.*, F. & F., 7/10/17.

MARTIN, George, *b.* York., *e.* York, 37184, Pte., *k. in a.*, F. & F., 25/4/18/

MARTIN, John, *b.* Greenwich, Kent., *e.* Bradford, Yorks. (Clayton, Yorks.), 4654, Pte., *k. in a.*, F. & F., 14/7/16.

MASON, Albert, *e.* Bradford, Yorks., 241854, Pte., *d.*, F. & F., 4/10/18.

MATHER, Joseph, *b.* Sheffield, *e.* Sheffield, 242718, Pte., *k. in a.*, F. & F., 9/12/17.

MATTHEWMAN, Charles, *b.* Bramley, Yorks., *e.* Bradford, Yorks. (Frizinghall, Yorks.), 2297, Pte., *k. in a.*, F. & F., 15/7/16.

MATTHEWMAN, Frank, *b.* Frizinghall, Yorks., *e.* Bradford, Yorks., 1277, Cpl., *k. in a.*, F. & F., 21/7/16.

MAWSON, Harry, *e.* Leeds (Rothwell, Yorks.), 306466, Pte., *d.*, F. & F., 23/6/18.

MAWSON, Samuel, *b.* Yeadon, Yorks., *e.* Yeadon, Yorks., 5506, Pte., *k. in a.*, F. & F., 15/8/16.

MAWSON, William, *e.* Leeds (Woodhouse, Leeds), 242964, Cpl., *k. in a.*, F. & F., 9/10/17.

MAY, Lawrence, *b.* Bradford, *e.* Bradford, Yorks., 260060, Pte., *d. of w.*, F. & F., 3/7/17.

MEAD, George, *b.* Borobridge, Yorks., *e.* Halifax, Yorks., 268629, Pte., *k. in a.*, F. & F., 9/10/17.

MEARS, Percy, John, *b.* Hackney, London, *e.* Hackney (Clapton, London) 54221, Pte., *k. in a.*, F. & F., 11/10/18.

METCALFE, John, Archie, *e.* Otley, Yorks. (Steeton, Yorks.), 201469. Pte., *k. in a.*, F. & F., 5/12/17.

METCALFE, Joseph William, *e.* Bradford, Yorks. (Bradford), 2969, Pte., *k. in a.*, F. & F., 22/5/15.

METCALFE, Walter, *b.* Saddleworth, Lancs., *e.* Leeds, 306613, Pte., *k. in a.*, F. & F., 25/4/18.

MIDGLEY, Jesse, *e.* Bradford, Yorks., 241278, Pte., *k. in a.*, F. & F., 9/10/17.

MIDGLEY, John Thomas, *b.* Hebden Bridge, Yorks., *e.* Halifax, Yorks., 205307, Pte., *k. in a.*, F. & F., 3/5/18.

MIDGLEY, Walter, *b.* Bradford, *e.* Bradford, Yorks., 1171, Dmr., *k. in a.*, F. & F., 19/11/15.

MILNER, Frederick, *b.* York., *e.* York., 201829, Pte., *k. in a.*, F. & F., 9/10/17.

MILNES, Frederick Charles, *b.* Nuneaton, Staffs., *e.* Bradford, Yorks., 2408, Pte., *d. of w.*, F. & F., 17/11/15.

MILNES, Harry, *e.* Bradford, Yorks. (Bradford), 242639, Pte., *d. home,* 22/5/17.

MINNISS, William Herbert, *b.* Leamside, Durham, *e.* Bury St. Edmunds, 242801, Pte., *d. of w.*, F. & F., 11/8/18.

MITCHELL, Frank, *b.* Leeds, *e.* Leeds, 67975, Pte., *d. of w.*, F. & F., 6/3/19.

MITCHELL, Joseph, *e.* Bradford, Yorks. (Bradford), 2573, Pte., *d. of w.*, F. & F., 4/9/16.

MITCHELL, Thomas, *e.* Leeds (Leeds), 34175, Pte., *k. in a.*, F. & F., 25/4/18.

MODLEY, Samuel, *e.* Bradford, Yorks. (Bradford), 3736, Pte., *k. in a.*, F. & F., 12/7/16.

APPENDIX

MOORE, Thomas Marshall, *b.* Tweedmouth, *e.* Gateshead, Durham, 242755, Pte., *k. in a., F. & F.,* 11/10/18.

MOORE, Avon, *b.* Bangor, Co. Down, *e.* Bradford, Yorks., 1630, Pte., *k. in a., F. & F.,* 1/7/16.

MOORE, George, *b.* Gateshead, Durham, *e.* Newcastle-on-Tyne, 46233, Pte., *k. in a., F. & F.,* 6/12/17, *formerly* King's Own Light Infantry, 44717.

MOORE, Norman, *b.* Bradford, *e.* Bradford, Yorks., 2480, Pte., *k. in a., F. & F.,* 17/11/15.

MOORE, Percy, *b.* Leeds, *e.* Leeds, 7292, Pte., *d. of w., F. & F.,* 8/11/16.

MOORHOUSE, Albert, *b.* Drighlington, Yorks., *e.* Bradford, Yorks., 240007, Coy. Quarter-Master Sergt., *k. in a., F. & F.,* 10/8/18.

MORAN, Francis, *b.* Bradford, *e.* Bradford, Yorks., 1614, Pte., *k. in a., F. & F.,* 28/8/16.

MORGAN, Fred, *e.* Bradford, Yorks., 5077, Pte., *d. of w., F. & F.,* 15/7/16.

MORLAND, Matthew, *b.* Shildon, Durham, *e.* Bishop Auckland, 242754, Pte., *k. in a., F. & F.,* 3/9/16, *formerly* 28412 Durham Light Infantry.

MORRELL, Francis, *e.* York (York), 200908, Sergt., *k. in a., F. & F.,* 20/9/18.

MORTON, John William, *b.* Bradford, *e.* Bradford, Yorks., 4409, Pte., *k. in a., F. & F.,* 3/9/16.

MUSHAM, Wilfred, *b.* Ilkley, Yorks., *e.* Bradford, Yorks., 5550, Pte., *k. in a., F. & F.,* 15/8/16.

MYERS, William Baines, *b.* Burley, Leeds, *e.* Leeds, 467, Pte., *d.* home, 22/1/17.

McARD, Joseph, *e.* Douglas, I. of M. (Douglas, I. of M.), 62903, Pte., *k. in a., F. & F.,* 13/7/18.

McCORMACK, William, *b.* Chelsea, London, *e.* Fulham, London, 14394, *d. of w., F. & F.,* 29/4/18.

McDONALD, William, *b.* Bradford, *e.* Bradford, Yorks., 241654, Pte., *k. in a., F. & F.,* 25/4/18.

McGRATH, John William, *b.* Bradford, *e.* Bradford, Yorks., 2077, L./Cpl., *k. in a., F. & F.,* 1/7/16.

McGREGOR, Charles, *b.* Leeds, *e.* Colsterdale, Yorks., 15/1341, Pte., *k. in a., F. & F.,* 9/10/17.

McINTYRE, Cormick, *b.* Leeds, *e.* Leeds, 306018, Pte., *d., F. & F.,* 9/10/17.

McPHAIL, Owen, *b.* Bradford, *e.* Bradford, Yorks., 240268, Sergt., *k. in a., F. & F.,* 25/4/18.

MᶜPHAIL, William, *b.* Bradford, *e.* Bradford, Yorks., 1689, Pte., *k. in a.*,
F. & F., 6/10/15.

NAISWITH, John William, *b.* Sunderland, *e.* Bradford, Yorks., 1026,
Cpl., *d. of w.*, F. & F., 8/5/15.

NAYLOR, Harry, *b.* Bradford, *e.* Bradford, Yorks., 4376, Pte., *d. of w.*,
F. & F., 29/8/16.

NEEDHAM, Jeremiah, *b.* Bradford, *e.* Bradford, Yorks., 240292, Pte.,
d. of w., F. & F., 28/12/17.

NELSON, Seymour, *b.* St. Margarets, Durham, *e.* Durham, 242839,
Pte., *k. in a.*, F. & F., 9/6/17, *formerly* 28402, Durham Light
Infantry.

NEWBY, Charles Allan, *b.* Bradford, *e.* Bradford, Yorks., 2505, Pte.,
k. in a., F. & F., 19/8/15.

NICHOL, William Edwin, *b.* Barkisland, Yorks., *e.* Halifax (Sowood,
Halifax), 203384, Pte., *k. in a.*, F. & F., 27/4/18.

NICHOLSON, Ernest, *e.* Bradford, Yorks. (Bradford), 3902, Pte., *k. in a.*,
F. & F., 1/7/16.

NICHOLSON, Stewart, *e.* Bradford, Yorks. (Bradford), 3691, L./Cpl.,
k. in a., F. & F., 25/7/16.

NICKSON, Albert Horace, *b.* Liverpool, 62908, Pte., *k. in a.*, F. & F.,
11/10/18, *formerly* 5/82285 Liverpool Regt.

NIGHTINGALE, Andrew, *b.* Southport, Lancs., *e.* Bradford, Yorks.
(Bradford), 2373, L./Cpl., *k. in a.*, F. & F., 19/12/15.

NOLAN, Francis, *b.* Leeds, *e.* York, 7298, Pte., *k. in a.*, F. & F., 25/11/16.

NORMINGTON, Fred, *e.* Bradford, Yorks., 2534, Pte., *k. in a.*, F. & F.,
23/5/15.

NORTH, Harold, *b.* Wortley, Leeds, *e.* Leeds, 306745, Pte., *d. of w.*,
F. & F., 12/2/18.

NORTHEND, William, *e.* Bradford, Yorks. (Bradford), 3183, Pte., *k. in a.*,
F. & F., 16/12/15.

NORTON, James, *b.* Bradford, *e.* Bradford, Yorks., 241835, Pte., *d. of
w.*, F. & F., 6/12/17.

O'BRIEN, John, *b.* West Hartlepool, *e.* West Hartlepool, 7150, Pte., *k. in
a.*, F. & F., 23/11/16, *formerly* 9052, Durham Light Infantry.

O'GRADY, Edward, *e.* Bradford, Yorks. (Bradford), 2946, Pte., *k. in a.*,
F. & F., 19/11/15.

OLIVER, James, *b.* Sunderland, *e.* Sunderland, 242883, Pte., *k. in a.*,
F. & F., 9/10/17, formerly 28273 Durham Light Infantry.

ONION, John, *b.* Bradford, *e.* Bradford, Yorks., 1704, Pte., *d. of w.*,
F. & F., 11/9/16.

OVERTON, George, Frederick, *e.* Bradford, Yorks., 681, Sergt., *k. in a.*,
F. & F., 7/9/15.

APPENDIX

OXLEY, John Robert, *e.* Bradford, Yorks. (Bradford), 241079, Pte., *d. of w., F. & F.,* 28/4/18.

PADLEY, George, *b.* Bradford, *e.* Bradford, Yorks., 4623, Pte., *k. in a., F. & F.,* 3/9/16.

PALEY, Benjamin, James, *b.* Glasgow, *e.* Bradford, Yorks., 2088, Pte., *k. in a., F. & F.,* 24/6/15.

PARKER, George, *b.* Shipley, Yorks., *e.* Bradford, Yorks., 2344, Pte., *k. in a., F. & F.,* 5/9/15.

PARKER, Harold, *b.* Nottingham, *e.* Nottingham, 47094, Pte., *k. in a., F. & F.,* 25/4/18, *formerly* 68411, Sherwood Foresters.

PARKER, Harold, *e.* Bradford, Yorks. (Bradford), 240959, L./Cpl., *k. in a., F. & F.,* 25/4/18.

PARKIN, Edward, *b.* South Hetton, Durham, *e.* Sunderland, 242892, Pte., *d. of w., F. & F.,* 13/10/17.

PARKINSON, Albert, *e.* Bradford, Yorks. (Bradford), 3503, Pte., *k. in a., F. & F.,* 1/7/16.

PARKINSON, Charles Henry, *e.* Sheffield (Rotherham), 242720, Pte., *d. of w., F. & F.,* 12/11/17.

PARKINSON, Henry, *e.* Bradford, Yorks. (Bradford), 3455, Pte., *k. in a., F. & F.,* 7/11/15.

PARKINSON, Lance, *b.* Queensbury, Yorks., *e.* Ripon, Yorks., 16/1739, Pte., *k. in a., F. & F.,* 7/10/17.

PARKINSON, Robert, *b.* Dewsbury, Yorks., *e.* Bradford, Yorks. (Bradford), 1659, Pte., *k. in a., F. & F.,* 21/7/16.

PARKINSON, William, *e.* Bradford, Yorks. (Bradford), 3171, Pte., *k. in a., F. & F.,* 1/7/16.

PARRATT, Edwin, *e.* Bradford, Yorks. (Bradford), 240482, Pte., *k. in a., F. & F.,* 3/9/16.

PARRY, Edward, *e.* Leeds (Leeds), 306008, Pte., *k. in a., F. & F.,* 25/4/18.

PATCHETT, John, *e.* Halifax, Yorks. (Hebden Bridge, Yorks.), 242618, Pte., *k. in a., F. & F.,* 25/4/18.

PATEFIELD, Ernest Edward, *e.* Bradford, Yorks., 2830, L./Cpl., *d. of w., F. & F.,* 20/7/16.

PAYTON, James, *e.* Bradford, Yorks., 3374, Pte., *k. in a., F. & F.,* 25/5/15.

PEARCE, Cyril, *b.* Bradford, *e.* Bradford, Yorks., 241779, L./Cpl., *k. in a., F. & F.,* 3/9/16.

PEEL, Thomas, *b.* South Shields, *e.* South Shields, 307309, Pte., *k. in a., F. & F.,* 7/12/17, *formerly* 3949, 7th Durham Light Infantry.

PERKINS, James, *e.* Bradford, Yorks. (Queensbury, Yorks.), 240761, Pte., *d. of w., F. & F.,* 24/7/17.

PETERSON, Lawrence, *b.* North Shields, *e.* Newcastle-on-Tyne, 242993, Pte., *k. in a.*, F. & F., 10/8/18, *formerly* 28851, Durham Light Infantry.

PHELPS, William Charles, *b.* Kendal, Westmoreland, *e.* Burnley, Lancs., 7131, Pte., *k. in a.*, F. & F., 22/10/16, *formerly* 30927, Durham Light Infantry.

PHILLIPS, William, *e.* Bradford, Yorks., 3361, Pte., *d. of w.*, F. & F., 17/8/16.

PICKARD, John Richard, *b.* Leeds, *e.* Leeds, 49724, Pte., *d.*, F. & F., 19/11/18.

PICKERING, Herbert, *e.* Bradford, Yorks. (Bradford), 240929, Pte., *k. in a.*, F. & F., 9/10/17.

PICKTHALL, Ronald, *b.* Market Harboro', Leicester, *e.* Leeds, 48577, Cpl., *k. in a.*, F. & F., 25/4/18.

PIGGOTT, Samuel, *b.* Anerley, London, *e.* Croydon, 325172, Pte., *k. in a.*, F. & F., 11/10/18, *formerly* 290923, Hants. Cyclist Battalion.

PILLING, John, *b.* Bacup, Lancs., *e.* Rawtenstall, 62949, Pte., *k. in a.*, F. & F., 11/10/18.

PINNER, Charles, *b.* Rotherham, *e.* Rotherham, Yorks., 242722, Pte., *k. in a.*, F. & F., 12/6/17.

PITMAN, Cyril Charles, *b.* Anerley, London, *e.* Cromar (Croydon), 56734, Pte., *d. of w.*, F. & F., 7/5/18, *formerly* R. F. A., 166091.

PLACKETT, Harry, *b.* Moorallerton, Leeds, *e.* Leeds, 305413, Sergt., *k. in a.*, F. & F., 25/4/18.

POLLARD, Henry, *b.* York, *e.* York, 242921, Pte., *d. of w.*, F. & F., 7/6/17.

POOL, Alfred, *e.* Bradford, Yorks., 241214, Sergt., *k. in a.*, F. & F., 25/4/18.

POOLE, George, *b.* Leeds, *e.* York, 7286, Pte., *d. of w.*, F. & F., 29/1/17.

POTTAGE, John, *b.* Bradford, *e.* Bradford, Yorks., 205, Coy. Sergt. Major, *k. in a.*, F. & F., 12/8/15.

POWELL, Richard, *b.* Bradford, *e.* Bradford, Yorks., 2653, Cpl., *d. of w.*, F. & F., 4/8/15.

PRIESTLEY, Richard Henry, *b.* Bradford, *e.* Bradford, Yorks., 240592, Cpl., *k. in a.*, F. & F., 14/4/18.

PRITCHARD, James, *b.* Liverpool, *e.* Bradford, Yorks. (Princeville, Bradford), 4402, Pte., *k. in a.*, F. & F., 1/7/16.

PULLAN, Prince, *b.* Bradford, *e.* Bradford, Yorks., 307642, Rfm., *k. in a.*, F. & F., 25/4/18.

RAIN, Harry, *b.* Bradford, *e.* Bradford, Yorks., 241763, Pte., *k. in a.*, F. & F., 3/9/16.

APPENDIX

RAKNSEN, Harry, *b.* Leeds, *e.* York, 32837, Pte., *k. in a.*, F. & F., 9/10/17.

RAMSBOTHAM, Roland, *b.* Bradford, *e.* Bradford, Yorks., 240594, Pte., *d. of w.*, F. & F., 27/4/18.

RAWLINGS, Charles, *b.* Bradford, *e.* Bradford, Yorks., 1145, Sergt., *k. in a.*, F. & F., 3/9/16.

RAYNER, James, *b.* Bradford, *e.* Bradford, Yorks., 1458, Pte., *k. in a.*, F. & F., 30/8/16.

REECE, Harold, *e.* Bradford, Yorks. (Bradford), 3117, Pte., *k. in a.*, F. & F., 3/9/16.

REGAN, William, *b.* Leeds, *e.* Leeds, 242680, Pte., *d.*, F. & F., 9/7/18.

RENNEY, Fred, *e.* Bradford, Yorks. (Bradford), 4269, Pte., *d. of w.*, F. & F., 4/7/16.

RESTALL, Eldred, *e.* Bradford, Yorks. (Bradford), 4000, Pte., *d. of w.*, F. & F., 29/8/16.

REYNOLDS, John William, *e.* Bradford, Yorks. (Bradford), 3100, Pte., *d. of w.*, home, 16/9/16.

RHODES, Percy, *e.* Bradford, Yorks. (Pudsey, Yorks.), 4588, Pte., *d. of w.*, F. & F., 12/7/16.

RICHARDSON, Albert, *b.* Durham, *e.* Bearpark, 7132, Pte., *k. in a.*, F. & F., 23/11/16, *formerly* 30085, Durham Light Infantry.

RICHARDSON, Sam, *b.* Leeds, *e.* Leeds, 28238, Pte., *d. of w.*, F. & F., 12/10/18.

RICK, George William, *b.* North Shields, *e.* Gateshead, 242762, Pte., *k. in a.*, F. & F., 9/10/17, *formerly* 28859, Durham Light Infantry.

RIDLEY, James, *b.* Hayton, near Carlisle, *e.* Seaham, 242763, Pte., *d. of w.*, F. & F., 19/3/17, *formerly* 28241, 17th Durham Light Infantry.

RILEY, Abraham, *b.* Leeds, *e.* Leeds, 263022, Pte., *d.*, F. & F., 9/10/18.

RILEY, Ernest, *e.* Bradford, Yorks. (Bradford), 6558, Pte., *k. in a.*, F. & F., 23/11/16.

ROBERTSHAW, Harold, *e.* Bradford, Yorks. (Allerton, Yorks.), 242611, Pte., *k. in a.*, F. & F., 28/12/17.

ROBERTSHAW, Simpson, *b.* Bradford, *e.* Bradford, Yorks., 4672, Pte., *d. of w.*, F. & F., 24/7/16.

ROBINSON, Charles, *e.* Bradford, Yorks. (Hyde, Cheshire), 3127, Pte., *k. in a.*, F. & F., 19/11/15.

ROBINSON, Fred, *e.* Bradford, Yorks., 3474, Pte., *k. in a.*, F. & F., 17/7/15.

ROBINSON, Harry, *e.* Bradford, Yorks. (Bradford), 3807, Pte., *d.*, at sea, 17/11/15.

ROBSON, George William, *b.* Newcastle-on-Tyne, *e.* Gateshead, 7076, Pte., *k. in a.*, F. & F., 23/11/16, *formerly* 30868 Durham Light Infantry.

ROLFE, Fred, *b.* Merton, Surrey, *e.* Whitehall (Wimbledon), 54177, Pte., *k. in a.*, F. & F., 11/10/18.

ROSS, Frederick Gilbert, *e.* Bradford, Yorks. (Bradford), 2766, Pte., *d. of w.*, F. & F., 6/7/16.

ROWLANDS, Matthew, *e.* Sunderland (Ryhope, Durham), 242885, Pte., *k. in a.*, F. & F., 3/7/17, *formerly* 30496, 23rd Durham Light Infantry.

RUDDEN, James, *e.* Bradford, Yorks., 241820, Pte., *k. in a.*, F. & F., 3/9/16.

RUDDICK, Frederick, *b.* Newby, Yorks., *e.* York, 200388, L./Cpl., *d.*, F. & F., 8/5/18.

RUDOLPH, George, *b.* Bradford, *e.* Bradford, Yorks., 1839, Pte., *k. in a.*, F. & F., 19/12/15.

RUSHTON, Eric., *b.* Bradford, *e.* Bradford, Yorks., 1880, Pte., *d. of w.*, F. & F., 3/7/16.

SABB, Harold, *b.* Cutsyke, Yorks., *e.* Castleford, Yorks., 43767, Pte., *d. of w.*, F. & F., 17/10/18, *formerly* 28194 King's Own Yorkshire Light Infantry.

SANDERSON, Richard, *b.* Leeds, *e.* Leeds, 49664, Pte., *k. in a.*, F. & F., 25/4/18.

SAWYER, Zeptha, *b.* Helmington, Durham, *e.* Bishop Auckland, 7259, Pte., *k. in a.*, F. & F., 22/10/16.

SAYERS, Joseph, *b.* West Bowling, Yorks., *e.* Bradford, Yorks. (Bradford), 2626, Sergt., *k. in a.*, F. & F., 15/7/16., D.C.M.

SAYERS, Reginald Herbert, *b.* Bow, Middlesex, *e.* Leyton (Leyton), 54196, Pte., *k. in a.*, F. & F., 11/10/18.

SCANLON, George William, *b.* Bradford, *e.* Bradford, Yorks., 4381, Pte., *d.*, F. & F., 16/2/16.

SCHOFIELD, Charles, *b.* Bradford, *e.* Bradford, Yorks., 240478, Pte., *d.*, F. & F., 31/10/18.

SCHOFIELD, Willie, *e.* Bradford (Bradford, Yorks.), 241846, Cpl., *d,.* F. & F., 1/8/18.

SCOTT, William, *b.* Harrogate, *e.* Harrogate, Yorks., 242628, Pte., *k. in a.*, F. & F., 11/10/18.

SELF, Rowland, Amos, *b.* Brampton, Suffolk, *e.* York, 21529, Pte., *k. in a.*, F. & F., 25/4/18, M. M.

SHARPE, William, *e.* Bradford, Yorks. (Bradford), 3831, Cpl., *d. of w.*, F. & F., 6/12/16.

APPENDIX

SHEPHERD, Charles, *b.* Leeds, *e.* Leeds, 306102, Pte., *k. in a.*, F. & F., 25/4/18.

SHIRLEY, John, *b.* Shoreditch, *e.* Walthamstow, 54191, Pte., *k. in a.*, F. & F., 11/10/18.

SHUTTLEWOOD, Harry, *b.* Roydon, Essex, *e.* Selby, Yorks., 242624, Cpl., *k. in a.*, F. & F., 9/10/17.

SIDDALL, Thomas, *b.* Richmond, Yorks., *e.* Richmond, Yorks., 260083, Pte., *k. in a.*, F. & F., 9/10/17, *formerly* Northumberland Fusiliers, 31554.

SILSBY, Bernard, *b.* Hitchin, Herts., *e.* Bradford, Yorks. (Bradford), 1173, Pte., *k. in a.*, F. & F., 12/7/16.

SILVERWOOD, Allen, *b.* Bradford, *e.* Bradford, Yorks., 241647, L./Cpl., *d. of w.*, F. & F., 11/11/17, D.C.M., M.M.

SIMPSON, Arthur, *b.* Bradford, *e.* Bradford, Yorks., 1722, Pte., *k. in a.*, F. & F., 19/11/15.

SIMPSON, George, Cuthbert, *b.* Bolton, Bradford, *e.* Bradford, Yorks., 1773, Coy. Quarter-Master Sergt., *k. in a.*, F. & F., 3/9/16., D.C.M.

SIMPSON, George, *b.* Hull, *e.* Leeds, 242942, Pte., *k. in a.*, F. & F., 25/4/18.

SIMPSON, William, *b.* Ripon, *e.* Ripon, 307466, Pte., *k. in a.*, F. & F., 25/4/18.

SKINNER, Frederick, James, *b.* Bexhill, Sussex, *e.* Maidstone, 62608, Pte., *d. of w.*, home, 2/11/18.

SMITH, Arthur, *b.* Windhill, Yorks., *e.* Bradford, Yorks., 2108, Pte., *k. in a.*, F. & F., 3/6/15.

SMITH, Albert Archer, *e.* Bradford, Yorks. (Bradford), 241237, Pte., *k. in a.*, F. & F., 3/9/16.

SMITH, Frederick Thomas, *b.* Blackburn, *e.* Blackburn, Lancs., 62976, Pte., *k. in a.*, F. & F., 11/10/18, *formerly* 2/66272 Manchester Regt.

SMITH, Harry, *e.* Bradford, Yorks., 2287, Pte., *k. in a.*, F. & F., 12/10/15

SMITH, Herbert Henry, *e.* Birmingham, 54194, Pte., *d., of w.*, F. & F., 15/10/18.

SMITH, John Thomas, *e.* Halifax, Yorks. (Wainstalls, Yorks.), 242619, Rfm., *d. of w.*, F. & F., 5/8/18.

SMITH, Lawrence, *e.* Bradford, Yorks. (Great Horton, Bradford), 242201, Pte., *k. in a.*, F. & F., 25/4/18.

SMITH, William, Henry, *b.* Shipley, Yorks., *e.* Bradford, Yorks., 240882, Pte., *k. in a.*, F. & F., 9/10/17.

SMITHIES, Thomas, *e.* Bradford, Yorks., 3031, Cpl., *k. in a.*, F. & F., 19/11/15.

SOUTH, George, *b.* Sanden, Herts., *e.* Bradford, Yorks., 18/1219, Pte., *k. in a., F. & F.,* 25/4/18.

SOUTHWELL, Fred, *b.* Norland, Yorks., *e.* Blatchley, Bucks., 27726, Cpl., *k. in a., F. & F.,* 11/10/18.

SOUTHWELL, Harry Jim., *b.* Nottingham, *e.* Glen Power, Wigston, 63728, Pte., *d. of w., F. & F.,* 16/10/18.

SOUTHWICK, Reginald, *b.* Watton, Yorks., *e.* Leeds, 48950, Pte., *k. in a., F. & F.,* 25/4/18.

SPARKES, Ernest John, *b.* Kensington, London, *e.* Hammersmith, London, 54197. Pte., *k. in a., F. & F.,* 10/8/18, *formerly* TR./-10/4257, Royal Sussex Regt.

SPENCER, Charles, *e.* Ashbourn (Ashbourne), 42098, Pte., *k. in a., F. & F.,* 3/5/18, *formerly* 69276, Sherwood Foresters.

SPENCER, Wilson, *b.* Windhill, Yorks., *e.* Bradford, Yorks., 4899, Pte., *k. in a., F. & F.,* 14/7/16.

SPINKS, Alfred, *b.* Hacknay, London, *e.* Stratford, London, 204189, Pte., *k. in a., F. & F.,* 11/10/18, *formerly* Rifle Brigade, 20968.

STANSFIELD, John, *b.* Shipley, Yorks., *e.* Bradford, Yorks. (Bradford), 1626, Pte., *k. in a., F. & F.,* 22/7/16.

STANTON, James, *e.* Bradford, Yorks. (Bradford), 2592, Pte., *k. in a., F. & F.,* 19/12/15.

STEAD, Lester, *b.* Bradford, *e.* Bradford, Yorks., 241528, Pte., *k. in a., F. & F.,* 25/4/18.

STEEL, Luther, *b.* Huddersfield, *e.* Huddersfield, Yorks., 16/1596, Pte., *k. in a., F. & F.,* 20/7/18.

STEVENS, Arthur Walter, *b.* Wilmington, Kent, *e.* Dartford, Kent, 51154, Pte., *d., F. & F.,* 17/10/18, *formerly* 33669 Worcestershire Regt.

STEVENSON, Edgar, *e,* Bradford, Yorks. (Bradford), 3619, Pte., *k. in a., F. & F.,* 15/7/16.

STOTT, Edgar, *b.* Bradford, *e.* Bradford, Yorks., 4636, Pte., *k. in a., F. & F.,* 17/2/16.

STRINGER, Herbert George, *b.* Bradford, *e.* Bradford, Yorks., 1412, Pte., *k. in a., F. & F.,* 5/9/15.

STYLE, Henry George, *b.* Canterbury, Kent, *e.* Holloway, London, 54272, L./Cpl., *d. of w., F. & F.,* 24/10/18.

STYLES, Cyril, *b.* Idle, Yorks., *e.* Bradford, Yorks. (Eccleshill, Yorks.), 263031, Pte., *d. of w., F. & F.,* 1/11/17.

SUTCLIFFE, Arnold, *b.* Bradford, *e.* Bradford, Yorks., 240551, Pte., *k. in a., F. & F.,* 3/9/16.

SUTCLIFFE, Joseph, *e.* Bradford, Yorks. (West Bowling, Yorks.), 2806, Pte., *k. in a., F. & F.,* 20/12/15.

APPENDIX

SWAIN, Thomas Lewis, *b.* Hunslet, Yorks., *e.* Leeds, 242523, Cpl., *k. in a., F. & F.*, 9/10/17.

SWAN, Robert, *b.* Houghton-le-Skerne, Durham, *e.* Darlington, 7184, Pte., *k. in a., F. & F.*, 3/9/16, *formerly* 15/153, Durham Light Infantry.

SWIFT, Joe Sykes, *e.* Harrogate (Wakefield), 5630, Pte., *d. of w., F. & F.*, 22/8/16, *formerly* 4028/3/1 Queen's Own Yorkshire Dragoons.

SYKES, Sydney William, *b.* Manchester, *e.* Manchester, 62975, Pte., *k. in a., F. & F.*, 11/10/18.

SYKES, Horace Frederick, *b.* Sheffield, *e.* Sheffield, 268117, Pte., *k. in a., F. & F.*, 25/4/18.

TAIT, Horace William, *b.* Sheffield, *e.* Sheffield, 270096, Pte., *k. in a., F. & F.*, 5/4/18.

TANE, Jerome, *e.* Bradford, Yorks. (Bradford), 307529, Pte., *d. of w., F. & F.*, 24/4/18.

TAYLOR, Albert, *b.* Bradford, *e.* Bradford, Yorks., 1906, Cpl., *k. in a., F. & F.*, 11/10/15.

TAYLOR, Joseph, *b.* Leeds, *e.* Leeds, 16487, Pte., *d., F. & F.*, 27/10/18, *formerly* 12392, East Yorks. Regt.

TAYLOR, John, *e.* Blyth (Cowper, Blyth), 46204, Pte., *k. in a., F. & F.*, 12/10/18, *formerly* 44414 King's Own Yorkshire Light Infantry.

DE-TCHERNIADIEFF, Vladimir, *b.* Russia, *e.* London, 54202, Pte., *k. in a., F. & F.*, 11/10/18.

TEMPEST, Fred, *b.* Bradford, *e.* Bradford, Yorks., 18/892, Pte., *d. of w., F. & F.*, 9/6/18.

TEMPLE, Thomas Charles, *b.* Stratford, *e.* Stratford, 54204, Pte., *k. in a., F. & F.*, 11/10/18.

TEMPLEMORE, Robert Frank, *b.* Hampstead, London, *e.* Whitehall, S.W. (Islington, London), 54200, Pte., *k. in a., F. & F.*, 11/10/18, *formerly* TR/10/109513 97th T. R.

THIRKILL, Edward, *e.* Bradford, Yorks., 241400, Pte., *k. in a., F. & F.*, 7/10/17.

THOMPSON, Albert, *b.* Tamworth, Staffs., *e.* Rugeley, 63735, Pte., *d. of w., F. & F.*, 15/7/18, *formerly* 22253, Machine Gun Corps.

THOMPSON, Alban Ruddock, *b.* Leeds, *e.* Leeds, 39773, Pte., *k. in a., F. & F.*, 25/4/18.

THOMPSON, William, *b.* Walker, Northumberland, *e.* Sunderland, 63736, Pte., *k. in a., F. & F.*, 11/10/18.

THOMPSON, Willie, *b.* Thornbury, Bradford, *e.* Bradford, Yorks., 2316, Pte., *k. in a., F. & F.*, 12/7/16.

THORNTON, Percy, *b.* Huddersfield, *e.* Huddersfield, Yorks., 32135, Pte., *k. in a., F. & F.*, 11/10/18.

THORNTON, Sydney, *b.* Bradford, *e.* Bradford, Yorks., 240272, **Pte.**, *k. in a.*, *F. & F.*, 3/9/16.

THORNTON, Willie, *e.* Bradford, Yorks. (Drighlington, Yorks.), 2917, Cpl., *k. in a.*, *F. & F.*, 22/10/16.

THORPE, George Henry, *b.* St. Lukes, Middlesex, *e.* Stratford, London, 52480, Pte., *k. in a.*, *F. & F.*, 25/4/18, *formerly* 34138, 5th Res. Cavalry Regt.

THROUP, William, *b.* Long Preston, Yorks., *e.* Keighley, Yorks. (Barnoldswick), 38132, Pte., *d. of w.*, *F. & F.*, 27/4/18.

TIMMS, John, *b.* St. Andrews, Newcastle-on-Tyne, *e.* Newcastle-on-Tyne, 268352, Pte., *k. in a.*, *F. & F.*, 11/10/18.

TINDALL, Frederick, *e.* Bradford, Yorks. (Bradford), 2590, Pte., *k. in a.*, *F. & F.*, 1/7/16.

TIPPING, Walter, *e.* Bradford, Yorks. (Bradford), 241505, Pte., *k. in a.*, *F. & F.*, 25/4/18.

TOFT, Arthur, *e.* York (York), 201209, Pte., *k. in a.*, *F. & F.*, 19/4/18.

TOMLINSON, John, *b.* Bradford, *e.* Bradford, Yorks., 1593, L./Cpl., *k. in a.*, *F. & F.*, 3/9/16.

TOMLINSON, James, *e.* Bradford, Yorks. (Bradford), 3657, L./Cpl., *k. in a.*, *F. & F.*, 15/7/16.

TONG, Edward, *b.* Leeds, *e.* Bradford, Yorks., 1236, L./Cpl., *k. in a.*, *F. & F.*, 3/9/16.

TOPHAM, Arthur Carr, *b.* Harrogate, *e.* Harrogate, 200060, L./Sergt., *k. in a.*, *F. & F.*, 11/10/18.

TUCKER, William, *b.* Esh Winning, Durham, *e.* Stanley, Durham, 47112, Pte., *k. in a.*, *F. & F.*, 12/10/18.

TURNBULL, Alfred, *b.* Sunderland, *e.* Sunderland, 242886, Pte., *d. of w.*, *F. & F.*, 23/7/17, *formerly* 23/50, Durham Light Infantry.

TURNER, George, *b.* Bradford, *e.* Bradford, Yorks., 1468, L./Cpl., *k. in a.*, *F. & F.*, 2/8/16.

TURNER, John Charles, *b.* Finsbury, *e.* Finsbury, 54199, Pte., *k. in a.*, *F. & F.*, 12/10/18.

TURPIN, Noah, *b.* Bradford, *e.* Bradford, Yorks., 2115, L./Cpl., *k. in a.*, *F. & F.*, 1/7/16.

TURPIN, Wilfred, *e.* Bradford, Yorks. (Bradford), 2596, Pte., *k. in a.*, *F. & F.*, 28/2/16.

TUXFORD, Sam, *b.* Bradford, *e.* Bradford, Yorks., 4697, Pte., *d. of w.*, *F. & F.*, 7/7/16.

UNDERWOOD, Stanley, *b.* West Bowling, Yorks., *e.* Bradford, Yorks., 240046, L./Sergt., *k. in a.*, *F. & F.*, 25/4/18.

VARLEY, Harry, *e.* Bradford, Yorks., 2306, Sergt., *k. in a.*, *F. & F.*, 14/8/16.

APPENDIX

VEAR, Thomas, *b.* York, *e.* York, 200513, Pte., *k. in a.*, F. & F., 25/4/18.

VENTRESS, Benjamin, *e.* Gildersome, Yorks. (Gildersome), 6600, Pte., *k. in a.*, F. & F., 23/11/16.

VIRR, George, *e.* Bradford, Yorks. (Bradford), 241728, Pte., *d.*, F. & F., 5/3/18.

VOINUS, Samuel, *e.* Bradford, Yorks. (Bradford), 3185, L./Cpl., *k. in a.*, F. & F., 12/7/16.

WADE, James Edward, *e.* Bradford, Yorks. (Bradford), 3789, Pte., *k. in a.*, F. & F., 26/8/16.

WADDINGTON, Arthur, *b.* Bradford, *e.* Bradford, Yorks., 4234, Pte., *k. in a.*, F. & F., 7/8/16.

WAGG, Harold Victor, *b.* Chesterfield, *e.* Chesterfield, Derbyshire, 60770, Pte., *k. in a.*, F. & F., 20/7/18.

WAITE, Ernest, *e.* Halifax, Yorks., 46311, Pte., *d.*, F. & F., 15/4/19.

WALKER, Charles, *b.* Bradford, *e.* Bradford, Yorks., 241713, Pte., *d. of w.*, F. & F., 17/4/18.

WALKER, Fred, *b.* Shipley, Yorks., *e.* Bradford, Yorks., 1498, Pte., *k. in a.*, F. & F., 10/8/15.

WALKER, Gilbert, *e.* Bradford, Yorks. (Bradford), 2549, Pte., *d. of w.*, F. & F., 12/5/15.

WALKER, John, *e.* Bradford, Yorks. (Bradford), 240910, L./Cpl. *k. in a.*, F. & F., 25/4/18. M.M.

WALKER, Nicholas, *e.* Bradford, Yorks., 240164, L./Cpl., *k. in a.*, F. & F., 25/4/18.

WALKER, Richard, *b.* Bradford, *e.* Bradford, Yorks., 4190, Pte., *d. of w.*, F. & F., 15/7/16.

WALLACE, Maurice, *b.* Stepney, London, *e.* Whitehall, S.W. (Bethnal Green), 54211, Pte., *k. in a.*, F. & F., 12/10/18.

WALLER, John, *e.* Bradford, Yorks. (Wibsey, Yorks.), 240659, Pte., *k. in a.*, F. & F., 2/3/17.

WALMSLEY, William, *b.* Bradford, *e.* Bradford, Yorks., 240011, Coy. Sergt.-Major, *d.*, F. & F., 27/10/18. Croix de Guerre.

WALSH, Richard, *b.* Wakefield, Yorks., *e.* Leeds (Leeds), 260071, Pte., *d. of w.*, F. & F., 29/4/18.

WALTON, Harold, *b.* Todmorden, Yorks., *e.* Halifax, Yorks., 242659, Pte., *d. of w.*, F. & F., 12/3/18.

WALTON, Norman, *b.* Durham, *e.* Durham, 242848, Pte., *k. in a.*, F. & F., 6/12/17.

WARDELL, John William, *b.* Swinton, Yorks., *e,* Bradford, Yorks., 1235, Pte., *d. of w.*, F. & F., 3/7/16.

WARNE, William Arthur, *e.* Leeds, 305776, Pte., *d.*, F. & F., 29/9/18.

WARRENER, George Arthur, *e.* Bradford, Yorks., 3113, L./Cpl., *k. in a.,* F. & F., 19/12/15.

WARRIOR, Edward, *e.* York (Mansfield, Notts.), 235083, Pte., *k. in a.,* F. & F., 25/4/18.

WARWICK, Harry, *b.* Bannam, Essex, *e.* Ilkley, Yorks. (Ben Rhydding, Yorks.), 263051, Pte., *d. of w.,* F. & F., 11/10/17.

WASTENEY, Walter, *b.* Bradford, *e.* Bradford, Yorks., 1458, Sergt., *d. of w.,* F. & F., 17/9/16.

WATERHOUSE, Duke William, *e.* Bradford, Yorks., 241150, Pte., *d.,* F. & F., 23/10/18.

WATERHOUSE, Edward, *b.* Leeds, *e.* Leeds, 307806, Pte., *k. in a.,* F. & F., 6/12/17.

WATERWORTH, Walter, *e.* Bradford, Yorks., 240682, L./Cpl., *d. of w.,* F. & F., 8/4/17.

WATKINS, William, *b.* Shipley, Yorks., *e.* Bradford, Yorks., 1374, Pte., *k. in a.,* F. & F., 29/8/15.

WATMOUGH, Harold Rawnsley, *b.* Bradford, *e.* Bradford, Yorks., 2460, Sergt., *k. in a.,* F. & F., 1/7/16.

WATSON, Ernest, *b.* Leeds, *e.* Leeds, 32447, Sergt., *k. in a.,* F. & F., 15/9/18.

WATSON, Eric Thomas, *b.* Bradford, *e.* Bradford, Yorks., 904, Sergt., *k. in a.,* F. & F., 23/11/16.

WHARTON, Charles, *b.* Ripon, *e.* Ripon, Yorks., 28237, Pte., *k. in a.,* F. & F., 25/4/18.

WHITAKER, Charles, *e.* Bradford, Yorks. (Clayton, Yorks.), 241300, L./Cpl., *d. of w.,* F. & F., 8/10/17.

WHITAKER, Thomas, *b.* Leeds, *e.* Gildersome, Yorks., 270280, Pte., *d.,* F. & F., 26/9/18.

WHITE, Victor, *b.* Bradford, *e.* Bradford, Yorks, 240210, Pte., *k. in a.,* F. & F., 25/4/18.

WHITEHEAD, Harry, *b.* Bradford, *e.* Bradford, Yorks., 240142, Pte., *k. in a.,* F. & F., 12/6/17.

WHITELEY, Ivo., *b.* Huddersfield, Yorks., *e.* Haworth, Yorks., 46146, Pte., *d.,* F. & F., 6/8/18.

WIGNALL, George, *b.* Bradford, *e.* Bradford, Yorks., 4559, Pte., *k. in a.,* F. & F., 3/7/16.

WILD, George, *e.* Bradford, Yorks. (Bradford), 5484, Pte., *k. in a.,* F. & F., 15/8/16.

WILD, George Arthur, *e.* Bradford, Yorks., 241345, Pte., *k. in a.,* F. & F., 9/10/17.

WILKINSON, Edgar James, *b.* Middlesboro, *e.* Bradford, Yorks., 1266, L./Cpl., *k. in a.,* F. & F., 11/8/16. D.C.M.

APPENDIX

WILKINSON, Harold, *b.* Bradford, *e.* Bradford, Yorks., 1455, Pte., *k. in a.*, F. & F., 25/1/17.

WILKINSON, Joseph Ernest, *b.* Bradford, *e.* Bradford, Yorks., 2449, Pte., *d. of w.*, F. & F., 17/11/15.

WILSON, James, *b.* Bradford, *e.* Bradford, Yorks., 242192, Pte., *k. in a.*, F. & F., 3/9/16.

WILSON, Leonard, *b.* Newcastle-on-Tyne, *e.* Bradford, Yorks. (Manningham, Yorks), 16/349, Sergt., *k. in a.*, F. & F., 11/10/18.

WILSON, Percy, *b.* Leeds, *e.* Leeds, 49628, Pte., *k. in a.*, F. & F., 25/4/18.

WILSON, Willie, *b.* Bradford, *e.* Bradford, Yorks., 240262, L./Cpl., *k. in a.*, F. & F., 9/10/17.

WINTERFLOOD, Thomas, *b.* Kensington, *e.* Kensington, London, 54212, Pte., *d. of w.*, F. & F., 14/10/18.

WOLFE, Sidney, *b.* Liverpool, *e.* Liverpool, 62991, Pte., *k. in a.*, F. & F., 11/10/18.

WOOD, Harry, *e.* Bradford, Yorks. (West Bowling, Yorks.), 2928, Pte., *k. in a.*, F. & F., 3/9/16.

WOOD, Joshua M., *b.* Bradford, *e.* Bradford, Yorks., 2519, Pte., *drowned at sea*, 17/11/15.

WOOD, Percy Herbert, *b.* Newcastle-on-Tyne, *e.* South Shields, 63746, Pte., *d. of w.*, F. & F., 18/6/18.

WOODCOCK, Samuel, *e.* Liverpool, 63743, Pte., *k. in a.*, F. & F., 11/10/18.

WOODHOUSE, Charles, *b.* Brotherton, Yorks., *e.* Pontefract, 48661, Pte., *k. in a.*, F. & F., 11/10/18.

WOODHOUSE, James, *e.* Bradford, Yorks. (Bradford), 2749, Pte., *d. of w.*, F. & F., 19/7/16.

WORSNOP, Albert, *b.* Leeds, *e.* Leeds, 307148, Pte., *k. in a.*, F. & F., 20/4/18.

WORTH, Louis, *e.* York, 3778, Pte., *d.*, F. & F., 11/3/17.

YEADON, Victor, *b.* Bradford, *e.* Bradford, Yorks., 1280, Pte., *k. in a.*, F. & F., 12/10/15.

YEOWART, David, *b.* Dearham, Cumberland, *e.* Gateshead (Gateshead), 242773, Pte., *k. in a.*, F. & F., 25/4/18, *formerly* 30465, 17th Durham Light Infantry.

YOUD, Joseph Laidler, *b.* Gateshead, *e.* Gateshead, 63758, Pte., *k. in a.*, F. & F., 11/10/18.

YOUNG, George Shields, *b.* Bradford, *e.* Bradford, Yorks., 4544, Pte., *d. of w.*, F. & F., 29/11/16.

YOUNG, Martin, *b.* Shilbottle, Northumberland, *e.* Alnwick, 59673, Pte., *k. in a.*, F. & F., 11/10/18.

APPENDIX IV.*

Nominal Roll of Officers of 1/6th Battalion West Yorkshire Regiment, who served with the Battalion abroad from 1915-1918.

c. Mobilized or commissioned.   *w.* Wounded.   *d.* Demobilized.

ANDERTON, H. L., Lt.-Col., *c.* 4/8/14, *w.* 7/2/16, 9/10/17, *d.* 13/1/19.
ABLITT, M.C., B.E., Capt., *c.* 26/9/14.
ARCHER, B., 2nd Lieut., *c.* 31/10/17, *p. of w.*, 6/5/18, *d.* 20/9/19.
ARMISTEAD, T. E., Capt., *c.* 10/9/14, *w.* 26/10/16, *k. in a.*, 3/5/17.
ATKINSON, H., 2nd Lieut., *c.* 10/10/18, *d.* 29/4/19.
AMBLER, G., Lieut., *c.* 25/10/16, *d.* 15/4/19.
ALBISTON, F. C., 2nd Lieut., *c.*, 3/10/17.
BARKER, H. W., Major, *c.* 4/8/14, *w.* 3/11/17, *d.* 26/3/19.
BACKHOUSE, W. H., 2nd Lieut., *k. in a.*, 13/3/18.
BELDON, E., Lieut., *c.* 27/6/17, *p. of w.*, 25/4/18.
BEHRENS, H. J., Capt., *c.* 10/9/14, *w.*, 13/7/17, *d.*, 28/1/19.
BERNHARD, F. H., Lieut., *c.* 5/11/14, *d.*, 16/8/17.
BISATT, G. N., Capt. and Adjt., *c.* 26/7/16.
BIRCH, D.S.O., W. L., 2nd Lieut., *c.*, 27/2/15, *w.*, 29/11/15, *d.*, 7/4/19.
BRIGGS, J. J., Lieut., *c.*, 10/9/14, *d.*, 28/3/19.
BROADWITH, E. W., Lieut., *c.* 26/9/16, *w.*, 23/11/16, *d.*, 30/1/19
BURROWS, J., Lieut., *c.* 12/7/15.
COLES, H., Lieut., *c.* 6/1/16.
CHEETHAM, H., 2nd Lieut., *c.* 6/1/16, *k. in a.*, 9/10/17.
CLOUGH, M.C., R., Lt.-Col., *c.*, 4/8/14, *w.*, 4/7/16, ; 11/10/18, *d.*, 29/3/19.
COOKSON, F., 2nd Lieut., *c.*, 17/7/17, *d.*, 22/3/19.
DAWSON, S. T., Lieut., *c.*, 5/8/16, *w.*, 21/7/17, *d.*, 3/7/19.
DE GROOT, W. L., Lieut., *c.* 8/7/16.
DOBSON, R. G., Capt. acting Major, *c.*, 21/8/14, *died*, 4/1/19 (previously transf. M.G.C.).
DODD, N., 2nd Lieut., *c.* 27/3/15, *k. in a.*, 1/7/16.
EDWARDS, F., Lieut., *c.*, 28/7/16, *d.*, 26/7/19.
EMMISON, P. C., Lieut., *c.* 30/11/15.

---

* It is regretted this Roll is incomplete, but it was decided not to delay any further the publication of the history.

APPENDIX

FAIRBANK, M.M., F. E., Lieut., *c.*, 26/4/17, *w.* and *p. of w.*, 25/4/18, *d.*, 20/9/19.

FAIRBANK, A. S., 2nd Lieut., *c.*, 26/4/17, *w.*, 13/2/16, *d.*, 29/3/19.

FAWCETT, M.C., R. A., Major, *c.*, 5/8/14, *w.*, 1/7/16, *d.*, 15/1/18.

FAWCETT, M.C., W. L., Capt., *c.* 10/9/14. To Indian Army.

FELL, R. G., Capt., *c.*, 5/12/14, *d.*, 14/6/19.

GARFITT, W., 2nd Lieut., *c.*, 26/9/17, *d.*, 22/4/19.

GORDON, M.C., J. S., Capt., *c.*, -/2/15, *w.*, 5/7/16, *p. of w.*, 25/4/18, *d.*, 6/2/19.

GORDON, S. J., Capt., *c.* 4/8/14.

GOODALL, J. A., Lieut., *c.*, 26/4/17, *w.*, 29/7/17, 10/1/18, *d.*, 1/11/19.

GREGORY, E. C., Capt., *c.*, 2/10/14, *w.*, 3/5/17, *d.*, 1/5/19.

GREENWOOD, M.C., L., 2nd Lieut., *c.*, 31/10/17, *w.*, 18/6/18, *d.*, 2/2/19.

GRICE, N., Capt., *c.*, 21/8/14, *w.*, 25/8/15, 1/7/16, 19/11/17, *d.*, 20/2/19.

HAMILTON, A., Capt., R.A.M.C., *c.*, 4/8/14, *w.*, 1/7/16, *d.*, 27/2/19.

HARRISON, A. R., 2nd Lieut., *c.*, 26/7/16, *w.*, 22/11/16, 30/3/18, *d.*, 28/3/19.

HARTNELL, J. W., Lieut., *c.* 16/11/15.

HARPER, C. R., 2nd Lieut., *k. in a.*, 15/7/16.

HAMILTON, J., 2nd Lieut., *c.*, 30/7/18, *d.*, 11/11/19.

HEARN, S. G., Capt., *c.*, 5/5/15, *w.*, 3/9/16, *d.*, 3/3/19.

HESELTON, D.S.O., J. L., Lt.-Col., *c.* 4/8/14, *w.*, 1/7/16, transf. Worcester Regt.

HEATON, S. T., 2nd Lieut., *k. in a.*, 27/9/16.

HENRICH, C. G., *c.* 21/11/15.

HEPBURN, D.L.I., 2nd Lieut., *c.* 1/8/17, *k. in a.*, 25/4/18.

HESKETH, J., 2nd Lieut., *c.*, 28/11/17, *k. in a.*, 14/10/18.

HESKETH, B., Lieut., *c.* 1/7/17.

HICK, M.C., B., Lieut., *c.*, 1/8/17, *w.*, 20/11/17, 17/10/18, *d.*, 20/2/20.

HIGGINS, C. G., 2nd Lieut., *c.*, 6/3/15, *d. of w.*, 1/7/16.

HILL, M. W., Capt., *c.*, 10/9/14, *w.*, 6/9/16, 17/3/17, *d.*, 19/4/19 (transf. M.G.C.).

HILL, M.C., W. H., Lieut.Col. and Q.M., *c.*, 4/8/14, *d.*, 1/4/20.

HICKSON, S. V. H., 2nd Lieut., *c.* 26/5/15, *w.* 1/7/16.

HOLLINGS, H., Lieut., *c.*, 18/11/15, *d.*, 25/3/19.

HORNSHAW, M.C., F. G., Lieut.-Col., *c.*, 10/9/14, *d.*, 15/11/19.

HUDSON, R.A., Lt.-Col., *k. in a.*, 11/10/17.

ILLINGWORTH, J., 2nd Lieut., *k. in a.*, 1/1/18.

JACKSON, H. E., 2nd Lieut., *c.* 6/7/16, *k. in a.* 12/6/17.

JOWETT, H. A., Capt., *c.*, 25/8/15, *w.*, 11/10/18.

JOWETT, H. E., Lieut., *p. of w.*, 25/4/18.
KITCHEN, H. B., Lieut., *c.*, 25/6/18, *d.*, 3/2/19.
KNOWLES, E. W., Capt., *c.*, 3/8/14, *w.*, 25/9/15, 24/7/16, *d.*, 6/6/18.
LAING, A. V. S., 2nd Lieut., *c.*, 31/10/17, *d.*, 11/2/19.
MARGERISON, T. C., Lieut., *c.*, 4/6/15, *w.*, 3/9/16, *d.*, 2/6/19.
MATTHEWS, G., 2nd Lieut., *k. in a.*, 2/7/18.
MARTIN, W. E., Lieut., *c.* 23/10/15.
MacLUSKY, M.C., W. B., Lieut. acting Capt., *c.*, 5/8/16, *d.*, 7/2/19.
MAUFE, C. G., Lieut., *c.* 7/5/16, *d.* 3/2/19.
McLAREN, J. M., Lieut., *c.*, 10/9/14, *d.*, 18/5/16.
McLEAN, R. D., Capt., *c.*, 20/8/15, *w.*, 22/4/18, *d.*, 21/3/19.
McLEAN, W., Lieut. acting Capt., *d. of w.*, 17/11/17.
MELHUISH, H., Lieut., *c.* 7/5/16. Transf. Indian Army.
MITCHELL, C. H., 2nd Lieut., *c.* 7/3/15, *k. in a.* 3/9/16.
MITCHELL, M.C., H., Lieut., *c.*, 30/11/15, *d.*, 26/1/19.
MIDDLETON, L. S., Capt., *c.*, 4/8/14, *w.*, 15/12/15, *d.*, 30/1/19.
MILNER, G. E., Capt., *c.*, 10/9/14, *w.*, 1/7/16, *d.*, 25/3/19.
MOORE, R., 2nd Lieut., *d. of w.*, 15/7/16.
MOSSOP, M.C., W. N., Capt. and Adjt., *c.* 10/9/14, *w.* 12/8/15, *d. of w.* 8/5/18.
MULLER, N., Capt., *c.*, 5/8/14, *k. in a.*, 28/7/18.
MULLER, D.S.O., M.C., J., Lt.-Col., *c.* 4/8/14, transferred to Welsh Regt. 1/7/16.
MUSGRAVE, M.C., F. W., Capt., *c.*, 14/8/14, *d.*, 27/3/19.
MYERS, M.C., E., Lieut., *c.*, 10/10/14, *w.*, 26/7/15, 1/7/16, 4/8/17, *d.*, 17/1/19.
NAREY, B. P., Lieut., *c.*, 6/7/16, *d.*, 4/2/19.
ODDY, J. L., Capt., *c.*, 4/8/14, *w.*, 1/7/16, *d. of w.*, 3/9/16.
PINKERTON, G. H., Lieut., *c.* 28/11/17.
PUCKRIN, G. M., Lieut., *c.* 29/8/17.
POLLARD, E. M., 2nd Lieut., *c.*, 3/10/14, *t. R.F.C.*, 3/11/15.
PEPPER, 2nd Lieut., *p. of w.*, 25/4/18.
RENNISON, W., Capt. and Adjt., *c.* 15/11/15.
RETBERG, H., Lieut., *c.* 27/6/17.
REES, G. F. G., Capt., *c.* 20/5/15.
RICHARDSON, E. B., 2nd Lieut., *c.*, 11/6/18, *d.*, 31/10/19.
RICHARDSON, C. E., Lieut., *k. in a.*, 11/10/18.
RILEY, M.C., B. M., Lieut., *c.*, 6/2/16, *w.*, 22/7/18, *d.*, 10/8/19.
ROBINSON, H. W., Lieut., *c.*, 24/12/15, *p. of w.*, 25/4/18, *d.*, 21/3/19.
ROBINSON, H. E., Capt. R.A.M.C., *k. in a.*, 25/4/18.
RUMNEY, Lieut., *c.* 28/11/17.
RUSSELL, H. R., Lieut., *c.* 26/9/17, *d.* 16/4/20.

APPENDIX

RYMER, N. A., 2nd Lieut. acting Capt., *c.*, 26/9/16, *w.*, 19/11/17, 13/10/18, *d.*, 6/4/19.

SAYES, J., *c.* 5/8/16.

SAVILL, S. C., Capt., *c.*, 22/8/14, *w.*, 19/5/15, 11/5/17, *resigned* 6/5/20.

SANDEMAN, M.C., G. R., Major and Adjt. Regular Army.

SANDERS, V.C., M.C., G., Capt., *c.* 27/6/17, *w. and p. of w.*, 25/4/18.

SARGENT, H. E., *c.* 5/6/15.

SCALES, M.C., W. A., Capt., *c.*, 1/3/15, *w.*, 1/7/16, *k.*, 6/1/18.

SCOTT, C. E., Lt.-Col., *c.*, 4/8/14, *w.*, 28/7/16, *d. of w.*, 9/8/16.

SENIOR, W. T., 2nd Lieut., *c.* 23/6/16, *k. in a.* 3/9/16.

SIMPSON, A., Lieut., *c.* 27/6/17.

SPEIGHT, M.C., G. H., Lieut., *c.* 12/6/15, *w.* 10/9/16, *d.* 11/3/19.

SPEIGHT, H. C., 2nd Lieut., *c.*, 22/10/15, *w.*, 18/12/15, 15/7/16, *resigned*, 6/3/17.

SPEIGHT, J. L., Capt., *c.* 11/1/16, *d. of w.* 9/10/17.

STANSFIELD, M.C., E. D., Major and Adjt., *c.* 29/11/15, *d.* 27/4/19.

STILLWELL, S. T. C., Lieut., *c.* 6/7/16.

STOREY, H. L., 2nd Lieut., *c.* 9/3/15, *d. of w.* 12/9/16.

STRACHAN, D. L., Capt., *c.* 15/5/15, *died* 29/12/16.

SUNTER, T., 2nd Lieut., *c.*, 1/8/17, *w.*, 15/4/18, *d.*, 22/3/19.

SUGDEN, 2nd Lieut., *p. of w.*, 25/4/18.

SHIELD, 2nd Lieut., *p. of w.*, 25/4/18.

TALBOT, J. H., 2nd Lieut., *c.*, 26/9/16, *resigned*, 28/3/19.

TAYLOR, J., Lieut., *c.* 3/3/15.

TEMPEST, D.S.O., M.C., E. V., Lieut. acting Capt., *c.*, 6/9/15, *w.*, 11/10/17, *d.*, 7/2/19.

TETLEY, W. G., Capt., *c.*, 4/8/14, *w.*, 11/10/15, 14/8/16, *d.*, 4/9/19.

THOMPSON, T. B., 2nd Lieut., *c.*, 1/8/17, *w.*, 13/9/18, *d.*, 3/3/19.

THRESH, M.C., A. E., Capt., *c.* 4/6/15, *d.* 25/7/19. (Transf. M. G. C.)

TODD, S. C., Lieut., *c.*, 18/9/15, *w.*, 1/7/16, 17/7/17, *d.*, 7/12/19.

TOMLINSON, C., Lieut., *c.*, 31/10/17, *d.*, 11/1/20.

TURLEY, J. F., Lieut., *c.*, 31/10/17, *w.*, 1/7/18, *d.*, 17/9/19.

TULEY, E., Lieut., *c.*, 29/5/18, *w.*, 11/10/18, *resigned*, 15/10/20.

TURNER, E. A., Lieut., *c.*, 25/10/16, *w.*, 13/11/15, 18/12/15, *k.*, 3/9/16.

TUNNAH, W., Lieut., *c.* 31/9/17.

VAUGHAN, A. L., Lieut., *c.*, 14/12/1, *w.*, 28/6/18, 18/9/18, *resigned*, 15/9/20.

WADE, D.S.O., H. O., Lt.-Col., *c.*, 4/8/14, *w.*, 1/7/16, *d.*, 21/6/19.

WALKER, F., Lieut. acting Capt., *c.*, 2/11/15, *d.*, 26/4/19.

WALKER, G. R. S., Capt., *c.*, 8/8/14, *w.*, 21/7/16, 22/11/17, *resigned*, 20/6/18.

WALKER, A. C. C., Capt., *c.*, 4/8/14, *t.* A.S.C. M.T., 29/6/16.

WARD, F. H., Lieut., *c.*, 1/7/15, *d.*, 23/3/19.
WATSON, J. C., 2nd Lieut., *c.* 10/9/14.
WALKER, N., Lieut., *c.* 1/7/17.
WARNER, W. E., Lieut., *c.* 26/9/17.
WEIGHILL, M.C., W. C. S., Lieut. acting Capt., *c.* 6/7/15, *w.* 14/7/16,
    -/6/17, 15/11/17, 16/5/18, *resigned,* 26/6/20.
WEATHERILL, G., 2nd Lieut., *c.*, 30/1/18, *p. of w.*, 18/9/18, *d.*, 19/2/19.
WHYTE, G. N. D., Lieut., *c.*, 19/10/15, *w.*, 9/5/15, 5/5/17, *d.*, 21/11/19.
WHITTERON, C., 2nd Lieut., *c.* 27/6/17, *k. in a.* 25/4/18.
WHINCUP, M.C., R., Capt. Rev., *c.*, 4/8/14, *d.*, 27/8/17.
WHITEHEAD, K. E., Capt. Rev., *c.* 4/5/16.
WHITTAM, C. C., Lieut., *c.* 1/7/16.
WHITTAKER, F. W., Capt., *c.* 2/7/15, *p. of w.* 25/4/18.
WILLIAMS, A., 2nd Lieut., *k. in a.*, 25/4/18.
WILSON, Arnold, 2nd Lieut., *c.* 1/3/17, *k. in a.* 3/5/17.
WISTANCE, D.S.O., M.C., Lt.-Col., *k. in a.* 25/4/18.
WIGGINS, H., 2nd Lieut., *c.*, 31/10/17, *p. of w.*, 27/5/18—13/12/18.
WORRALL, H. V., 2nd Lieut., *c.* 9/7/15.
WOOD, J. A. S., 2nd Lieut., *k. in a.*, 12/6/17.
WRIGHT, R. B., 2nd Lieut., *c.*, 3/8/17, *k. in a.*, 8/7/18.
WOOD, E. A. H., Lieut., *k. in a.*, 11/8/17.
WHITING, W. C., 2nd Lieut., *c.* 30/4/16.
YORKE, G., Lieut., *c.*, 27/7/15, *w.*, 5/9/17, *d.*, 15/11/19.

APPENDIX V.

Nominal Roll of Warrant Officers and Company Quarter Master Sergts., 1/6th Battalion West Yorkshire Regiment. April 15th, 1915, to November 11th, 1918 (Armistice Day).

Regimental Sergeant Majors.

Freeman, C. L.	15/4/15 to 29/1/16	To Hospital.
Barker, M.C., D.C.M., H.	2/3/16 to 25/4/18	Missing.
Moss, R.	26/4/18 to 15/7/18	For Commission.
Sugden, D.C.M., M.S.M., A.	16/7/18 to 11/11/18	

Regimental Quarter Master Sergeants.

Welch, G.	15/4/15 to 16/8/17	For Commission
Woodhead, M.S.M., C. H.,	17/8/17 to 11/11/18	

Bandmaster.

King, G. M.	9/3/18 to 11/11/18

Company Sergeant Major (A Company).

Pottage, J.	15/4/15 to 12/8/15	Killed in Action.
Rhodes, H. E.	13/8/15 to 14/1/16	Time Expired.
Banks, D.C.M., H.	4/3/16 to 27/8/16	Wounded.
Simpson, D.C.M., C. G.,	29/8/16 to 3/9/16	Killed in Action.
Finney, C. G.	4/9/16 to 10/10/17	Wounded.
Hutchinson, J. B.	11/10/17 to 12/3/18	For Commission.
Stanton, M.M., W. E.	13/3/18 to 25/4/18	Prisoner of War.
Barker, E.	1/7/18 to 11/11/18	

Company Quarter Master Sergeants (A Company).

Dawson, H.	15/4/15 to 3/6/15	Died of Wounds.
Rhodes, H. E.	4/6/15 to 12/8/15	To C. S. M.
Griffiths, I. E.	13/8/15 to 29/4/16	To Hospital.
Simpson, D.C.M., C. G.,	30/4/16 to 28/8/16	To C. S. M.
Wilkinson, R.	29/8/16 to 11/11/18	

Company Sergeant Majors (B Company).

Mackay, T.	15/4/15 to 30/7/16	To Hospital.
Humphreys, D.C.M., G.	1/8/16 to 2/9/16	Wounded.
Baxter, F.	4/9/16 to 25/3/17	For Commission.
Howard, F.	26/3/17 to 25/4/18	Prisoner of War.
Vickers	1/6/18 to 30/9/18	To England (Substitution).
Padgett, M.M., C.	1/10/18 to 11/11/18	

Company Quarter Master Sergeants (B Company).

Woodhead, M.S.M., C. H., 15/4/15 to 17/8/17   To R. Q. M. S.
Chapman, F.   18/8/17 to 21/3/18   Wounded.
Hardaker, R.   24/4/18 to 11/11/18

Company Sergeant Majors (C Company).

Barker, M.C., D.C.M., H.   15/4/15 to 12/7/15   Wounded.
Walmsley, W.   13/7/15 to 25/4/18   Missing (Died Prisoner of War).
Bradley, D.C.M., E.   26/4/18 to 11/11/18

Company Quarter Master Sergeant.

Packett, E. A.   15/4/15 to 22/1/16   Time Expired.
Moorhouse, A.   1/2/16 to 10/8/18   Killed in Action.
Davis, S.   25/9/18 to 11/11/18

Company Sergeant Major (D. Company).

Hanson, A.   15/4/15 to 16/3/16   Time Expired.
King, M.M., H. R.   17/3/16 to 26/7/16   Wounded.
Parsey, D.C.M., J. L.   27/7/16 to 13/1/17   For Commission.
Moorhouse, W.   14/1/17 to 25/4/18   Prisoner of War.
Wallace, A.   16/7/18 to 11/11/18

Company Quarter Master Sergeants.

Vaughan, C. St. J.   15/4/15 to 30/6/15   To Hospital.
Matthews, H.   1/7/15 to 15/12/15   To Hospital.
King, M.M., H. R.   16/12/15 to 16/3/16   To C.S.M.
Parsey, D.C.M., J. L.   17/3/16 to 26/7/16   To C.S.M.
Honour, R.   27/7/16 to 12/2/18   For Commission.
Scott, A.   7/4/18 to 11/11/18

Supernumerary—Company Sergeant Major.

Banks, D.C.M., H.   22/10/18 to 11/11/18

APPENDIX VI.

LIST OF HONOURS AND AWARDS OBTAINED BY THE 1/6TH BATTALION WEST YORKSHIRE REGT.

V.C. (1)

Regt. No.

1147   Sergt. S. Meekosha.

D.S.O. (3)

Lt.-Col. H. O. Wade.
Lt.-Col. W. Wistance, M.C.
Lt. E. V. Tempest, M.C., 146th Inf. Bde. H. Q.

M. C. (24)

Lt.-Col. Wistance, W., D.S.O.
Major Clough, R.
Major Hornshaw, F. G.
Capt. Sandeman, G. R.
Capt. Muller, J., 146th I.B.H.Q.
Capt. Fawcett, R. A.
Capt. Fawcett, W. L.
Capt. Hill, W. H.
Capt. Gordon, J. S.
Capt. Weighill, W. C. S.
Capt. Mossop, W. N.
Capt. Sanders, G., V.C.
Capt. Stansfield, E. D.
Capt. Rees, G. F. G.
Rev. Whincup, R., 146th Inf. Bde. H.Q
Lieut. Tempest, E. V.
Lieut. Mitchell, H.
Lieut. MacLusky, W. B.
2/Lieut. Scales, W. A.
2/Lieut. Speight, G. H.

2/Lieut. Hick, B.
2/Lieut Greenwood, L.
2/Lieut. Illingworth, J.
R. S. M. Barker, H.

BAR to M.C. (2)

Capt. Stansfield, E. D.
Lieut. MacLusky, W. B.

D.C.M. (24)

Regt. No.

9	R.S.M. Barker, H.,M.C.
11572	R.S.M. Sugden, A.
298	C.Q.M.S. Parsey, J. L.
79	Sergt. Banks, H.
242637	Cpl. Brown, A. P.
3539	Sergt. Bradley, E.
241048	Sergt. Browne, W.
2474	Cpl. Ellison, W.
240180	Pte. Evans, H.
2315	Pte. Francis, W.
3225	Lc.-Cpl. Johnson, E.
1140	Sergt. Kelly, J. W.
2190	Pte. Kermode, E. M.
18104	Pte. King, H.
31822	Pte. Nicholson, W.
2424	Preston, E.
1773	Sergt. Simpson, C. G.
2626	Sergt. Sayers, J.
1165	Cpl. Smith, A.
3727	Lc.-Cpl. Simpson, W. G., M.M.

Regt. No.

4539	Lc.-Cpl. Silverwood, A., M.M.
1266	Lc.-Cpl. Wilkinson, E. J.
1360	Lc.-Cpl. Wilcock, H.
2111	C. S. M. Humphreys, G.

M. M. (70)

2091	Lc.-Cpl. Airey, N. G.
9230	Sergt. Bagnall, T.
241764	Cpl. Bradley, G.
1756	Pte. Bradley, T.
21717	Pte. Butler, D.
241856	Sergt. Chew, R.
72577	Cpl. Clacey, E.
1249	Lc.-Cpl. Corke, A.
1263	Pte. Cooke, B.
3808	Pte. Cawthra, M.
1608	Pte. Coupland, A.
242826	Pte. Charlton, W.
240344	Pte. Cassarley, V.
2623	Sergt. Dracup, J.
241215	Cpl. Davis, J.
2503	Pte. Dawson, J. H.
242897	Pte. Dodds, C.
16/1532	Pte. Dalby, H.
2372	Cpl. Emmott, G.
2044	Sergt. Fairbank, F. E.
1799	Cpl. Foster, R. J.
4274	Pte. Greenwood, W.
1500	Cpl. Hutchinson, W.
241394	Lc.-Cpl. Hird, W.
1418	Pte. Hodgson, G. H.
242747	Pte. Howe, A. G.
242878	Pte. Horner, A. J.
240174	Pte. Hainsworth, A.
242520	Pte. Hirst, W.
202059	Pte. Hanson, R.

Regt. No.

62621	Pte. Hitman, A. J.
238233	Pte. Hawkins, E. T.
63690	Pte. Hardy, D.
50749	Pte. Johnson, T. J.
324	Sergt. King, H. R.
1706	Sergt. McIvor, R. G.
1908	Cpl. Mee, H.
242490	Lc.-Cpl. Middleton, W.
2292	Pte. Moss, E.
3107	Pte. Marshall, A. T.
241548	Pte. Marton, E.
241126	Lc.-Cpl. O'Donnell, G.
260007	C. S. M. Padgett, C.
242864	Lc.-Cpl. Poole, E. P.
62911	Pte. Porte, A. D.
15/1622	Pte. Pawson, R.
15887	Pte. Pickles, B.
54179	Lc.-Cpl. Rough, C. E.
54181	Pte. Rawling, H. T.
62611	Pte. Reed, G. W.
1259	Sergt. Stanton, W.
240883	Cpl. Stott, W.
3727	Lc.-Cpl. Simpson, W. G., D.C.M.
3301	Lc.-Cpl. Sutcliffe, W.
4539	Lc.-Cpl. Silverwood, A., D.C.M.
20/37	Lc.-Cpl. Smithies, D.
42398	Lc.-Cpl. Shepherd, G. F.
62922	Lc.-Cpl. Smythe, C. G.
3506	Pte. Smith, C.
242614	Pte. Sweet, J.
62974	Pte. Swinton, A. R.
240143	Cpl. Turton, H.
242770	Lc.-Cpl. Thomas, D.
211568	Pte. Thistlethwaite, L.
240144	C. S. M. Wallace, A.
4616	Cpl. White, W.
240737	Lc.-Cpl. Woolham, H.
240710	Pte. Walker, J.

APPENDIX

240787 Pte. Woddiwiss, C. B.
240980 Sergt. Powell, F.

BAR to M. M. (1)
241126 Lc.-Cpl. O'Donnell, G.

M. S. M. (6)
240197 Sergt. Chapman, S.
242634 Sergt. Sharp, B.
11572 R. S. M. Sugden, A.,

D.C.M.
2450 Sergt. Sunter, T.
240398 Sergt. Ward, J.

1809 C. Q. M. S. Woodhead, C. H.

CROIX DE GUERRE. (1)
229 C. S. M. Walmsley, W.

BELGIAN CROIX DE GUERRE (1)
240037 C. S. M. Moorhouse, W.

RUSSIAN CROSS OF ST. GEORGE (1)
4th Class.
3539 Sergt. Bradley, E., D.C.M.

APPENDIX VI.

MEMORIAL WINDOW TO THE 6th BATTALION WEST YORKSHIRE REGIMENT—BRADFORD CATHEDRAL.*

IN the centre is a figure of an Infantryman lying mortally wounded amidst the desolation of the battlefield. He lies with gas mask at the alert, and clasping his rifle. Near him is his steel helmet and around him are barbed wire entanglements. In the distance is a ruined Church, shell-torn trees and the setting sun. As the day closes, he looks up and sees Him who made the Great Sacrifice. " Greater love hath no man than this, that a man lay down his life for his friend."

Below the soldier between two graves is the Badge of the Battalion. On the left is a soldier's grave behind the Line, upon which his comrades have placed a cross and a wreath. On the other side is a battlefield grave ; the soldier has been buried in action and his comrades, with haste, yet with reverence, have placed his rifle and helmet to mark the spot. Behind the graves are poppies, the symbol of death. In front are the White Roses of York.

Around the side lights is the History of the Battalion.

At the bottom of the left-hand light are the Arms of Bradford.

In the first illustration is shown the landing of Troops in France by night. In a corner is a shield showing a Fleur de lys, also the Badge of the Battalion Scouts. Above these we see Ypres. The ruin of the Cloth Hall is shown as it was in 1915. Near this is a soldier in fur coat and gumboots—he is on guard and is wearing the gas mask of that period on his forehead. In front of him is the gas flag showing the wind "at danger." Opposite him are the Arms of Ypres.

Next is shown the Leipzig Redoubt—a typical German strong point. Above is shown the storming and capture of Thiepval. Near here is a small medallion, the first of a series, showing the specialists of the Battalion. This one shows the Bombers. In the border a " stokes " and a 50-pounder Trench Mortar represent the work of the Trench Mortar men. Next is shown Nieuport and a Torpedo Boat Destroyer representing the Royal Navy who were the " left flank " of our line. In the border above is shown a spade and trowel representing the Pioneers. Next is shown Passchendaele Ridge—a barrage of fire

---

* This description is supplied by the Bromsgrove Guild, Birmingham.

and smoke and a German Pill Box in action. A little scene shows the work of the Stretcher Bearers. Above this the 49th Divisional Mark is surrounded by a Laurel Wreath. At the extreme top of the window Aeroplanes represent the Air Force.

In the top of the right-hand light is an observation balloon, and surrounded by a Laurel Wreath is the " mark " of the 62nd Division. Below is Bullecourt—the Battalion holding the Line. In the border is a pack mule as a tribute to the work of the Horses and Mules of the Transport. The next panel indicates the Battle of Cambrai—the Tanks advancing through the smoke barrage. Near this are the Arms of Cambrai. Then Kemmel Hill—the hill is shown with the burning windmills on the top, and near this is a medallion showing the Signallers at work. Next is shown Iwuy and above is a captured German Gun. Below in the border is a scroll with the word " FAMARS." Above this is the badge of the First Battalion of the West Yorkshire Regiment and the trumpet and drums, together with the words of their march, " Ça Ira." Then is shown the final advance through Valenciennes, together with the Arms of that Town.

At the Base of the Window is seen the Bridge of Boats on the Rhine with Cologne in the distance. Near here at the end of the Dedication Scroll is shown the Arms of the See of Bradford. In the two centre lights of the tracery are St. Michael of Belgium and St. George of England. Below there are the shields of Britain, America, Belgium, Japan, Russia and Portugal. On the left-hand light is shown St. Louis the Soldier Saint and King of France, and below the Shield of France. On the extreme left is shown St. Ambrose of Italy and the National Shield. On the right is shown St. Sava of Serbia and the Serbian Shield, and in the extreme right is shown St. Methodius of Roumania and the Roumanian Shield. These symbolize all the Nations who fought with us.

Printed in Great Britain
by Amazon

23389948R10243